Lecture Notes in Computer Science 3590

Commenced Publication in 1973
Founding and Former Series Editors:
Gerhard Goos, Juris Hartmanis, and Jan van Leeuwen

T0223553

Kurt Bauknecht   Birgit Pröll
Hannes Werthner (Eds.)

E-Commerce and Web Technologies

6th International Conference, EC-Web 2005
Copenhagen, Denmark, August 23-26, 2005
Proceedings

 Springer

Volume Editors

Kurt Bauknecht
University of Zurich, Department of Informatics (IFI)
Winterthurer Str. 190, 8057 Zurich, Switzerland
E-mail: baukn@ifi.unizh.ch

Birgit Pröll
Johannes Kepler University, Institute for Applied Knowledge Processing (FAW)
Softwarepark Hagenberg, 4232 Hagenberg, Austria
E-mail: bproell@faw.uni-linz.ac.at

Hannes Werthner
Leopold Franzens University, Department for Information Systems, e-tourism (ISET)
Universitätsstr. 15, 6020 Innsbruck, Austria
E-mail: hannes.werthner@uibk.ac.at

Library of Congress Control Number: 2005930718

CR Subject Classification (1998): H.4, K.4.4, J.1, K.5, H.3, H.2, K.6.5

ISSN   0302-9743
ISBN-10   3-540-28467-2 Springer Berlin Heidelberg New York
ISBN-13   978-3-540-28467-3 Springer Berlin Heidelberg New York

Springer is a part of Springer Science+Business Media

springeronline.com

© Springer-Verlag Berlin Heidelberg 2005
Printed in Germany

Typesetting: Camera-ready by author, data conversion by Scientific Publishing Services, Chennai, India
Printed on acid-free paper   SPIN: 11545163   06/3142   5 4 3 2 1 0

Preface

We welcome you to the 6th International Conference on E-Commerce and Web Technology (EC-Web 2005) held in Copenhagen, Denmark. It was held in conjunction with DEXA 2005. This conference was organized for the first time in Greenwich, UK, in 2000, and it has been able to attract an increasing number of participants and interest, reflecting the progress made in the field. As in the five previous years, EC-Web 2005 served as a forum that brought together researchers from academia and practitioners from industry to discuss the current state of the art in e-commerce and Web technologies. We are sure that inspirations and new ideas emerged from the intensive discussions that took place during the formal sessions and social events.

Keynote addresses, research presentations and discussions during the conference helped to further develop the exchange of ideas among current researchers, developers and practitioners.

The conference attracted 139 paper submissions and each paper was reviewed by three Program Committee members. The Program Committee selected 39 papers for presentation and publication (an acceptance rate of 28%). And we have to confess that this task was not that easy due to the high quality of the submitted papers.

We would like to express our thanks to our colleagues who helped with putting together the technical program: the Program Committee members and external reviewers for their timely and rigorous reviews of the papers, and the Organizing Committee for their help in the administrative work and support. We owe special thanks to Gabriela Wagner for her helping hand concerning the administrative and organizational tasks of this conference.

Finally, we would like to thank all the authors who submitted papers, authors who presented papers, and the participants who made this conference an intellectually stimulating event. We hope that all attendees enjoyed the hospitality of Copenhagen.

August 2005   Birgit Pröll and Hannes Werthner

Organization

General Chairperson
Kurt Bauknecht, University of Zurich, Switzerland

Conference Program Chairpersons
Birgit Pröll, Johannes Kepler University, Linz, Austria
Hannes Werthner, Leopold Franzens University, Innsbruck, Austria

Program Committee
Sourav S. Bhowmick, Nanyang Technological University, Singapore
Martin Bichler, TU Munich, Germany
Niels Bjørn-Andersen, Copenhagen Business School, Denmark
Susanne Boll, University of Oldenburg, Germany
Walter Brenner, University of St. Gallen, Switzerland
Stephane Bressan, National University of Singapore, Singapore
Tanya Castleman, Deakin University, Australia
Wojciech Cellary, Poznan University of Economics, Poland
Jen-Yao Chung, IBM T.J. Watson Research Center, USA
Roger Clarke, Xamax Consultancy Pty. Ltd., Australia
Eduardo Fernandez, Florida Atlantic University, USA
Elena Ferrari, University of Insubria at Como, Italy
Farshad Fotouhi, Wayne State University, USA
Karl A. Fröschl, Electronic Commerce Competence Center, Austria
Yongjian Fu, Cleveland State University, USA
Chanan Glezer, Ben Gurion University of the Negev, Israel
Rüdiger Grimm, University of Technology, Ilmenau, Germany
Manfred Hauswirth, EPFL, Switzerland
Thomas Hess, University of Munich, Germany
Yigal Hoffner, IBM Zurich Research Laboratory, Switzerland
Christian Huemer, University of Vienna, Austria
Gregory E. Kersten, University of Ottawa, Canada
Hiroyuki Kitagawa, University of Tsukuba, Japan
Gabriele Kotsis, Johannes Kepler University, Linz, Austria
Winfried Lamersdorf, University of Hamburg, Germany
Alberto Laender, Federal University of Minas Gerais, Brazil
Juhnyoung Lee, IBM T.J. Watson Research Center, USA
Leszek Lilien, Purdue University, USA
Ee-Peng Lim, Nanyang Technological University, Singapore
Huan Liu, Arizona State University, USA
Heiko Ludwig, IBM T.J. Watson Research Center, USA
Sanjay Kumar Madria, University of Missouri-Rolla, USA
Bamshad Mobasher, DePaul University, USA

Natwar Modani, IBM India Research Lab, India
Mukesh Mohania, IBM India Research Lab, India
Gustaf Neumann, Vienna University of Economics and BA, Austria
Wee Keong Ng, Nanyang Technological University, Singapore
Rolf Oppliger, eSECURITY Technologies, Switzerland
Oscar Pastor, Valencia University of Technology, Spain
Günther Pernul, University of Regensburg, Germany
Evangelia Pitoura, University of Ioannina, Greece
Giuseppe Psaila, University of Bergamo, Italy
Gerald Quirchmayr, University of Vienna, Austria
Indrakshi Ray, Colorado State University, USA
Werner Retschitzegger, Johannes Kepler University, Linz, Austria
Tomas Sabol, Technical University of Kosice, Slovakia
Nandlal L. Sarda, Indian Institute of Technology, Bombay, India
Steffen Staab, University of Koblenz-Landau, Germany
Michael Stroebel, BMW Group, Germany
Roger M. Tagg, University of South Australia, Australia
Kian-Lee Tan, National University of Singapore, Singapore
Stephanie Teufel, University of Fribourg, Switzerland
Bruce H. Thomas, University of South Australia, Australia
A Min Tjoa, Technical University of Vienna, Austria
Aphrodite Tsalgatidou, National and Kapodistrian University of Athens, Greece
Krishnamurthy Vidyasankar, Memorial University of Newfoundland, Canada
Hans Weigand, Tilburg University, The Netherlands
Christof Weinhardt, University of Karlsruhe, Germany

External Reviewers

Nitin Agarwal, Arizona State University, USA
George Athanasopoulos, National and Kapodistrian University of Athens, Greece
Peter Bednar, Technical University of Kosice, Slovakia
Panagiotis Bouros, National and Kapodistrian University of Athens, Greece
Lars Braubach, University of Hamburg, Germany
Radoslav Delina, Technical University of Kosice, Slovakia
Wolfgang Dobmeier, University of Regensburg, Germany
Marin Husemann, University of Hamburg, Germany
Yoshiharu Ishikawa, University of Tsukuba, Japan
Eleni Koutrouli, National and Kapodistrian University of Athens, Greece
Krishna Kummamuru, IBM India Research Lab., India
Marian Mach, Technical University of Kosice, Slovakia
Norbert Meckl, University of Regensburg, Germany
Laurent Mignet, IBM India Research Lab., India
Peter Mihok, Technical University of Kosice, Slovakia
Javier Muñoz, Technical University of Valencia, Spain
Björn Muschall, University of Regensburg, Germany
Michael Pantazoglou, National and Kapodistrian University of Athens, Greece
Niyati Parikh, Arizona State University, USA
Lance Parsons, Arizona State University, USA

Table of Contents

XII Table of Contents

Recommender Systems

A Collaborative Filtering Recommendation Methodology for
Peer-to-Peer Systems
Hyea Kyeong Kim, Jae Kyeong Kim, Yoon Ho Cho 98

A Framework for Session Based Recommendations
Natwar Modani, Yogish Sabharwal, S. Karthik 108

Automatic Knowledge Recommending System Using E-Mail
DooHyun Kim, WonHyuck Choi, BurmSuk Seo, JungGoo Seo,
ByoungWon Hwang 118

E-Negotiation and Agent Mediated Systems

Narrowing the Gap Between Humans and Agents in e-Commerce: 3D
Electronic Institutions
Anton Bogdanovych, Helmut Berger, Simeon Simoff, Carles Sierra ... 128

Standard K-Languages as a Powerful and Flexible Tool for Building
Contracts and Representing Contents of Arbitrary E-Negotiations
Vladimir A. Fomichov 138

Automated Negotiation Based on Contract Net and Petri Net
Fu-Shiung Hsieh 148

Business Process / Strategic Issues and Knowledge Discovery

Linking the Balanced Scorecard to Business Models for Value-Based
Strategic Management in e-Business
Chien-Chih Yu 158

The Framework of Web-Based Voice of the Customers Management for
Business Process Management in Service Industry
Chong Un Pyon, SungMin Bae, Ji Young Woo, Sang Chan Park 168

E-Business Perceptions Versus Reality: A Longitudinal Analysis of
Corporate Websites
Niels Bjørn-Andersen, Steve Elliot 178

Knowledge Discovery in Web-Directories: Finding Term-Relations to
Build a Business Ontology
Sandip Debnath, Tracy Mullen, Arun Upneja, C. Lee Giles 188

Applications and Case Studies in E-Commerce

Performance Issues in E-Commerce

Web Usage Mining

E-Payment Approaches

Security and Trust in E-Commerce

Web Services Computing

Architecture of a Semantic XPath Processor. Application to Digital Rights Management

Rubén Tous, Roberto García, Eva Rodríguez, and Jaime Delgado

Universitat Pompeu Fabra (UPF), Dpt. de Tecnologia, Pg. Circumval.lació,
8, E-08003 Barcelona, Spain
{ruben.tous, roberto.garcia, eva.rodriguez, jaime.delgado}@upf.edu

Abstract. This work describes a novel strategy for designing an XPath processor that acts over an RDF mapping of XML. We use a *model-mapping approach* to represent instances of XML and XML Schema in RDF. This representation retains the node order, in contrast with the usual *structure-mapping* approach. The processor can be fed with an unlimited set of XML schemas and/or RDFS/OWL ontologies. The queries are resolved taking into consideration the structural and semantic connections described in the schemas and ontologies. Such behavior, schema-awareness and semantic integration, can be useful for exploiting schema and ontology hierarchies in XPath queries. We test our approach in the Digital Rights Management (DRM) domain. We explore how the processor can be used in the two main rights expression languages (REL),: MPEG-21 REL and ODRL.

1 Introduction

1.1 Motivation

Usually XML-based applications use one or more XML schemas. These schemas are mainly used for instance validity check. However, it is sometimes necessary to consider the inheritance hierarchies defined in the schemas for other purposes, e.g. when evaluating queries or conditions that can refer to concepts not directly present in the data, but related to them through an inheritance chain. Today it is also becoming common the use of RDFS[25]/OWL[24] ontologies to define semantic connections among application concepts. All this *structural* and *semantic* knowledge is hard to access for developers, because it requires a specific treatment, like defining multiple extra queries for the schemas, or using complex RDF[26] tools to access the ontologies information.

To overcome this situation we present the architecture of a schema-aware and ontology-aware XPath processor. The processor can be fed with an unlimited set of XML schemas and/or RDFS/OWL ontologies. The queries are resolved taking in consideration the structural and semantic connections described in the schemas and ontologies. We use a *model-mapping approach* to represent instances of XML and XML Schema in RDF. This representation retains the node order, in contrast with the usual *structure-mapping* approach, so it allows a complete mapping of all XPath axis.

K. Bauknecht et al. (Eds.): EC-Web 2005, LNCS 3590, pp. 1–10, 2005.

1.2   Related Work. Model-Mapping vs. Structure-Mapping

The origins of this work can be found in a research trend that tries to exploit the advantages of an XML-to-RDF mapping [1][2][3][4][5][6][7]. However, the concepts of *structure-mapping* and *model-mapping* are older. In 2001, [8] defined these terms to differentiate between works that map the structure of some XML schema to a set of relational tables and works that map the XML model to a general relational schema respectively.

   More recently, [4] takes a *structure-mapping* approach and defines a direct way to map XML documents to RDF triples ([2] classifies this approach as *Direct Translation*). [1], [2], and [3] take also a *structure-mapping* approach but focusing on defining semantic mappings between different XML schemas ([2] classifies their own approach as *High-level Mediator*). They also describe some simple mapping mechanisms to cover just a subset of XPath constructs. Other authors like [5] or [6] take a slightly different strategy (though within the *structure-mapping* trend) and focus on integrating XML and RDF to incorporate to XML the inferencing rules of RDF (strategies classified by [2] as *Encoding Semantics*). Finally it's worth mention the RPath initiative [7], that tries to define an analogous language to XPath but for natural (not derived from XML) RDF data (this last work doesn't pursue interoperability between models or schemas).

   The target to achieve a semantic behavior for XPath/XQuery has also been faced in [23]. This approach consists also in translating the XML schemas to OWL, but the authors define an XQuery variant for the OWL data model called SWQL (Semantic Web Query Language). The difference between this approach and ours is that our work does not need a translation between the semantic queries (instances of SWQL in the related approach) and XPath/XQuery expressions. We have developed a new XPath processor that manipulates conventional queries but taking in consideration the semantic relationships defined in the schemas and/or ontologies.

2   Architecture of the Semantic XPath Processor

2.1   Overview

Figure 1 outlines how the processor works. The key issue is the XML-to-RDF mapping, already present in other works, but that we face from the *model-mapping* approach. In contrast with the *structure-mapping* approach, that maps the specific structure of some XML schema to RDF constructs, we map the XML Infoset [9] using RDFS and OWL axioms. This allows us to represent any XML document without any restriction and without losing information about node-order. We use the same approach with XSD, obtaining an RDF representation of the schemas. Incorporating alternative OWL or RDFS ontologies is straightforward, because they are already compatible with the inference engine. In the figure we can see also that an OWL representation of the XML model is necessary. This ontology allows the inference engine to correctly process the different XPath axis and understand how the XML elements relate to the different XSD constructs.

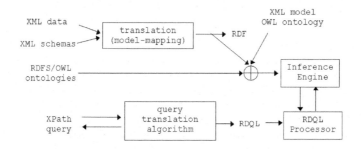

Fig. 1. Semantic XPath processor architecture overview

2.2 An OWL Ontology for the XML Model (XML/RDF Syntax)

We have tried to represent the XML Infoset [9] using RDFS and OWL axioms. A simplified description of the ontology in Description Logics syntax ($\mathcal{SHIQ}$-like style [17]) would be:

$$Document \sqsubseteq Node$$
$$Element \sqsubseteq Node$$
$$TextNode \sqsubseteq Node$$
$$childOf \sqsubseteq descendant$$
$$parentOf \sqsubseteq ancestor$$
$$childOf = parentOf^-$$
$$\mathcal{T}rans(ancestor)$$
$$ancestor \sqsubseteq ancestorOrSelf$$
$$self \sqsubseteq descendantOrSelf$$
$$self \sqsubseteq ancestorOrSelf$$
$$self = sameAs$$
$$immediatePrecedingSibling \sqsubseteq precedingSiblinng$$
$$immediateFollowingSibling \sqsubseteq followingSibling$$
$$immediatePrecedingSibling = immediateFollowingSibling^-$$
$$\mathcal{T}rans(followingSibling)$$

2.3 XPath to RDQL Translation Algorithm

RDQL [13] is the popular RDF query language from HP Labs Bristol. Each XPath *axis* can be mapped into one or more triple patterns of the target RDQL query. Analogously each *nodetest* and *predicate* can be mapped also with just one or more triple patterns. The output RDQL query always takes the form:

```
SELECT *
WHERE
  (?v1, <rdf:type>, <xmloverrdf:document>)
  [triple pattern 2]
  [triple pattern 3]
  ...
  [triple pattern N]
```

The translation can be deduced from the XPath formal semantics. For example, the *following* axis is described as:

$$A_{following}(x) = \{x_1 \mid x_1 \in A_{descendant-or-self}(x_2)$$
$$\wedge\ x_2 \in A_{following-sibling}(x_3)\}$$
$$\wedge\ x_3 \in A_{ancestor-or-self}(x)\}$$

So the *following* axis must be translated to:

```
(?vi-2, <xmloverrdf:ancestor-or-self>, ?vi-3)
(?vi-1, <xmloverrdf:following-sibling>, ?vi-2)
(?vi, <xmloverrdf:descendant-or-self>, ?vi-1)
```

2.4   Example Results

An example query could be:

```
/child::movies/child::movie/child::title
(in abbreviated form /movies/movie/title)
```

That is translated to:

```
SELECT *
WHERE
          (?v1, <rdf:type>, <xmloverrdf:document>)
        , (?v2, <xmloverrdf:childOf>, ?v1)
        , (?v2, <xmloverrdf:hasName>, "movies")
        , (?v3, <xmloverrdf:childOf>, ?v2)
        , (?v3, <xmloverrdf:hasName>, "movie")
        , (?result, <xmloverrdf:childOf>, ?v3)
        , (?result, <xmloverrdf:hasName>, "title")
```

3   Incorporating Schema-Awareness

3.1   Mapping XML Schema to RDF

Having an XML instance represented with RDF triples opens a lot of possibilities. As we have seen before, we can use OWL constructs (*subPropertyOf, transitiveProperty, sameAs, inverseOf*, etc.) to define the relationship between the different properties defined in the ontology. In our ontology for the XML model, the object of the *hasName* property is not a literal but a resource (an RDF resource). This key aspect allows applying to *hasName* all the potential of the OWL relationships (e.g. defining ontologies with names relationships). So, if we want our XPath processor to be schema-aware, we just need to translate the XML Schema language to RDF, and to add to our XML/RDF Syntax ontology the necessary OWL constructs that allow the inference engine to understand the semantics of the different XML Schema components. The added axioms in Description Logics syntax ($\mathcal{SHIQ}$-like style [17]) would be:

$$hasName \sqsubseteq fromSubstitutionGroup$$
$$\mathcal{T}rans(fromSubstitutionGroup)$$
$$hasName \sqsubseteq fromType$$
$$\mathcal{T}rans(fromType)$$
$$fromType \sqsubseteq subTypeOf$$

3.2 A Simple Example of Schema-Aware XPath Processing

The next example ilustrates the behaviour of our processor in a schema-related XPath query. Take this simple XML document:

```
<A>
  <B id='B1' />
  <B id='B2'>
   <C id='C1'>
    <D id='D1'></D>
   </C>
  </B>
  <B id='B3'/>
</A>
```

And its attached schema:

```
<schema>
 <complexType name='BType'>
   <complexContent>
      <extension base='SUPERBType'></extension>
   </complexContent>
 </complexType>
 <element name='B'
         type='BType' substitutionGroup='SUPERB' />
</schema>
```

When evaluating the XPath query *//SUPERB*, our processor will return the elements with IDs 'B1', 'B2' and 'B3'. These elements have a name with value

'B', and the schema specifies that this name belong to the substitution group
'SUPERB', so they match the query. Also, when evaluating the query //SU-
PERBType, the processor will return 'B1', 'B2' and 'B3'. It assumes that the
query is asking for elements from the type SUPERBType or one of its subtypes.

4   Implementation and Performance

The work has been materialised in the form of a Java API. We have used the
Jena 2 API [11] for RDQL computation and OWL reasoning. To process XPath
expressions we have modified and recompiled the Jaxen XPath Processor [10].
An on-line demo can be found at *http://dmag.upf.edu/contorsion*.

Though performance wasn't the target of the work, it is an important aspect
of the processor. We have realised a performance test over a Java Virtual Machine
v1.4.1 in a 2GHz Intel Pentium processor with 256Mb of memory. The final
delay depends mainly on two variables, the size of the target documents, and
the complexity of the query. Table 1 shows the delay of the inferencing stage
for different document depth levels and also for some different queries.

The processor behaves well with medium-size documents and also with large
ones when simple queries are used (queries that do not involve transitive axis),
but when document size grows, the delay related to the complex queries increases
exponentially. Some performance limitations of the Jena's OWL inference engine
have been described in [18]. We are now working on this problem, trying to obtain
a more scalable inference engine. However, the current processor's performance
is still acceptable for medium-size XML documents.

Table 1. Performance for different document depth levels

expression	5d	10d	15d	20d
/A/B	32ms	47ms	47ms	62ms
/A/B/following-sibling::B	125ms	46ms	48ms	47ms
/A/B/following::B	125ms	62ms	63ms	47ms
/A//B	172ms	203ms	250ms	219ms
//A//B	178ms	266ms	281ms	422ms

5   Testing in the DRM Application Domain

The amount of digital content delivery in the Internet has made Web-scale
Digital Rights Management (DRM) a key issue. Traditionally, DRM Systems
(DRMS) have dealt with this problem for bounded domains. However, when
scaled to the Web, DRMSs are very difficult to develop and maintain. The solution is interoperability of DRMS, i.e. a common framework for understanding
with a shared language and vocabulary. That is why it is not a coincidence that
organisations like MPEG (Moving Picture Experts Group), OMA (Open Mobile
Alliance), OASIS (Organization for the Advancement of Structured Information Standards), TV-Anytime Forum, OeBF (Open eBook Forum) or PRISM
(Publishing Requirements for Industrial Standard Metadata) are all involved in

standardisation or adoption of rights expression languages (REL). Two of the main REL initiatives are MPEG-21 REL [22] and ODRL [20].

Both are XML sublanguages defined by XML Schemas. The XML Schemas define the language syntax and a basic vocabulary. These RELs are then supplemented with what are called Rights Data Dictionaries [21]. They provide the complete vocabulary and a lightweight formalisation of the vocabulary terms semantics as XML Schemas or ad hoc ontologies. ODRL and MPEG-21 REL have just been defined and are available for their implementation in DRMS. They seem quite complete and generic enough to cope with such a complex domain. However, the problem is that they have such a rich structure that they are very difficult to implement. They are rich in the context of XML languages and the "traditional" XML tools like DOM or XPath. There are too many attributes, elements and complexTypes (see Table 2) to deal with.

Table 2. Number of named XML Schema primitives in ODRL and MPEG-21 REL

	Schemas	xsd:attribute	xsd:complexType	xsd:element	Total
ODRL	EX-11	10	15	23	127
	DD-11	3	2	74	
MPEG-21	EL-R	9	56	78	330
	REL-SX	3	35	84	
	REL-MX	1	28	36	

5.1 Application to ODRL License Processing

Consider looking for all constraints in a right expression, usually a rights license, that apply to how we can access the licensed content. This would require so many XPath queries as there are different ways to express constraints. For instance, ODRL defines 23 constraints: industry, interval, memory, network, printer, purpose, quality, etc. This amounts to lots of source code, difficult to develop and maintain because it is very sensible to minor changes to the REL specs. Hopefully there is a workaround hidden in the language definitions.

As we have said, there is the language syntax but also some semantics. The *substitutionGroup* relations among *elements* and the *extension/restriction base* ones among *complexTypes* encode generalisation hierarchies that carry some lightweight, taxonomy-like, semantics. For instance, all constraints in ODRL are defined as XML elements substituting the *o-ex:constraintElement*, see Figure 2. The difficulty is that although this information is provided by the XML Schemas, it remains hidden when working with instance documents of this XML

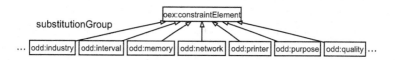

Fig. 2. Some ODRL constraint elements defined as *substitutionGroup* of *constraintElement*

Schemas. However, using the semantics-enabled XPath processor we can profit from all this information. As it has been shown, the XML Schemas are translated to OWL ontologies that make the generalisation hierarchies explicit, using *subClassOf* and *subPropertyOf* relations. The ontology can be used then to carry out the inferences that allow a semantic XPath like "//o-ex:constraintElement" to retrieve all *o-ex:constraintElement* plus all elements defined as its *substitutionGroup*.

5.2   Application to the MPEG-21 Authorisation Model

MPEG-21 defines an authorisation algorithm that is a decision making process resolving a central question *"Is a Principal authorized to exercise a Right such a Resource?"*. In this case, the semantic XPath processor help us when determining if the user has the appropriate rights taking into account the rights lineage defined in the RDD (Rights Data Dictionary).

In contrast with ODRL, that uses XMLSchemas both for the language and dictionary definitions, MPEG-21 has an ontology as dictionary (RDD). The semantics that it provides can also be integrated in our semantic XPath processor. To do that, the MPEG-21 RDD ontology is translated [19] to the ontology language used by the Semantic XPath Processor, i.e. OWL. Once this is done, this ontology is connected to the semantic formalisation build up from the MPEG-21 REL XML Schemas. Consequently, semantic XPath queries can also profit from the ad hoc ontology semantics. For instance, the acts taxonomy in MPEG-21 RDD, see Figure 3, can be seamlessly integrated in order to facilitate license checking implementation. Consider the following scenario: we want to check if our set of licenses authorises us to uninstall a licensed program. If we use

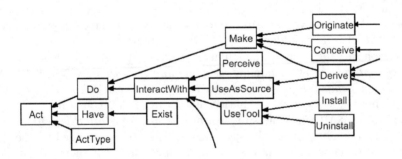

Fig. 3. Portion of the acts taxonomy in MPEG-21 RDD

XPath, there must be a path to look for licenses that grant the *uninstall* act, e.g. "//r:license/r:grant/mx:uninstall". Moreover, as it is shown in the taxonomy, the *usetool* act is a generalisation of the *uninstall* act. Therefore, we must also check for licenses that grant us *usetool*, e.g "//r:license/r:grant/mx:uninstall". An successively, we should check for *interactwith*, *do* and *act*.

However, if we use a semantic XPath, the existence of a license that grants any of the acts that generalise *uninstall* implies that the license also states that the *uninstall* act is also granted. This is so because, by inference, the presence of the fact that relates the license to the granted act implies all the facts that relate the license to all the acts that specialise this act. Therefore, it would suffice to check the semantic XPath expression "//r:license/r:grant/mx:uninstall". If any of the more general acts is granted it would match. For instance, the XML tree */r:license/r:grant/dd:usetool* implies the trees */r:license/r:grant/dd:install* and */r:license/r:grant/dd:uninstall.*

6   Conclusions and Future Work

In this paper we have described a novel strategy for designing a semantic XPath processor that acts over an RDF mapping of XML. We use a *model-mapping approach* to represent instances of XML and XML Schema in RDF. This representation retains the node order, in contrast with the usual *structure-mapping* approach. The obtained processor resolves the queries taking into consideration the structural and semantic connections described in the schemas and ontologies provided by the user. It can be used to express schema-aware queries, to face interoperability among different XML languages or to integrate XML with RDF sources.

In the context of DRM implementation, the Semantic XPath Processor has shown its benefits. First of all, less coding is needed. The Semantic XPath processor allows reusing the semantics hidden in the XML Schemas so we do not need to recode them. Moreover, the code is more independent from the underlying specifications. If there is a change in the specifications, which causes a modification of the XML Schemas, it is only necessary to regenerate the corresponding ontologies. Now we are working to embed the processor in an XQuery implementation to achieve the semantic behaviour also for XQuery expressions.

References

1. A. Y. Halevy, Z. G. Ives, P. Mork, I. Tatarinov: Piazza: Data Management Infrastructure for Semantic Web Applications, 12th International World Wide Web Conference, 2003
2. Cruz, I., Xiao H., Hsu F. An Ontology-based Framework for XML Semantic Integration. University of Illinois at Chicago. Eighth International Database Engineering and Applications Symposium. IDEAS'04. July 7-9, 2004 Coimbra, Portugal.
3. B.Amann,C.Beeri,I.Fundulaki,and M.Scholl.Ontology-Based Integration of XML Web Resources. In Proceedings of the 1st International Semantic Web Conference (ISWC 2002),pages 117-131,2002.
4. M.C.A.Klein. Interpreting XML Documents via an RDF Schema Ontology. In Proceedings of the 13th International Workshop on Database and Expert Systems Applications (DEXA 2002),pages 889-894, 2002.
5. L.V.Lakshmanan and F.Sadri.Interoperability on XML Data. In Proceedings of the 2nd International Semantic Web Conference (ICSW 03), 2003.

6. P.F.Patel-Schneider and J.Simeon.The Yin/Yang web:XML syntax and RDF semantics.In Proceedings of the 11th International World Wide Web Conference (WWW2002), pages 443-453,2002.

7. RPath - RDF query language proposal http://web.sfc.keio.ac.jp/ km/rpath-eng/ rpath.html

8. M. Yoshikawa, T. Amagasa, T. Shimura and S. Uemura, XRel: A Path-Based Approach to Storage and Retrieval of XML Documents using Relational Databases, ACM Transactions on Internet Technology, Vol. 1, No. 1, June 2001.

9. XML Information Set (Second Edition) W3C Recommendation 4 February 2004 http://www.w3.org/TR/xml-infoset/

10. Jaxen: Universal Java XPath Engine http://jaxen.org/

11. Jena 2 - A Semantic Web Framework http://www.hpl.hp.com/semweb/jena.htm

12. RDF/XML Syntax Specification (Revised) W3C Recommendation 10 February 2004 http://www.w3.org/TR/rdf-syntax-grammar/

13. RDQL - A Query Language for RDF W3C Member Submission 9 January 2004 http://www.w3.org/Submission/RDQL/

14. XML Path Language (XPath) 2.0 W3C Working Draft 23 July 2004 http://www.w3.org/TR/xpath20/

15. Dave Reynolds. Jena 2 Inference support http://jena.sourceforge.net/inference/

16. OWL Web Ontology Language Overview. W3C Recommendation 10 February 2004 http://www.w3.org/TR/owl-features/

17. Ian Horrocks, Ulrike Sattler and Stephan Tobies. Practical reasoning for expressive description logics. In Proc. of the 6th Int. Conf. on Logic for Programming and Automated Reasoning (LPAR99), number 1705 in Lecture Notes in Artificial Intelligence, pages 161180. Springer, 1999.

18. Dave Reynolds. Jena 2 Inference support http://jena.sourceforge.net/inference/

19. J. Delgado, I. Gallego and R. Garcia. Use of Semantic Tools for a Digital Rights Dictionary. E-Commerce and Web Technologies: 5th International Conference, 2004. LNCS Volume 3182 (338-347) Springer-Verlag.

20. R. Iannella. Open Digital Rights Language (ODRL), Version 1.1. World Wide Web Consortium 2002 (W3C Note). http://www.w3.org/TR/odrl.

21. G. Rust and C. Barlas. The MPEG-21 Rights Data Dictionary. IEEE Transactions on Multimedia, 2005 volume 7 number 2.

22. X. Wang and T. DeMartini and B. Wragg and M. Paramasivam. The MPEG-21 Rights Expression Language. IEEE Transactions on Multimedia 2005 volume 7 number 2.

23. Lehti and Fankhauser (2004). XML Data Integration with OWL: Experiences & Challenges, SAINT 2004: 160-170.

24. OWL Web Ontology Language Semantics and Abstract Syntax. W3C Recommendation, 10 February 2004. http://www.w3.org/TR/owl-semantics/.

25. RDF Vocabulary Description Language 1.0: RDF Schema. W3C Recommendation, 10 February 2004. http://www.w3.org/TR/rdf-schema/ .

26. Resource Description Framework (RDF): Concepts and Abstract Syntax. W3C Recommendation, 10 February 2004. http://www.w3.org/TR/rdf-concepts/.

Conceptual and Formal Ontology Model of e-Catalogs

Hyunja Lee and Junho Shim

Department of Computer Science,
Sookmyung Women's University,
Seoul 140-742, Korea
{hyunjalee, jshim}@sookmyung.ac.kr

Abstract. Ontology concerns with the nature and relations of being. Electronic catalog contains rich semantics associated with products, and serves as a challenging practical domain for ontology application. It is beneficial to model e-Catalogs based not only on the definition of each product class and the taxonomic hierarchy of classes but also on the associated semantic knowledge. Ontology can play an important role in e-Commerce as a formalization of e-Catalogs. However, an ontological modeling should not be technically too complicated to represent and comprehend the e-Catalog domain for a domain expert who has little knowledge in the formal language. In this paper, we present an ontological representation of e-Catalogs, which is both conceptual and formal. We take an Extended Entity Relationship approach to denote the fundamental set of modeling constructs, and present corresponding description logic representation for each construct. We also consider the modeling language to be reasonably practical with regard to its expressiveness and complexity. We illustrate sample e-Catalog modeling scenarios to demonstrate the practical feasibility of our modeling approach.

1 Introduction

E-Commerce, ranging from e-marketplace and e-procurement to supply chain management and business intelligence, is one area of application that would benefit greatly from the systematic management of rich semantics [10,6,12]. Electronic Catalog (e-Catalog), a key component of any e-Commerce system, contains information such as pricing, features, and terms about the goods. Semantically enriched yet precise information provided by the ontology may enhance the quality and effectiveness of electronic transactions [3,7]. Ontology can play a critical role here.

A dominant and well-known modeling approach for building an ontology application is to directly employ a formal ontology language such as DAML+OIL [6] and OWL [12], to represent the domain knowledge. This approach, mainly favored by the research community with deep computer science background, may be beneficiary for integrating the domain ontology model with an inference engine for the language. However, this approach is deficient in that it is technically too complicated to represent and comprehend the domain for a domain expert who has little knowledge in the formal language. Instead, we claim that a modeling process should moderate

K. Bauknecht et al. (Eds.): EC-Web 2005, LNCS 3590, pp. 11–20, 2005.
© Springer-Verlag Berlin Heidelberg 2005

the conceptual domain knowledge for the perspective of the domain experts, into a formal ontology model described in a formal ontology language. Our goal is to achieve an ontological representation of e-Catalogs, which is both conceptual and formal.

In this paper, we present an ontological modeling of e-Catalogs. Our goal is to represent the semantic information of e-Catalog in a conceptual model, and then to construct a formally sound ontology using description logics.

We take an Extended Entity Relationship approach for conceptual modeling method, and present the fundamental set of modeling constructs and corresponding description language representation for each construct. Additional semantics that cannot be represented in EER are modeled directly in DL. Since each basic construct can be mechanically translated into a corresponding description language block, the resulting model is in pure DL. Our modeling language currently stands within SHIQ(d) [5] which is known reasonably practical with regard to its language expressiveness and algorithmic complexity.

The rest of this paper is organized as follows. Section 2 provides an overview of the related work. Section 3 illustrates our e-Catalog modeling approach. Section 4 provides a scenario to demonstrate the use and benefits of our modeling approach. And finally, Section 5 draws the contribution and conclusion of our work.

2   Related Work

Applying ontology into e-Catalog is described in [2,11,10]. [2] presents the issues of B2B integration, focusing on product information. [11] presents a practical model for eCl@ss and touches upon the practical issues for classification schemes. These previous works have addressed various issues of e-Catalog management, but are limited in that the underlying model was assumed to be the simple code-based hierarchical model. [10] is a recent work to support the ontological needs for designing an enterprise-scale ontology system such as e-Catalog system. Their work is focused on providing programmatical issues including APIs and query languages to manipulate ontologies, rather than modeling the semantic information of e-Catalog.

The need for semantic model of e-Catalog is illustrated in the area of integration of multiple classification code schemes [7,14]. [7] presents that one needs to take a more flexible view of a product instead and its semantics should be captured and represented in a machine-readable form. However, their semantic model for e-Catalogs is limited to the semantic inclusion relationship, and concentrated to find out the subsumption relationships between parent-child classes. [14] also uses the specific types of semantic relationships between product classes, such as synonym or antonym, in order to approach the catalog integration.

We claim that in order to realize e-Catalog ontology, product information should be enriched with *intensional* knowledge using a set of agreed upon concepts and axioms. That is the reason why we employ the description logic. Formally described information in pure DL, however, may be hardly understood for the people who have little knowledge on DL. Therefore we use the Extended Entity Relationship to conceptually and pictorially represent the basic semantic information. A general translation scheme from EER model to DL may be found at [1]. In our preliminary work [8], we introduced a modeling framework to adopt the EER to DL translation scheme for the e-Catalog domain.

For any semantic modeling to be suitable for its application domain, it is crucial to investigate what semantic concepts and relationships are desirable for the domain and to capture them in the model. More specifically, as mentioned in [3], ontological modeling of e-Catalog requires specifying a conceptualization of e-Catalog in terms of classes, properties, relationships, and constraints. We participated in a project [9] to building an operational product ontology database for a public procurement service agency, and learned what concepts, in terms of classes, properties, relationships, and constraints, may be fundamental to represent the products and services. In this paper, we include those concepts in our model.

Finally, we present a scenario to illustrate the practical usability of our conceptual yet formal modeling approach in an e-Catalog domain, which is another unique feature distinguished to our previous work.

3   Modeling of E-Catalogs

3.1   Extended Entity-Relationship

For the conceptual representation of the fundamental model of e-Catalog, we use an Extended Entity-Relationship approach. (Figure 1) Basic modeling elements are entities, denoting a set of product objects, and relationships between entities. Since an entity can participate in the same relationship with different roles, a unique role name is assigned to each ER-roles. A relationship between two entities may represent arbitrary semantic relationship between entities. An important relationship in e-Catalog is the inclusion relationship which consists of the following two types: class inclusion (isa) or meronymic inclusion (part-whole), where the former is depicted by triangle as the later by pentagon.

Figure 1 illustrates a simple catalog model for the computer products in EER. As explained in the following sections, each modeling construct in EER is then translated into the corresponding description language syntax.

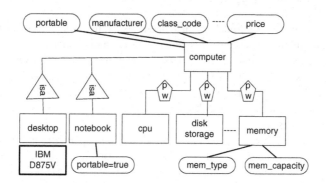

Fig. 1. A simple e-Catalog model in EER

3.2   Classes and Objects for e-Catalogs

A class is a set of objects (or items), with the same set of attributes. Each class is represented as a concept inclusion TBox in description language. Each attribute is atomic and has one of the following predefined domains: Integer, Real, String, and Boolean. If a class C contains single valued attributes $A_1,...,A_n$, and each attribute has $D_1,...,D_n$, respectively, then we express it as following: $C \sqsubseteq \forall A_1.D_1 \sqcap =1A_1 \sqcap ... \sqcap \forall A_n.D_n \sqcap =1A_n$. The number restriction $=1A_i$ represents A_i is a single valued. If a class has a multi-valued attribute, then the maximum cardinality of the attribute can be represented as $\leq maxA_i$. Integer, Real, String, and Boolean are concrete domain attributes (predefined classes) and have concrete type expressions such as $\leq_d$, $\geq_d$, $>_d$, $<_d$, $\geq_d \sqcap \leq_d$, $=_d$. Finally, each individual product object is represented as a ABox in DL.

For example, as shown in the Figure 1, *Computer* class has *portable, manufacturer, class_code*, and *price* attributes, and each attribute has Boolean, String, and Integer concrete domain data type, respectively. And *IBMD875V* is an individual computer product of which product class code is 43211508. It is not portable, manufactured by IBM and its price is $2500. Then they can be formally described as following.

$Computer \sqsubseteq \forall portable.Boolean \sqcap = 1portable \sqcap \forall mfr.String \sqcap = 1mfr \sqcap \forall class\_code.String \sqcap = 1class\_code \sqcap \forall price.Integer \sqcap = 1price,$

$Computer(IBMD875V), portable(IBMD875V, False), mfr(IBMD875V, 'IBM'), class\_code(IBMD875V, '43211508'), price(IBMD875V, 2500)$

Our experience of analyzing a practical e-Catalog domain shows that the following four types of classes should be regarded as the most conceivable ones: *products, classification scheme, attributes,* and *UOMs* [9]. The products, the most important concept, are for the goods or services. For example, all the classes shown in Figure 1 are products. The classification scheme and the attributes are used for the classifications and descriptions of products, respectively. The UOM is short for the unit-of-measures and it is associated with the attributes. The classes may have relationships each other and the relationships are covered in the following section.

3.3   Relationships for e-Catalogs

The types of semantic relationships has been researched for a long time in multi discipline areas including cognitive science, logics, and databases. A classification scheme by [13] presents one of the various viewpoints of classifying the semantic relationships. Based on both their work and our field experience [9], we have a taxonomy of semantic relationships as in Figure 2, in which top-level relationships include the general domain relationships, e-Catalog domain specific relationships, and user-defined relationships.

The relationships for general domain include *inclusion, attribution,* and *synonym*. As in [14], they are semantically generic to various domains, and we should consider them as meaningful semantic relationships for the e-Catalog domain as well.

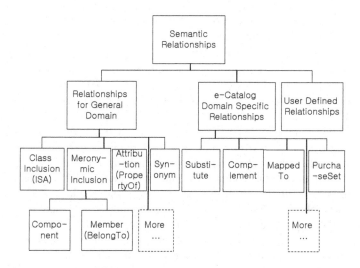

Fig. 2. A taxonomy of semantic relationships for e-Catalog

The *inclusion* relationship describes cases in which an entity type contains other entity types, and it can be classified into the *class inclusion* or *meronymic inclusion*. The *class inclusion* represents the standard subtype/supertype relationship. If C is a subtype of D, then it is written as $C \sqsubseteq D$ in DL. The attributes of D are inherited to C. Those inherited attributes need not reappearing in C, in that inheritance is already embodied within the semantic of $\sqsubseteq$.

The *meronymic inclusion* between C and D represents a *part-whole* relationship, i.e., C is a part of D (D is the whole of C), or simply C has D. For example, HDD and CPU are the parts of computer, and the beef-stew has beef, garlic, and onion. There are different semantic interpretations of this part-whole relationship. Similar to [13] we found part-whole relationships to include *component-of*, *substance-of*, *member-of*, *portion-of*, and *feature-of* relationships. For example, *Computer* has *Hdd*, and *Hdd* has *Dcspindle* motor as its part. This part-whole(has) relationship is an example of the *component-of*, and it can be written in DL as following.

$Hdd \sqsubseteq \exists component\text{-}of.Computer, \quad Hdd \sqsubseteq \exists component\text{-}of_t.Computer,$
$Dcspindle \sqsubseteq \exists component\text{-}of.Hdd, \quad Dcspindle \sqsubseteq \exists component\text{-}of_t.Hdd,$
$component\text{-}of \sqsubseteq composed\text{-}of^{-1}, \quad component\text{-}of_t \sqsubseteq composed\text{-}of_t^{-1},$
$composed\text{-}of \sqsubseteq component\text{-}of^{-1}, \quad composed\text{-}of_t \sqsubseteq component\text{-}of_t^{-1},$
$component\text{-}of_t, composed\text{-}of_t \in S+$

The *component-of* and *composed-of* have inverse property each other, i.e., $component\text{-}of^{-1} \sqsubseteq composed\text{-}of$, $component\text{-}of \sqsubseteq composed\text{-}of^{-1}$. In order to handle indirect part-whole relationship, we need the transitive property $x \ pw \ y \ \& \ y \ pw \ z \Rightarrow x \ pw \ z$. We employ *component-of* and *component-of_t* for corresponding to direct and indirect respectively, and specify $component\text{-}of_t \in S^+$ (and similarly *composed-of_t* as well).

The *attribution* describes situation where an entity type describes property or characteristic of other entity types. And finally, the *synonym* relationship describes an entity type contains similar semantics to other entity types, and represented as $C{\equiv}D$, i.e., $C \sqcap D \wedge C \sqcap D$. For example, if *Laptop* computer is identical to *Notebook*, but referenced in either way, then we may define $Laptop \equiv Notebook$.

The next set of semantic relationships is particularly conceivable relationships for the e-Catalog domain. It includes *substitute, supplement (or complement), purchase-set,* and *mapped-to* relationships. For examples, a pencil is a *substitute* of a ballpoint pen, and a LCD monitor is a *substitute* of a CRT monitor in that each may role as a replacement of the other. The *supplement* relationship represents that one may be added to another in order to complete a thing or extend the whole. For example, an antiglare filter is a *supplement* to a CRT monitor. And similar but not identical to these, we may also see that such products as monitors, OS, and mouse are also purchased with a personal computer. This is represented as *purchase-set,* i.e., a personal computer has *purchase-set* relationships with monitors, OS, and mouse.

While such substitute, supplement, or purchase-set are relationships among product classes, the *mapped-to* relationship is to assign a product into a specific class code within a classification scheme, or to map a class code of a classification scheme into the codes of different classification schemes. For example, a LCD panel product is *mapped to (belonged to)* 43172410 commodity class under a certain standard classification scheme. Then, a product class may be defined or classified differently depending on classification schemes. For example, the product personal computer is mapped to 43171803 in UNSPSC classification system, and 8471-10 or 8471-41 in HS code system.

Note that those e-Catalog semantic relationships may be written in DL in similar ways for the generic ones, and due to the page limit we do not illustrate the details in this paper. And finally we may have user-defined semantic relationships to represent the specific purposes.

4 An Example Scenario

In this section, we present a scenario to illustrate the practical feasibility of use of our modeling approach in an e-Catalog domain. The scenario is for the Customs Service Administration to regulate their export-embargo product classes. For example, let us assume that the electronic industry has developed a new DC spindle motor with diameter less than 0.1". Since such a motor especially manufactured by IBM has some features which could be borrowed for manufacturing the massive destructive device, the administration wants to prohibit any product internally containing the IBM motor from being exported. The objective is to have their product catalog modeled in a conceptual and formal way to support such an export embargo.

In order to do this, first of all, their catalog should have part information for electronic device products. A device may be a part of another device, and such direct and indirect part semantics must be modeled and made available by a Custom Service Administration domain expert (conceptual modeling). Figure 3 shows an EER view of hardware products and their parts. The pictorial donation of EER modeling method helps the conceptual representation of the semantics.

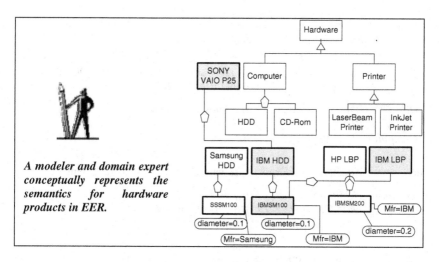

Fig. 3. Customs Service e-Catalog model in EER

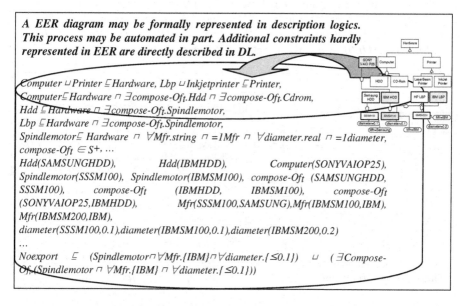

A EER diagram may be formally represented in description logics. This process may be automated in part. Additional constraints hardly represented in EER are directly described in DL.

$Computer \sqcup Printer \sqsubseteq Hardware$, $Lbp \sqcup Inkjetprinter \sqsubseteq Printer$,

$Computer \sqsubseteq Hardware \sqcap \exists compose\text{-}Of_t.Hdd \sqcap \exists compose\text{-}Of_t.Cdrom$,

$Hdd \sqsubseteq Hardware \sqcap \exists compose\text{-}Of_t.Spindlemotor$,

$Lbp \sqsubseteq Hardware \sqcap \exists compose\text{-}Of_t.Spindlemotor$,

$Spindlemotor \sqsubseteq Hardware \sqcap \forall Mfr.string \sqcap =1Mfr \sqcap \forall diameter.real \sqcap =1diameter$,

$compose\text{-}Of_t \in S^+, ...$

$Hdd(SAMSUNGHDD)$, $Hdd(IBMHDD)$, $Computer(SONYVAIOP25)$,

$Spindlemotor(SSSM100)$, $Spindlemotor(IBMSM100)$, $compose\text{-}Of_t$ $(SAMSUNGHDD,$

$SSSM100)$, $compose\text{-}Of_t$ $(IBMHDD,$ $IBMSM100)$, $compose\text{-}Of_t$

$(SONYVAIOP25,IBMHDD)$, $Mfr(SSSM100,SAMSUNG),Mfr(IBMSM100,IBM)$,

$Mfr(IBMSM200,IBM)$,

$diameter(SSSM100,0.1),diameter(IBMSM100,0.1),diameter(IBMSM200,0.2)$

...

$Noexport \sqsubseteq (Spindlemotor \sqcap \forall Mfr.\{IBM\} \sqcap \forall diameter.\{\leq 0.1\}) \sqcup (\exists Compose\text{-}Of_t.(Spindlemotor \sqcap \forall Mfr.\{IBM\} \sqcap \forall diameter.\{\leq 0.1\}))$

Fig. 4. A formal model in DL corresponding to Fig. 3

The part of EER model we are interested in can be translated into description logic in Figure 4. The export embargo list should include not only electronic devices which use the IBM motor as its direct part, but also other hardware products which contain the motor internally as its indirect part. In the figure, *IBMSM100* is the individual product (object) which satisfies the embargo condition: *Spindlemotor* $\sqcap \forall Mfr.\{IBM\}$ $\sqcap \forall diameter.\{\leq 0.1\}$, where the data type of *diameter* is Real which has concrete domain interpretation on the equality comparison operator. Other spindle motors such as *IBMSM200* and *SSSM100* do not match the condition.

Then *IBMSM100* is a part of both *IBM HDD* and *IBM LBP* products which are an individual product (object) of HDD and Laser-beam Printer product classes, respectively. And *SONY VAIO P25* product uses the *IBM HDD* product as its part.

> *Hdd(IBMHDD) ⊑ Hardware ⊓ ∃compose-Of.{IBMSM100}*
> *Lbp(IBMLBP) ⊑ Printer ⊓ ∃compose-Of.{IBMSM100}*
> *Computer(SONYVAIOP25) ⊑ Hardware ⊓ ∃compose-Of.{IBMHDD}*

Then, we may declare a *NoExport* hardware product class as following:

> *Noexport ⊑ (Spindlemotor ⊓ ∀Mfr.{IBM}*
> *⊓ ∀diameter.{ ≤0.1})⊔ (∃Compose-Of.*
> *Spindlemotor⊓ ∀Mfr.{IBM}⊓ ∀diameter.{ ≤0.1}))*

Our e-Catalog model represented in DL may be translated into a DL-based ontology language. This means that we can implement the model into a knowledgebase in that language which has a run-able reasoning engine. For example, we can implement the scenario in RACER, a description logic reasoning tool [5], and Figure 5 shows that the tool returns *Noexport* as *{SONY VAIO P250, IBMHDD, IBMLBP, IBMSM100}*, which is the right set of export embargo product classes.

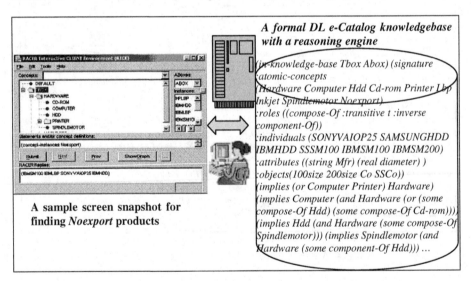

Fig. 5. A screen snapshot of finding *Noexport* using a reasoning tool [5]

5   Conclusion

Modeling e-Catalogs, as for any other domain, demands domain expertise and experience. It also requires the ability to analyze the ontological expressiveness and complexity necessary for the domain. In addition, clear understanding of description logics (DL) is another requirement to develop a formal ontology.

We have introduced an ontological modeling for the e-Catalog domain. The objective of our work is to present a both conceptual and formally sound e-Catalog ontology model. The approach is based on EER and description logic. We claim this work to be a preliminary groundwork towards the practical application of ontological concepts into the e-Catalog domain.

DAML+OIL or its superset follower OWL has a theoretical background on DL, and they all have common features. Our model in DL may be easily translated into them. The expressiveness and complexity of modeling constructor provided by OWL should be selectively looked into along with its practical usage in the e-Catalog domain.

Finally, in our approach, an EER diagram is formally represented in description logics. One of our ongoing works is to build a modeling tool to automate this translation process. The interface of our tool may be similar to an existing tool like [4], but distinguished as well in ways that it includes a variety of specialized modeling features for the e-Catalog domain and EER to OWL translation capability as well as EER to DL.

Acknowledgement

This Research was supported by the Sookmyung Women's University Research Grants 2005.

References

1. D. Calvanese, M. Lenzerini, and D. Nardi, "Unifying Class-Based Representation Formalisms," Journal of Artificial Intelligence Research, Vol. 11, AI Access Foundation and Morgan Kaufmann Publishers, 1999.
2. Z. Cui, D. Jones, and P. O'Brien, "Semantic B2B Integration: Issues in Ontology-based Approaches," SIGMOD Record, Vol. 31(1), ACM, 2002.
3. D. Fensel, Y. Ding, B. Omelayenko, E. Schulten, G. Botquin, M. Brown, and A. Flet, "Product Data Integration in B2B E-Commerce," IEEE Intelligent Systems, Vol. 16, IEEE Society, 2001.
4. E. Franconi and G. Ng, "The i•com Tool for Intelligent Conceptual Modelling," 7th. International Workshop on Knowledge Representation meets Databases (KRDB'00), 2000.
5. V. Haarslev and R. Möller, "Description Logic Systems with Concrete Domains: Applications for the Semantic Web," 10th International Workshop on Knowledge Representation meets Databases (KRDB'03), 2003.
6. F. van Harmelen, P.F. Patel-Schneider, and I. Horrocks (Editors), Reference description of the DAML+OIL ontology markup language, http://www.daml.org/2001/03/reference, 2001.
7. D. Kim, J. Kim, and S. Lee, "Catalog Integration for Electronic Commerce through Category-Hierarchy Merging Technique," 12th International Workshop on Research Issues on Data Engineering (RIDE2002), IEEE Society, 2002.

8. H. Lee, J. Shim, and D. Kim, "Ontological Modeling of e-Catalogs using EER and Description Logics," Proc. of the International Workshop on Data Engineering Issues in E-Commerce (in conjunction with ICDE 2005), IEEE Society, 2005.

9. I. Lee, S. Lee, T. Lee, S. Lee, D. Kim, J. Chun, H. Lee, and J. Shim, "Practical Issues for Building a Product Ontology System," Proc. of the International Workshop on Data Engineering Issues in E-Commerce (in conjunction with ICDE 2005), IEEE Society, 2005.

10. J. Lee and R. Goodwin, "SNOBASE, for Semantic Network Ontology Base," http://www.alphaworks.ibm.com/aw.nsf/bios/snobase.

11. J. Leukel, V. Schmitz, and F. Dorloff, "A Modeling Approach for Product Classification Systems," Proc. of the Database and Expert Systems Applications, 13th International Conference (DEXA 2002), Springer-Verlag, 2002.

12. M.K. Smith, C. Welty, and D.L. McGuinness, "OWL Web Ontology Language Guide – W3C Recommendation," http://www.w3c.org/TR/owl-guide/, 2004.

13. V. C. Storey, "Understanding Semantic Relationships," VLDB Journal, Vol. 2, VLDB Endowment, 1993.

14. G. Yan, W. K. Ng, and E. Lim, "Product Schema integration for Electronic Commerce - A Synonym Comparison Approach," IEEE Transaction on Knowledge and Data Engineering, Vol. 14(3), IEEE Society, 2002.

Automatic Ontology Mapping for Agent Communication in an e-Commerce Environment

Marina Mongiello and Rodolfo Totaro

Dipartimento di Elettrotecnica ed Elettronica,
Politecnico di Bari, Bari - Italy
{mongiello, r.totaro}@poliba.it

Abstract. Internet-based e-commerce provides a high level of flexibility and openness though presenting many drawbacks due to the heterogeneity of the exchanged information. Ontologies are a key technology to solve many of the problems of e-commerce, in fact many companies use ontologies as a method of exchanging meaning between different agents. As ontology usage becomes more prevalent, the need for ontology reconciliation increases. In fact, ontology mapping methods can contribute to solve the problem of knowledge communication and interchange.

In this paper we present an automatic method for ontology mapping. The method is made up of two phases: a lexical-semantic analysis based on the WordNet thesaurus and a structural analysis based on a matching algorithm that finds semantic mappings between two ontologies expressed in Attributive Language with Number description ($\mathcal{ALN}$) Description logic. The mapped ontologies describe the same conceptualization through a set of rules that join related concepts. We deployed the proposed approach in a prototype system that currently is employed for large scale experiments. A simple experiment with a case study domain has shown a good correspondence with human mapping manually conducted and the system provided results.

1 Introduction

Web-enabled e-commerce helps user contact a large number of potential clients, hence it needs to be open to a large numbers of suppliers and buyers. However the open and flexible e-commerce requires to deal with the question of heterogeneity in the product, catalog and document description standards of the trading partners. Hence it is necessary to provide solutions to the problem of openness, heterogeneity and dynamic nature of the exchanged content, through the normalization, mapping and updating of the exchanged data. Intelligent solutions that help to mechanize the process of structuring, aligning and standardizing are key requisites to successfully overcoming the current bottlenecks of e-commerce and enabling its further growth. Ontology technology can solve many of this problems, in fact they are used as a method of exchanging meaning between different agents. As ontology usage becomes more prevalent, the need for ontology reconciliation increases. Ontology mapping methods can contribute to solve the problem of knowledge communication and interchange. Approaches to carry

K. Bauknecht et al. (Eds.): EC-Web 2005, LNCS 3590, pp. 21–30, 2005.

out the mapping process either in a completely automated or semi-automatic fashion have been proposed. A comprehensive review of the state of the art in the semantic integration using ontologies is in [17,10]. However, let us recall the more relevant approaches. A semi-automatic mapping is proposed in [15]: SKAT system requires the interaction with a human expert to find the best set of mapping rules. A different approach is the method proposed in [20]. It can be applied when two agents with different ontologies would interact and have some common individuals in their knowledge bases. The method assumes that there are common individuals. A method based on a statistical approach is implemented in Glue [5] system that uses an automatic method for ontology mapping by estimating concepts similarity between ontologies comparing individuals stored in knowledge bases. Glue system works only on taxonomy of concepts in ontologies. Prompt [18] performs merging of ontologies. Ontomorph [4], Chimaera [13], Hical [9] use a variety of heuristics to match ontology elements. Anchor-Prompt [19] treats ontology as a graph with classes as nodes and slots as links. In [11] similarity between the nodes of two taxonomy is computed based on an TDF/IF model. In [8] the author reformulate the matching problem as that of propositional satisfiability.

In this paper we propose an algorithm for matching the concepts of two ontologies with the aim to completely automate the mapping. The algorithm is composed by a lexical-semantic analysis based on WordNet [7] thesaurus and a structural analysis based on a matching algorithm. The lexical-semantic analysis gives a measure of similarity between concept names in ontologies and returns the possible sets of mapping rules. After that, the structural analysis gives an evaluation of each set of mapping rules and chooses the best set.

With respect to existing methods, our approach is completely automated. This is an advantage since the manual specification of correspondences between concepts would be a time-consuming and error-prone process. Besides, it considers not only the hierarchical structure of concepts in the ontologies but also relations between them. This is important for conducting the structural analysis in which it is possible to reason also on the relations between concepts. A third feature of our method is the fact that it does not use individuals hence it is well-suited for reasoning also on not data-oriented ontologies. We deployed the proposed approach in a prototype system. While large scale experiments are in progress, a simple experiment with a case study ontology has shown a good correspondence with human mapping manually conducted and the system provided results.

The remaining of the paper is organized as follows. In Section 2 we briefly recall the formalism we use for representing ontologies and the tools for conducting lexical and structural analysis, after that we define the method through the description of the lexical and the structural analysis. Section 3 describes an application of the method in an applicative scenario concerning the apartment rental environment. Section 4 and 5 describe respectively our implementation and empirical evaluation. Last section concludes the paper and proposes further developments.

2   Two-Phases Ontology Mapping

In this section we describe the proposed method that is made up of two phases, a lexical-semantic analysis and a structural one. We use formalisms and tools to support our method. More precisely, we use Description Logics (DL) [6], [1] to describe ontologies and CLASSIC reasoner [2] for the implementation of the algorithm developed for ontology mapping. The lexical-semantic analysis is based on WordNet [14,7] thesaurus. To determine the measure of semantic similarity between two concepts we use the Leacock and Chodorow measure [3]. It is based on the length of paths between concepts in a taxonomy and to WordNet for the representation of concepts.

Our method can be applied to ontologies described in $\mathcal{ALN}$ logic [6].

Lexical-semantic analysis. The first phase of the analysis is a lexical semantic analysis for comparing the names of concepts in ontologies. The analysis follows the method proposed by Cupid [12] through a normalization step and the evaluation of a similarity measure. Semantically similar concept names contain abbreviations, acronyms, punctuation, etc. that make them syntactically different. To make them comparable, according to Cupid method, we normalize them into sets of name tokens.

First of all we perform *Tokenization*, (parsing names into tokens based on punctuations and acronyms): the names are parsed into tokens by a customizable tokenizer using punctuation, upper case, special symbols, digits, etc. e.g. $POLines \Rightarrow \{PO, Lines\}$. The second step is *Expansion* (identifying abbreviations and acronyms) in which abbreviations and acronyms are expanded, e.g. $\{PO, Lines\} \Rightarrow \{Purchase, Order, Lines\}$. The third step is the *Elimination* (discarding prepositions, articles, etc.): tokens such as articles, prepositions or conjunctions are marked to be ignored during comparison. Concept names not included in WordNet are normalized like a composed-word. After that each concept is represented by a set of tokens. Finally we compute *Similarity measure*. Given two ontologies O_1 and O_2, let T_1 and T_2 be respectively a set of tokens in O_1 and O_2; we compute a similarity measure between the two sets as:

$$ns(T_1, T_2) = \frac{\sum_{t_1 \in T_1} [max_{t_2 \in T_2} sim(t_1, t_2)] + \sum_{t_2 \in T_2} [max_{t_1 \in T_1} sim(t_1, t_2)]}{|T_1| + |T_2|}$$

where $sim(t_1, t_2)$ is the Leacock-Chodorow similarity measure and t_1 and t_2 are tokens.

The resulting measure allows us to distinguish between different categories of similarity depending on the relation of the similarity with two threshold parameters α and β. We computed these parameters as an average of similarity measure between pairs of words that normally are considered synonyms and subsumee-subsumer by knowledge engineers respectively. We use $\alpha = 2.85$ and $\beta = 2.16$; anyway their value can be tuned in the prototype system. The sets that can be determined are *Synonym* (if $ns(T1, T2) > \alpha$); *Related* (if $\beta < ns(T1, T2) < \alpha$); *Not related* (if $ns(T1, T2) < \beta$); *Antinomy*. We consider a pair of sets as antinomy if there is a pair of tokens (t_1, t_2), $t_1 \in T_1$ and $t_2 \in T_2$, that WordNet considers antinomy. If a token is not indexed in WordNet, the semantic measure belongs to the set *Not related*, thus the choice depends on the structural analysis phase. Anyway in our prototype it is possible to adopt also different solutions.

Definition 1. *Given a concept C we denote with $Syn(C)$ the set of synonyms of the concept C and with $Rel(C)$ the set of concept related to C.*

Structural analysis and the distance algorithm. In this subsection we present the structural analysis and an algorithm for computing semantic distance between concepts.

Discovering potentially acceptable mappings. First of all we determine all the potentially acceptable mappings. To this purpose let us give some useful definitions.

Definition 2. *Given two ontologies O_1 and O_2 and a concept C in O_1, $A(C)$ is the set of possible associations of the concept C with concepts of O_2. $A(C)$ is defined as follows: $A(C) = Syn(C)$ if $Syn(C) \neq \emptyset$ and $A(C) = Rel(C) + \{\perp\}$ if $Syn(C) = \emptyset$*

Definition 3. *Given two ontologies O_1 and O_2, a mapping rule is a pair (C,D) where C is a concept of O_1 and $D \in A(C)$. $rule(O_1, O_2)$ is the set of mapping rules between O_1 and O_2.*

Definition 4. *An empty rule is a mapping rule (C, D) with $D \equiv \perp$*

The *empty rule* represents the possibility that the destination ontologies do not provide a corresponding concept in a source ontology.

Definition 5. *Given two ontologies O_1 and O_2 to map, a potentially acceptable mapping is a set of mapping rules defined as follows:*

$$Map = \{(C_i, D) \in rules(O_1, O_2) | i = 1, ...n_{O_1} \wedge C_1 \neq C_2 \neq ...C_{n_{O_1}}\}$$

where n_{O_1} is the number of concepts in the ontology O_1.

After having considered rules between concepts, rules between roles should be considered. They are determined considering that there is a match between pair of roles that joins pairs of matching concepts. Each potentially acceptable mapping is completed with rules between roles according to the previously defined rule, that have a similarity measure greater than a prefixed threshold.

Evaluation of potentially acceptable mappings. The evaluation of a potentially acceptable mapping is obtained through an auxiliary ontology. The concept names in the source ontology are replaced with the names of matched concepts in the destination one according to the rules of the potentially acceptable mappings. Names are replaced only in the right side of the concept definitions. Rules between roles are applied only if they have the same direction in the two ontologies. The number of times in which these rules cannot be applied is computed and used as a parameter for the mapping evaluation.

During the previous phases inconsistences can be determined in the knowl-edge base, this can happen while loading the destination and auxiliary ontology in the same KB; in this case uncorrect mappings are marked.

The measure for the evaluation of the correctness of potentially acceptable mapping is computed as average of concept distance, i.e. the structural similar-ity between two concepts in a rule. Such a value is returned by an algorithm we will describe later. In fact, since concepts in the destination and auxiliary ontologies use the same vocabulary, for a given rule in the potentially acceptable mapping we can compute the distance between two DL descriptions. Evalua-tion of Potentially acceptable Mappings, EPM is computed using the following measure:

$$EPM = \frac{\sum_{i=1}^{N} conceptDistance(C_i^1, C_i^2) - 2 \cdot K \cdot N_R}{2 \cdot N}$$

where N is the number of rules between not atomic concepts that are in the potentially acceptable mapping, N_R is the number of not applicable rules be-tween roles and K is a weight varying in the range $[0, 1]$. The obtained measure is an average between $conceptDistance$ values corrected by $K * N_R$ since a not applicable rule gives an increment of the $conceptDistance$ value. The value is returned by algorithm $conceptDistance$. K is a parameter whose value can be set through the system interface. Let us now describe the algorithm; it extends an algorithm for matchmaking that some of us contributed to define [16], and provides a symmetric measure of concept distance. The algorithm applies to normal form of input concepts.

```
Algorithm conceptDistance(C, D);
input CLASSIC concepts C, D, in normal form,
output distance n ≥ 0, where 0 means that C ≡ D
begin algorithm
    if  C ⊓ D is not satisfiable
        return ∞
    let n := 0 in
        /* add to n the number of concept names in D */
        /* which are not among the concept names of C and viceversa */
        1. n := n + |D_{names+} - C_{names+}| + |C_{names+} - D_{names+}|;
        /* add 2 to n for each number restrictions of D */
        /* that is not in C */
        2. for each concept (≥ x R) ∈ D_♯
        such that there is no concept (≥ y R) ∈ C_♯ with y ≥ x
                n := n + 2;
        3. for each concept (≤ x R) ∈ D_♯
        such that there is no concept (≤ y R) ∈ C_♯ with y ≤ x
                n := n + 2;
        /* for each universal role quantification in D */
        /* add the result of a recursive call */
        4. for each concept ∀R.E ∈ D_{all}
            if  there does not exist ∀R.F ∈ C_{all}
                then n := n + conceptDistance(⊤, E) + conceptDistance(⊤, F);
                else n := n + conceptDistance(F, E);
        return n;
end algorithm
```

Selection of the final mapping. Among all the evaluated potentially acceptable mappings we select the final mapping as the one that satisfies some conditions.

First of all it must have the minimum value of minimum EPM; the second condition to be verified is the minimum number of rules between concepts (for a given EPM); finally it must have the maximum average of the lexical-semantic similarity measure for the rules that appear in the potentially acceptable mappings. The second condition is necessary because if adding a new mapping rule to a possible mapping its EPM does not decrease, the new rule may be uncorrect. In this case, for a given EPM, the mapping with a minor number of rules is selected.

3   Scenario

In this Section we describe an application of the proposed method in a e-commerce scenario as shown in Figure 1. Let us consider two or more agents for e-commerce that can communicate; each agent has an engine and manages several ontologies concerning different domains. The knowledge base concerning a particular domain stores several descriptions of requests. The agent receives a request by an end-user, searches for a description in its knowledge base that satisfies user's request. If the search does not provide satisfactory results, the agent may try to find in an external knowledge base a description better fitting the request. Hence it could forward the request to another agent. To this purpose the request should be mapped in the corresponding ontology. Once determined the mapping rules between the two ontologies, the source description is translated in the destination description. The agent that manages the destination ontology searches for a description that satisfies the request. Finally, the set of results is sent to the client and the final selection is submitted to the end-user. As an example, we refer to an apartment rental environment. The agent should satisfy user's requests concerning, for example, a searched apartment, if the request could not be satisfied, it can be forwarded to another agent.

Let us now describe how to use mapping rules to translate descriptions of concepts belonging to the source ontology to descriptions of corresponding concepts

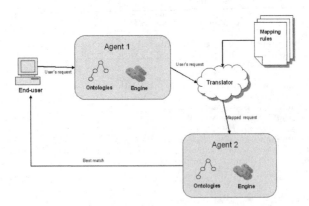

Fig. 1. Scenario

Table 1. How to use mapping rules

Source Concept	Rules	Translated concept
$Flat$	$Flat-> apartment$	$apartment$
$\forall hasRoom.SingleRoom$	$SingleRoom-> single\_room$	$\forall contains\_room.single\_room$
	$hasRoom-> contains\_rooms$	
$(\geq 2\ hasRoom)$	$hasRoom-> contains\_rooms$	$(\geq 2\ contains\_room)$
$\forall occupants.Student$	$occupants-> occupants$	$\forall occupants.student$
	$Student-> student$	
$\forall hasFacilities.ADSL$	$ADSL-> adsl$	$---$

belonging to the destination ontology. A concept description is a conjunction of concepts S_i of the source ontology: $C \equiv S_1 \sqcap S_2 \sqcap ... \sqcap S_n$. The translated description will represent only concepts S_i for which there exist mapping rules for all concepts used in the description of S_i. As an example, let us consider the mapping rules described in Table 1 and the following description:

$Flat \sqcap \forall hasRoom.SingleRoom \sqcap (\geq 2\ hasRoom) \sqcap \forall occupants.Student \sqcap$
$\sqcap \forall hasFacilities.ADSL$

Translation of a description is performed by considering for each concept in the conjunction the proper rules. A concept is omitted if the corresponding rule is not available, thus obtaining a more general description that is anyway useful for retrieval. Using mapping rules, we obtain the following translated description:
$apartment \sqcap \forall contains\_room.single\_room \sqcap (\geq 2\ contains\_room) \sqcap \forall occupants.student$
In the previous description, "$\forall hasFacilities.ADSL$" is not present in the translated description, since a rule for "$hasFacilities$" is not available.

4   A Prototype System

To validate the proposed approach a prototype system for mapping between ontologies has been implemented. The system, as shown in the component diagram in Figure 2, embeds NeoClassic reasoner and WordNet dictionary.

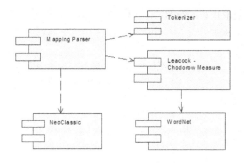

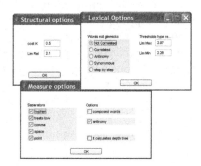

Fig. 2. Component diagram of the prototype system architecture

Fig. 3. Options

The module Mapping Parser extracts concepts from the two ontologies, uses the two modules Leacock-Chodorow measure and the Tokenizer. It computes semantic similarity between concept names, extracts and evaluates the potentially acceptable mappings through the concept distance algorithm and NeoClassic reasoner, a C++ implementation of the CLASSIC reasoner. The Tokenizer module implements the tokenization described in the Section 2; we can configure Tokenizer options through the Measure Options Window shown in the Figure 3 that shows also the Lexical Options Window and the Structural Options one. In the Lexical Options Window we can set α and β thresholds (respectively Lim Min and Lim Max in the figure) or choose a default set for the measures that can not be computed, if a term is not indexed in WordNet. In the Structural Options Window we can set the K parameter and the threshold for semantic relation similarity.

5   Empirical Evaluation and Discussion

The algorithm has been evaluated in the apartment rental domain. The test was performed on three ontologies created by different expert users. This choice of different users was due to the need of ensuring different models of the given domain, in fact, generally different person models in different way the same domain. This ensures that the ontologies are different both for the vocabulary for expressing concept names and for the choice of relations between concepts. Let us refer to the following example:

Ontology 1: $SeaVilla \equiv House \sqcap \forall isLocated.Sea$; $Flat \sqsubseteq House$;

Ontology 2: $SeaHouse \sqsubseteq House$; $Apartment \sqsubseteq House$.

To evaluate the performances of the algorithm, we compared the set of mapping rules returned by the algorithm with those of a manually conducted mapping.

We chose two parameters to evaluate the performance of the algorithm: the percentage of exact mapping rules, i.e. perfect match and the percentage of acceptable mapping rules, i.e. acceptable rules, obtained as the sum of exact mapping rules and imprecise ones.

Exact mapping rules are those in which the system returns the same rules selected in the manual mapping. Imprecise rules are those found by the system that are not uncorrected but that anyway are not the best ones.

In the previous example, the relation between *SeaHouse* in the second ontology and *House* in the first one is assumed as an imprecise rule since *SeaHouse* is however a *House* but it could be better associated to *SeaVilla* in the first ontology.

We performed the mapping on the three ontologies, determining a range of 63%-81% for Perfect Match and 71%-88% for Acceptable match. Figure 4 demonstrates the results for the various mappings.

Such a variability in the percentage can be explained by considering the single rules found out by the algorithm. It was noticed that the algorithm behaves in a more efficient manner when the compared ontologies are strongly connected inside, hence there is a high number of relations between concepts. On the other

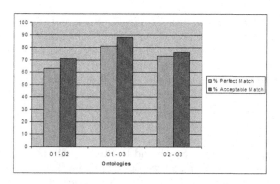

Fig. 4. Empirical evaluation

hand, it is less effective when ontologies have a predominant hierarchical structure, hence the usefulness of the structural analysis is strongly reduced.

Experiments highlighted the ability of the system to find relations between concepts having different semantic but the same name. In fact the system finds the correct associations through structural analysis, though the algorithm found several alternatives for those terms during the lexical analysis and the ontologies are strongly connected.

The parameter K was set to 0.7 in the performed test; it was used for managing inverse relations in the auxiliary ontologies, since such type of relations can not be expressed in the adopted $\mathcal{ALN}$ logic.

6   Conclusion and Future Work

We described an automatic method for semantic mapping of ontologies. The method consists of two phases, a lexical-semantic analysis and a structural one. An application in an e-commerce scenario of the proposed algorithm is described. We deployed the proposed approach in a prototype system. An experiment with a case study domain has shown a good correspondence with human mapping manually conducted and the system provided results. We are currently working on an extension of the distance algorithm to more expressive logics; besides we aim to refine the proposed method in order to reduce the computational time of the structural analysis.

The authors would like to thank Francesco M. Donini, A. Halevy and Natasha Noy for their thoughtful and helpful comments on earlier draft of the paper.

References

1. F. Baader, I. Horrocks, and U. Sattler. Description logics. In S. Staab and R. Studer, editors, *Handbook on Ontologies in Information Systems*, pages 385–405. Springer, 2003.

2. R. J. Brachman et al. Living with CLASSIC: When and How to Use a KL-ONE-Like Language. In J. Sowa, editor, *Principles of Semantic Networks: Explorations in the Representation of Knowledge*, pages 401–456. MK, 1991.

3. Leacock C. and Chodorow M. Combining local context and wordnet similarity for word sense identification. In Fellbaum, editor, *WordNet an electronic lexical database*, pages 265–283. MIT Press, London, England, 1998.

4. H. Chalupsky. Ontomorph: a translation system for symbolic knowledge. In *Principles of knowledge representation and reasoning*, 2000.

5. A. Doan, J. Madhavan, P. Domingos, and A. Halevy. Ontology matching: A machine learning approach. In S. Staab and R. Studer, editors, *Handbook on Ontologies in Information Systems*, pages 385–405. Springer, 2003.

6. F. M. Donini, M. Lenzerini, D. Nardi, and A. Schaerf. Reasoning in Description Logics. In Gerhard Brewka, editor, *Principles of Knowledge Representation*, Studies in Logic, Language and Information, pages 193–238. CSLI Publications, 1996.

7. C. Fellbaum, editor. *Wordnet: an electronic lexical database*. MIT press, 1999.

8. F. Giunchiglia and P. Shvaiko. Semantic matching. *Knowledge Engineering Review Journal*, 18(3):265–280, 2004.

9. R. Ichise, H. Takeda, and S. Honiden. Rule induction for concept hierarchy alignement. In *Proc. of workshop on ontology learning at IJCAI 2001*, 2001.

10. Y. Kalfoglou and M. Schorlemmer. Ontology mapping: the state of the art. *The knowledge engineering review*, 18(1):1–31, 2003.

11. M. Lacher and G. Groh. facilitating the exchange of explicit knowledge through ontology mappings. In *Proc. of FLAIRS 2001*, 2001.

12. J. Madhavan, P. A. Bernstein, and E. Rahm. Generic schema matching with cupid. In *Proceedings of the 27th VLDB Conference*, Roma, Italy, 2001.

13. D. McGuinnes, R. Fikes, J. Rice, and S. Wilder. The chimaera ontology environment. In *Proc. of AAAI 2000*, 2000.

14. G. A. Miller, R. Beckwith, C. Fellbaum, D. Gross, and K. Miller. Introduction to wordnet: an on-line lexical database. *Journal of Lexicography*, 3(4):235–244, 1990.

15. P. Mitra, G. Wiederhold, and J. Jannink. Semi-automatic integration of knowledge sources. In *Proc. of Fusion '99*, Sunnyvale, USA, 1999.

16. T. Di Noia, E. Di Sciascio, F.M. Donini, and M. Mongiello. A system for principled Matchmaking in an electronic marketplace. In *Proc. of WWW-03*, pages 321–330, 2003.

17. N. Noy. Semantic integration: a survey of ontology-based approaches. *Sigmod record*, 33(4), 2004.

18. N. Noy and M. Musen. Prompt: an algorithm and tool for automated ontology merging and alignment. In *Proc. of AAAI 2000*, 2000.

19. N. Noy and M. Musen. Anchor-prompt: using non-local context for semantic matching. In *Proc. of workshop on ontologies and information sharing at IJCAI 2001*, 2001.

20. F. Wiesman, N. Roos, and P. Vogt. Automatic ontology mapping for agent communication. In G. Schreiber & M. van Someren (Eds.) B. Krose, M. de Rijke, editor, *Proc. of BNAIC2001*, pages pp. 291–298, Amsterdam: Universiteit van Amsterdam., 2001.

An Ontology-Based Two-Level Clustering for Supporting E-Commerce Agents' Activities

Domenico Rosaci

DIMET Department, University Mediterranea of Reggio Calabria,
Via Graziella Loc. Feo di Vito 89060 Reggio Calabria, Italy
domenico.rosaci@unirc.it **

Abstract. This paper presents an approach for determining clusters of customer agents having both similar interests and buying behaviour. On the one hand, a seller can exploit such a clustering for improving its activities, e.g. for adapting the presentation of its Web Site or for proposing suitable offers to each agent cluster. On the other hand, a customer agent can realize with the other agents of its cluster various kinds of collaboration. In our approach, each agent is provided with an ontology that representing interests and behaviour of its human owner and the clustering technique we propose, that is performed at two levels of detail, is based on the extraction of semantic similarities between agent ontologies.

1 Introduction

In a Business-to-Customer E-Commerce Community the sellers, on the one hand, have the necessity to classify their customers in order to either propose to each of them a customized offer or adapt the product presentation to customer typology. Each customer, on the other hand, often needs to determine which customers are similar to him, in order to realize a fruitful cooperation. These necessities become crucial in the case we desire to automatize both seller and customer activities by using software agents. A software agent is a computing entity capable of perceiving dynamic changes in the environment and, consequently, of autonomously performing user delegated tasks. Agents that support customers and sellers have to be able to perform agent clustering. This problem can be solved by determining agent similarities, and a way for determining these similarities is that of representing by a unique formalism, called *ontology*, both agent interests and behaviour. Most of the approaches proposed in the last few years for representing the Semantic Web, are capable of modeling agent knowledge. This is the case of XML-Schema [11], that is designed for allowing user to define its own XML data types that can be used into XML documents and RDF Schema (RDFS), that provides a basic type system for use in RDF models. However, XML-Schema and RDFS only allow to represent information schemas but it does not support reasoning. Other ontology languages, as OML (Ontology Markup Language)

** This work has been funded by the Project SESTANTE, Programma Interreg III-B.

K. Bauknecht et al. (Eds.): EC-Web 2005, LNCS 3590, pp. 31–40, 2005.

[9], CKML (Conceptual Knowledge Markup Language) [3], DAML+OIL [4] and OWL [11], allow to include descriptions of classes, properties and their instances, and in addition specify how to derive logical consequences from a given ontology. Ontologies have been already exploited for clustering agent ontologies. In particular, in [10,8], some approaches for clustering software agents on the basis on ontology similarities have been proposed, however in these approaches only similarities among concepts are considered, while similarities with respect to agent behaviour are not taken into account. In [2], an approach for clustering e-commerce agents, exploiting both content-based and ontology-based similarities, is presented. However, this approach considers only the agent behaviour in visiting seller sites, and does not deal with more general logic relationships as, for instance, the negotiation behaviour.

The main contribution of this paper is in proposing a technique for automatically clustering customer agents. This technique is based on the extraction of some inter-ontology similarities, that give a measure of the closeness between two agent ontologies with respect to both the ontology concepts and the agent behaviour. Clustering is done at two level of detail. At a first level, we derive clusters of agents having similar concepts and concept relationships in their ontologies. At a second level, we further re-cluster the first level clusters on the basis of behaviour similarities.

Section 2 introduces the reference customer agent's ontology model, while Section 3 presents the definitions of inter-ontology similarity and Section 4 describes our clustering algorithm. Finally, Section 5 presents an experiment of e-commerce agent clustering and draws some conclusions.

2   The Customer Agent's Ontology Model

In this section, we introduce our customer ontology model. We can observe that different kinds of knowledge need to be represented. First of all, the ontology has to represent some products relating to the customer, each product having a set of associated *properties (e.g., the* price).

We call *schema* the objects' representation, where a schema may be a primitive data type (e.g. an integer), or it may have a more complex structure. Moreover, schemas are semi-structured, in the sense that each property can appear in actual objects with an arbitrary multiplicity. Each object (i.e., a a book) can be viewed as an instance of a schema. We assume that, for each property of an object schema, a set of objects may appear into an object of the schema, and we associate two integer variables with the property for representing the maximum and the minimum cardinality of the property set. We introduce the constant MUL for representing the maximum value admissible for the maximum cardinality. We call *required* a property that has both minimum and maximum cardinality equal to 1 and *optional* a property having minimum (resp. maximum) cardinality equal to 0 (resp. 1). We use a set BS of primitive object schemas for representing *integer, real, boolean* and *string* values, as well as the schema *void* that represents a *null* value and *propositional* for propositional variables.

Definition 1. An *object schema* s is either: (i) a basic object schema or (ii) a set $\{p_1, p_2, ..., p_n\}$, where each p_i, $i = 1..n$, that we call *property* of s, is a triplet $(p, minCard, maxCard)$ such that p is an object schema and both $minCard$ and $maxCard$ are integer objects with $0 \leq minCard \leq maxCard$.

$title = \{(string, 1, 1)\}$ is an example of object schema that contains only one *required* basic property. Instead, the schema $author = \{(firstName, 1, 1), (lastName, 1, 1)\}$ has two *required*, non basic, properties. Finally, the schema $book = \{(author, 1, MUL), (title, 1, 1), (editor, 0, MUL), (price, 0, 1)\}$ has both *required*, *optional*, *zero-or-more* and *one-or-more* properties.

Furthermore, an ontology should be capable of representing a *collection* of objects, as the *products* purchased by the customer, that may be composed, in its turn, by other sub-collections as a collection of books and a collection of CDs. For this purpose, we define the notion of *collection schema*.

Definition 2. A *collection schema* cs is either an empty set or a set $\{c_1, c_2, ..., c_n\}$, where $c_1, c_2, ..., c_n$ are collection schemas.

A collection having schema cs is an instance of cs.

It is also necessary to use functions that operate on objects and collections. To this purpose, we define the notion of *function schema*, as a triplet that contains a set of object and collection schemas of input, a set of object and collection schemas of output, and a returned schema. Each actual function can be viewed as an instance of its schema.

Definition 3. A *function schema* fs is a triplet $(input, output, returned)$, where (i) *input* (resp. *output*) is a set $\{oi_1, oi_2, ..., oi_m, ci_1, ci_2, ..., ci_n\}$ (resp. $\{oo_1, oo_2, ..., oo_h, co_1, co_2, ..., co_k\}$) such that $oi_l, l = 1,.., m$ (resp. $oo_l, l = 1,.., h$) is an object schema and $ci_r, r = 1,.., n$ (resp. $co_r, r = 1,.., k$) is a collection schema, and (iii) *returned* is an object schema or a collection schema.

As an example, in order to represent the action performed by a customer c when, in the context of a negotiation with a merchant, he reacts to a new *proposed_price* of the merchant by making a new *offer*, we may use the function schema $new\_off = (\{real, real\}, \{real\}, void)$, and implement it by a function $c\_new\_off = (\{proposed\_price, offer\}, \{offer\}, void)$.

In the reality of an agent, there exist some situations that may happen or not. In order to represent such situations, we use propositional objects, that we call *events*. For instance, suppose a customer has the possibility to decide to make or not an offer for the product that is currently evaluating. We represent such a situation with the event $makeO$. Often, we want to represent an event that is the *negation* of another event. We represent this kind of situation by an event $\neg e$ that is the *classical negation* of e and that means the negation of e happens. However, in other cases, we want to represent the fact that *there is no evidence that an event happens*. To this purpose, we use the *default negation*. If e is an event, the default negation of e, denoted by $\sim e$, means that e is assumed to be *false* for default. Extended Logic Programming (ELP) [5] is a formalism to represent logical rules dealing with both classical and default negation. In the agent reality, there exist some relationships between events that can be suitably represented by ELP rules. For instance, suppose to represent the following situation: the customer makes an offer for the current book if both he considers interesting it and the price proposed by the seller is not too high. We model such a situation by the rule: $makeOff \leftarrow intBook, \neg tooHigh$. Generally, in representing an agent ontology, we have to consider a (finite) set of clauses, that form an *extended logic program*. The semantics of extended programs is an extension of the stable model semantics [1] and it is represented by the *answer sets*.

Often, when an event happens in the world of a customer or a seller, an action is consequently produced. For instance, suppose that, when a customer decides to make an offer in a negotiation, the value of the offer is equal to the mean between his previous offer and the price proposed at the present by the seller. We can thus say that, when the event $makeO$ is true, a function, that we denote by new_off, is called that sets the value of the object $offer$ equal to $(proposed\_price + offer)/2$. We call *action* a 5-tuple composed by an event, as $makeO$, a function, as new_off, that is activated by the event, a set of objects, as $\{proposed\_price\}$, that are the arguments of the function, and another two sets of objects and events, as $\{offer\}$ and $\{end\}$, respectively, whose state is modified by the function.

Definition 4. An *action* is a set $\{e, f, os1, es, os2\}$ where e is en event, f is a function, $os1, os2$ are object sets, es is an events set, such that the function f is activated if $e = true$ by passing it as input arguments the objects belonging to $os1$ and f modifies both the value of the objects belonging to $os2$ and the events belonging to the es and returns a value $f(os1, es, os2)$.

The set $\mathcal{O}$ of all the schemas describing an agent reality is called the *ontology* of the agent.

Definition 5. An *ontology* is a 6-tuple $\langle OS, CS, FS, \varepsilon, \mathcal{P}, A \rangle$, where: (*i*) OS is a set of object schemas; (*ii*) CS is a set of collection schemas; (*iii*) FS is a set of function schemas; (*iv*) ε is a set of events; (*v*) $\mathcal{P}$ is an extended logic program; (*vi*) A is a set of actions.

3   Inter-ontology Similarities

3.1   Content-Based Similarities

We define the terminological similarity $T_{s_1 s_2}$ between two schemas as a real coefficient, belonging to [0,1], that measures how much the names of s_1 and s_2 are synonyms. This coefficient can be derived by a standard thesaurus (e.g. Wordnet [7]). We assume that for each property of $s1$ there is at most only a property of $s2$ with a non-zero terminological similarity. We compute the similarity between two object schemas $s1$ and $s2$ recursively. If both $s1$ and $s2$ are basic schemas, we assign a similarity equal to 1 if the schemas are the same, 0 otherwise. If one of the schemas is basic and the other is non-basic, we assign 0 to the similarity. In the general case of two non-basic schemas, we compute the similarity as the product of the terminological similarity and the mean value of some terms, each term associated with a pair (x, y) of properties, where x (resp. y) is a property of $s1$ (resp. $s2$). Each term is computed as the product of the similarity between x and y, the terminological similarity between x and y and a factor that takes into account both maximum and minimum cardinalities.

Definition 6. Let $x = \{(p_1^x, m_1^x, M_1^x), (p_2^x, m_2^x, M_2^x), ..., (p_n^x, m_n^x, M_n^x)\}$ and $y = \{(p_1^y, m_1^y, M_1^y), (p_2^y, m_2^y, M_2^y), ..., (p_k^y, m_k^y, M_k^y)\}$ be two object schemas and let $l = max(n, k)$. The *similarity* between x and y is defined as $SS_{xy} =$

$$
\begin{cases}
1, & \text{if } x, y \in BS \text{ and } x = y \\
0, & \text{if } (x, y \in BS \text{ and } x \neq y) \\
& \text{or } (x \in BS \text{ and } y \notin BS) \\
& \text{or } (y \in BS \text{ and } x \notin BS) \,; \\
TS_{xy} \cdot \frac{1}{l} \sum_{i=1}^{n} \sum_{j=1}^{k} SS_{p_i^x, p_j^y} \cdot \alpha_{p_i^x p_j^y} \cdot TS_{p_i^x p_j^y}, & \text{if } x, y \notin BS.
\end{cases}
$$

where $\alpha_{p_i^x p_j^y} =$

$$
\begin{cases}
1, & \text{if } m_i^x = m_j^y \text{ and } M_i^x = M_j^y; \\
0, & \text{if } m_i^x \neq m_j^y \text{ and } M_i^x \neq M_j^y; \\
0.5, & \text{if } (m_i^x = m_j^y \text{ and } M_i^x \neq M_j^y) \text{ or } (m_i^x \neq m_j^y \text{ and } M_i^x = M_j^y).
\end{cases}
$$

As an example, consider the two schemas $book1 = \{(author_{book1}, 1, MUL), (title_{book1}, 1, 1), (price, 0, 1)\}$ and $book2 = \{(author_{book2}, 1, 1), (title_{book2}, 1, 1)\}$, where $author_{book1} = author_{book2} = \{(String, 1, 1)\}$. The only property pairs with non-zero terminological similarity are $(author_{book1}, author_{book2})$ and $(title_{book1}, title_{book2})$, that have similarity equal to 1, since they are composed by two basic properties with terminological similarity equal to 1 and with the same maximum and minimum cardinality. Moreover, $\alpha_{title_{book1} title_{book2}} = 0.5$ and $\alpha_{author_{book1} author_{book2}} = 1$. Also suppose that $T_{book1, book2} = 0.95$. Thus, the similarity between these two schemas is $0.95 \cdot \frac{1}{3} \sum (0.5 + 1) = 0.475$.

We also define the similarity between two collections X and Y. If both X and Y are collections that do not contain any subcollection, the similarity is equal to the terminological similarity. Otherwise, it is computed as the mean value of the similarities between each pair (a, b) of subcollections, where a (resp. b) is a subcollection of X (resp. Y). We assume that for each subcollection of X there is at most only a subcollection of Y with a non-zero terminological similarity.

Definition 7. Let X and Y be two collection schemas. The similarity between X and Y is defined as:

$$
SS_{XY} =
\begin{cases}
TS_{XY}, & \text{if } X = Y = \emptyset; \\
TS_{XY} \cdot \frac{1}{l} \sum_{i=1}^{n} \sum_{j=1}^{k} SS_{c_i^X c_j^Y} \cdot TS_{c_i^X c_j^Y}, & \text{if } X = \{c_1^X, c_2^X, ..., c_n^X\} \\
& \text{and } Y = \{c_1^Y, c_2^Y, ..., c_k^Y\}.
\end{cases}
$$

where $l = max(n, k)$

For instance, consider the collections $books1 = \{narrative, poetry\}$ and $books2 = \{romances, essays\}$. We suppose that all the involved subcollections are empty schemas. Also suppose that $T_{books1,books2} = 0.95$ and $T_{narrative,romances} = 0.66$ is the only subcollection pair with non-zero terminological similarity. Thus, the similarity between $books1$ and $books2$ is $0.95 \cdot 0.66/2 = 0.32$.

Finally, we define the similarity between two function schemas $f1$ and $f2$. In this case, if the cardinalities of the respective input and output sets are different, the similarity between $f1$ and $f2$ is assumed equal to 0, otherwise, it is computed as the mean value of all the similarities between each corresponding parameter.

Definition 8. Let $f1 = (input_1, output_1, returned_1)$ and $f2 = (input_2, output_2, returned_2)$ be two function schemas, where (i) $input_1$ is a set $\{oi_1^1, oi_2^1, ..., oi_m^1, ci_1^1, ci_2^1, ..., ci_n^1\}$ such that $oi_1^1, oi_2^1..., oi_m^1$ are object schemas and $ci_1^1, ci_2^1, ..., ci_n^1$ are collection schemas, (ii) $input_2$ is a set $\{oi_1^2, oi_2^2, ..., oi_m^2, ci_1^2, ci_2^2, ..., ci_n^2\}$ such that $oi_1^2, oi_2^2...oi_m^2$ are object schemas and $ci_1^2, ci_2^2, ..., ci_n^2$ are collection schemas, (iii) $output_1$ is a set $\{oo_1^1, oo_2^1..., oo_h^1, co_1^1, co_2^1, ..., co_k^1\}$ such that $oo_1^1, oo_2^1...oo_h^1$ are object schemas and $co_1^1, co_2^1, ..., co_k^1$ are collection schemas, (iv) $output_2$ is a set $\{oo_1^2, oo_2^2..., oo_h^2, co_1^2, co_2^2, ..., co_k^2\}$ such that $oo_1^2, oo_2^2...oo_h^2$ are object schemas and $co_1^2, co_2^2, ..., co_k^2$ are collection schemas, (v) $returned_1$ (resp. $returned_2$) is an object schema or a collection schema.

The similarity between $f1$ and $f2$ is computed as: $SS_{f1f2} = \frac{1}{z}(\sum_{i=1}^{m} SS_{oi_i^1 oi_i^2} + \sum_{i=1}^{n} SS_{ci_i^1 ci_i^2} + \sum_{i=1}^{h} SS_{oo_i^1 oo_i^2} + \sum_{i=1}^{k} SS_{co_i^1 co_i^2} + SS_{returned_1 returned_2})$, where $z = m + n + h + k + 1$.

The definitions above allow us to compute the overall content-based similarity between two ontologies $\mathcal{O}_1$ and $\mathcal{O}_2$, as the mean of all the semantic similarities between each pair of object, collection and function schemas (s_1, s_2), where $s1$ belongs to $\mathcal{O}_1$ and s_2 belongs to $\mathcal{O}_2$.

Definition 9. Let $\mathcal{O}_1 = (\mathcal{O}_1.\mathcal{V}, \mathcal{O}_1.I)$ and $\mathcal{O}_2 = (\mathcal{O}_2.\mathcal{V}, \mathcal{O}_2.I)$ be two ontologies. The content-based similarity between $\mathcal{O}_1$ and $\mathcal{O}_2$ is computed as $CBS_{\mathcal{O}_1 \mathcal{O}_2} = \frac{\sum_{i=1}^{|OS_1|} \sum_{j=1}^{|OS_2|} SS_{os_i^1 os_j^2} + \sum_{i=1}^{|CS_1|} \sum_{j=1}^{|CS_2|} SS_{cs_i^1 cs_j^2} + \sum_{i=1}^{|FS_1|} \sum_{j=1}^{|FS_2|} SS_{fs_i^1 fs_j^2}}{|OS_1| \cdot |OS_2| + |CS_1| \cdot |CS_2| + |FS_1| \cdot |FS_2|}$ where OS_1, CS_1 and FS_1 (resp. OS_2, CS_2 and FS_2) are the object schema set, the collection schema set and the function schema set of $\mathcal{O}_1.\mathcal{V}$ (resp. $\mathcal{O}_2.\mathcal{V}$) .

3.2   Behaviour-Based Similarities

Here we define the similarity between two ontologies $\mathcal{O}_1$ and $\mathcal{O}_2$ with respect to the behavioural component, represented by logic programs and actions. Firstly, we assume that there exists the possibility to determine if two events $e_1 \in \mathcal{O}_1$ and $e_2 \in \mathcal{O}_2$ are synonyms and, in the affirmative case, we choose to indicate with a unique common event e both e_1 and e_2. Then, if A_1 and A_2 are two event sets, we indicate with $CE_{A_1 A_2}$ the set of events common to A_1 and A_2. Let $\mathcal{P}_1$ (resp. $\mathcal{P}_2$) be the logic program of $\mathcal{O}_1$ (resp. $\mathcal{O}_2$) and let AS^1 (resp. AS^2) be the answer sets collection of $\mathcal{P}_1$ (resp. $\mathcal{P}_2$). In order to compute the similarity

$S_{\mathcal{P}_1 \mathcal{P}_2}$ between the two programs, first we compute, for each answer set AS_i^1 of AS^1, the similarity $S_{AS_i^1 AS_j^2}$ with each answer set AS_j^2 of AS^2. This similarity is computed as the ratio between (i) the number of events common to AS_i^1 and AS_j^2, and (ii) the number of events present in the largest of the two involved answer sets. Finally, we compute the *program similarity* $S_{\mathcal{P}_1 \mathcal{P}_2}$ as the mean of all the $S_{AS_i^1 AS_j^2}$, for each AS_i^1 (resp. AS_j^2) belonging to AS^1 (resp. AS^2).

Definition 10. Let $\mathcal{P}_1$ (resp. $\mathcal{P}_2$) be the logic program of $\mathcal{O}_1$ (resp. $\mathcal{O}_2$). Let AS^1 (resp. AS^2) be the answer sets collection of $\mathcal{P}_1$ (resp. $\mathcal{P}_2$). Let $S_{AS_i^1 AS_j^2} = |CE_{AS_i^1 AS_j^2}|/max(|AS_i^1| + |AS_j^2|)$ be the similarity between $AS_i^1 \in AS^1$ and $AS_j^2 \in AS^2$. We compute $S_{\mathcal{P}_1 \mathcal{P}_2}$ as the mean of all the $S_{AS_i^1 AS_j^2}$, for each AS_i^1 (resp. AS_j^2) $\in AS^1$ (resp. AS^2).

As an example, consider the two programs:

$$\mathcal{P}_1: \begin{array}{l} makeOff \leftarrow intBook, \sim end \\ end \leftarrow \sim makeOff \\ intBook \leftarrow \\ \neg highPrice \leftarrow \end{array} \qquad \mathcal{P}_2: \begin{array}{l} makeOff \leftarrow intBook, \neg highPrice, \sim end \\ end \leftarrow \neg makeOff \\ intBook \leftarrow \\ \neg highPrice \leftarrow \end{array}$$

where $\mathcal{P}_1$ means that (i) a customer makes an offer for a book if this is interesting and there is no evidence that the negotiation phase is ended yet and (ii) the negotiation ends if there is no evidence the customer makes an offer. $\mathcal{P}_2$ corresponds instead to a customer that makes an offer for a book if this is interesting, the price is not high and the negotiation is not ended yet; moreover, the negotiation ends if the customer does not make an offer anymore. The answer sets of $\mathcal{P}_1$ are $AS_1^1 = \{intBook, makeOff\}$ and $AS_2^1 = \{intBook, end\}$, while the unique answer set of $\mathcal{P}_1$ is $AS_1^2 = \{intBook, \neg highPrice, makeOff\}$. AS_1^1 has a similarity with AS_1^2 equal to $2/3{=}0.75$, while AS_2^1 has a similarity with AS_1^2 equal to $1/3{=}0.33$, thus the overall similarity is $(0.75+0.33)/2{=}0.54$.

Now, we define the *action similarity* between two actions A_1 and A_2. It is computed as the mean of all the similarities between each element of A_1 and the corresponding element of A_2.

Definition 11. Let $A^1 = \{e^1, f^1, o1^1, e^1, o2^1\}$ and $A^2 = \{e^2, f^2, o1^2, e^2, o2^2\}$ be two actions. We define $S_{e^1 e^2} = \begin{cases} 1, \text{ if } e^1 = e^2; \\ 0, \text{ otherwise.} \end{cases}$, $S_{f^1 f^2} = \begin{cases} 1, \text{ if } f^1 = f^2; \\ 0, \text{ otherwise.} \end{cases}$

$S_{o1_i^1 o_j^2} = \begin{cases} 1, \text{ if } o1_i^1 = o1_j^2; \\ 0, \text{ otherwise.} \end{cases}$ $S_{o2_i^1 o2_j^2} = \begin{cases} 1, \text{ if } o2_i^1 = o2_j^2; \\ 0, \text{ otherwise.} \end{cases}$ $S_{e^1 e^2} = \begin{cases} 1, \text{ if } e^1 = e^2; \\ 0, \text{ otherwise.} \end{cases}$

The overall similarity between A_1 and A_2 is computed as $S_{A_1 A_2} =$

$$\frac{S_{e^1 e^2} + S_{f^1 f^2} + \sum_{i=1}^{|o1^1|} max_{j=1}^{|o1^2|}(S_{o1_i^1 o1_j^2}) + \sum_{i=1}^{|o2^1|} max_{j=1}^{|o2^2|}(S_{o2_i^1 o2_j^2}) + \sum_{i=1}^{|e^1|} max_{j=1}^{|e^2|}(S_{e_i^1 e_j^2})}{2 + max(|o1^1|, |o1^2|) + max(|o2^1|, |o2^2|) + max(|e^1|, |e^2|)}.$$

If AS^1 and AS^2 are two sets of actions, we compute the similarity between AS_1 and AS_2 as the mean of all $S_{AS_i^1 AS_j^2}$, where $AS_i^1 \in AS^1$ and $AS_j^2 \in AS^2$.

Definition 12. Let AS^1 and AS^2 be two sets of actions. The similarity between AS_1 and AS_2 is computed as $S_{AS^1 AS^2} = \frac{\sum_{i=1}^{|AS^1|} \sum_{j=1}^{|AS^2|} (S_{AS_i^1 AS_j^2})}{|AS^1| \cdot |AS^2|}$.

Finally, we can define the overall behavioral-based similarity between two ontologies as the mean of the program similarity and the action similarity.

Definition 13. Let $\mathcal{O}_1$ and $\mathcal{O}_2$ be two ontologies. The behavioral-based similarity between $\mathcal{O}_1$ and $\mathcal{O}_2$ is computed as follows: $BBS_{\mathcal{O}_1 \mathcal{O}_2} = \frac{SS_{\mathcal{P}_1 \mathcal{P}_2} + S_{A_1 A_2}}{2}$ where $\mathcal{P}_1$ and $\mathcal{A}_1$ (resp. $\mathcal{P}_2$ and $\mathcal{A}_2$) are the logic program and the action set of $\mathcal{O}_1$ (resp. $\mathcal{O}_2$), respectively. .

4   The CBSC Two-Level Clustering

In our approach, the process of determining customer agent clusters is equivalent to clustering agent ontologies, since we associate an ontology to each agent. In order to determine clusters, we introduce an algorithm, that we call *Content and Behaviour Similarities-based Clustering* (CBSC), based on the well known Hierarchical Clustering [6]. Our algorithm is composed by two phases: The first one aims to realize a clusterization based only on content-based similarities, while the second one, for each cluster produced in the first phase, operates a further clusterization based on behaviour based similarities.

Content-Based Clustering: This first phase takes in input (i) a set $O = \{o_1, o_2, ..., o_N\}$ of N ontologies to be clustered, (ii) an NxN matrix $C = \{C_{ij}\}$ where C_{ij} is the content-based similarity between the ontologies o_i and o_j belonging to O, (iii) a real parameter $\rho \in [0, 1]$. The algorithm yields as output (i) a set $CC = \{CC_1, CC_2, ..., CC_k\}$, where each $CC_i, i = 1, ..., k$ is a set of ontologies belonging to O, called *content-based cluster*, (ii) a matrix $CS = \{CS_{ij}\}$ where $CS_{ij}, i = 1, ..., k, j = 1, ..., k$ is the content-based similarity between the clusters CC_i and CC_j belonging to CC and (iii) a vector $CL = \{CL_i\}$ where CL_i gives a measure of the homogeneity level of the cluster CC_i. The algorithm is composed by two phases: The first phase computes the set CC as follows: It starts by assigning each ontology to a cluster, so that initially CC is composed by N clusters, each containing just one ontology. Let the similarities between the clusters be the same as the content-based similarities between the ontologies they contain and let $LC_i = 0, \forall CC_i \in CC$. Next, we perform the following two steps: (1) We find the closest (most similar) pair of clusters (CC_i, CC_j) and merge them into a single cluster called CC_m, so that now we have one cluster less. We assign to this cluster a level $L_m = C_{ij}$; (2) Then, we compute similarities between the new cluster and each of the old clusters, where the similarity between two clusters is defined as the greatest similarity from any member of one cluster to any member of the other cluster. We repeat steps (1) and (2) until the phase (1) is not able anymore to form a new cluster with a level greater then the threshold ρ.

Behaviour-Based Clustering: This second phase takes in input the set CC of the K content-based clusters built in the previous phase, and the N*N matrix

$B = \{B_{ij}\}$ where B_{ij} is the behaviour-based similarity between the ontologies o_i and o_j belonging to O, (iii) a real parameter $\psi \in [0,1]$. The algorithm yields as output (i) k sets $BC^j = \{BC_1^j, BC_2^j, ..., BC_{h_j}^j\}, j = 1..., k$, where each $BC_i^j, i = 1, ..., h_j$ is a set of ontologies belonging to CC_j, called *behaviour-based cluster*, (ii) k matrices $BS^j = \{BS_{lm}^j\}, j = 1, ..., k$ where $CS_{lm}^j, l = 1, ..., h_j, j = 1, ..., h_j$ is the behaviour-based similarity between the clusters BC_l^j and BC_m^j belonging to BC_j and (iii) k vectors $BL^j = \{BL_i^j\}, j = 1, ..., k$ where $BL_i^j, i = 1, ..., h_j$ gives a measure of the homogeneity level of the cluster BC_i^j. The algorithm, for each cluster $CC_i \in CC$ applies the procedure shown in previous content-based clustering phase, with the only difference that it uses the behaviour-based similarities rather than the content-based similarities and the parameter ψ as threshold.

5   Experiments and Conclusions

In order to evaluate the presented clustering approach, we have applied it to the case of a Web bookshop, having four book collections, namely *narrative*, *poetry*, *essay* and *manuals*. *narrative* has the three sub-collections *fantasy*, *science_fiction* and *literature*; *poetry* is partitioned into the sub-collections *theatre* and *lyrics*; *essay* is formed by the sub-collections *hystory* and *science*. *manual* has not any sub-collection. We have built an ontology vector O containing the ontologies of 800 simulated customers of the site, each of them belonging to a pre-defined cluster having particular characteristics w.r.t. customer interests and behaviour. Clusters are the following:

A. Customers of this clusters are interested only in narrative and poetry books. This cluster has been partitioned into two sub-clusters, on the basis of the customer behaviour:
   A1. These customers, when they buy a narrative book, they also buy a poetry book, without taking into account book price.
   A2. These customers buy either a narrative or a poetry book, without taking into account book price.
   A2. These customers buy either a narrative or a poetry book, but only if the book price is lesser than a pre-fixed threshold.
B. Customers of this cluster are interested only in essays. This cluster has been partitioned into two sub-clusters, on the basis of the customer behaviour:
   B1. These customers buy a book only if there is a discount on it.
   B2. These customers buy a book also if there is not a discount on it.
C. Customers of this clusters are interested only in manuals.

Note that the clusters are all disjoints and have the same size (160 customers for each cluster) and that each customer behaviour has been represented by the logic program of its ontology. We have computed the matrix C (resp. B) of content-based (resp. behaviour-based) similarities, and we have used the ontology vector O and the matrix C as inputs of the content-based clustering presented in the previous section. Next, we have used both the clusters produced in this phase and the matrix B as inputs of the behaviour-based clustering, by obtaining the final clusterization. The algorithm has generated three content-based clusters and five clusters. We have named as cluster A^* (resp. B^*, C^*, $A1^*$, $A2^*$, $B1^*$, $B2^*$) the generated cluster containing most of the customers belonging to A (resp. B, C, $A1$, $A2$, $B1$, $B2$) and we have computed the percent p_A (resp. p_B, p_C, p_{A1}, p_{A2}, p_{B1}, p_{B2}) of customers of A (resp. B, C, $A1$, $A2$, $B1$, $B2$) that have been correctly placed by the clustering algorithm into A^* (resp. B^*, C^*, $A1^*$, $A2^*$, $B1^*$, $B2^*$). These percents are reported in Table 5, that also shows for each of the produced clusters the mean content-based similarity $\overline{CS}$ and the mean behaviour-based similarity $\overline{BS}$. The results show that the CBSC algorithm clusters the customers with a high accuracy degree, by also producing clusters with high content-based and behaviour-based similarity. We observe that the presented clusterization takes into account only schema similarities. This is, in our opinion, the main limitation of the CBSC algorithm. In order to overcome this limit, we are working on the definition of similarity measures considering also extensional data as actual objects, schemas and functions.

Table 1. Results of the CBSC Clustering on the bookstore customers test set

parameter/cluster	A	B	C	$A1$	$A2$	$B1$	$B2$
p	0.97	0.96	0.99	0.93	0.92	0.95	0.91
$\overline{CS}$	0.91	0.87	0.92	0.88	0.89	0.87	0.86
$\overline{BS}$	0.89	0.86	0.90	0.87	0.88	0.85	0.86

References

1. G. Brewka and T. Eiter. Preferred answer sets for extended logic programs. *Artificial Intelligence*, 109:297–356, 1999.
2. F. Buccafurri, D. Rosaci, G.M.L. Sarné, and D. Ursino. An agent-based hierarchical clustering approach for e-commerce environments. In *Proc. of the 3th EC-WEB Conf.*, pp. 115–118, Aix-en-Provence, France, 2002. Springer.
3. CKML URL. http://www.ontologos.org/ckml/ckml/ckml%200.2.html. 2005.
4. DAML+OIL URL. http://www.daml.org/2001/03/daml+oil-index.html. 2005.
5. M. Gelfond and V. Lifschitz. Classical negations in logic programs and disjunctive databases. *New Generation Computing*, 9:365–386, 1991.
6. S.J. Johnson. Hierarchical Clustering Schemes. *Psychometrika*, 2:241–254, 1967.
7. A.G. Miller. WordNet: A lexical database for english. *Comm. of the ACM*, 38(11):39–41, 1995.
8. E. Ogston, M. van Steen, and F. Brazier. Group Formation Among Decentralized Autonomous Agents. *Applied Artificial Intelligence*, 10(9-10):953–970, 2004.
9. OML URL. http://www.ontologos.org/oml/oml%20root.html. 2005.
10. P.R.S. Visser, V.A.M. Tamma. An Experiment with Ontology-Based Agent Clustering. In *Proc. of the IJCAI-99 Workshop on Ontologies and Problem-Solving Methods*, Stockholm, Sweden, 1999.
11. W3C Recommendation URL. http://www.w3.org. 2005.

Specifying Workflow Web Services Using Petri Nets with Objects and Generating of Their OWL-S Specifications

Eric Andonoff, Lotfi Bouzguenda, and Chihab Hanachi

IRIT Laboratory,
University Toulouse 1, 1 Place Anatole France,
31042 Toulouse Cedex, France
{andonoff, lotfi.bouzguenda, hanachi}@univ-tlse1.fr

Abstract. This paper deals with Workflow Web Services (W2S). By W2S, we mean services automating business processes, and whose description and execution are accessible through the Web. In a first step, we use the Petri Net with Objects (PNO) formalism to graphically and formally model W2S, and then, in a second step, we provide rules to derive OWL-S specifications from PNO specifications automatically. The two main advantages of our approach are, first, to ease the design, the simulation and the verification of a workflow service thanks to PNO, and second, to publish it thanks to OWL-S, which is a semantic Web service description language. Consequently, PNO can be seen as a formalism providing an operational semantic to OWL-S since it defines formal and executable specifications to analyze, simulate, check and validate OWL-S specifications.

1 Introduction

Web services brought an evolution to the Web, transforming it to a provider of services. A Web service is defined as a software component that can be accessed over the Internet by other software components. Web services changed the Web to make it the place of choice for all type of activities including for instance e-commerce, business to business or enterprise application integration [1]. Nowadays, we are witnessing the overrun of Web services because of the broad adoption of their XML-based standards such as WSDL [2], SOAP [3] and UDDI [4].

Today, Web services evolve towards semantic Web services [5]: the objective is to describe Web services in a machine-understandable fashion applying to Web services concepts of the semantic Web [6]. Thus, semantic Web services increase the interoperability between Web services using for instance ontology to facilitate the communication between these applications. Semantic Web services correspond to intelligent Web services able to address tasks such as automatic Web service discovery, automatic Web service invocation, automatic Web service composition and interoperation, and automatic Web service execution monitoring.

In this paper we are interested in Workflow Web Services (W2S). By W2S, we mean workflow services whose description and execution are accessible through the Web. W2S differ from Web services because they must allow the expression of the three workflow complementary and interacting models that is the organizational, the informa-

K. Bauknecht et al. (Eds.): EC-Web 2005, LNCS 3590, pp. 41–52, 2005.
© Springer-Verlag Berlin Heidelberg 2005

tional and the process models. The organizational model structures the workflow actors and gives them authorization, through the notion of role, to perform tasks making up the processes. The informational model defines the structure of the documents and data required and produced by the processes. The process model defines component tasks, their coordination as well as the required resources (information, actors).

W2S are particularly interesting in the context of loose Inter-Organizational Workflow [7]. Inter-Organizational Workflow (IOW) is a technology allowing the cooperation of distributed and heterogeneous workflow (business) processes running in different organizations [8]. Thus, IOW helps organizations to face the emergence of the open and dynamic worldwide economy since it allows them to put in common resources and skills, and coordinate their respective workflow processes in order to reach a common goal corresponding to a value-added service. Loose IOW refers to occasional cooperation between organizations, free of structural constraints, where the organizations involved and their number are not pre-defined but should be selected at run time in an opportunistic way. One possible way to select these organizations is to sub-contract the research to a mediator, as it is presented in [9], thanks to a matchmaker. The aim of the matchmaker is to connect workflow service requesters to workflow service providers according to the following protocol: (i) a workflow service provider advertises the proposed service to the matchmaker, (ii) the matchmaker stores the advertisement, (iii) a workflow service requester asks the matchmaker whether it knows providers offering the desired service, and finally (iv) the matchmaker matches the request against the stored advertisements and returns the result as a set of workflow service providers. In this way, and as the Web provides many facilities for inter-organizational communication, the use of a matchmaker finally requires the definition of a Workflow Web Service description language allowing providers to publish through the Web their capabilities and requesters to express their needs, capabilities and needs being expressed in the terms of a common ontology whose role is to solve semantic problems between partners.

Most of the existing languages proposed in the context of Web services do not meet the previous requirements for W2S. Indeed, Web services languages, such as WSDL [2], do not allow the expression of the process concept as it is defined in the workflow, i.e. as a set of coordinated tasks. Regarding composition Web services languages, such as BPEL4WS [10] or WSFL [11], neither they completely describe the organizational and informational models, nor they integrate semantics aspects through ontology. If we consider workflow technology, the proposed languages, such as YAWL [12] or XPDL [13], describe the three workflow models, and tools are provided to derive XML workflow specifications. Unfortunately, these XML specifications solve only syntactic conflicts between organizations, while in loose IOW, the heterogeneous context requires semantics conflicts solving mechanisms.

On the other hand, languages proposed in the context of semantic Web services, and more particularly OWL-S [14], which is recommended by the World Wide Web consortium, seems to be appropriate to W2S. Indeed, first OWL-S captures the concepts involved in the three workflow models, second it allows the description of workflow services referencing ontology, and third it enables their publication in a semantic Web accessible format.

However, OWL-S has two main drawbacks: first, it does not provide any graphical tool to specify services, and, second, it lacks theoretical foundations with an operational semantics to analyze, simulate and validate the services. To compensate these drawbacks, this paper proposes a solution based on the two following principles:

- (i) The use of a graphical and formal language, namely Petri Nets with Objects (PNO), to describe workflow services. PNO [15] are used as a graphical tool to help a designer to define a workflow service; they also provide formal and executable specifications to analyze, simulate, check and validate the described workflow service.
- (ii) The proposition of rules to derive a PNO onto OWL-S specifications.

Thus, PNO can be seen as a graphic tool making easier the specification of a workflow service, and avoiding the designer to know OWL-S' syntax. It can also be seen as a formalism providing an operational semantic to OWL-S since it defines formal and executable specifications to analyze, simulate, check and validate specifications that will be derived onto OWL-S specifications.

The remainder of this paper is organized as follows. Section 2 introduces the PNO formalism and explains why this formalism is convenient for workflow service specification and validation. Section 3 presents OWL-S and justifies why we have chosen OWL-S as a target language. Section 4 gives an operational semantics to OWL-S by formalizing its service profile and service process using PNO. This section first presents our approach, and then specifies the rules we propose to derive a PNO onto OWL-S specifications. Section 5 briefly compares our proposition to related works and concludes the paper.

2 Petri Nets with Objects: A Language for Workflow Services

2.1 What Are Petri Nets with Objects?

Petri Nets with Objects (PNO) [15] are a formalism combining coherently Petri nets (PN) technology and Object-Oriented (OO) approach. While PN are very suitable to express the dynamic behavior of a system, OO approach enables the modeling and the structuring of its active (actor) and passive (information) entities. In a conventional PN, tokens are atomic, whereas they are objects in a PNO. As any PN, a PNO is made up of places, arcs and transitions, but in PNO, they are labeled with inscriptions referring to the handled objects. More precisely, a PNO features the following additive characteristics:

- Places are typed. The type of a place is a (list of) type of an (list of) object(s). A token is a value matching the type of a place such as a (list of) constant (e.g. 2 or 'hello'), an instance of an object class, or a reference towards such an instance. The value of a place is a set of tokens it contains.
- Arcs are labeled with parameters. Each arc is labeled with a (list of) variable of the same type, as the place the arc is connected to. The variables on the arcs surrounding a transition serve as formal parameters of that transition and define the flow of tokens from input to output places. Arcs from places to a transition determine the enabling condition of the transition: a transition may occur (or is enabled) if there exists a binding of its input variables with tokens lying in its input places.
- Each Transition is a complex structure made up of three components: a precondition, an action and emission rules. A transition may be guarded by a precondition, i.e.

a side-effect free Boolean expression involving input variables. In this case, the transition is enabled by a binding only if this binding evaluates the precondition to be true. Preconditions allow for the fact that the enabling of a transition depends on the location of tokens and also on their value. Most transitions also include an action, which consists in a piece of code in which transition's variables may appear and object methods be invoked. This action is executed at each occurrence of the transition and it processes the values of tokens. Finally, a transition may include a set of emission rules i.e. side-effect free Boolean expressions that determine the output arcs that are actually activated after the execution of the action.

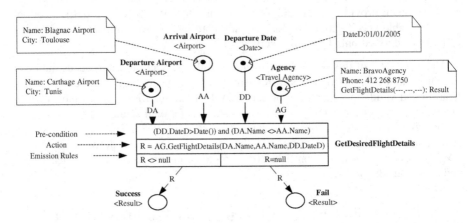

Fig. 1. Example of a PNO

Figure 1 gives an example of a PNO describing a simple task providing the references of a flight, given the departure and arrival airports, the traveling date and the agency in charge of finding the flight. This PNO is composed of a transition, four input places and two output places. Each place is typed with one of the four following object classes: *Airport, Date, TravelAgency* and *Result*. Each input place contains a token whose value is indicated by a comment linked to it by an arrow. From left to right, the first two input places called *DepartureAirport* and *ArrivalAirport* contain one token corresponding to an Airport. The object class *Airport* has two attributes *{Name,City}* and we can read that the flight requested is between Tunis and Toulouse. With the same principle, we can deduce from the *DepartureDate* and *Agency* input places that the travel date is 01/01/2005 and the travel agency in charge of finding the flight is *Bravo Agency*. Let us also remark that the *TravelAgency* object class, in addition to three attributes *{Name,Phone,Address}*, features a method *{GetFlightDetails}* as well. Now let us consider the transition *GetDesiredFlightDetails*. It has a precondition *{(DD.DateD>Date()) and (DA.Name<>AA.Name)}* which indicates that the departure date must be in the future and departure and arrival airports are different. Let us notice that this precondition is expressed with the formal parameter of the input arcs (*DD, DA* and *AA*). If this precondition is satisfied, the action is executed and the object *Travel Agency* is asked to execute the *GetFlightDetails* method. According to the result R, returned by this method, the emission rules will direct the process through one path or another. If a flight is found, the result R is not null and then a token is put in the *Success* output place. In the other case, a token is put in the *Fail* output place.

2.2 Motivations for Using Petri Nets with Objects

Petri nets are widely used for workflow service specification [16]. Several good reasons justify their use:

- *An appropriate expressive power* that allows the description of the different tasks involved in a workflow service and their coordination.
- *A graphical representation* that eases the workflow service specification.
- *An operational semantics* enabling an easy mapping from specification to implementation.
- *Theoretical foundations* allowing analysis and validation of behavioral properties and simulation facilities.

Unfortunately, Petri nets focus on the process definition and do not capture the organizational and the informational dimensions of a workflow. As mentioned previously, Petri nets with Objects extend Petri nets by integrating high-level data structure represented as objects and therefore provide the possibility to integrate in a coherent way the two dimensions missing in Petri nets. Thus, using PNO, actors of the organizational model are directly represented as objects and they may be invoked through methods in the action part of a transition. In the same way, data and documents of the informational model are also represented by objects flowing in the PNO and transformed by transitions. In the previous example (cf. figure 1), the object *Agency* refers to an actor of the organizational model while the *DepartureAirport, ArrivalAirport* and *DepartureDate* objects are data of the informational model.

To summarize, PNO are convenient for workflow service specification because they really take into account the informational, organizational and process models of a workflow: a PNO specification makes the glue between these models since it permits the description, in a same representation, of actors of the organizational model, data and documents of the informational model, and tasks of the process model. Moreover, we use PNO as a graphical tool to specify a workflow service, and as a formal tool to define executable specifications in order to analyze, simulate, check and validate a workflow service. Thus, PNO can be seen as a formalism providing an operational semantic to OWL-S.

3 OWL-S: A Semantic Web Service Language for W2S

3.1 Brief Overview of OWL-S

OWL-S is a semantic markup language that enables the description of Web services in order to be selected, invoked and composed [14]. OWL-S refers to an ontology of services that defines and structures the concepts for handling Web services. The resulting conceptual model is defined through a hierarchy of classes that may be variably refined according to the business domain considered. The essential properties of a service are described by the three following classes: ServiceProfile, ServiceModel and ServiceGrounding.

The *ServiceProfile* provides all the necessary information for a service to be found and possibly selected. The Service Profile is described by three groups of attributes. The first group describes the identity of the service with attributes such as *serviceName*, *textDescription* or *contactInformation* defining respectively the identity of the service, a natural-language description of it, and the organization providing it. The second group gathers attributes to classify a service (e.g. *serviceCategory*, *serviceParameter*) or to evaluate or compare it to others having the same capabilities (e.g. *qualityRating*). The third group expresses the functional capabilities of the service with four attributes that are *input*, *output*, *precondition* and *effect*. These attributes respectively define the required entries for starting the service, the results the service is able to produce, the constraints that must be satisfied by the input, and the output properties guaranteed after the service execution.

In OWL-S, services are viewed as processes. So, the *ServiceModel* describes the service in terms of a process model composed of two specifications: a service process and a process control. The *ServiceProcess* defines the structure of the process using three types of processes: atomic, simple and composite processes. Atomic processes correspond to operations that the service can directly execute; they have no sub-processes. Simple processes correspond to abstractions of atomic processes and are not directly invocable. Composite processes are collections of processes coordinated by control constructs including sequence, loops, conditionals and concurrency. Four attributes are defined for these processes: *inputs, outputs, preconditions* and *effects* having the same semantic as the functional capabilities of the ServiceProfile. Regarding the *ProcessControl*, OWL-S represents informally all the useful attributes for monitoring the execution of the service, notably its possible states at run-time (e.g. ready, ongoing, suspended, aborted…).

The *ServiceGrounding* defines how to access to the service by specifying the communication protocols and messages, and the port numbers to be used.

3.2 Motivations for Using OWL-S

The first reason that lead us to choose OWL-S is that OWL-S is appropriate to workflow service description for two main reasons. On the one hand, it is possible to describe, using the service profile and the service model of OWL-S, the three different interrelated models of a workflow i.e. the organizational, informational and process models. Regarding the process, there is a direct mapping between the service model of OWL-S and the process model of a workflow. In OWL-S, the described service is broken down into tasks and their coordination is specified using control constructs such as sequence, loops, conditional, concurrency. In the process model of a workflow, the process is also broken down into tasks and workflow patterns are used to coordinate them. Even if OWL-S does not include all the PNO patterns, it provides the necessary control constructs to describe the majority of workflow process models since it allows the modeling of sequence, loops, conditional and concurrency. Regarding the informational and organizational aspects, OWL-S, through the service profile and the service process, gives the support for the description of actors, information (data or documents) and their availability as required in a workflow. This is made possible thanks to the set of inputs (actors, data and documents), preconditions (actors able to play specific roles, empty documents), outputs (data and documents) and effects (documents well filled, compliant with a specific norm). On the other hand, OWL-S, which is a semantic Web service language, enriches Web Services description based on WSDL with semantic information about the properties (Service-Profile) and the structure of the service (ServiceModel). Moreover, these semantic information are based on an ontology, extensible according to the domain and described with a well defined mark up language. Ontology makes possible, in the context of loose IOW in which several heterogeneous organizations cooperate, to solve semantic conflicts between these organizations by defining a shared business view based on a common vocabulary. Moreover, OWL-S ontology has a first-order logic representation [17] that enables deduction and eases the implementation of matchmaking mechanisms (e.g. subsumption) useful to compare Workflow Services. Such mechanisms are very important when selecting partners.

The second reason that lead us to choose OWL-S is the easy mapping between PNO and OWL-S concepts since, firstly, the OWL-S service profile can be derived from the input and output places of a PNO, secondly, the OWL-S service process can be built from the places and transitions of a PNO, and, finally, all the OWL-S control constructs have a corresponding PNO pattern.

The third reason that lead us to choose OWL-S is that OWL-S is recommended by the World Wide Web consortium, which is not the case for WSMO [18], another interesting semantic Web language.

4   Formalizing Service Profile and Service Process Using PNO

4.1   Our Approach

The idea is to use PNO as a graphic tool to specify, analyze, simulate and validate a workflow Service and to deduce from this specification the corresponding OWL-S service profile and service process.

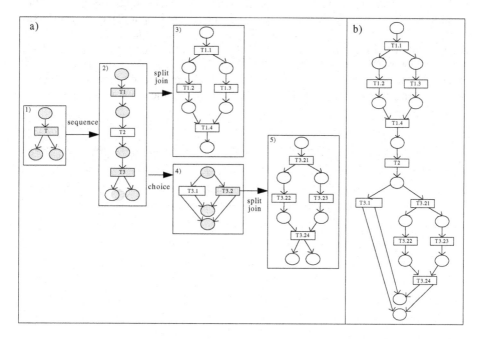

Fig. 2. Hierarchical Design of a Workflow Service and Final PNO

The design process of a PNO workflow service, i.e. a workflow service designed using PNO, is a hierarchical construction as it is the case for a OWL-S service process specification. The designer first specifies a unique transition with input and output places. If this transition does not correspond to an atomic task (immediately executable), the designer refines it, using only the PNO patterns which have a corresponding control construct in OWL-S, that is *sequence, split, split-join, choice, iterate, unordered, repeat-until, repeat-while*, and *if-then-else*. The result is the definition of others transitions expanding the previous one, and having input places and producing output places. The so-defined transitions can themselves be refined if necessary. This top-down decomposition approach is repeated until we obtain only atomic transitions.

Figure 2a above illustrates this hierarchical design process. The first transition, named T, is first defined. It includes one input and two outputs with their corresponding conditions (respectively preconditions and post-conditions). This transition is refined using the *sequence* pattern. Three new transitions, named T1, T2 and T3, are defined and replace the previous one. Among these three transitions, T1 and T3 are refined while T2 is atomic. T1 is refined using the *split-join* pattern while T3 is refined using the choice pattern. These transitions replace the refined ones. Finally, a new transition of T3, named T3.2, is in turn refined using the *split-join* pattern.

The final result is a global PNO describing a workflow service (see figure 2b). This PNO can be represented as a tree where non-terminal nodes are the refined transitions and terminal nodes (leaves) are atomic transitions. Each node (terminal or non-terminal) of the PNO tree include a data structure which indicates the name of the transition, the PNO pattern used when refining the transition (null for atomic transitions), and its corresponding inputs, outputs, preconditions and post-conditions. More precisely, for each input place of each transition we have a couple (InputName, Pre-Condition) where InputName is the name of the considered input place and PreCondition is the precondition of the transition in case where this input place is involved in the precondition. In the similar way, for each output place of each transition, we have a couple (OutputName, EmRule) where OutputName is a name of the considered output place and EmRule is the emission rule associated to the considered output place. Figure 3 below visualizes the tree corresponding to the previous PNO.

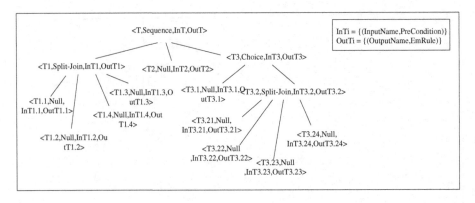

Fig. 3. PNO Tree

Finally, before deriving the OWL-S service profile and service process specifications, the designer can use one of the PNO analysis techniques to simulate, check and validate the corresponding workflow service. Validation concerns a certain number of properties such as for instance Ending (does a process effectively ends?), Liveness (is a given task (transition) always possible?), Boundedness (does the number of possible configurations of a process is finite?), and Reachability (is there an evolution of the process leading to a given configuration (desired or not)?).

4.2 From PNO to OWL-S Service Profile and Process

The starting point of the derivation is the global PNO. We consider three types of places: *begin* places which are exclusively input places, *intermediate* places which are input and output places, and finally *end* places which are exclusively output places. In this step, only *begin* and *end* places are to be considered. Table 1 below summarizes the different derivation rules. In this table, the variable I represents the set of input places of the global PNO while O represents its set of output places.

As shown previously in section 4.1, the result of the decomposition process used for designing a PNO workflow service is a PNO tree. This tree is the starting point to derive the OWL-S service process. We consider two types of nodes: *terminal* nodes and *non-terminal* nodes. Table 2 below summarizes the different derivation rules. In this table, N is the set of the PNO tree nodes (terminal and non terminal) and T is the set of its terminal nodes ($T \subset N$).

Derivation algorithms which implement the previous rules are not, because of space limitation, presented in the paper. The interested reader can find them in [19].

Table 1. Mapping PNO with OWL-S Service Profile

PNO	OWL-S Service Profile
Begin place $b \in B$, $B=I-(I \cap O)$	Parameter Name of an Input
End place $e \in E$, $E=O-(O \cap I)$	Parameter Name of an Output
Precondition associated to a Begin place $b \in B$	Parameter Name of a Precondition
Emission rule associated to an End place $e \in E$	Parameter Name of an Effect

Table 2. Mapping PNO tree with OWL-S Service Process

PNO tree	OWL-S Service Process
Name of a Node $n \in N$	Name of a Process
(InputName, PreCondition) of a node $n \in N$	Input of a Process Precondition associated to the Input
(OutputName, EmRule) of a node $n \in N$	Output of a Process Effect associated to the Output
Terminal Node $t \in T$	Atomic Process
Non Terminal Node $n \in N\text{-}T$	Composite Process

5 Discussion and Conclusion

This paper deals with Web Workflow Services description language devoted to organizations involved in a loose IOW for helping them to describe their workflow needs and/or workflow capabilities. In this paper, we propose to use:

- *PNO for workflow services specification and validation*. First, PNO are convenient to workflow services specification: a PNO specification makes the glue between the different workflow models since it permits the description, in a same representation, of actors of the organizational model, data and documents of the informational model, and tasks of the process model. Moreover, this specification is graphical and thus reduces the complexity of workflow services definition. Second, PNO are convenient to workflow services validation since they define formal and operational specifications. Thus, PNO can be seen as a formalism providing an operational semantic to OWL-S.
- *OWL-S for W2S specification*. First, as shown in section 3.2, OWL-S is appropriate to workflow services description. Secondly, OWL-S includes ontology that makes possible, in the context of loose IOW in which several heterogeneous organizations cooperate, to solve semantic conflicts between these organizations by defining a shared business view based on a common vocabulary, and to ease the implementation of matchmaking mechanisms (e.g. subsumption) useful to compare workflow services. Such mechanisms are very important when selecting partners. Second, the mapping between PNO and OWL-S is easy since the concepts of these two languages are close the ones to the others.

This paper also defines rules to derive PNO specifications onto OWL-S service profile and service process specifications.

This work is implemented in a simulator called MatchFlow [9] whose objective is to connect workflow service requesters to workflow service providers, offers and requests being described using PNO and published according to OWL-S. MatchFlow implements the rules previously given and the corresponding algorithms (presented in [19]).

We found in the literature some works about specification of workflow services accessible through the Web. Some are relevant to workflow technology while others are relevant to semantic Web service technology.

Regarding workflow technology, the main proposition, to our opinion, is the one of YAWL [12]. YAWL permits a graphical specification of workflow services, validates them using a Petri Net representation, and provides tools to derive XML specifications. However, this proposition has two major drawbacks. Firstly, YAWL focus, when specifying a workflow service, on the modeling of the process model and the formalism used do not really make the glue between the three workflow models. Secondly, YAWL derive XML specifications which solve only syntactic conflicts between organizations, while in loose IOW, the heterogeneous context requires semantics conflicts solving mechanisms.

Regarding semantic Web services technology, [20] describes the OWL-S Editor Tool for visual modeling of OWL-S services. This tool permits the description of Web services using standard UML Activity Diagrams and derives the corresponding OWL-S specifications. However, this proposition has two major drawbacks. Indeed, on the one hand, UML Activity Diagrams focus on the modeling of the process model and not really make the glue between the three workflow models, and, on the other hand, UML Activity Diagrams do not provide an operational semantic to validate the described services. Besides, at the meantime, OWL-S only provides a first-order logic representation [17], and, the work described in [21] must be fitted to OWL-S. However, we believe that classical Petri nets used in [21] are less adequate to workflow services specification than PNO.

We plan to complete this work refining the OWL-S ontology for integrating some workflow processes particularities. Indeed, the analyze and simulation of a PNO enable the deduction of process properties (ending, reachability...) and some performance evaluations (average throughput time, average waiting time...) which are not taken into account in the current OWL-S ontology. These information are however relevant and useful for workflow requester to compare providers. Hence, we propose to refine the Service Model class by adding a specific sub-class describing these process properties.

References

1. Medjahed, B., Bouguettaya, A., Elmagarmid, A.: Composing Web Services on the Semantic Web. Int. Journal on Very Large DataBases (2003) 12(4) 333–351
2. World Wide Web Coalition: the Web Service Description Language. Documentation available at: http://xml.coverpages.org/wsdl.html
3. World Wide Web Coalition: the Simple Object Access Protocol. Documentation available at: http://xml.coverpages.org/ni2003-06-24-a.html
4. World Wide Web Coalition: Universal Description Discovery and Integration. Documentation available at: http://xml.coverpages.org/ni2005-02-02-a.html
5. McIlraith, S., Son, TC., Zeng, H.: Semantic Web Services. Int. Journal on Intelligent Systems 16(2) (2001) 46–53
6. Berners-Lee, T., Hendler, J. Lassila, O.: The Semantic Web. Scientific American Magazine 284(5) (2001) 34–43
7. Divitini, M., Hanachi, C., Sibertin-Blanc, C.: Inter Organizational Workflows for Enterprise Coordination. In: Omicini, A., Zambonelli, F., Klusch, M., Tolksdorf, R. (eds): Coordination of Internet Agents, Springer-Verlarg, Berlin Heidelberg New-York (2001) 46–77
8. van der Aalst, W.: Inter-Organizational Workflows: An Approach Based on Message Sequence Charts and Petri Nets. Int. Journal on Systems Analysis, Modeling and Simulation 34(3) (1999) 335–367
9. Andonoff, E., Bouzguenda, L., Hanachi, C., Sibertin-Blanc, C.: Finding Partners in the Coordination of Loose Inter-Organizational Workflow. 6th Int. Conference on the Design of Cooperative Systems (2004) Hyères (France) 147–162
10. BEA, IBM, Microsoft: Business Process Execution Language for Web Services. Documentation available at: http://xml.coverpages.org/bpel4ws.html
11. IBM: Web Services Flow Language. Documentation available at: http://xml.coverpages.org/wsfl.html
12. van der Aalst, W., Alderd, L., Dumas, M., ter Hofstede, A.: Design and Implementation of the YAWL System. 16th Int. Conference on Advanced Information System Engineering (2004) Riga (Latvia) 142–159
13. Workflow Management Coalition: XML Process Definition Language. Documentation available at: http://xml.coverpages.org/XPDL20010522.pdf

14. OWL Services Coalition: Ontology Web Language for Services Version 1.0. Documentation available at: http://xml.coverpages.org/ni2004-01-08-a.html
15. Sibertin-Blanc, C.: High Level Petri Nets with Data Structure. 6th Int. Workshop on Petri Nets and Applications (1985) Espoo (Finland)
16. van der Aalst, W.: The application of Petri Nets to Workflow Management. Int. Journal on Circuits, Systems and Computers 8(1) (1998) 21–66
17. Berardi, D., Gruninger, M., Hull, R., McIlraith, S.: Flows: A First-Order Logic Ontology for Web Services. Available at: www.wsmo.org/papers/presentations/ FLOWS-WSMO-06-30-04.ppt
18. Lara, R., Roman, D., Polleres, A., Fensel, D.: A Conceptual Comparison of WSMO and OWL-S. 2nd International Conference on Web Services Europe (2004) Erfurt (Germany) 254–269
19. Andonof, E., Bouzguenda, L., Hanachi, C.: Specifying Workflow Web Services using Petri Net with Objects and OWL-S. Technical Report IRIT/UT1/SOC (2004)
20. Scicluna, J., Abela, C., Montebello, M.: Visual Modeling of OWL-S Services. Available at: http://www.daml.org/services/owl-s/pub-archive.html
21. Narayanan, S., McIlraith, S.: Simulation, Verification and Automated Composition of Web Services. 11th Int. World Wide Web Conference (2002) Honolulu (Hawaii) 77–88

Improving Web Design Methods with Architecture Modeling[*]

Santiago Meliá[1], Jaime Gómez[1], and Nora Koch[2]

[1] Universidad de Alicante, Spain
{santi, jgomez}@dlsi.ua.es
[2] Ludwig-Maximilians-Universität München,
and F.A.S.T GmbH, Germany
kochn@pst.ifi.lmu.es

Abstract. Many approaches have been developed for modeling the functional aspects of Web applications, but there is a lack of a modeling language for their architectural concerns. This paper proposes such a modeling language defined as a UML 2.0 profile, which allows the specification of domain-specific models for the architectural view of Web applications. The profile is part of the Web Software Architecture (WebSA) approach, which follows the Model Driven Architecture (MDA) principles. The modeling elements proposed for each WebSA model (subsystem, configuration and integration models) are both represented graphically and formalized by means of the profile and the metamodel, respectively. In this article we will focus on the Configuration model and how it is used to model the well-known Petstore example.

1 Introduction

In the Web domain, customers and users impose increasingly complex needs on the Web software being developed. In order to face such growing demands, during the last years the Web engineering community has proposed several languages, architectures, methods and processes for the Web. Among others, several methodologies, such as OO-H [2], UWE [11], WebML [3], have been proposed for the analysis and design of Web applications, and have shown their suitability for the specification of the functional requirements, in particular the navigational requirements posed by Web information systems. However, the design of architectural aspects of Web applications are almost always ignored, or postponed until the implementation phase with disadvantages related to scalability, platform-independence or security. Architecture models are fundamental in an MDA process, which consists in building and transforming platform-independent models and platform-specific models of the Web application. The objective is to generate only in the last steps platform-specific models and code. Such vision will have enormous consequences for the development and maintenance of the increasing amount of Web software that is being produced.

In order to overcome this lack of modeling elements for the early design of Web architectures the WebSA – Web Software Architecture – approach has been defined [12]. WebSA enriches Web engineering proposals with techniques for the

---

[*] This research has been partially sponsored by the Spanish METASING (TIN2004-00779) and the EC 5th FP AGILE (IST-2001-32747).

K. Bauknecht et al. (Eds.): EC-Web 2005, LNCS 3590, pp. 53–64, 2005.

development of software architectures for the Web and it is based on the Model Driven Architecture (MDA) paradigm [14]. The approach proposes a set of architectural models and a set of transformations that permit the integration of these architectural models with a pre-existing functional model, defined by any of the above mentioned methodologies. The WebSA architecture models, namely the Subsystem Model, the Configuration Model and the Integration Model, provide a Web architecture perspective that includes the subsystems, Web components and connectors that make up the Web application.

The focus in this paper is set up on the modeling elements of the WebSA profile defined for the Configuration Model, which extends one of the new models in the UML 2.0 [17]: the composite structure. This model allows for a specification of software architecture following a properly component-based notation. The benefits of the composite structure are, by means of the Configuration Model, extended to the Web application domain. In addition, we show how to apply the profile to the architecture definition of the Petstore [19] Web application.

The rest of the paper is organized as follows: Sect. 2 provides a brief overview of the WebSA approach. Sect. 3 focuses on the metamodel and profile of the Configuration Model. Sect. 4 describes how the Configuration Model has been applied to model the architecture of the Web application Petstore and how this architectural model fits with traditional navigation models provided by Web design methods. Sect. 5 gives an overview of related work and finally, Sect. 6 outlines some conclusions and proposes further lines of work.

2   An overview of the WebSA Approach

WebSA is a proposal whose main target is to cover all the phases of the Web application development focusing on software architecture. It contributes to cover the gap currently existing between traditional Web design models and the final implementation. In order to achieve this, it defines a set of architectural models to specify the architectural viewpoint which complements current Web engineering methodologies such as [2, 11]. Furthermore, WebSA allows for the integration of the different viewpoints of a Web application by means of transformations between models.

The WebSA approach proposes three architectural models:

- **Subsystem Model (SM):** determines the subsystems that make up our application. It is mainly based on the classical architectural style defined in [1] – the so called "layers architecture" – where a layer is a subsystem encapsulating a certain level of abstraction. Furthermore, it makes use of the set of architectural patterns defined in [18] that determine which is the best layer distribution for our system.
- **Configuration Model (CM):** defines an architectural style based on a structural view of the Web application by means of a set of Web components and their connectors, where each component represents the role or the task performed by one or more common components identified in the family of Web Applications. This is explained with more detail in Sect. 3.
- **Integration Model (IM):** merges the functional and the architectural views into a common set of concrete components and modules that will make up the Web application. This model is inferred from the mapping of the components which are

defined in the configuration model, the subsystem model and the models of the functional view.

The formalization of these models is obtained by means of a MOF-compliant [15] repository metamodel (part of the OMG proposed standards) that specifies (1) which is the semantics associated with each model element, (2) which are the valid configurations and (3) which constraints apply.

Furthermore, WebSA proposes a development process based on the *MDA development process* [10], which includes the same phases as the traditional life cycle (Analysis, Design, and Implementation). However, unlike in the traditional life cycle, the artifacts that result from each phase in the MDA development process must be a computable model. These models represent the different abstraction levels in the system specification and are, namely: (1) Platform Independent Models (PIMs) defined during the analysis phase and the conceptual design, (2) Platform Specific Models (PSMs) defined in the low-level design, and (3) code.

In order to meet these requirements, the WebSA development process establishes a correspondence between the Web-related artifacts and the MDA artifacts. As a main contribution, WebSA defines a transformation policy driven by the architectural viewpoint, that is, is an "architectural-centric" process [9] (see Fig. 1).

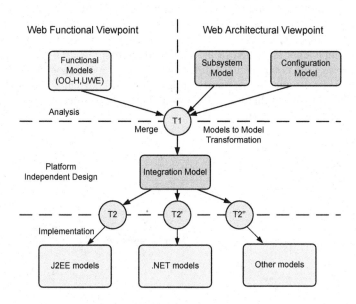

Fig. 1. The WebSA Development Process

Fig. 1 shows how in the analysis phase the Web application specification is divided vertically into two viewpoints. The functional-perspective is given by the Web functional models provided by approaches such as OO-H [2] or UWE [11], while the Subsystem Model (SM) and the Configuration Model (CM) define the software architecture of the Web Application. In the analysis phase, the architectural models are based on two different architectural styles to define the Web application. These models fix the application architecture orthogonally to its functionality, therefore allowing for their reuse in different Web applications.

The PIM-to-PIM transformation (T1 in Fig. 1) from analysis models to platform independent design models provides a set of artifacts in which the conceptual elements of the analysis phase are mapped to design elements where the information about functionality and architecture is integrated. The model obtained is called Integration Model (IM), which merges in a single architectural model the information gathered in the functional viewpoint (e.g., from Conceptual and Navigational models in OO-H and Conceptual, Navigational and Process models in UWE) with the information provided by the Configuration and Subsystem models.

It is important to note that the Integration model, being still platform independent, is the basis on which several transformations, one for each target platform (see e.g., T2, T2' and T2'' in Fig. 1). The output of these PIM-to-PSM transformations is the specification of the Web application for a given platform.

In the rest of the article we will focus on the Configuration Model since it represent the core of the WebSA architectural viewpoint.

3   Configuration Model (CM)

The Configuration model defines an architectural style based on the structural view of the Web application by means of a set of Web components and their connectors, where each component represents the role or the task performed by one or more common components identified in the family of Web applications. In this way, CM uses a topology of components defined in the Web application domain, and this allows us to specify the architectural configuration without knowing anything about the problem domain. At this level, we can define architectural patterns for the Web application as a reuse mechanism.

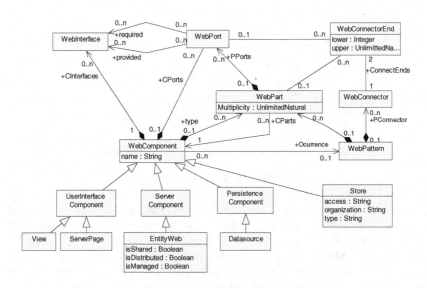

Fig. 2. Simplified CM Metamodel

A diagram for the Configuration model is built by means of a UML 2.0 Profile of the new composite structure model, which is well-suited to specify the software architecture of Web applications. The main modeling elements of the CM are *WebComponent, Web Connector, WebPart* and *WebPattern*.

In order to formalize the Configuration model elements and their relationships, we define the Configuration metamodel (see Fig. 2).

3.1 WebComponent

A WebComponent represents an abstraction of one or more software components with a shared functionality or role in the context of a Web application. For example, a ClientPage is a WebComponent that contains presentation data and/or user interaction code. Note how a Web component does not necessarily map to a single physical page but reflects a general task that must be performed by the application, such as showing certain information to the user. The most important properties of a WebComponent are defined by the classes WebPort, WebInterface and WebPart.

The WebComponent is the root class of a type hierarchy that represents the different roles or tasks that may be performed by the components identified in the family of Web Applications. For example, the subclass EntityWeb is an object representing a concept of the application domain (see Fig. 2). In addition to the subtypes of WebComponent, which are shown in Fig. 2, the Petstore example (Sect. 4) will in addition use the following subtypes: ProcessComponent, UserAgent, DAC, LegacyView, Controller, View and EntityData. The complete topology of the WebSA components can be seen in [13].

3.2 WebPort

WebPort is an interaction point between a WebComponent and its environment. It decouples the internals of the component from the interaction with other components, making that component reusable in any environment that conforms to the interaction constraints imposed by its WebPorts. In this way, a WebComponent can only communicate with the outside through its WebPorts.

3.3 WebInterface

WebInterface represents the functionality the component to which it is associated offers to or requires from the rest of the system in order to be able to perform its task. Each WebInterface is associated with a WebPort specifying the nature of the interactions that may occur over this WebPort (see Fig. 2). On the one hand, the required interfaces of a WebPort characterize the requests which may be made from the WebComponent to its environment. On the other hand, the provided interfaces of a WebPort characterize requests the environment makes to the WebComponent.

3.4 WebConnector

WebConnector specifies a link that allows the communication in the system between two or more WebComponents or/and WebParts of the WebComponents (see 3.6). This communication is established through the WebPorts. However, in the case of a WebPart this relationship may affect either a WebPort or the whole WebPart. Each WebConnector has associated two WebConnectorEnds (see Fig. 2).

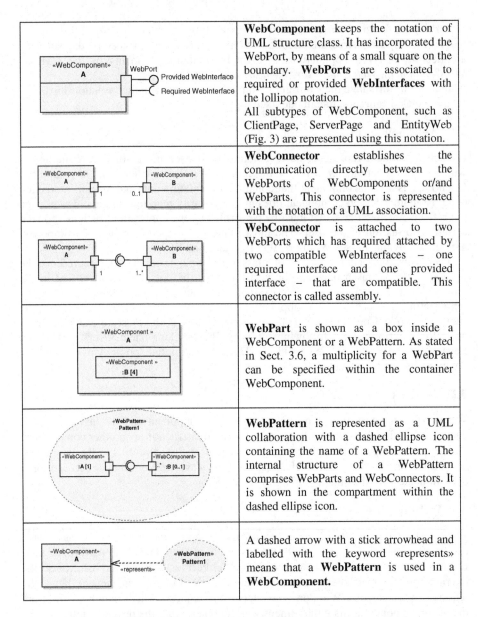

«WebComponent» A WebPort Provided WebInterface Required WebInterface	**WebComponent** keeps the notation of UML structure class. It has incorporated the WebPort, by means of a small square on the boundary. **WebPorts** are associated to required or provided **WebInterfaces** with the lollipop notation. All subtypes of WebComponent, such as ClientPage, ServerPage and EntityWeb (Fig. 3) are represented using this notation.
«WebComponent» A «WebComponent» B 1 0..1	**WebConnector** establishes the communication directly between the WebPorts of WebComponents or/and WebParts. This connector is represented with the notation of a UML association.
«WebComponent» A «WebComponent» B 1 1..*	**WebConnector** is attached to two WebPorts which has required attached by two compatible WebInterfaces – one required interface and one provided interface – that are compatible. This connector is called assembly.
«WebComponent » A «WebComponent » :B [4]	**WebPart** is shown as a box inside a WebComponent or a WebPattern. As stated in Sect. 3.6, a multiplicity for a WebPart can be specified within the container WebComponent.
«WebPattern» Pattern1 «WebComponent» :A [1] «WebComponent» :B [0..1]	**WebPattern** is represented as a UML collaboration with a dashed ellipse icon containing the name of a WebPattern. The internal structure of a WebPattern comprises WebParts and WebConnectors. It is shown in the compartment within the dashed ellipse icon.
«WebComponent» A «WebPattern» Pattern1 «represents»	A dashed arrow with a stick arrowhead and labelled with the keyword «represents» means that a **WebPattern** is used in a **WebComponent.**

Table 1. Notation used in a Configuration Model

3.5 WebConnectorEnd

WebConnectorEnd represents an endpoint of the connector that attaches the connector to a WebPort or a WebPart. The WebConnectorEnd has two properties: (1) *lower* which specifies the lower bound of elements which could be connected with the WebConnectorEnd. (2) *upper* which specifies the upper bound of elements which could be connected with the WebConnectorEnd.

3.6 WebPart

WebPart represents a set of instances that are owned by composition belonging to a WebComponent instance. A WebPart has a property multiplicity, which using the notation [x{...y}] specifies the initial instance or the amount of instances (x) when the WebComponent is created, and the maximum amount of instances at any time (y).

3.7 WebPattern

WebPattern represents a Web architectural pattern, which is specified by a composite element made up of a set of WebConnectors, and WebParts that corresponds to Web components playing roles to accomplish a specific task or function. WebPattern instances are elements of reuse in a configuration model. For example, the Petstore application has two WebPatterns called *MVC2* (see Sect. 4.1) and *Façade* (see Sect. 4.2) which contain some possible configuration of elements that represent the patterns Model-View-Controller [1] and Façade [6].

In order to represent the architectural style defined by the Configuration Model, the CM Profile has been defined as an extension of the UML Composite Structure model including Web components and properties of the Web application domain.

In this way, the CM profile has incorporated all the classes of its metamodel as stereotypes, extending the UML metaclasses. The CM stereotyped classes will add the domain specific semantic defined in the Configuration metamodel to the semantic that they inherit from the UML metaclasses.

For the visual representation of the CM profile elements we stick to the notation of the corresponding UML metaclass elements. These modeling elements are described in Table 1.

4 A Case Study: Petstore

For the proof-of-concept of the CM profile, we have chosen the J2EE Petstore example [19]. This application constitutes a blueprint that uses best practices and design guidelines for a distributed component Web application.

As stated above, the CM represents an architectural style and it is made up of a set of Web components and their connectors. This model is independent of the application functionality and the development platform. Therefore in this article we will only focus on its architectural aspects. We first give an overview of the Petstore configuration model and then dive into two applied patterns *MVC2* and *Façade*.

Fig. 3 shows a general view of the CM representing the Petstore architecture, which is made up of a set of components and connectors that are described next.

In the front-end part of the model we find the UserAgent (e.g., a browser) which receives the user's requests and renders the ClientPage set. Each ClientPage contains the interface and functionality information and is responsible for sending messages to the *MVC2* WebPattern (described in detail in Sect. 4.1). The *MVC2* WebPattern receives the requests through the WebPort *ClientHandler* and establishes the interface reaction through the WebPort *ScreenData*, which is defined by the ServerPage components.

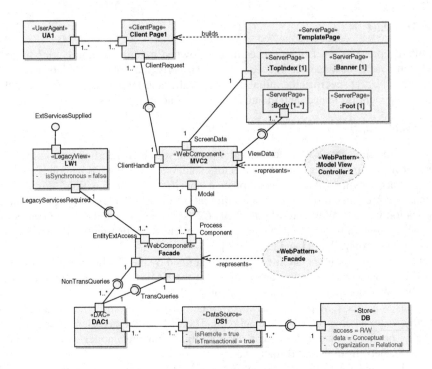

Fig. 3. Configuration Model of Petstore

The ServerPages of Petstore are specified following the pattern *Master Template* defined by Conallen [4]. Following this pattern, in Fig. 3 we have defined a *TemplatePage* that builds the client pages by instantiation of the WebParts *TopIndex*, *Banner*, *Foot* and *Body*. Each instance of a Body ServerPage needs an interface to access the required data objects. Such interface is provided by the WebPort *ViewData* of the *MVC2* Web Pattern. Looking at the MVC2, we can observe that the MVC2 component needs information from the components that implement the business logic, which is obtained through the *BLogic* interface offered by the *Façade* WebPattern (described in detail in Sect. 4.2). The *Façade* invokes the DAC (Data Access Component, based on the Data Access Object pattern [6]), which contains the data access methods and decouples the business logic from the data. In our example DAC offers two interfaces, one for the non transactional queries, i.e. the data retrieval queries which are accessed through the WebPort process component of *Façade*, and one for the transactional queries (insert, update and delete) which are accessed through the *Entity* port of *Façade*. The WebComponent *Façade* is in turn related to the component LegacyView, which offers a series of services coming from the *EntityExtAccess* port to other applications and converts the received asynchronous calls into requests to the business logic. Finally, the specified remote and transactional data sources allow for the connection to Store that contains the information modelled in the conceptual model of the functional view of the Web application Petstore, and specifies a read/write access, as well as a relational organization.

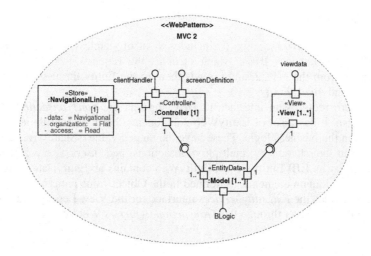

Fig. 4. Model-View-Controller 2 Pattern

4.1   Model View Controller 2 Pattern

Fig. 4 depicts the components of the *MVC2* WebPattern, a variant of the classic MVC. This pattern is made up of a controller component that has two Web Interfaces, one for receiving the requests from the client page and one for building the pages. It is connected to a Store component which contains information about the links among pages. The fact that links are contained in a Store supports the separation of navigation from presentation. Also, the controller needs the information contained in the component EntityData, which contains both data coming from the classes of the conceptual model and the connectivity through the BLogic WebInterface.

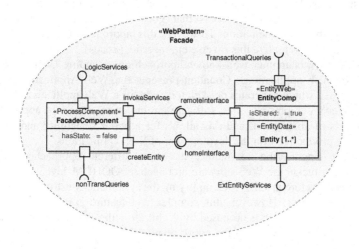

Fig. 5. Façade Pattern

4.2 Façade Pattern

The Façade WebPattern (see Fig. 5) includes a set of stateless ProcessComponents (e.g., a Session Stateless EJB), which receives the requests through the *BLogic* WebInterface from the *MVC2*, and resends them to the Entity through the interfaces *createEntity* and *invokeEntity*.

This pattern requires an interface to DAC through the *nonTransactionalQueries* interface. Also, it has a set of EntityWeb components that represent the elements of the domain in the business logic. These have the tagged value isShare=true indicating that they can be shared by multiple transactions and users (e.g., it could be implemented by an EJB Entity). Each EntityWeb contains an EntityData representing the state of the domain elements, as defined in the ObjectValue pattern [6]. Note how this entity provides the *ExtEntityServices* interface for the View Legacy and sends the requests to the data layer through the *TransactionalQueries* WebInterface.

5 Related Work

The modern Web architecture emphasizes scalability, independent deployment, and interaction latency reduction, security enforcement, and legacy systems encapsulation. For instance, approaches such as Representational State Transfer (REST) [5] architectural style, to represent Web architectures, with focus upon the generic connector interface of resources and representations. However, REST has only served both as a model for design guidance, and as test for architectural extensions to the Web protocols. WebSA is based on some concepts of the REST architecture style to define a process development for the production of Web applications.

Hassan and Holt [7] present an approach aimed at recovering the architecture of Web applications. The approach uses a set of specialized parsers/extractors that analyze the source code and binaries of Web applications. They describe the schemas used to produce useful architecture diagrams from highly detailed facts. Conversely, WebSA follows the opposite process that goes from the representation of the architecture to the implementation. However, this approach does not describe the transformation rules to realize this reverse engineering process.

Conallen's work is another well-known approach on extending UML [4] to model the design of Web applications. Conallen presents the Web Application Extension (WAE) for UML, which generates de skeleton code for a Web application. Unlike this approach, WebSA represents the software architecture of Web applications at different levels of abstraction, and this allows for a better scalability and reusability improving the productivity on the development of Web applications.

In the Web Engineering community moreover different approaches have been developed which tackle the Web software architecture. OOHDM-Java2 [8] proposes a product line architecture in J2EE for simplifying the systematic construction of different families of applications. However, this complex architecture is only useful for J2EE platforms. Another approach is proposed by WebRatio – the WebML tool [3]. WebML is a modeling language based on the entity relationship of data that provides its own notation and proposes a static architecture based on the J2EE struts framework.

6   Conclusions and Further Work

WebSA is an approach that complements the currently existing methodologies for the design of Web applications with techniques for the development of Web architectures. WebSA comprises a set of models and transformations, a modeling language and a development process. The development process also includes the description of the integration of these architectural models with the functional models of the different Web design approaches setting the base for an MDA

In this paper we have presented a UML 2.0 Profile for WebSA. We want to stress the importance of the UML compliance of this modeling language, which allows the use of any UML 2.0 CASE tool. Furthermore, it is the basis for the specification of the transformations that rely on the QVT standard.

Currently, we are working on the set of QVT [16] transformation models to support the WebSA refinement process. This work will formalize the transformations while guaranteeing the traceability between those models and the final implementation.

References

1. F. Buschmann, R. Meunier, H. Rohnert, P. Sommerlad, M. Stal. Pattern-Oriented Software Architecture – A System of Patterns, John Wiley & Sons Ltd. Chichester, England, 1996
2. C. Cachero. OO-H. Una extensión de los métodos OO para el modelado y generación automática de interfaces hipermediales http://www.dlsi.ua.es/ ~ccachero/pTesis.htm, 2003
3. S. Ceri, P. Fraternali, M. Matera. Conceptual Modeling of Data-Intensive Web Applications, IEEE Internet Computing 6, No. 4, July/August 2002, 20–30
4. J. Conallen. Building Web Applications with UML, 2nd Edition, Addison-Wesley Longman, September 2002
5. R. Fielding, R. Taylor. Principled Design of the Modern Web Architecture, ACM Transactions on Internet Technology 2(2), May 2002, 115-150
6. E. Gamma, R. Helm, R. Johnson, J. Vlissides. Design Patterns: Elements of Reusable Object-Oriented Software, Addison-Wesley, 1995
7. A. Hassan, R. Holt. Architecture Recovery of Web Applications, International Conference on Software Engineering (ICSE'02), Orlando, Florida, May 2002
8. M. D. Jacyntho, D. Schwabe, G. Rossi. A Software Architecture for Structuring Complex Web Applications, Journal of Web Engineering, 1(1),37-60, 2002
9. I. Jacobson, G. Booch, J. Rumbaugh. The Unified Software Development Process, Addison-Wesley, 1999
10. A. Kleppe, J. Warmer, W. Bast. MDA Explained. The Model Driven Architecture, Practice and Promise, Addison-Wesley, 2003
11. N. Koch, A. Kraus. The Expressive Power of UML-based Web Engineering, In Proc. of the 2nd. IWWOST, CYTED, Málaga, Spain, June 2002, 105-119
12. S. Meliá, C. Cachero. An MDA Approach for the Development of Web Applications, In Proc. of 4th ICWE, LNCS 3140, July 2004, 300-305
13. S. Meliá. The WebSA Configuration Model Profile. Technical Report TR-WebSA2, http://www.dlsi.ua.es/~santi/pPublicaciones.htm, November 2004
14. OMG. Model Driven Architecture, OMG doc. ormsc/2001-07-01
15. OMG. Meta Object Facility (MOF) v1.4, OMG doc. formal/02-04-03

16. OMG. RFP: MOF 2.0 Query / Views /Transformations, OMG doc. ad/2002-04-10
17. OMG. UML 2.0, Final Adopted Specification, OMG doc. ptc/2003-08-02
18. Klaus Renzel, Wolfgang Keller. Client/Server Architectures for Business Information Systems: A Pattern Language, PLoP Conference, 1997
19. TM J2EE Blueprint. Java Petstore 1.1.2, http://developer.java.sun.com/developer/releases/petstore/petstore1_1_2.html, November 2004

Developing E-Commerce Applications from Task-Based Descriptions*

Pedro Valderas, Joan Fons, and Vicente Pelechano

Department of Information Systems and Computation,
Technical University of Valencia,
Camí de Vera s/n, 46022 Valencia, Spain
{pvalderas, jjfons, pele}@dsic.upv.es

Abstract. In the development of E-commerce applications several decisions must be taken to provide the information, functionality and navigation that better fills to the commercial needs of an organization. These decisions define the requirements that an E-commerce application must satisfy. Although there are a significant number of proposals for modelling and developing E-commerce applications, very few of them clearly state how to elicit and represent E-commerce requirements, and how to go from the requirements specification to the Web conceptual model with a sound methodological basis. This work presents an approach to capture E-commerce application requirements by means of: (1) the identification of the tasks that users must be able to achieve and (2) the description of these tasks from the point of view of the interaction that the user requires of the web application. In addition, we show how the web conceptual model of the OOWS method can be systematically derived from a task description.

1 Introduction

E-commerce applications must provide the information, functionality and navigation structure that better adjust to the commercial needs of an organization. To develop an E-commerce application, several decisions must be taken: (1) which data of the products is more adequate to be shown and which mechanism should be provided for accessing to this data (searches, indexed lists, etc), (2) which functionality can execute users (add products to cart, make reservations, etc.) and (3) which navigational structure fits the usability requirements that the purchase process should take into account in order to improve the commercial exchange. These decisions define most of the requirements that an E-commerce application must satisfy.

From a methodological point of view, the most outstanding approaches (OOHDM [3], WebML [6], WSDM [1], UWE [7], OOWS [4]. etc.) allow analysts to develop E-commerce applications from web conceptual models where E-commerce applications are described at a high level of abstraction. However, very few approaches clearly

---

* The work reported in this paper has been funded by the MEC under grant TIN2004-03534 and cofinanced by FEDER.

K. Bauknecht et al. (Eds.): EC-Web 2005, LNCS 3590, pp. 65–75, 2005.

state with how to elicit and represent E-commerce requirements, and how to go from the requirements specification to the conceptual schema with a sound methodological basis. In this sense, when dealing with complex E-commerce applications, it might be difficult to manually define the conceptual schema that satisfies every requirement.

In this work, we present an approach to capture E-commerce application requirements and systematically obtain the web conceptual model from them. To do this, we propose: (1) to identify the tasks that users of the E-commerce application must achieve and (2) to describe these tasks from the point of view of the interaction that the user requires of the web application. In addition, we show how the navigational model of the OOWS method can be systematically derived from a task description.

This work is organized as follow: Section 2 introduces a brief overview of the whole process that we propose to develop E-commerce applications. Section 3 presents a task-based method to capture E-Commerce application requirements. Section 4 presents an overview of the OOWS method and how its navigational model can be systematically defined form a task description. Conclusions and further work are presented in Section 5. The Amazon web site has been taken as a case study to clearly map the new concepts and abstraction mechanisms and their implementation in a real Web environment.

2   E-Commerce Application Development Process

The process that we propose to develop an E-Commerce application is divided into three main stages: requirements elicitation, conceptual modelling and implementation. This process is graphically presented in Figure 1.

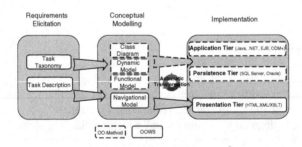

Fig. 1. E-Commerce Application Development Process

In the requirements elicitation step, tasks that users must be able to achieve are identified and described. To do this, a hierarchy of tasks is first defined. Next, each leaf task of the hierarchy is described from the interaction that the user requires of the web application by means of activity diagrams.

In the conceptual modelling stage, the web conceptual schema of the OOWS method is defined. The OOWS conceptual schema is made up of several models which describe the different aspects of an E-commerce application. The system static structure and the system behaviour are described in three models (*class diagram* and *dynamic*-and *functional* models) that we borrow from an object oriented software production method called OO-Method [8]. The navigational aspects of a Web application are described in a *navigational model* [4] .In this work we focus on the systematic derivation of the navigation model from the task description. How the other models are systematically obtained from the requirements elicitation stage is explained in [10].

In the last stage, the E-commerce application is implemented by using a specific technology following a three-tier architecture. The implementation is automatically achieved from the information defined in the conceptual schema [4]. The process of automatic implementation is supported by the OLIVANOVA tool [11].

Next, we introduce both the task description defined at the requirements elicitation stage and how the OOWS navigational model of an E-commerce application can be systematically derived from these descriptions.

3 Task-Based Descriptions of E-Commerce Applications

In this section, we introduce a method for describe E-commerce applications from: (1) the identification of the set of tasks that users must achieve and (2) the description of these tasks from the system-user interaction.

3.1 Task Identification

In order to easily identify tasks, we propose the construction of a task taxonomy taking a *statement of purpose*, which describes the goal for which the application is being built, as the starting point. The statement of purpose is considered as the most general task. From this task, a progressive refinement is performed and more specific tasks are obtained. Tasks are decomposed into more specific ones until *elementary tasks* are obtained. An *elementary task* is defined as a task that when divided into subtasks, atomic actions are obtained. In addition, we propose to enrich this taxonomy by indicating temporal relationships among tasks. To do this, we use the relationships introduced by the CTT approach (ConcurTaskTree) [2]. Due to space problem, we only present the four relationships that have been used in the example of this work:

- T1 []>> T2, *Enabling with information passing*: when T1 task is terminated then task T2 is activated; in addition when T1 terminates it provides some value for T2;
- T1 |> T2, *Suspend-Resume*: T1 can be interrupted by T2. When the T2 terminates then T1 can be resumed.
- T1 [] T2, *Choice*: One of the tasks can be chosen and only the chosen task can be performed.
- T1*, *Iteration*: the task is iterative.

Figure 2 shows the task taxonomy that we obtain from the statement of purpose of the Amazon Web site (*Purchase Products*). To easily identify the elementary tasks they are circled with a thicker line. We briefly describe the task taxonomy:

- The task *Purchase Products* (the statement of purpose) is decomposed into *Collect Items* and *Checkout*. The relation between them is *enabling with information exchange.* Indeed, first items should be collected into de shopping cart before checkout is possible. The information that needs to be exchange is the shopping cart.

- *Collect Items* is decomposed into *Add Product to Shopping Cart* (which can be repeated) and *Inspect Shopping Cart*. The relation between both tasks is *suspend-resume*, which indicates that *Add Product to Shopping Cart* can be interrupted by *Inspect Shopping Cart* at any point and will be reactivated from the state reached before the interruption once *Inspect Shopping Cart task* is ended.
- The task *Add Product to Shopping Cart* is decomposed into *Add CD*, *Add Software* and *Add Book*. The user can either (*Choice relationship*) add a CD, some software or a book.
- To checkout, first the user should login (*Login*) and then the payment handling is done (*Handle Payment*).

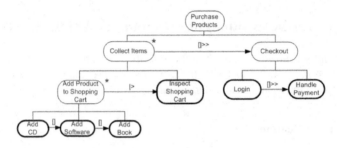

Fig. 2. Amazon Task Taxonomy

Tasks inherit the temporal constraints of the ancestors. For instance, in Figure 2, *Add Book* is a sub-task of *Add Product to Shopping Cart* and since *Add Product to Shopping Cart* can be suspended by *Inspect Shopping Cart,* this constraint will also apply to *Add Book*.

Once elementary tasks are identified we must describe how they should be achieved. Next, we introduce a strategy to do this.

3.2 Task Description

Once the task taxonomy is built, elementary tasks are described to define how user can achieve them. To do this, we extend traditional description where user and system actions are described by introducing information about the *system-user interaction*, indicating explicitly when (at which exact moment) it is performed. To do this we introduce the concept of **interaction point (IP).** Two kinds of interactions can be performed in an IP:

   (1) *Output Interaction*: the system provides the user with information and/or access to operations which are related to an entity[1]. The user can perform several actions with both the information and the operations: the user can select information (as a result the system provides the user with new information) or the user can activate an operation (as a result the system carries out an action).

---

[1] Any object of the real world that belongs to the system domain (e.g. client, product, invoice, etc).

(2) *Input Interaction*: the system requests the user to introduce information of an entity. The system uses this information to correctly perform a specific action (for instance, the client information needed to carry out an on-line purchase). In this case, the only action that user can perform is the information introduction.

In this way, a task is described as a process where the system carries out several *actions* sometimes delaying them in order to *interact* with the *user* by means of an IP. As far as the system actions, two kinds are proposed: *(1) Functionality Execution* that are actions that change the system state and *(2) Information Search* that are actions that only query the system state.

In order to perform descriptions based on IPs we propose the use of UML *activity diagrams* [5] where (see Figure 3):

- Each node (activity) represents an IP (solid line) or a system activity (dashed line). IPs are stereotyped with the *Output* or the *Input* keyword to indicate the interaction type. System actions are stereotyped with the *Function* or the *Search* keyword to indicate their types.
- In the *Output IPs* the number of information instances[2] that the IP includes (cardinality) is moreover depicted as a small circle in the top right side of the primitive.
- As far as the *Input IPs,* we have said that they are used by the system to correctly perform a specific action. To capture that this kind of IPs exclusively depends on a system action and it does not take part in the general process of the task, nodes that represent both elements (input IP and system action) are encapsulated into dashed squares.
- Finally, each arc represents (1) a user action (selection or introduction of information and activation of operations) if the arc source is an IP or (2) a node sequence if the arc source is a system action.

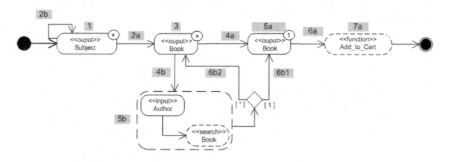

Fig. 3. Description of the task *Add Book*

Continuing with the Amazon web site, the *Add Book* elementary task is described in Figure 3 (the shaded numbers are not part of the notation). This task starts with an *Output* IP where the system provides the user with a list (cardinality *) of subjects (1).

---

[2] Given a system entity (e.g. client), an information instance is considered to be the set of data related to each element of this entity (Name: Joseph, Surname: Elmer, Telephone Number: 9658789).

From this list, the user can select a subject (2a and 2b). If the subject has sub-subjects the system provides again the user with a list of (sub) subjects (2b). If the selected subject has not sub-subjects (2a) the system informs about the Books of the selected subject by means of an *Output* IP (3). From this IP the user can perform two actions: **A)** select a book (4a) and then the system provides the user with a description of the selected book (5a). **B)** Activate a search operation (4b) and then the system performs a system action which searches the books of an author (5b). To do this, the user must introduce an author by means of an *Input* IP. If the search returns only one book, the system provides the user with its detailed description (6b1). Otherwise, the system provides the user with a set of books (6b2). Finally, when the user has obtained a book description (5a) he/she can activate the *Add_to_Cart* operation (6a) and then the system performs an action which adds the selected book to the shopping cart (7a).

IPs allow us to describe elementary tasks from the user-system interaction. In each IP, the user and the system perform an information exchange. However, any detail of this information is specified (we just indicate the entity which the information is related to). These details are described using an information template technique that is next introduced.

Describing the system data. The information that must be stored in the system is defined by means of a template technique that is based on data techniques such as the CRC Card [8]. We propose the definition of an information template (see Figure 4) for each entity identified in the description of a task. In each template, we indicate an identifier, the entity and a *specific data* section. In this section, we describe the information in detail by means of a list of specific features associated to the entity. For each feature we provide a name, a description and a data type. In addition, we use these templates to indicate the information shown in each IP. For each feature we indicate the IP/s where it is shown (if there is any). To identify an IP we use the next notation: *Output (Entity, Cardinality)* for the Output IPs and *Input (Entity, System Action)* for the Input IPs.

According to the template in Figure 4, the information that the system must store about a book is (see the specific data section): the book title, the author name, the

Identifier:	O1			
Entity:	Book			
Specific Data:	*Name*	*Description*	*Type*	*IPs*
	Title	Title of the book	String	Output(Book,*), Output(Book,1)
	Edition	Editorial of the book	String	Output(Book,1)
	Author name	Author that has written the book	String	Output(Book,*), Output(Book,1)
	Commentary	A brief commentary of the book	Text	Output(Book,1)
	Cover	Book cover.	Image	Output(Book,*), Output(Book,1)
	Price	Price of the book	Number	Output(Book,1)
	List Price	Amazon Price	Number	Output(Book,*), Output(Book,1)
	Saving	Saving by purchasing in Amazon	Number	Output(Book,1)
	Used price	Price of a used book	Number	Output(Book,1)
	Availability	Number of books in Stock	Number	Output(Book,1)
	Purchase times	Times that the book has been purchased	Number	
	Client Profiles	Profiles of the clients that have purchased the book	String[]	

Fig. 4. Information template

cover and the list price that are shown in the Output(book,1) and Output(book,*) IPs (IPs defined in the *Add Book* elementary task, see Figure 3); the edition, the price, the saving, the used price, the availability and some comments about the book that are shown only in the Output(book,1) IP; and finally, times that a book has been bought and client profiles that usually purchase it which are not shown in any IP.

4   Deriving the Navigational Model from the Task Description

In this section we introduce the navigational model of the OOWS method [4] and how it can be systematically derived from the task-based description presented above.

Navigational structure. The OOWS navigational model is represented by a directed graph (which defines the navigational structure) whose nodes are *navigational contexts* and its arcs denote *navigational links* (see Figure 5, OOWS side). A navigational context (represented by an UML package stereotyped with the *«context»* keyword) defines a view on the class diagram that allows us to specify an information recovery. A navigational link represents navigational context reachability: the user can access a navigational context from a different one if a navigational link between both has been defined.

Identification from a task description: On one hand, each output IP defines a navigational context except for those IPs than both inform about multiple instances of one entity (cardinality *) and allow the user to access to another IP which informs about only one instance of the same entity (cardinality 1). These situations are explained below. On the other hand, a navigational link between two navigational contexts is defined if the IPs which the contexts have been detected from are: (1) connected by means of an arc or (2) connected through an IP which has not generated any context.

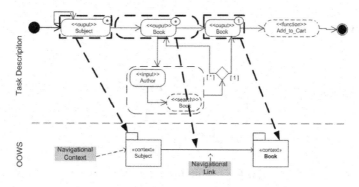

Fig. 5. Identification of the navigational structure

Figure 5 shows the navigational structure defined from the *Addt Book* elementary task. The Output(Subject,*) IP defines the *Subject* navigational context. The Output(Book,1) IP defines the *Book* navigational context. Any context is generated from the Output(Book,*) IP because it allow the user to access to Output(Book,1) IP (same entity, only one instance). A navigational link is defined between Subject and

Book navigational contexts because the Output(Subject,*) IP and the Output(Book,1) IP (IPs which contexts are detected from) are connected through the Output(Book,*) IP (which has not generated any context).

Context definition. A navigational context is made up of a set of *navigational classes* that represent class views over the classes of the class diagram (including attributes and operations). Each navigational context has one mandatory navigational class, called *manager class* (see OOWS side of Figure 6, *Book* class) and optional navigational classes to provide complementary information of the manager class, called *complementary classes* (see OOWS side of Figure 6, *Author* class). All navigational classes must be related by unidirectional binary relationships, called *navigational relationships* that are defined upon an existent relationship in the class diagram.

Identification from a task description: The manager class of a navigational context is detected from the entity associated to the IP that has generated the context. In addition, information templates allow us to identify the manager class attributes and the complementary navigational classes. Each template feature that is shown in an IP maps to an attribute of the manager class of the navigational context detected from this IP. However, if the feature makes reference to an entity different from the template entity the feature maps to a complementary class (instead of an attribute). On the other hand, each *function* system action that is activated from an output IP which has generated a navigational context maps to an operation of the manager class of the context.

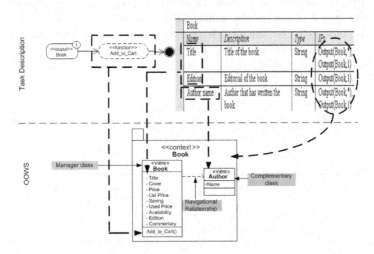

Fig. 6. Identification of context definition

Figure 6 shows the definition of the *Book* navigational context. Each feature defined in the *Book* entity template (which are shown in the Output(Book,1) IP) defines a manager class attribute except for the *Author Name* feature. This feature references to the *Author* entity and then, the *Author* complementary class is defined. Furthermore, the *Add_to_Cart* operation is defined in the manager class because the *Add_to_Cart* system action can be activated from the Output(Book,1) IP.

Information Access Mechanisms. For each context, we can define: (1) Search filters (see OOWS side of Figure 7): mechanisms that allow us to filter the space of objects that retrieve the navigational context. (2) Indexes (see Figure 7): structures that provide an indexed access to the population of objects. Indexes create a list of summarized information allowing the user to choose one item (instance) from the list. This selection causes this instance to become active in the context.

Identification from a task description: On one hand, indexes are detected from those output IPs that both informs about multiple instances of one entity (cardinality *) and provides the user with access to another IP that informs about only one instance of the same entity (cardinality 1). In this case, the first IP defines an index in the navigational context detected from the second IP. Index attributes are detected from the template features that are shown in the first IP. On the other hand, search filters are detected from *search* system actions. Each *search* system action that is activated from an output IP which has defined either a navigational context or an index of a navigational context maps to a search filter of the navigational context. Filter attributes are defined from the template features that are shown in the input IP which allow the user to introduce the search criterion.

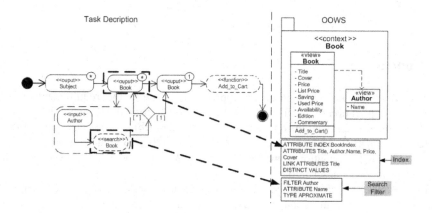

Fig. 7. Identification of information access mechanisms

Figure 7 shows the information access mechanisms of the *Book* navigational context. On one hand, the Output(Book,*) IP defines an index whose attributes are detected from the template features that are shown in the IP. On the other hand, a search filter is defined into the *Book* navigational context because a search system action can be activated from the IP that generates an index of this context, (Output(Book,*)). Attributes of the filter are obtained from the template features that are request in the input IP that allows the user to introduce the author information.

Implementation Issues. Figure 8 shows the implementation of the contexts derived from the task *Add Book*. Figure 8A shows the implementation of the context *Subject*. Figures 8B and 8C implement the context Book (index of books and book description).

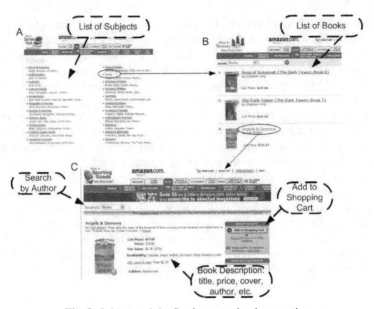

Fig. 8. *Subject* and the *Book* context implementation

5   Conclusions

In this work we have presented an approach to capture the requirements of E-commerce application by (1) identifying the tasks that define the business process that the E-commerce application must support and (2) describing these tasks from the of the interaction that the user requires of the web application. In addition, we have shown how the navigational model of the OOWS method can be systematically derived from a task description.

Furthermore, we have applied our approach to a real case study (the Amazon web site, www.amazon.com). First, we have identified the tasks that define the Amazon product purchase process by means of a task taxonomy. Next, we have described these tasks by means of activity diagrams. Finally, we have shown how the OOWS navigational model of the Amazon web site can be derived from its task description.

Finally, we are currently defining a wizard that asks the user by means of a guided process in order to systematically detect and describe tasks. This wizard will allow us to hide the possible complexity of our notation making the definition of complex E-Commerce applications easier.

References

1. O. De Troyer and C. Leune. WSDM: A user-centered design method for Web sites. In Proc. of the 7th International World Wide Web Conference, 1998.
2. F. Paternò, C. Mancini and S. Meniconi, 1997. "ConcurTaskTrees: a Diagrammatic Notation for Specifying Task Models", In Proceedings of INTERACT'97, Chapman & Hall, 368-366.

3. D. Schwabe, G. Rossi, and S. Barbosa. Systematic Hypermedia Design with OOHDM. In ACM Conference on Hypertext, Washington, USA, 1996.
4. J. Fons, V. Pelechano, M. Albert and O. Pastor. Development of Web Applications from Web Enhanced Conceptual Schemas. In ER'03, pp 232-245. Chicago, EE.UU, 13 - 16 October 2003.
5. Object Management Group. Unified Modeling Language (UML) Specification Version 2.0 Final Adopted Specification. www.omg.org, 2003.
6. S. Ceri, P. Fraternali, S. Bongio. Web Modeling Language (WebML): a Modeling Language for Designing Web Sites. In WWW9, Vol. 33 (1-6), pp 137-157. Computer Networks, 2000.
7. N. Koch, M. Wirsing: Software Engineering for Adaptive Hypermedia Applications. In: 3rd Workshop on Adaptive Hypertext and Hypermedia. (2001).
8. R. Wirfs-Brock, B. Wilkerson and L. Wiener. *Designing Object–Oriented Software.* Prentice–Hall, 1990.
9. O. Pastor, J. Gomez, E. Insfran, V. Pelechano. "The OO-Method Approach for Information Systems Modelling: From Object-Oriented Conceptual Modeling to Automated Programming". Information Systems 26, pp 507–534 (2001).
10. E. Insfrán, O. Pastor and R. Wieringa, Requirements Engineering-Based Conceptual Modelling. Journal "Requirements Engineering" (RE), March 2002. 7(2): p. 61-72.
11. Olivanova Model Execution System. Care technologies (www.care-t.com).

Information Aggregation Using the Caméléon# Web Wrapper

Aykut Firat[1], Stuart Madnick[2], Nor Adnan Yahaya[3], Choo Wai Kuan[3], and Stéphane Bressan[4]

[1] Northeastern University, Boston, MA, USA
a.firat@neu.edu
[2] Massachusetts Institute of Technology, Cambridge, MA, USA
smadnick@mit.edu
[3] Malaysia University of Science and Technology, Petaling Jaya, Malaysia
{noradnan, wkchoo}@must.edu.my
[4] National University of Singapore, Singapore
steph@nus.edu.sg

Abstract. Caméléon# is a web data extraction and management tool that provides information aggregation with advanced capabilities that are useful for developing value-added applications and services for electronic business and electronic commerce. To illustrate its features, we use an airfare aggregation example that collects data from eight online sites, including Travelocity, Orbitz, and Expedia. This paper covers the integration of Caméléon# with commercial database management systems, such as MS SQL Server, and XML query languages, such as XQuery.

1 Introduction

We have argued [12] and illustrated in a case study [15] that information aggregation plays a critical role in the success of electronic business and electronic commerce services. Indeed, extraction and aggregation provide the foundation for added services leveraging the large amounts of data available on the public Internet and on Intranet that are waiting to be put in context and turned into information.

In this paper, we present the technology and tools that we have developed to achieve effective and efficient information extraction and aggregation: Caméléon#. Caméléon# is a web data extraction and aggregation tool that automates form submission; and dynamically converts semi-structured data into relational tables and XML documents. These converted data can then be queried with SQL and XQuery to facilitate interoperability across heterogeneous platforms. Caméléon#'s design and implementation make it Web service compliant and allow a seamless integration into a service oriented architecture. We introduce the features of Caméléon# by means of simple yet challenging examples.

In the financial information aggregation example shown in Fig. 1, internal and external semi-structured data sources are treated as if they were relational tables and aggregated into an MS Excel sheet using SQL through the use of Caméléon#.

K. Bauknecht et al. (Eds.): EC-Web 2005, LNCS 3590, pp. 76–86, 2005.

Caméléon# associates each web source with a simple specification (spec) file that contains a virtual schema declaration with form submission and data extraction rules. Although we do not offer fully-automatic spec file generation, spec file creation is remarkably simple.

During the last decade or so, we have been successfully employing Caméléon# (and its predecessors) for research and teaching purposes. It is part of a larger semantic integration framework ECOIN [5], and has been used in a number of courses to introduce web data management concepts. Compared to other commercial and academic tools, we find Caméléon# better in its balance of simplicity and expressiveness; and capability to connect to problematic sites (e.g., sites that require "on the fly" javascript interpretation).

In the next section, we start with a quick background on wrappers. Then we explain the features of Caméléon# with a practical airfare example that collects price information from eight online airfare sources including Travelocity, Expedia, Orbitz, etc. We also discuss the integration of Caméléon# with a commercial database management system (MS SQL Server) and the XML query language XQuery.

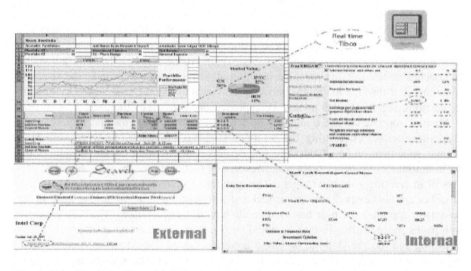

Fig. 1. Caméléon# in Financial Information Aggregation: Internal and External information sources are aggregated as if they were relational tables into an MS Excel sheet with SQL

2 Background

During the boom years of the Internet, especially with the emergence of aggregators [12], there has been a proliferation of data extraction technologies, often-called Web wrappers (or wrappers for short).

A web wrapper is an engine capable of responding to some type of query by retrieving a web page S, based on:

1. A specification of path and parameterized inputs to get to the Web page S containing a set of implicit objects (and any other page S' similar to S); and then extracting data items based on:
2. A mapping specification W that postulates a data repository R with the objects in S. The mapping W must also be capable of recognizing and extracting data from any other page S' similar to S (see [11]).

We can classify wrappers according to how they treat documents (Web pages); how their mapping specifications are generated; and how declarative they are.

Wrappers treat Web pages either as a document tree or as a data stream. Wrapper engines like W4F [14] and Lixto [2] parse Web pages using Document Object Model (DOM) into a tree, and mapping specifications are expressed primarily in terms of the DOM. Other wrapper engines such as TSIMMIS [6] and Caméléon# ignore the HTML tag-based hierarchy and treat Web pages as a sequence of characters. Mapping specifications in this category are usually expressed in terms of regular expressions.

Wrappers can be manual, semi-automatic, or automatic based on how their mapping specifications are generated. In the manual approach (e.g., Jedi [7]), users create general extraction rules by analyzing a representative set of web pages, and are responsible for updating the specification files when necessary. In automatic generation, users first have to annotate a number of training examples through a visual interface (e.g., SoftMealy [8]). Machine learning algorithms, such as inductive learning, are then applied to generate the mappings (e.g., Wien [10], Stalker [13]). Semi-automatic approaches do not use any machine-learning algorithms but try to make the spec file creation easier through mappings between the visual and text/DOM views, by making suggestions on patterns that need to be approved or modified by the user.

Manual approaches are known to be tedious, time-consuming and require some level of expertise concerning the wrapper language. In addition, when web sites change, specification files have to be updated manually as well. Given the state of the art in automatic wrapper creation, however, automatic approaches are not very successful in creating *robust* wrappers. The maintenance costs of current automatic approaches are also comparable to manual and semi-automatic approaches, since in the automatic approach the user has to annotate new training samples when the wrapped web pages are modified. In fact, as noted by [9], it is unrealistic to assume that a user is willing and has the skills to browse a large number of documents in order to identify a set of informative training examples. While new approaches are being suggested that require a small number of training samples [9], their applicability is limited to simpler Web pages that do not contain various sorts of exceptions. On difficult web pages the lack of informative examples would lead to low accuracy.

A third grouping can be made according to how declarative mapping specifications are. In this context, *"declarative"* implies a clear separation of mapping specifications from the computational behavior of the wrapping engine. "Lowly declarative" wrapper engines mix mapping specifications with a programming language (e.g., W4F with Java) or offer a programming language of their own (e.g., Compaq's WebL) (see [4]). In "highly declarative" wrapper engines, extraction rules are separated from the computation logic and do not require any compilation of the rules into executable code.

Based on these three dimensions, existing academic wrappers can be classified as shown in Table 1. A recent survey of commercial engines can be found in [4].

Table 1. Classification of Web Wrapper Projects (see [4] and [11] for references)

	Highly Declarative		Lowly Declarative	
	DOM-based	*Stream-based*	*DOM-based*	*Stream-based*
Manual		Tsimmis	Jedi	Araneus
Semi-automatic	NoDoSe	Caméléon#	W4F	
Automatic	Lixto	WIEN, Stalker	XWrap	

3   Airfare Aggregation with Caméléon#

One of several applications built with Caméléon# is 'Mega Air Fare Aggregator' shown in Fig. 2 (after an execution to find prices between Boston and San Francisco).

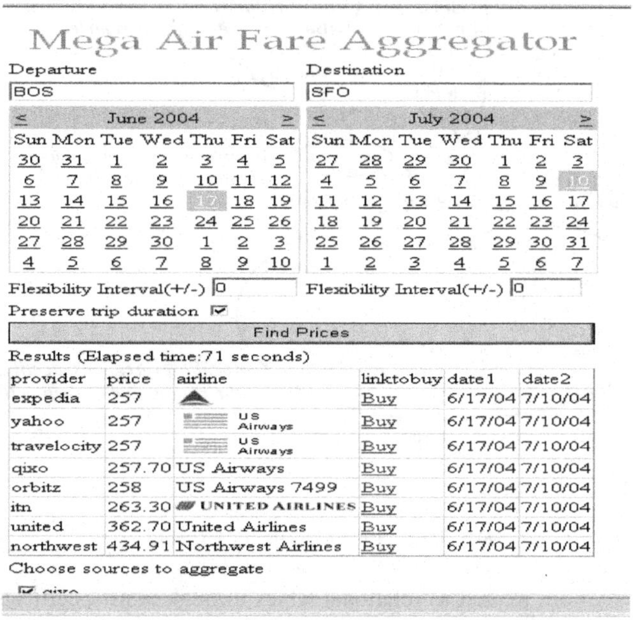

Fig. 2. Mega Airfare Aggregator

The core of this application is a SQL query in the form of
```
(Select provider, price, airline, linktobuy, date1,
date2
From expedia
Where date1= '6/17/04' and date2= '7/10/04' and Depar-
ture= 'BOS' and Destination = 'SFO'
UNION
...
UNION
```

```
Select provider, price, airline, linktobuy, date1,
date2
From travelocity
Where date1= '6/17/04' and date2= '7/10/04' and Depar-
ture= 'BOS' and Destination = 'SFO')
Order By price ASC
```

Fig. 3. Specification File for Expedia

Here, web sites are treated as relational tables through their specification files. As an example, the spec file for the Expedia web site is shown in Fig. 3. In this example, air fare prices from Expedia are obtained through a single form submission; therefore the spec file has a single source declaration. Despite single page traversal, Expedia is a difficult site for two reasons. First, there are cookies, which are set in a non-standard way through Javascript. Because of that, automatic cookie handling will not be able to acquire and supply them. In Caméléon#, custom cookies can be specified as shown in Fig. 3. Second, the Expedia site requires an input form parameter (Time) whose value is determined by some Javascript code. Failure to interpret Javascript will also make it impossible for wrappers to connect to this site. In Caméléon#, we take advantage of Microsoft's .Net framework, which allows mixing different languages with the provision of common intermediate layer CLR (like Java's bytecode). This way, we are able to interpret Javascript code dynamically.

In Fig. 3, after specification of form parameters (those enclosed with # signs are input parameters that are expected in the where clause of a SQL query to Caméléon#), the name of the attribute and its data type are specified. For each attribute, regular expressions inside begin and end tags denote a region in a document, and the expression inside the pattern tag extracts the values for the attribute.

Once spec files for all the airfare sites are constructed, they can be treated as relational tables. It then becomes trivial to construct the airfare aggregation previously shown.

4 Integration with RDBMS

While *core* Caméléon# creates the illusion of an RDBMS to query web data sources, its query support is limited to simple queries in the form of 'Select ... From ... Where'. To support full SQL, additional steps must be taken. Below we explore three ways of achieving this goal.

4.1 OLE-DB Provider for Caméléon#

OLE-DB is Microsoft's way of building common access to data sources including text and XML files, (although they are being deprecated and replaced by .NET data providers). Sources with OLE-DB providers can be linked to SQL Server and utilize its industry strength query planner and execution engine.

We have built an OLE-DB provider for Caméléon#, and the details of it are described in [3]. With this OLE-DB provider, it is possible to issue arbitrary SQL queries with the help of openrowset function (in SQL Server).

```
select   *
from openrowset ('OLEDBCamProv.CamProv', '', ' Select
provider, price, airline, linktobuy, date1, date2 from
expedia where date1= '6/17/04' and date2= '7/10/04' and
Departure= 'BOS' and Destination = 'SFO'')
```

One problem with the openrowset function, however, is that the SQL Server query planner treats it as a black box; and does not use it in the planning and optimization phase of the query. Queries in the openrowset are executed as they are without any optimization. To overcome this problem, Caméléon# engine must satisfy minimum conformance requirements to SQL 92, which is not a trivial task to undertake in developing OLE-DB providers. Besides, there is no clear indication that OLE-DB providers can be developed for functional sources, which require certain input parameters to be specified every time a query is issued against existing tables.

Ignoring optimization issues, the OLE-DB provider for Caméléon# does provide integration with SQL Server.

4.2 Parameterized Views

In SQL-Server it is possible to model web data as functions that return tables. For example, the Expedia web site could be modelled with the following function like a parameterized view:

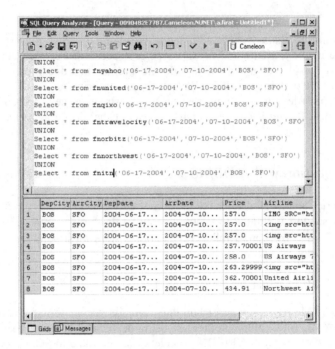

Fig. 4. Parameterized Views & SQL Server Client

```
CREATE FUNCTION fnexpedia (@DepDate smalldatetime,
@ArrDate smalldatetime, @DepCity char(3), @ArrCity
char(3))
returns @fnexpedia table (DepCity char(3),
ArrCity char(3), DepDate smalldatetime, ArrDate small-
datetime, Price real, Airline varchar(30))
AS
BEGIN
DECLARE @query VARCHAR(255)
DECLARE @Date1 char(8), @Date2 char(8)
SET @Date1=CONVERT(char(8), CAST (@DepDate AS small-
datetime), 1)
SET @Date2=CONVERT(char(8), CAST (@ArrDate AS small-
datetime), 1)
SET @query = 'CaméléonSQL "Select Price, Airline From
expedia where Departure="' + @DepCity +'" and Destina-
tion="' + @ArrCity + '" and Date1="' + @Date1 +'" and
Date2="' + @Date2 + '" "'
EXEC master..xp_cmdshell  @query
insert    @fnexpedia
Select  @DepCity , @ArrCity, @DepDate, @ArrDate, Price,
Airline From expedia
RETURN
END
```

In the above function Caméléon# executes the query, creates a temporary table and bulk loads the results into that table. The users can then call the Expedia web site as if it was a parameterized view as follows:

```
Select *
from fnexpedia('06-17-2004','07-10-2004','BOS','SFO')
```

Airfare prices can then be obtained from SQL Server Client as shown in Fig. 4.

One difficulty with this approach, however, is that it is not possible to use these functions with variables in a SQL statement. For example, the following statement would not be meaningful in SQL:

```
Select price
from fnexpedia('06-17-2004','07-10-2004','BOS',Des),
targetcitycodes t
where  Des = t.Destination
```

Furthermore, contrary to expectation this union query in SQL Server is not executed in parallel.

4.3   Custom Planner/Optimizer/Execution Engine

Finally, we mention our "capabilities aware" custom planner, optimizer and execution (POE) engine that works on top of the Caméléon# core. The central concept in this custom POE engine is the concept of a capability record to represent the capability restrictions of Web sources. An example capability record for a currency exchange web site, olsen, is shown below:

```
relation(cameleon, olsen, [ ['Exchanged',string], ['Ex-
pressed',string], ['Rate',number],
['Date',string]],cap([[b(1),b(1),f,b(1)]],
['<','>','<>','<=','>=']])).
```

This simple capability record expresses binding restrictions as a list of all possible binding combinations of the attributes in the virtual relation. A binding combination specifies attributes that need to be bound; attributes that need to be free; and attributes that can be either free or bound. It is represented with a list of binding specifiers for each of the attributes in the relation. A binding specifier can be one of the following: b, b(N), f, and ?. b indicates that the attribute has to be bound. b(N) indicates that the attribute has to be bound with N keys-at-a-time binding restriction. f indicates that the attribute must be free. ? indicates that the attribute can be either bound or free. The record for operator restrictions is a list of the operators, which cannot be used in queries on the relation.

Note that key-at-a time restrictions are quite common among the web wrapped relations. The olsen source can only bind one key at a time for its attributes Exchanged, Expressed, and Date. Key-at-a-time restrictions that can bind more than key at a time (N>1) are also common. A good example of this is a stock quote server like finance.yahoo.com, which allows up to 50 stock quote symbols to be entered at one time.

Based on capability records our custom POE engine produces an optimized plan respecting the capability restrictions. The core Caméléon# and a local RDBMS are then used to execute the plan. More details on this can be found in [1].

5 Integration with XQuery

Since Caméléon# can return results in XML, it becomes trivial to integrate it with XQuery. The airfare results can be obtained with the following XQuery:

```
<Airfare>
{let $travelocity :=
doc(http://interchange.mit.edu/Cameleon_sharp/camserv.asp
x?query=Select Airline, Price from expedia where Destina-
tion="SFO" and Departure="BOS" and Date1="6/12/04" and
Date2= "7/12/04"&amp; format=xml")//price

            ...
let $expedia :=
doc(http://interchange.mit.edu/Cameleon_sharp/camserv.asp
x?query=Select Airline, Price from expedia where Destina-
tion="SFO" and Departure="BOS" and Date1="6/12/04" and
Date2= "7/12/04"&amp; format=xml")//price

            ...
return
  <Results>
            <travelocity>{ $travelocity }</travelocity>
            <itn>{ $itn }</itn>
            <qixo>{ $qixo }</qixo>
            <yahoo>{ $yahoo }</yahoo>
            <orbitz>{ $orbitz }</orbitz>
            <united>{ $united }</united>
            <northwest>{ $northwest }</northwest>
            <expedia>{ $expedia }</expedia>
  </Results>
  }
  </Airfare>
```

XQuery implementations execute this query in parallel, and under a minute, which is quite remarkable given that in SQL-Server the union query took almost 5 minutes to complete.

6 Spec File Management

Caméléon# reduces the effort of aggregating data to the definition of the spec file. Yet, this effort is not insignificant. The scalability of the Caméléon# approach depends on opportunities for re-using and sharing spec files in communities of users.

For this reason, we developed a spec file management system to help store, manage and share spec files, as shown in Fig. 5.

A public repository is created to archive all spec files within a community of interest (a company, a group of users, etc.). Public here does not mean its access is not controlled, it is public within a community. There is only one such repository.

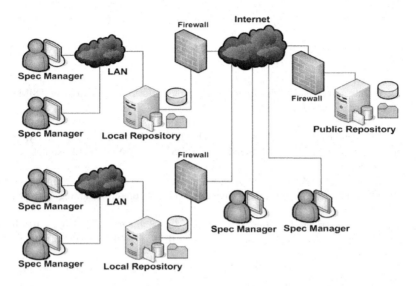

Fig. 5. Spec File Repository Architecture

However, it is connected to several local repositories. Local repositories are usually available only to the internal network of a community. The local repositories periodically communicate their spec files to the public repository. The architecture of the spec file repository is shown in Fig. 5.

The spec manager is a suite developed to assist user in the spec file creation, edition and publication. The spec manager client consists of tools such as web browser, spec file editor, spec file tester, regular expression tester and spec file searcher.

7   Conclusion

We described Caméléon#, a tool for extraction and aggregation of data from various sources. We illustrated the simplicity of use and the power of Caméléon# with the example construction of an application such as the mega airfare aggregator. Caméléon# is used in research and teaching as well as in industrial applications.

References

1. Alatovic, T.: Capabilities Aware, Planner, Optimizer, Executioner for Context Interchange Project. Thesis (S.M.) M.I.T, Dept. of EE & CS (2001)
2. Baumgartner, R., Flesca, S., Gottlob, G. (2001). "Declarative Information Extraction, Web Crawling, and Recursive Wrapping with Lixto". In Proc. LPNMR'01, Vienna, Austria, 2001.
3. Chan, C.: OLE DB for the Context Interchange System. Thesis (S.M.) M.I.T, Dept. of EE & CS (2000)

4. Chuang, S.W.: A Taxonomy and Analysis of Web Wrapping Technologies. Thesis (S.M.) M.I.T, Technology and Policy Program (2004)
5. Firat, A.: Information Integration Using Contextual Knowledge and Ontology Merging Thesis (Ph.D.) M.I.T. (2003)
6. Garcia-Molina, H., Hammer, J., Ireland, K., Papakonstantinou, V., Ullman, J., Widom, J. (1995). Integrating and Accessing Heterogeneous Information Sources in TSIMMIS. In Proceedings of the AAAI Symposium on Information Gathering, pp. 61-64, Stanford, California, March 1995
7. Huck, G., Fankhauser, P., Aberer, K., Neuhold, E. J.: JEDI: Extracting and Synthesizing Information from the Web; submitted to COOPIS 98, New York; IEEE Computer Society Press, (1998)
8. Hsu, C., and Dung, M. (1998). Wrapping semistructured web pages with finite-state transducers. In Proceedings of the Conference on Autonomous Learning and Discovery CONALD-98.
9. Knoblock, C., Lerman, K., Minton, S., Muslea, I.: Accurately and reliably extracting data from the web: A machine learning approach, IEEE Data Engineering Bulletin, 23(4), (2000)
10. Kushmerick, N., Doorenbos, R., Weld., D. (1997) Wrapper Induction for Information Extraction. IJCAI-97, August 1997.
11. Laender, A., Ribeiro-Neto, B., Silva, A. and Teixeira, J.: A Brief Survey of Web Data Extraction Tools, SIGMOD Record, 31(2), (2002)
12. Madnick, S. and Siegel, M: Seizing the Opportunity: Exploiting Web Aggregation, MIS Quarterly Executive, 1(1), (2002)
13. Muslea, I., Minton, S., and Knoblock, C. (1998) STALKER: Learning extraction rules for semistructure, Web-based information sources. In Proc. of AAAI'98: Workshop on AI and Information Integration.
14. Sahuguent, A. and Azavant, F.: W4F: the WysiWyg Web Wrapper Factory. Technical Report, University of Pennsylvania, Department of Computer and Information Science, (1998)
15. Zhu, H., Siegel, M. and Madnick, S.: Information Aggregation – A Value-added E-Service, Proc. of the International Conference on Technology, Policy, and Innovation: Critical Infrastructures, (2001)

Data Cleansing for Service-Oriented Architecture[*],[**]

Jung-Won Lee, Eunyoung Moon, and Byoungju Choi[***]

Dept. of Computer Science and Engineering, Ewha Womans University,
11-1 Daehyun-dong, Sudaemun-ku, Seoul, Korea
{jungwony, mney, bjchoi}@ewha.ac.kr

Abstract. Service-Oriented Architecture (SOA) is a new paradigm for integrating distributed software, especially e-Business application. It is essential to exchange reliable data between services. In this paper, we propose a methodology for detecting and cleansing dirty data between services, which is different from cleansing static and large data on database systems. We also develop a data cleansing service based on SOA. The service for cleansing interacting data makes it possible to improve the quality of services and to manage data effectively for a variety of SOA-based applications. As an empirical study, we applied this service to clean dirty data between CRM and ERP services and showed that the dirty data rate could be reduced by more than 30%.

1 Introduction

Recently, distributed software integration technology started using web services for loosely coupling e-Business applications, not for tightly coupling some software in the enterprise. However, web service is only an implementation technology for Service-Oriented Architecture (SOA), which simply regulates what and where to describe services and how to browse services. Therefore, it is distinguished from SOA itself, which provides specific fundamentals for service composition and management in order to support business interactions inside and outside the enterprise [1].

When services are integrated based on SOA, it is possible to verify the connection among services by simulating the entire system operation. At this time, however, it is only possible to verify whether input and output specifications of each service are correctly matched but not possible to verify whether correct data is used. Though the objective of SOA [2] is to compose, integrate, and manage services with ensuring the quality of service (QOS), the responsibility for ensuring the quality of data exchanged between services so that they can execute their tasks correctly still remains with the developers. Currently, the process of dirty data detection and cleansing is applied without fail to such fields as data mining where the quality of prepared data seriously affects the accuracy of the result, using statistical methods [3]. However, if data cleansing to support SOA depends solely on one data cleansing tool of single database or data mining system, the following problems may arise.

---

[*] This work was partially supported by Grant No.R04-2003-000-10139-0 from the Basic Research Program of the Korea Science & Engineering Foundation.
[**] This work was partially supported by University IT Research Center Project.
[***] Corresponding author.

K. Bauknecht et al. (Eds.): EC-Web 2005, LNCS 3590, pp. 87–97, 2005.

First, it is impossible to guarantee the quality of data exchanged between services. For example, if there is a data set ($D=\{d_1, d_2,...,d_k,...,d_n\}$) exchanged between two interacting services (Services A and B), and Service B had deleted or cleansed d_2 and d_k using a cleansing tool in the system, Service A may keep waiting for response to the original values of d_2 and d_k without knowing it. Therefore, a data cleansing service that can monitor data interactions among services is required.

Second, SOA-based system developers should modify the inside of a service in order to regulate the constraints for data input and output between services. For example, let's assume that you are creating a new service by connecting Services A and B. Also assume that A has output data $D=\{d_1,d_2,d_3,...,d_k,...,d_n\}$ and B processes only $D'=\{d_1,d_2,d_3',...,d_k'\}$ as its input. Unlike d_1 and d_2 with the completely same data format and meaning, d_3' and d_k' have the same data types but different ranges. So, you need to modify the inside of B and thus have to develop independent services that allow separately managing only the data exchanged between services.

Third, even though there is a cleansing tool developed as an independent component, flexible dirty data detection is still impossible. In other words, even if a cleansing tool developed as a component is used between Services A and B, the cleansing engine should be repeatedly updated in order to establish rules to detect errors in data sent from Service A and to reflect any changes in the rules. Therefore, it is needed to develop services that can flexibly handle changes in data set and constraints using XML as the standard supporting SOA.

In this paper, we present a method, which as an independent service can detect and cleanse errors in data exchanged between services while sticking to the fundamentals of SOA. The developed dirty data cleansing service improves the quality of services composed based on SOA, reduces developers' efforts in composing services, and efficiently manages data in systems having a lot of interactions such as e-business system. By applying the service to integrating CRM and ERP services based on SOA, we found that errors in the data exchanged between two services were reduced by more than 30%.

The reminder of this paper is organized as follows. Section 2 describes the background of this study; Section 3 proposes taxonomy of dirty data and a method for detecting and cleansing interactive data between services; Section 4 explains the development process of the service for cleansing data based on the SOA; and Chaper 5 provides its application and the lessons from an empirical study.

2   Background

Data quality problems arise when data is not compatible with the system specification, when the user cannot completely understand data due to its complexity or metadata fault, or when the selected data is not what the user expected [3]. Efforts to solve these problems cost a lot of money and time in many fields [4].

Studies to find out proper methods to cleanse data whose quality is in doubt are in progress in many fields such as database and data mining. These studies mainly focus on identifying dirty data in database, like identifying redundant values in one table in database [5,6] or cleansing data that cause conflict in names or structures at the time of schema mapping [7]. On the other hand, other research efforts to identify suspicious or lost data in data sets using statistical methods are also actively researched [8]. However, if data cleansing methods take into account only the database where all data are already collected, there is no way to consider the quality of data exchanged between SOA-based systems using web services. As already mentioned in Introduction, considering cleansing of dirty data merely as one of internal problems of service causes other problems. On this, we present a method to cleanse data at the time of service integration. This method satisfies both the efforts to improve data quality during software development process and the fundamentals for composing and managing SOA-based services.

A variety of applications based on data mining such as ERP and CRM employ data cleansing tools. MonArch, SLAAM, ZipIt, and HummingBird are the examples of data cleansing tools. However, these tools apply only to specific data types (e.g., mail address, address change, searching the duplicated person, etc.) of specific applications developed based on data mining. Though they were developed independently, it is hard to reuse them for SOA where inter-service routing occurs frequently. Therefore, in this paper, we present a data quality cleansing service that can operate independently of the system or application to which it belongs.

3 Detecting and Cleansing Dirty Data

This Section presents the taxonomy of dirty data and proposes the rule for detecting and cleansing dirty data.

3.1 Taxonomy of Dirty Data Between Services

For feasibility test, we classified errors that may arise in database during data collection, integration, and storing into 33 types [9]. To define the data errors that may arise during interaction between services, we have to rearrange the 33 dirty data types. As the taxonomy of dirty data presented in [9] is established based on the completeness of taxonomy, however, no more taxonomy would be added for classifying interaction data and thus it is necessary to select the error types for interaction data from the established taxonomy.

As shown in Table 1 below, data types that can be handled as dirty data exchanged between services were 'Selected' from 33 types of dirty data. 'Detectable' indicates whether the dirty data can be detected by the constraints set by the service developer (O) or by using a special tool (X). Of 33 dirty data types, only 12 dirty data were selected as interaction data errors and the other data are those mainly arising in database or those determined to be dirty only through comparison with other data sets. Of 12 selected dirty data, only 6 data were determined to be detectable according to the service developers' constraints. As data errors such as misspelling, extraneous data entry, ambiguous data, and incomplete context can be detected using a special type of tools such as a spelling checker and thesaurus and mostly related to natural language processing, we do not include these data types in the scope of this study.

3.2 The Rules for Detecting and Cleansing Dirty Data

The rules for detecting 6 data types selected to be detectable in Table 1 are outlined in Table 2 (Rule numbers follow those of error numbers used in Table 1). As the error

Table 1. Types of Detectable Interaction Data Errors

No.	Type	Selected/ Detectable
1	missing data without the constraint of not allowing null	√/O
2	missing data with the constraint of not allowing null	√/O
3	wrong data type (violating data type constraint, including value range)	√/O
4	dangling data (violating referential integrity violation)	
5	duplicated data (violating non-null uniqueness constraint)	√/O
6	mutually inconsistent data	
7~9	lost update, dirty read, or unrepeatable read data due to lack of concurrency control	
10	lost transaction (due to lack of proper crash recovery)	
11	wrong categorical data (e.g., out of category range data)	√/O
12	outdated temporal data (violating temporal valid time constraint)	
13	inconsistent spatial data (violating spatial constraint)	
14	erroneous entry (e.g., age mistyped as 26 instead of 25)	√/X
15	Misspelling (e.g., principle instead of principal)	√/X
16	extraneous data (e.g., name an title, instead of just name)	√/X
17	entry to wrong field (e.g., address in the name field)	√/X
18	wrongly induced field data (due to function or computing error)	
19	inconsistency among tables and files	
20	different data for the same entity in several databases	
21	Ambiguous data because of using abbreviation	√/O
22	incomplete context (homonyms)	√/X
23	abbreviation (ste for suite, hwy for highway)	√/X
24~33	compound data not in compliance with the standard	

Table 2. The Rules for Detecting and Cleansing Dirty Data by Error Types

Rule	Detecting Rule(D) / Cleansing Rule(C)
1	(D) Search empty data, which allows 'null' but does not have any value.
	(C) Replace the empty data with null value or a representative value specified in the developers' constraints.
2	(D) Search empty data, which does not have any value, including 'null' value.
	(C) Generate feedback message for the value out of allowable range. If a value that can indicate dirty data is set in the developer's constraint, replace data with the value.
3	(D) Identify data out of allowable value range.
	(C) Generate feedback message for the value out of allowable range.
5	(D) Check if data with the constraint of not being duplicated is duplicated in the collected data sets.
	(C) Generate feedback message for the duplicated data, and ask for deletion.
11	(D) Identify data out of allowable category range, using category lookup table or pre-built computerized abstraction hierarchy. * Category lookup table (1) Arithmetic Expression (2) Number Expression (3) Date (4) Postal Code (5) Phone Number (6) E-Mail Address (7) Home Page (8) URL (9) File Name
	(C) Present the reason for being out of category range, with warning message.
21	(D) Check whether the data exists in the user-defined library.
	(C) Recommend to generalize the data in the dictionary, with warning message.

detection technique set forth in Rule 11 is not the one filtering errors out of data using a special tool or thesaurus, it is impossible to identify all errors. But, partial error detection is possible using regular expressions such as yy/mm/dd, yyyy/mm/dd for dates, number of digits in postal codes or telephone numbers, string@string(.string)+ for mail addresses, and http://(string.)+string(.string)* for web sites and URLs.

4 Data Cleansing Service

This Section proposes a basic service for data quality control on SOA, using the rule for detecting and cleansing dirty data presented in Section 3. The service consists largely of conversion, detection, and cleansing processes as shown in Figure 1.

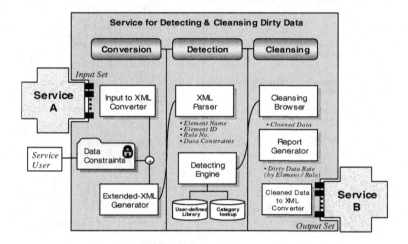

Fig. 1. Block Diagram of Service for Detecting and Cleansing Dirty Data

The service consists of 'Conversion' process for combining input data and the user's data constraints, 'Detection' process for extracting information required for dirty data detection and detecting the dirty data according to the specified rules, and 'Cleansing' process for cleansing dirty data through the browser showing the detected dirty data, displaying the statistics data on dirty data, and displaying the cleansed data. The following describes the essence of each process of the service.

- *From Input to XML Converter*: For this paper, all specifications related to input and output were written in XML, the standard format for exchanging data, at the time of service development and the rules were also specified in XML for extendibility. Data input from Service A are mapped to XML elements, and given a hierarchical structure if necessary. Figure 2(a) illustrates an example of a customer order service form of CRM, where interface form is converted to XML.
- *Data Constraints*: First, the constraints to be applied to input data are received from service user. For example, as <OrderID> data is a sequential order ID that must have a unique value, null should not be allowed (Rule 2), and the value range should be given (Rule 3), and the order ID should not be duplicated (Rule 5). Therefore, the

service user should provide the information about such data constraints according to the procedure specified by the service.

- *Generating Extended-XML with Data Constraints*: Data constraints obtained in this way are combined with the input documents converted into XML document, to be extended to an XML document in which constraints for each data are specified. As input data and constraints are combined for flexible processing, the XML document should be extended based on XML Document Type Description (DTD) as shown in Figure 2(b). This DTD is divided into 4 parts: rule declaration part, category declaration part for filtering out particularly 'wrong category data' (like Rule 11), data declaration part for values of elements and data received as input specification, and attribute declaration part for constraints for each element.

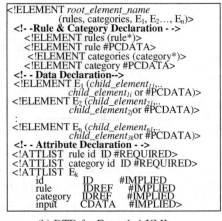

```
<?xml version="1.0" encoding="UTF-8" ?>
- <Order>
    <OrderID>654435</OrderID>
    <CustomerID>987651</CustomerID>
    <Email>ayrton@fiorano.com</Email>
  - <ShipDetails>
      <Mode>Air</Mode>
      <Address>Fiorano Software Inc., 718 University Avenue, Suite
        212, Los Gatos, California.</Address>
      <Country>USA</Country>
      <PostalCode>95032</PostalCode>
      <PhoneNumber>408.354.3210</PhoneNumber>
    </ShipDetails>
    <Product>CISCO 1601R ROUTER</Product>
    <Quantity>1</Quantity>
    <Price>1000$</Price>
    <BillAmount>1000$</BillAmount>
    <OrderDate>15/02/04</OrderDate>
  </Order>
```

(a) XML Specification of a Customer Order Service Form

```
<!ELEMENT root_element_name
          (rules, categories, E₁, E₂..., Eₙ)>
<!--Rule & Category Declaration -->
  <!ELEMENT rules (rule*)>
  <!ELEMENT rule #PCDATA>
  <!ELEMENT categories (category*)>
  <!ELEMENT category #PCDATA>
<!-- Data Declaration-->
<!ELEMENT E₁ (child_element₁ᵢ...
          child_element₁ᵢ or #PCDATA)>
<!ELEMENT E₂ (child_element₂ᵢ...
          child_element₂ᵢor #PCDATA)>
      :
<!ELEMENT Eₙ (child_elementₙᵢ...
          child_element₃ₖor #PCDATA)>
<!-- Attribute Declaration -->
<!ATTLIST rule id ID #REQUIRED>
<!ATTLIST category id ID #REQUIRED>
<!ATTLIST Eₖ
     id          ID          #IMPLIED
     rule        IDREF       #IMPLIED
     category    IDREF       #IMPLIED
     input       CDATA       #IMPLIED>
```

(b) DTD for Extended-XML

Fig. 2. XML Conversion

- *Parsing Extended-XML*: Only the required information is extracted from the extended-XML document using XML parser. As a result of parsing, element name, element ID, rule number to be processed, category number, and conditions for the rule are extracted for each data.
- *Detecting Dirty Data*: Based on the data information obtained from parsing, the detection rule presented in Section 3.2 is applied. Brief algorithm for detection is shown in Figure 3. The detection rule is applied to data referring to *ruleNo* in the element list. If data violates the rule, the algorithm sets an error type. Here, category lookup table specifies regular expressions for the category of each data for Rule 11. If the expression to be checked is changed, it is needed to change the category lookup table only. In addition, user-defined library for Rule 21 arranges general words and their abbreviations such as (Doctor, Dr.), (Drive, Dr.), and (road, rd), which can be updated continuously.
- *Cleansing*: Information for cleansing provides both name and value of the data detected to be dirty. So far, most studies put cleansing process under the domain experts charge. Therefore, in this paper, if the subject of cleansing activity is service user but the service user cannot cleanse the detected dirty data, the data is not processed any more and feedback message is sent to the follwing service.

```
procedure Detecting( ruleNo^{1..i} : pairs of rule No. and rule name,
                    category^{1..j} : pairs of category No. and category name,
                    element ^{1..n}: list including element name, ID, ruleNo, category, conditions, data)
returns element ^{1..n} including detected error types
begin
   move all pairs of ruleNo to rule_table;  move all pairs of category to cat_table;
   for (k=1; k<=n; k++)
   begin
   switch (ruleNo) {
      case 1: if data == empty then error_type = 1;
      case 2: if (data == 'Null' or empty) then error_type = 2;
      case 3: if (data < codition1) and (data > condition2) then error_type = 3;
      case 5: compareC&P(data); // compare data of current and data with identical element name of
                                          previous data stream, find duplicated data

         case 11: // category lookup
                   if (category == 1)  // arithmetic expression
                   then check data if the form follows [0-9]+{[+-*/]+[0-9]+}+;
                   else if (category == 2) // number expression
                   then check data if the form follows [A-Za-z]*[0-9]+[A-Za-z]*;
                    else if (category == 3) // date
                   then check data if the form follows 'yyyy/mm/dd or yy/mm/dd';
                    else if (category == 4) // postal code
                   then check data if the form follows 'd=[0-9], ddddd or ddd-ddd';
                    else if (category == 5) // phone number
                   then check data if the form follows 'd=[0-9], ddd-ddd-ddddd';
                    else if (category == 6) // e-mail address
                   then check data if the form follows 'string@string(.string)';
                    else if (category == 7 or 8) // home page or URL
                   then check data if the form follows 'http://(string.)+string(.string)*';
                    else if (category == 9) // file name
                   then check data if the form follows 'string(.string)*';
         case 21: if data is not in user-defined library for abbreviation
                   then error_type = 21;
      }
      append error_type to the end of the list (element^k);
   end
end
```

Fig. 3. Algorithm for Detecting Dirty Data

- *Report Generation*: Report is generated mainly based on the statistics on dirty data. In other words, it is shown how many errors were cleansed, by comparing the dirty data rate before and after cleansing.
- *Converting Cleaned Data to XML*: XML document in the same form as shown in Figure 2 (a) is used as it is. But, if there is any data cleansed, the data value is replaced with the cleansed one.

5 Application

In this section, we presents the implementation of data cleansing service and also show how efficient this service is for dirty data control, applying it to integration of the actual distributed system.

5.1 Implementation of the Data Cleansing Service Using ESB

Data cleansing service is implemented based on Java 2 Enterprise Edition 1.4.2 in Windows 2000 server environment. To provide this service on ESB that supports SOA, we used FioranoESB™, the Fiorano Business Integration Suite. ESB transmits message in the form of standard XML, using Java Messaging Server (JMS). We applied the developed service to construction of a system configured with total 9 services as shown in the Figure 4.

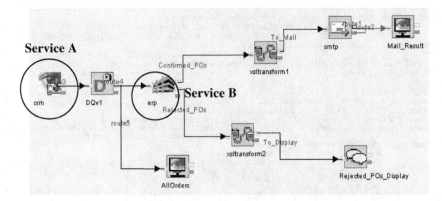

Fig. 4. Example of Data Cleansing Service Application: Combination of CRM and ERP

Centering on CRM system for ordering products (Service A) and ERP for approving or rejecting orders (Service B), we constructed the system by integrating numbers of services that converts transaction information to XML document (xslttransform 1 and 2), transfers the information (SMTP), and displays the result (Mail_Result, Rejected_POs_Display, AllOrders). When Service A and Service B are integrated, Dirty Data Detecting and Cleansing Service (DQv1), the service we developed for controlling errors in data exchanged between the two systems, is inserted. The buyer sends purchase information together with his or her personal information to ERP system (the product management system) through CRM system

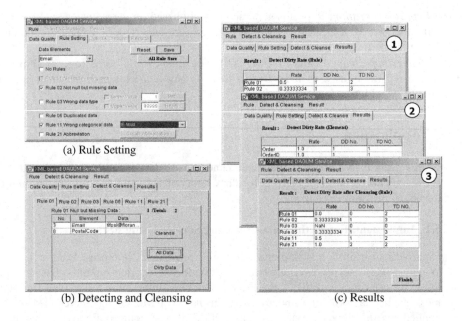

(a) Rule Setting

(b) Detecting and Cleansing

(c) Results

Fig. 5. Service Execution

(the customer information management system). ERP decides whether to approve or to reject the order using the information it received, and then sends the approved message to the buyer by e-mail (Confirmed_POs path, following 'ERP') or displays the rejected result on the dialog window (Rejected_POs path).

This is a representative example of application, where several systems are integrated and a large amount of data travels among the systems. If the implemented DQv1 service is inserted as an independent service between CRM and ERP systems, it can detects dirty data in the interaction between CRM and ERP from the user's point of view, including wrong selection made by the buyer, inconsistency of range of data processing between services, and data transmission error due to network error, according to the objectives designated by the user.

When receiving data sets from CRM system (see Figure 2 (a), for data example), the data detecting and cleansing service receives data constraints from the service user through the interface as shown in Figure 5 (a). Internally, extended-XML is generated, which is sent to the detecting process. In the detecting process, the service detects dirty data using the dirty data detection algorithm and displays the detected dirty data to the user, to provide an environment for the user to cleanse the dirty data (Figure 5 (b)). Figure 5 (b) shows the screen where all data to which Rule 1, the constraint for collecting dirty data, which is empty even though 'null' is allowed, is applied. The number of data to which this rule is applied is 2. They are 'Email' and 'PostalCode'. The dirty error detection result displayed on the screen shows that only one data is violated (that is, Rule 01 Null but Missing Data: 1/Total:2). According to this result, the user understands that 'Email' is not empty data and thus cleanses 'PostalCode', the empty data. The user can cleanse the dirty data by entering necessary data to 'PostalCode' ('12-340' for example). In addition, the service can display all data information ('All Data') or dirty data only to the user. When the dirty data detecting and cleansing process is finished, the result is displayed as shown in Figure 5 (c). ① shows the dirty data rate according to the rules ('TD' means the total number of data and 'DD' means the number of dirty data.), ② shows the dirty data rate according to each data, and ③ shows the dirty data rate after cleansing.

5.2 Empirical Study

Previous section presented service execution for one data transmission event. In order to determine how effective the service developed for this paper is for cleansing dirty data, we generated total 200 data events between CRM and ERP. Figure 6 shows the comparison between the dirty data rates for each data/rule before and after cleansing with this service.

In Figure 6 (a), Data No. 1 ('Order') and No. 5 ('ShipDetails') are formal data to represent the hierarchical structure of XML document but do not have any value, so that no dirty data detection rule is not applied. For Data No. 2 (OrderID), it is shown that the dirty data rate was reduced from 25% to 10% after this service was applied as the service detected dirty data according to Rules 2, 3 and 5 and cleansed them through dirty data feedback. On the other hand, of input data, Data No. 4 (Email), 7 (Address), 11 (Product), 13 (Price), and 14 (BillAmount) showed relatively low cleansing rate. It is because even though Data No. 4, 11, and 13 should have been detected as dirty data by Rules 11 and 21 and cleansed, they were detected but not cleansed as correct data values were unknown. For 'Email' as an example, 'tifosiafiorano.com' is detected as dirty data because it violates the rule of 'string@string(.string)+'. If its correct e-mail address is known, it can be replaced with 'tifosi@fiorano.com'. But, even the domain expert cannot be sure of it, so that it cannot be cleansed. Therefore, as shown in 6 (b), detecting dirty data by applying Rules 1, 2, 3 and 5 that check null or value range showed high cleansing rates, while detecting by applying Rules 11 and 21 that do not have information about what is correct data showed low cleansing rate. In general, it is shown that the dirty data rate was reduced from 18.08% for the entire input data to 12.31% for the data cleansed by applying this service, which has the same effect as reducing dirty data by about 31.91%. The reason why higher cleansing rate was not achieved results from the fact that this service is limited to the data exchanged between services and does not use any natural language processing technique or commercial tool.

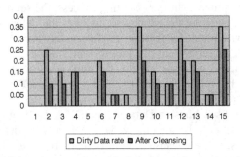

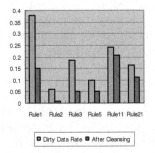

(a) Dirty data rate for each data: x-axis is numbered in series according to the order of data input from CRM to ERP, and y-axis indicates the dirty data rate.

(b) Dirty data rate for each rule: x-axis shows the rule number applied, and y-axis indicates the dirty data rate.

Fig. 6. Comparison of Dirty Data Rates

Through the empirical study performed to verify the effects of this service, it was shown that if the dirty data detecting and cleansing service developed here was applied to data exchanged between services when services were composed and integrated based on SOA, even dirty data would be made effective by giving feedback to the user rather than making it obsolete data.

6   Conclusion

In this paper, we presented the development of a dirty data detecting and cleansing service based on SOA, focusing on data exchanged between services, unlike the existing dirty data cleansing techniques for static and large data. The developed dirty data cleansing service can be useful for data quality control when services with frequent interactions such as e-business are integrated, and provides flexibility for the service user in setting the data constraints by allowing the user to set detection rules using XML. In addition, it was shown through the empirical study that the dirty data rate was reduced by applying the dirty data detecting and cleansing service to the data exchanged between two services when CRM and ERP services were combined based on SOA. At present, a study of construction of data ontology for XML-based e-business transaction is in progress in order to enhance the dirty data cleansing rate by employing a special tool and minimize the user constraints.

References

[1] G. Lee and G. C. Lee, "Standardization Trend and Development Direction of Web Services", Database Research Journals of KISS, Vol. 19, No. 1, pp80-87, 2003.3

[2] M.P.Papazoglou and D.Georgakopoulos, "Service-Oriented Computing", Communication of the ACM, Vol.46, No.10, pp25-28, 2003.10

[3] T. Johnson, and T. Dasu, "Data Quality and Data Cleaning", Tutorials of 10th SIGKDD, 2004.8

[4] T. Dasu, T. Johnson, S. Muthukrishnan, V. Shkapenyuk, "Mining Data Structure; Or, How to Build a Data Quality Browser", In Proceedings of SIGMOD Conf., pp 240-251, 2002

[5] M. Hernandez and S. Stolfo, "Real-world data is dirty: data cleansing and the merge/purge problem", Data Mining and Knowledge Discovery, Vol.2(1), pp9-37, 1998

[6] M. Lee, H Lu, T Ling, and Y. Ko., "Cleansing Data for Mining and Warehousing", In Proceedings of 10th DEXA, 1999.

[7] M. Hernandez, R. Miller, and L. Hass, "Schema Mappings as Query Discovery", In Proceedings of Intl. Conf. VLDB, 2001

[8] M. M. Breunig, H.-P. Kriegel, R. Ng, J. Sander, "LOF: Identifying Density-Based Local Outliers", In Proceedings of SIGMOD Conf., 2000

[9] W. Kim, B. Choi, E-K. Hong, S-K. Kim, D. Lee, "A Taxonomy of Dirty Data", The Data Mining and Knowledge Discovery Journal, Vol7 No.1, pp81-99, 2003.1

A Collaborative Filtering Recommendation Methodology for Peer-to-Peer Systems

Hyea Kyeong Kim[1], Jae Kyeong Kim[1,*], and Yoon Ho Cho[2]

[1] School of Business Administration, KyungHee University,
1, Hoeki-dong, Dongdaemoon-gu, Seoul, 130-701, Korea,
Tel: +82-2-961-9355, Fax: +82-2-967-0788
{kimhk, jaek}@khu.ac.kr
[2] School of E-Business, KookMin University,
861-1 Jungnung, Sungbuk, Seoul, 136-702, Korea,
Tel: +82-2-910-4950, Fax: +82-2-910-4519
www4u@kookmin.ac.kr

Abstract. To deal with the image recommending problems in P2P systems, this paper proposes a PeerCF-CB (Peer oriented Collaborative Filtering recommendation methodology using Contents-Based filtering). PeerCF-CB uses recent ratings of peers to adopt a change in peer preferences, and searches for nearest peers with similar preference through peer-based local information only. The performance of PeerCF-CB is evaluated with real transaction data in S content provider. Our experimental result shows that PeerCF-CB offers not only remarkably higher quality of recommendations but also dramatically faster performance than the centralized collaborative filtering recommendation systems.

1 Introduction

According to a recent report, 93% of information produced worldwide is in digital form and the unique data added each year exceeds one exabyte, and more than 513 million people around the world are now connected to the global information resource [8]. However, many of those people have problems to search for digital contents they are most interested in. This trend calls for recommender systems with scalable searching capability. A recommender system is defined as a system that assists users in finding the items they would like to use. It has been used to help users search for products or multimedia contents in Web environment. One of the most successful recommendation techniques is Collaborative Filtering (CF), which has been widely used in a number of different applications [1], [2], [4], [5], [6], [7]. Collaborative filtering is an information filtering technique that depends on human beings' evaluations of items. It identifies users whose tastes are similar to those of a given user and it recommends items those users have liked in the past.

The peer-to-peer (P2P) systems are developed to facilitate direct communication or collaboration between two or more agents, such as personal computers or

---

* Corresponding author.

K. Bauknecht et al. (Eds.): EC-Web 2005, LNCS 3590, pp. 98–107, 2005.

devices. P2P applications such as Napster and Gnutella are increasingly popular for file sharing through direct exchange. These applications offer the advantages of decentralization by distributing the storage capacity and load across a network of peers and scalability by enabling direct and real-time communication [10]. For example, to search for contents, the agent of peer broadcasts a search request to peers connected, and propagates the requests to their own peers and so on. An increasing number of P2P users and shared contents also raise a serious complexity for the users selecting their desired contents. Accordingly recommender systems in P2P systems are emerging as a successful solution to overcome these difficulties [1], [6], [7]. However, existing research and practice in recommender systems are mostly based on centralized client-server architecture.

In this paper, we propose an adaptive CF recommendation methodology in P2P systems, PeerCF-CB (Peer oriented Collaborative Filtering recommendation methodology using Contents-Based filtering), to deal with the problems we face in recommending images. Although CF has been used successfully as a recommendation technique for client-server architecture, it is necessary to adapt the CF methodology for recommending images in P2P systems. For such a purpose, Content-based image retrieval (CBIR) is employed, which performs similarity-based image retrieval using its visual features such as color, texture and shape [4], [9]. In CBIR, the peer describes visual characteristics of desired images using a query that is a set of example images. To learn about the peer's true intention, the peer's current preference on the presented images needs to be fed back so that CBIR can learn from this preference to retrieve images more similar to the one the peer really wants. This learning process is an essential mechanism for a faster search of desired images in PeerCF-CB.

PeerCF-CB essentially follows the ground principle of CF and CBIR techniques, while we suggest the following modification to be applied in the P2P systems; *an event-driven recommendation* - whenever a peer finds relevant contents, the contents are forwarded to other peers in real time, *a recent rating-based filtering* - recent observations can better represent the current peer's interests than the past observations, and *a dynamic neighbor re-formation* - to reflect the change in recent interests, neighbor peer set is frequently re-formed using peer-based local information only, which results in the performance improvement with much less computation time.

Several experiments are performed to compare the performance of PeerCF-CB with that of a centralized CF system using real transaction data in S content provider, and their results are discussed.

2   Peer Model

Peer network in P2P system consists of interconnected peers and they collaborate each other by exchanging preference information. It is assumed that peers have distinctive preference and they are willing to share what images they prefer. Each peer, named as a *host peer* participates in the peer network, and has an individual *peer model*. The peer model is composed of three parts, *host peer profile, neighbor peer set,* and   *target peer set.* A host peer profile includes information about what images a host peer prefers. Such information is used to find similar peers as neighbor peer set to receive recommendations. Target peer set is composed by requests of other peers, and a host peer forwards images to them as recommendations.

The success of recommendation depends to a large extent on the ability to represent the host peer's actual preference. Images saved on a host peer's computer include information about peer's preference on images. Therefore, saved images, called as a *preferred image set* are used to create host peer profile. Whenever a host peer h saves or deletes an image, the preferred image set is updated. Preferred image set, P^h consists of multiple images, and is defined as $\{q_1^h, q_2^h, ..., q_i^h, ...q_L^h\}$, which denotes that host peer h has L saved images on his/her personal computer. Each image is represented as collection of all possible visual features that describe its perceptual properties such as HSV (i.e. hue, saturation, and value of color) based color moment, shape and texture. q_1^h is composed of S-dimensional visual feature values, and defined as $\{q_{i1}^h, q_{i2}^h, ..., q_{is}^h, ...q_{iS}^h\}$ where S denotes the number of visual features, and q_{is}^h denotes sth feature value on image i of the host peer h. Each image in a preferred image set is represented as a point in the multidimensional space of those features.

Host peer h receives recommendations from its neighbor peers. Each peer estimates *neighbor similarity, NS(h,n)*, between host peer h and other peer n, to select neighbor peers, which have higher $NS(h,n)$ than others. A neighbor peer set of h, N^h is defined as $\{n_1^h, n_2^h, ..., n_j^h, ...n_M^h\}$ where M is the predefined number of neighbor peers. Once a peer is selected as a neighbor peer, it is dynamically exchanged with a more similar peer in candidate neighbor set. In PeerCF-CB, the neighbor peer set of host peer h's most similar neighbor peer set is defined as a candidate neighbor set, CN^h, to limit the exploration boundary. When one of the candidate neighbor peers who has higher neighbor similarity than a neighbor peer is detected, the peer becomes a new neighbor of h.

Target peer set, T^h is a peer set which is recommended by host peer. T^h is defined as $\{t_1^h, t_2^h, ..., t_e^h, ...t_N^h\}$ where N is the predefined number of target peers. The target peer set is organized by the request of other peers with similar tastes.

3   Recommendation Procedure

PeerCF-CB consists of the following three cooperating distinct procedures, *an Event-driven recommendation procedure, a CBIR procedure, and a Neighbor reformation procedure.*

3.1   Event-Driven Recommendation Procedure

Event-driven recommendation is generated with a push way, which is that whenever a peer saves an image, the newly saved image is added to the preferred image set of the peer and forwarded to other peers in real time. The push way can particularly emphasize the most recent ratings of neighbor peers, which leads to faster spread of newly obtained images. Host peer is allowed to push the newly saved image to only limited number of target peers, however recommendations of host peer can reach away beyond target peers.

3.2 CBIR Procedure

The pushed images from neighbor peers are accumulated in a queue of host peer. And the CBIR procedure selects top-k recommendation list among the images in the queue.

In CBIR procedure, a distance between each preferred image of a host peer and each image in a queue is calculated based on visual features and k images having the shortest distance are selected as top-k recommendation list. The pushed image set, X^h in the queue of h is defined as $\{x_1, x_2, ..., x_C\}$, where C is the maximum number of images in a queue. A queue keeps on maintaining recently received C images. P^h is used as a query for searching similar images. The query, which is internally represented as multiple query points, is continuously updated by adding the newly saved images to the query points in P^h. Since a query is allowed to have multiple query points, the distance function between an image x_i, and a query P^h aggregates multiple distance components from the image to related query points. We use the following aggregate distance function;

$$Dist(x, P^h) = \sqrt{\frac{L}{\sum_{i=1}^{g} 1/dist^2(x, q_i)}}, \qquad (1)$$

where L is the number of query points in a query P^h, q_i is the ith query point of P^h, and $dist(x, q_i)$ is a distance function between an image x and a query point q_i. We derived the equation (1) from the FALCON's formula [11]. It treats an image with the shortest distance component to any one of query points as the image with the shortest aggregate distance. The $dist(x, q_i)$ in Equation (1) is defined as;

$$dist(x, q_i) = \sqrt{\sum_{s=1}^{S} w_s(x_s - q_{is})^2}, \qquad (2)$$

where S is the number of dimensions of feature space, w_s is a weight of the sth dimension in the feature space, and x_s and q_{is} are coordinates of an image x and a query point q_i on the sth dimension, respectively. w_s is defined as $1/\sigma_s$ where σ_s is a standard deviation of coordinates of sth dimension of images. Note that σ_s is calculated using all images in P^h.

CBIR procedure generates top-k recommendation list for the host peer. The retrieved k images are presented to the peer and the peer skims through the list to see if there are any images of interest. Then, the peer may save desired images on the peer's computer.

3.3   Initial Neighbor Formation Procedure

Neighbor re-formation procedure decides whom to keep as neighbors in accordance with distance-based neighbor similarity. Before explaining neighbor reformation, this section explains about building an initial neighbor peer set to participate in the peer network. As an initial neighbor peer set, M nearest neighbor peers are generated based on the similarity between host peer and other peers using an average inter-cluster distance function[3]. To take an initial neighbor set for h, the agent calculates *Neighbor similarity, NS(h,n)*. Given P^h and P^n , $NS(h,n)$ is defined as;

$$NS(h, n) = 1 - \left(\frac{1}{|P^h||P^n|} \sum_{q^h \in P^h} \sum_{p^n \in P^n} sim(q^h, q^n) \right), \tag{3}$$

$$where \; sim(q^h, q^n) = \sum_{s=1}^{S} |q_s^h - q_s^n|, \tag{4}$$

$|P^h|$ and $|P^n|$ are the size of the P^h and the P^n respectively, q^h and q^n are images in the P^h and the P^n respectively, and $sim(q^h, q^n)$ is a feature-based distance function between P^h and P^n. In equation (4), S is the number of dimensions of the feature space and q^h and q^n are coordinates of q_s^h and q_s^n on the sth dimension respectively.

Using the $NS(h,n)$, initial neighbor peer set is determined by comparison of the degree of similarity between saved image sets. Note that for a new peer without any saved image, an initial neighbor set is composed of peers having the most frequently saved images. As preferred image set is often updated by newly saved images, the similarity is also changed with the passage of time. Neighbor reformation procedure attempts to adapt the change in real time, i.e., dynamic neighbor reformation is occurred.

3.4   Neighbor Re-formation Procedure

The neighbor re-formation procedure is implemented with a learning algorithm to constitute better relevant neighbor peer set. In the procedure, each host peer decides whom to disconnect from neighbor peer set and whom to add to the neighbor peer set. The neighbor peers with consistently similar preference to a host peer are kept as neighbors. But when the preference of a neighbor peer becomes different from the host peer, the neighbor peer is disconnected from the neighbor peer set. For the replacement of a disconnected neighbor, PeerCF-CB makes the host peer explore the candidate neighbor set, CN^h . If a more similar peer is discovered among the CN^h than any n_i, the cn^h is included to the N^h and the n_i is discarded. This always leads N^h to be composed of peers with more similar preferences.

Figure 1 illustrates the neighbor re-formation procedure, where neighbor peer A is the most similar neighbor peer, and neighbor set of peer A are candidate neighbor peer set. If peer C has higher neighbor similarity than current neighbor

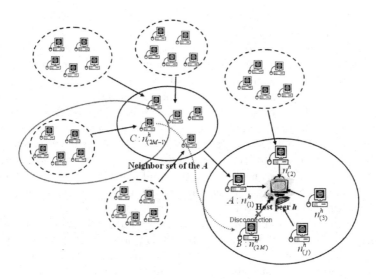

Fig. 1. Neighbor re-formation

peer B, the peer C becomes new neighbor peer of host peer h, while peer B is excluded from h's neighbor set. According to this mechanism, any neighbor peer of peer C may be also included in neighbor peer set of host peer h later time.

4   Experimental Evaluation

4.1   Experiment

The performance of PeerCF-CB is compared with that of two centralized benchmark recommender systems, *CentralizedCF-CB* and *CentralizedCF*. The *Centralized CF-CB* is similar to PeerCF-CB, but neighbor re-formation procedure of *CentralizedCF-CB* uses all peers' ratings. And CBIR procedure of *CentralizedCF-CB* is performed based on all past ratings of neighbor set. *CentralizedCF* is similar to *CentralizedCF-CB*, but it follows a pure CF principle. The *Centralized CF* adapts PLS(Purchase Likeliness Score) [4] to select top-k recommendation list instead of a CBIR procedure of *CentralizedCF-CB*.

The systems to perform our experiments were implemented using Visual Basic 6.0 and ADO components. MS-Access is used to store and process all the data necessary for our experiments. We run our experiments on Windows 2003 based PC with Intel Pentium IV processor having a speed 2.80 GHz and 1GB of RAM.

The comparative experiment is performed with real transaction data offering character images from S content provider, a leading Korean company, in mobile commerce. The data contain 8,776 images, 1,921 customers, and 55,321 transactions during the period between June 1, 2004 and August 31, 2004. The transaction data during the three months are divided into two sets, a training set and a test set. Host peers are determined as the users who have purchased at least one image during the training period, and initial preferred image set of each host peer is generated from transaction records of the training period. Initial neighbor peer set is then formed based on the initial preferred image set. Each host peer receives recommendations from his/her neighbor peers at each connection date for the test period, and then we observe whether the recommended images match the real purchased images of each host peer or not.

HSV (Hue, Saturation, and Value of color) based color moment was selected as visual features characterizing images [4], [9]. For all pixels in images, we translated the values of three-color channels (i.e. RGB; red, green, and blue) into HSV values. Then, the mean, standard deviation and skewness for HSV values were calculated to represent images as vectors in nine dimensional feature spaces.

This research employs two metrics, **hit ratio** and **response time** for the evaluation of accuracy and performance of suggested recommendation methodology respectively. The hit ratio is defined as the ratio of hit set size to the test set size, where hit set size means the success number of recommendations, in our experiment, and test set size means the number of connections. The response time is defined as the amount of time required to generate recommendations for the test set.

4.2   Results and Discussion

This section presents experimental results performed by different parameter set, and the performance of PeerCF-CB is compared with those of CentralizedCF-CB and CentralizedCF.

Among different parameter set, the queue size of each peer and neighbor peer size are determined to be most important parameters impacting on the recom-

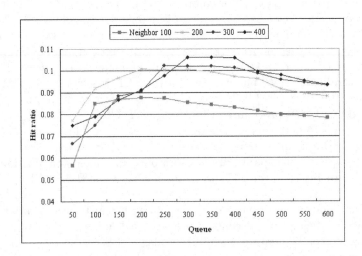

Fig. 2. Neighbor re-formation

mendation quality. Experiments are performed as we varied the queue size from 50 to 600 with an increment 50 at each neighbor peer size from 100 to 400. Figure 2 shows the results. From the results, we make an important observation over all neighbor peer sizes that the quality of recommendation improves as the queue size is increased. As the queue of each peer stores images recommended from its neighbors, recommendation based on large queue size will have a higher hit ratio especially in the domains of newly released images. But after a certain level the improvement slows down and eventually the recommendation quality becomes worse. This indicates that the excessive queue size may cause violation of reflecting the current preference, which leads to lower quality of recommendations. It confirmed that our recent rating-based filtering using queue is a reasonable suggestion to enhance the quality of recommendations.

To compare with the centralized benchmark systems, the experiments were carried out with varied number of neighbors at top-20 recommendation list, and computed the corresponding hit ratio and response time. Note that, to make the comparisons fair with the centralized benchmark systems, we also experimentally determined the optimal queue size of PeerCF-CB for each number of neighbors and tune the system to perform to its ideal level.

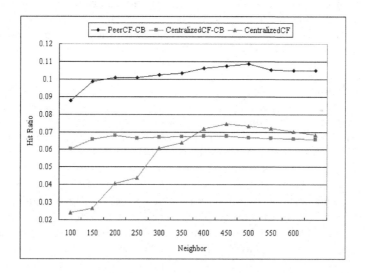

Fig. 3. Recommendation quality comparison

Figure 3 shows the sensitivity of the neighbor size from 100 to 650 with an increment 50. The recommendation quality of CentralizedCF improves as the neighbor size is increased, and after a certain point the improvement slows down and eventually the recommendation quality becomes flat. This result is similar to those of other CF recommender systems [2], [5]. On the other hand, the results of PeerCF-CB and CentralizedCF-CB do not have much variance over all neighbor size, similarly to other content-based filtering systems. Figure 3 also shows that

PeerCF-CB gains improvement of over 40% on the average from the results of centralized benchmark systems. From these results, we make an observation that PeerCF-CB works better than the centralized benchmark systems at all neighbor sizes and the recommendation quality of PeerCF-CB is robust.

Table 1. Performance comparison

	PeerCF-CB	CentralizedCF-CB	CentralizedCF
Response Time (sec)	0.0497	2.3620	2.0484

Table 1 shows the performance comparison represented by average response time. The PeerCF-CB is about 47 times and 41 times faster than CentralizedCF-CB and CentralizedCF respectively. When top-k list is generated, the benchmark centralized procedure uses all past ratings of its neighbors. But PeerCF-CB uses only recent ratings in the queue, which makes PeerCF-CB reflect the up-to-date preference of peers. This makes the PeerCF-CB offer not only higher accuracy but also dramatically faster performance improvement. Moreover, the benchmark centralized procedures perform neighbor re-formation using the preferred image sets of all peers, while PeerCF-CB uses the preferred image sets of neighbor peers and neighbor peer's neighbor peers only, which leads to the dramatically improvement of response time.

5   Conclusion

With the pervasive deployment of personal computers, P2P systems are receiving increasing attention in research and practice. In this paper, we suggest an adaptive CF-based recommendation methodology in P2P systems, PeerCF-CB, to deal with the problems we face in recommending multimedia contents. The characteristics of PeerCF-CB is as follows. First, using the queue of each peer, PeerCF-CB reflects the most current preference of peers, which results in significant quality improvement. Second, each Peer's event, such as saving an image, triggers recommendations with push way which leads to faster spread of new contents without centralized control. Finally, similar neighbor peers are dynamically determined based on peer-based local information only, which results in dramatically faster performance. Our experiment shows that PeerCF-CB offers not only remarkably higher quality of recommendations but also dramatically higher performance than the centralized benchmark procedures. These results give much implication to developing recommender systems in P2P systems, because the number of contents and that of peers grow very fast and personal computers have inherently a limited computing power only. PeerCF-CB is expected to be a realistic solution to the problems currently encountered in multimedia content recommendations in P2P systems.

PeerCF-CB has flexibility to share any multimedia contents, therefore we plan to extend PeerCF-CB to varying contents, such as music and text as a further research area. Furthermore, it will be also a promising research area to develop a robuster recommender system with high degree of tolerance against errors and attack.

References

1. Canny, J.: Collaborative filtering with privacy, In Proc. of the IEEE Symposium on Re-search in Security and Privacy. (2002) 45-57
2. Cho, Y.H., Kim, J.K.: Application of Web usage mining and product taxonomy to collaborative recommendations in e-commerce. Expert Systems with Applications. 26 (2004) 233-246
3. Jiawei H., Micheline K.: Data Mining Concepts and Techniques. Morgan Kaufmann Pub-lishers. (2001)
4. Kim, C.Y., Lee, J.K., Cho, Y.H., and Kim, D.H.: VISCORS: a Visual Contents Recom-mender System on the Mobile Web, IEEE Intelligent Systems, Special issue on Mining the Web for Actionable Knowledge, Vol. 19, pp.32-39.
5. Kim, J.K., Cho, Y.H.: Using Web Usage Mining and SVD to Improve E-commerce Recom-mendation Quality. Lecture Notes in Computer Science. 2891 (2003) 86-97
6. Olsson, T.: Bootstrapping and Decentralizing Recommender Systems. Ph.D. The-sis, Dept. of Information Technology, Uppsala Univ. (2003)
7. Peng, H., Bo, X., Fan, Y., Ruimin, S.: A scalable P2P recommender system based on dis-tributed collaborative filtering. Expert Systems with Applications. 27 (2004) 203-210
8. Prete, C.D., McArthur, J.T., Villars, R.L., Nathan, R. I., Reinsel, L. D.: Indus-try develop-ments and models, Disruptive Innovation in Enterprise Computing: storage. IDC. February. (2003)
9. Porkaew, K., Chakrabarti, K. Mehrotra, S.: Query Refinement for Multimedia Similarity Re-trieval in MARS, In Proc. Of the 7th ACM Multimedia Conference. (1999) 235-238.
10. Ramanathan, M. K., Kalogeraki, V., Pruyne, J.: Finding Good Peers in Peer-to-Peer Net-works. HP Labs. Technical Report HPL-2001-271. (2001)
11. Wu, L., Faloutsos, C., Sycara, K., Payne, T.: FALCON: Feedback Adaptive Loop for Con-tent-Based Retrieval. In Proc. 26th VLDB Conference. (2002). 297-306

A Framework for Session Based Recommendations

Natwar Modani[1], Yogish Sabharwal[1], and S. Karthik[2,*]

[1] IBM India Research Lab, Block-I, IIT Delhi, New Delhi 110016, India
{namodani, ysabharwal}@in.ibm.com
[2] Dept of Comp Sc and Engg, IIT Madras, Chennai 600036, India
sk@meenakshi.cs.iitm.ernet.in

Abstract. In this paper, we introduce a new problem which we call as Online Probabilistic Weighted Bipartite Graph Matching. Consider a weighted bipartite graph with a source node set, a target node set, an edge set and a set of weights for the edges. The source nodes arrive in an online fashion based on a stochastic process. When a source node arrives, it needs to be matched with a target node before the arrival of next source node. Since the arrival process is stochastic, all the source nodes need not arrive and their order of arrival is also not known a priori. The objective is to match the arriving source node with a target node such that the expected sum of weights of the matching over the arrival process is maximized. We present some heuristics that perform well for this problem. We demonstrate the application of our formulation for session based recommendation [5]. Here the source nodes correspond to the web pages, the target nodes correspond to the advertisement that can be shown and the edge weights correspond to the revenue generated by showing the given advertisement on the given web page. The user traversal of web pages corresponds to the arrival process of the source nodes.

1 Introduction

The Weighted Bipartite Graph Matching is a well established problem with polynomial time solutions that solve the probelm exactly [4] [11]. However, in many practical cases the source nodes arrive in an online fashion whereas the rest of the information is known a priori. The arrival of source nodes is governed by a stochastic process. To the best of the authors knowledge, this case has not been examined in the literature. Here we formulate this problem and call it the *Online Probabilistic Weighted Bipartite Graph Matching* problem. Consider a weighted bipartite graph with a source node set S, a target node set T, an edge set E and a set of weights W for the edges. The source nodes arrive in an online fashion based on a stochastic process P and each source node can arrive atmost once. When a source node $s \in S$ arrives, it needs to be matched with a target node $t \in T$ before the arrival of the next source node. Since the arrival process

---

* Work done when the author was at IBM India Research Lab, New Delhi.

K. Bauknecht et al. (Eds.): EC-Web 2005, LNCS 3590, pp. 108–117, 2005.

P is stochastic, all the source nodes need not arrive and their order of arrival is also not known a priori. Also, let S^u represent the set of source nodes that have already arrived and let T^u represent the set of target nodes which have been matched to the nodes in S^u. The objective is to match the arriving node $s \in S$ with a target node $t \in T$ such that $t \notin T^u$ and the expected sum of weights of the matching over the arrival process is maximized. Since the number of possible arrival patterns can be exponential in the number of remaining source nodes, clearly it is a hard problem to solve.

The session based recommendation problem can be modeled as a practical application of our problem definition. Consider a web site which is interested in providing recommendations to the users to their site. Let the source nodes correspond to the web pages and the target nodes correspond to the recommendations (e.g., advertisements). Also let there be space for only one recommendation per web page and let the revenue generated by showing a recommendation on a given page correspond to the edge weight for the edge joining the corresponding source and target nodes. Since the user traversal pattern is clearly probabilistic [8] [10], the set of pages that would be visited by the user and the order of their traversal is not known a priori. However, the probabilistic characterization of the arrival process can be assumed to be known. The objective of the web site owner is to maximize the expected revenue for the user over the entire session. Note that having a matching solution means we do not allow repetitions of the pages or recommendation as we can imagine that if a page is being revisited, it might be served from the cache and hence there is no chance to show a different recommendation. Also, there is no incentive to show any recommendation more than once.

The rest of the paper is organized as follows. First we provide a more formal definition of our problem in the section 2. Then we discuss the related work in section 3. We discussion some heuristics in section 4 and explain our experiments in section 5. We conclude with our results and directions for future research.

2   Formal Definition

Let $\mathcal{G} = (S \cup T, E, W)$ be a weighted bipartite graph, where S and T are the two partitions and $W \colon E \times \mathcal{B} \to \Re^+$ be the weight function. The vertices of S *arrive* one after another and have to be matched to vertices in T on arrival. Let $\mathcal{U}$ be the set of scenarios, where a scenario $U \in \mathcal{U}$ is a two-tuple (X, p), where X is a sequence of nodes from U that appear (without repetitions) in the scenario and p is the probability of occurence of the scenario. Let X_i denote the ith element in the sequence X. Further, let $n = |S|$ and $m = |T|$. Clearly, the number of possible subsets of S itself can be as large as 2^n and since $\mathcal{U}$ has an element corresponding to every possible sequence, $|\mathcal{U}|$ can be as large.

We use the notation $X \preceq Y$ to denote that X is a sequence prefix of Y, i.e., $Y_i = X_i$ for all $1 \leq i \leq |X|$. We additionally use the notation $X \prec Y$ when $X \preceq Y$ and $|X| < |Y|$.

Let $\mathcal{V}$ denote the set of all prefix sequences occuring in the scenarios, i.e., $\mathcal{V} = \{X'|X' \preceq X \text{ and } (X,p) \in \mathcal{U}\}$. We define an assignment function as a function

$$F: \mathcal{V} \to T \cup \{\Gamma\}, \text{ such that, } F(S_1) \neq F(S_2) \; \forall S_1 \prec S_2, \; F(S_2) \neq \Gamma, \; S_1, S_2 \in \mathcal{V}.$$

An assignment function is a representation of a solution to our online matching problem. A sequence S represents the nodes in order of arrival. $F(S)$ maps S to a node of T that is matched with the last appearing node, i.e., $S_{|S|}$, when the nodes $S_1, ..., S_{|S-1|}$ have already appeared before in the same order as they appear in the sequence. $F(S) = \Gamma$ corresponds to the last node not being matched with any node of T. The condition in the definition ensures that the same target node from T is not matched twice in a given scenario (however, of course, two nodes may be unmatched in a given scenario).

Let $\mathcal{F}$ denote the family of all functions satisfying the above conditions. The goal of our problem is to find an assignment function that maximizes the total expected weight, i.e.,

$$argmax_{F \in \mathcal{F}} \{ \sum_{(X,p) \in \mathcal{S}} p \cdot (\sum_{X' \preceq X} F(X')) \}$$

In our problem, we are assuming that the arrival process is stochastic. In particular, we will examine two types of arrival processes. We will describe only one of these in the paper due to space constraint. In this scenario, the arrival of the next node is dependent on the last arrived node. In particular, let the probability of arrival of node s_j immediately after s_i be $m_{ij} = f(i,j)$ if s_j has not arrived yet, and 0 otherwise. It is almost a Markovian model in that the probability of a given node s_j coming next depends only on the current node s_i if s_j has not arrived already. If the Markov chain that governs the arrival process is acyclic, then we do not need to make any change to the usual definitions.

3   Related Work

Targeting and recommender systems is a well studied area [6] [7] [9]. However, most of the work in the past has been concentrated on finding *a good recommendation* for a user when she is on a given page. In our work, we assume that we know the *goodness* of the recommendations and address the issue of scheduling the recommendations in the face of uncertainity of the user traversal path, with the objective of maximizing the expected reward over the entire user session. Modani et al [5] discuss the problem of session based targeting. They formulate the problem with comprehensive details about how to model the arrival process and the reward calculation etc. However, the problem formulation there becomes too specific to the web advertising situation and does not provide a problem definition of wider interest.

We model our recommendation scheduling problem as an Online Probabilistic Weighted Bipartite Graph Matching problem. Weighted Bipartite Graph Matching is a well known problem [4] [11]. An online version of the Weighted Bipartite

Graph Matching was proposed by [2], where the source nodes arrive one by one and have to be matched before the arrival of the next source node. However, in this setting the edge weight for the edges incident on a source node are revealed only on the arrival of that source nodes. It is shown in [2] that the best deterministic solution under these circumstances is a greedy approach and a competitive ratio [1] of 3 is proved. Note that, here, it does not matter whether all the nodes arrive or not; nor the order of arrival as the edge weights are revealed only after arrival of the corresponding source node.

Another related problem is the two stage stochastic version of the weighted bipartite graph matching [3], where there are two sets of edge weights. A first stage weight set is provided to begin with and a set S of scenarios is also provided. A scenario $s \in S$ consist of the second stage edge weights and the probability of the scenario occurring. The problem is to have a first stage matching solution first and then one of the scenarios is materialized. After the scenario is materialized, a second stage matching has to be performed for the nodes not matched in the first stage. The objective is to maximize the expected total weight of the combined (first and second stage) matching. It is shown to be a hard problem and the authors proposea factor $\frac{1}{2}$ approximation algorithm for the problem.

It is tempting to think that the problem described in this paper can be modeled as a sequence of two stage stochastic weighted bipartite graph matching problems. We give an example below to illustrate that it would lead to incorrect formulation of our problem.

Example: Consdier a scenario where there are three source nodes s_1, s_2 and s_3 and three target nodes t_1, t_2 and t_3 (Figure 1) with the weights as shown.

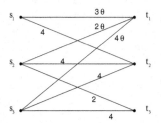

Fig. 1. An example to show incorrectness of 2-stage modelling of our problem

Suppose there are two possible scenarios $< s_1, s_2, s_3 >$ and $< s_1, s_2 >$ each occuring with probability $1/2$. When node s_1 appears, if s_1 is matched to t_1, then a best matching for the scenario $< s_1, s_2, s_3 >$ is $< t_1, t_2, t_3 >$ and a best matching for the scenario $< s_1, s_2 >$ is $< t_1, t_2 >$. The average matching value is therefore $\frac{(3\theta+8)+(3\theta+4)}{2} = 3\theta + 6$. On the other hand consider the case when s_1 is matched to t_2. Then a best matching for the scenario $< s_1, s_2, s_3 >$ is $< t_2, t_3, t_1 >$ and that for $< s_1, s_2 >$ is $< t_2, t_1 >$. The average matching value is therefore $\frac{(4\theta+6)+(2\theta+4)}{2} = 3\theta + 5$. Therefore, one would pick to match s_1 to t_2. The total weight accumulated so far is 1.

Now, consider when node s_2 arrives. If s_2 is matched to t_1, the best matching value is $2\theta + 4$ for scenario 1 and 2θ for scenario 2, resulting in an average matching value of $2\theta + 2$. If s_2 is matched to t_3, the best matching value is $4\theta + 2$ for scenario 1 and 2 for scenario 2, resulting in an average matching value of $2\theta + 2$. Thus in either case, the average matching value (along with the accumulated cost of 1 due to the decision of matching s_1 with t_2) does not exceed $2\theta + 3$. Note that this value is much less than the average matching value that was computed for this case ($3\theta + 5$), when we had matched s_1 with t_2.

The problem lies in the fact that when we had independently found the possible matching for the 2 scenarios when we were evaluating the decision for matching s_1 with t_2, we had matched s_2 with different target nodes in the 2 solutions, whereas, in practice, we must match them with the same target node.

4   Heuristics

We present some heuristics for the Online Probabilistic Weighted Bipartite Graph Matching problem. Our choice of heuristics is motivated by the following reasons. We choose static matching based heuristic as our first heuristic as this is the optimal solution to the standard matching problem. Then we choose Greedy since it is the best possible approach known in case of online version of the problem. We then describe a sample based heuristic which is motivated by the two stage stochastic matching problem. Finally, we present a heuristic that makes the best use of information present in our problem setting.

To illustrate our heuristics, we will take the following example. Let there be a bipartite graph with 3 nodes on each side. Let the edge weight matrix be as given below, where a 0 represents no edge connecting the nodes. Also, let the arrival be governed by a Markov chain with transition probabilities as given below. Note that since the Markov Chain does not have cycles, so the usual definition of the Markov process can be used to find the various probabilities.

$W(a,b)$	1 2 3
1	3 2 4
2	1 0 5
3	0 2 6

$M(i,j)$	1 2 3
1	$0\ \frac{1}{3}\ \frac{1}{3}$
2	$0\ 0\ \frac{1}{2}$
3	$0\ 0\ 0$

In the above Markov chain, $\Sigma_i M(i,j) \neq 1$. The residual probability, i.e. $1 - \Sigma_i M(i,j)$ is the probability of the arrival process halting after vertex a_i arrives. Also, let the particular path instance be (s_1, s_3), i.e., first the node s_1 arrives followed by node s_3.

4.1   The Static Matching Approach

Here, we find an optimal matching on the entire graph as a preprocessing step. Then, as the source nodes arrive one by one, we just look up that in the preprocess step, which target node the arriving source node was matched to, and return that target node. Here the preprocessing cost is to find an optimal matching for the entire graph and the run time cost is to just look up the matching (constant time in best case). For our example mentioned above, the optimal matching is $(s_1 - t_1), (s_2 - t_3), (s_3 - t_2)$ and the optimal value is 10. So according to this heuristic, when the source node s_1 arrives, we match it with t_1 and when the source node s_3 arrives, we match it with t_2. The total value obtained is 5.

4.2   The Greedy Approach

Greedy is a simple approach where we choose a target node t_j such that $t_j \notin T^u$ and $w_{ik} \leq w_{ij} \forall k \notin T^u$ to match with the arriving source node s_i, i.e., to choose a target node such that it has not been used before, and amongst all such target node, and is adjacent to the edge with maximum weight. In other words, choose node t_j to match with s_i such that

$$j = argmax_{(k \ s.t. \ t_k \notin T^u)} w_{ik}.$$

Clearly this would have a run time complexity of $O(n)$ where $n = |T|$. In our exapmle, when the source node s_1 arrive, it will assign t_3 as the match. Now, when the next source node s_3 arrives, it has to match it with t_2. So the total value obtained is 6.

4.3   The Sampling Approach

In this approach, the idea is to solve the problem over a randomly samples set of paths from the paths that can appear at any stage. We try all possible matchings from the source node to unused target nodes and determine the average matching value from a randomly sampled set of paths drawn independently from the possible scenario set. We finally select the matching that gives us the best average matching value.

For example, when the source node s_1 arrives, it tries to obtain sample paths for the remaining nodes. The sample paths with their respective probabilityies are $S_1 = \{\} \ w.p. \ \frac{1}{3}, S_2 = \{s_2\} \ w.p. \ \frac{1}{6}, S_3 = \{s_3\} \ w.p. \ \frac{1}{3},$ and $S_4 = \{s_2, s_3\} \ w.p. \ \frac{1}{6}$. After necessary computations, it can be seen that the best decision here would be to match s_1 with t_1. Now, when source node s_3 arrive, the only possible remaing path is a null path and hence the best decision is to match s_3 with t_3. In this case, the total value derived is 9. The running time of this approach is high, polynomial in the number of nodes and edges, since we could be required to solve as many as m matching problems for each sample path, where m is the number of remaining target nodes. However, it evades handling of exponential number of scenarios by randomly sampling senarios from the given distribution.

4.4   The Probabilistic Heuristic

We now present a heuristic which is specifically geared for our problem formulation. Let v_{ik} represent the probability of s_k arriving some time in future during the session provided s_i arrives. This can be compute either from the transition probability matrix for Markovian arrival, or can be estimated by generating some sample path and finding this probability by counting the number of paths where s_i arrives, (not necessarily immediately) followed by s_k. By definition, we take $v_{ii} = 1$. Let the newly arriving source node be s_i. Then we compute a new matrix, called auxiliary matrix A, where the elements are $a_{ij} = v_{ik} * w_{kj}$. Then we find the optimal matching on this A matrix and match the arriving source node based on this match. In our example, it is easy to see that initially, the V and A matrices would be

$V(i,k)$	1	2	3		$A(i,j)$	1	2	3
1	1	$\frac{1}{3}$	$\frac{1}{2}$		1	3	2	4
2	0	1	$\frac{1}{2}$		2	$\frac{1}{3}$	0	$\frac{5}{3}$
3	0	0	1		3	0	1	3

When we compute the optimal matching on this A matrix on the arrival of s_1, the optimal matching on A would match s_1 with t_1. Then when the source node s_3 arrives, the V and A matrices are

$V(i,k)$	1	2	3		$A(i,j)$	1	2	3
1	0	0	0		1	0	0	0
2	0	0	0		2	0	0	0
3	0	0	1		3	0	2	6

Clearly, the optimal matching now on A would match s_3 with t_3. The total value obtained is 9. The run time of this heuristic at each step consists of finding the V matrix and then computing one optimal matching.

4.5   Discussion

From the run time complexity point of view, the static matching is the fastest, followed by Greedy, Probabilistic and Sampling based heuristics in that order. It is intuitively clear that the static matching would perform very well in the cases when almost all the source nodes arrive (i.e., long path) and may perform badly when very few source nodes arrive (short paths). This is because in case of short paths, the source for which the good target nodes were reserved, may not even appear. On the other hand, the Greedy would perform very well for when very few source nodes arrive (short paths), but it will start faltering when more source nodes arrive (long paths), since it may have exhausted the good target nodes too early. The sampling based and probabilistic heuristics try to strike a balance. However, the running time of sampling based heuristic may become too high for large graphs.

5   Experiments

To study the performance of the proposed heuristics, we conducted several simulations. Our results showed similar trends in all the experiments, so we will discuss only one set of experiments in detail. The particular experiment we describe here is inspired by our application, namely the session based recommendations. In this setting, we used approximately Markovian arrivals and a weight matrix which is composed of various parts, suitable for recommendation set up.

5.1   Data Generation

First, we fix the size of the Bipartite graph and kept the number of nodes on the source and target sides as equal. The graph was taken to be fully connected with a weight matrix computed in fashion similar to [5]. Namely, each element w_{ij} of the matrix W was computed as $w_{ij} = a_i * b_j * c_{ij}$, where all the factors were i.i.d. random samples from a uniform $[1, 10]$ distribution on integers. This implies that the minimum and maximum values for the w_{ij} were 1 and 1000, respectively.

A typical user navigation pattern on a web site can be adequately modeled as a Markovian arrival process. However, whenever a source node was visited, we made the transition probabilities to this node (from all other nodes) as zero. This is to ensure that no source node was visited more than once. The transition probability matrix was generated by drawing i.i.d. random samples from a uniform distribution. This matrix had size 1 more than the number of source nodes, where the extra node represented the probability of termination of the arrival process (an absorbing state in Markovian terminology). The probability for a source node to be the first arriving node was taken as an independent random sample which was quadratically inversely dependent to the a_i as described in the weight matrix generation.

5.2   Simulation Process

We choose 8 sizes for the graph, (5, 10, 15, 20, 25, 50, 75, 100) nodes on each side. For each graph size, we generated 10 independent scenarios (i.e., the weight matrix, the initial arrival probabilities and the Markov Transition probabilities). For each scenario, we generated 100 paths on the source node set. So in all we had 8000 data points. We run all our heuristics on size $5, 10, 15, 20, 25$ graphs, but did not run the sampling heuristic for the size $50, 75, 100$ graphs as it was very time consuming. We then found the post facto optimal matching value for each data point by computing the matching with only the source side nodes which appear in the given path. We scaled our results for the heuristics by the post facto optimal matching value. Even though the post facto optimal is not achievable, it provides a good reference point to compare with. We draw one graph for each graph size with the independent variable being the path length.

5.3   Results and Discussion

Intuitively, one would expect that for the short paths (relative to the number of total source nodes), the Greedy heuristic would do well and the Static Matching based heuristic will not do well. On the other hand, for long paths (almost all the source nodes arrive), the reverse is expected to be true. In our results (Figure 2), both the intuitions are confirmed. Also, it can be noted that the cross over point (when the Static Matching starts performing better than Greedy) is when the path length is about $\frac{2}{3}$ of the total number of source nodes.

The other two heuristics, namely the Sampling based and Probabilistic, perform at almost similar level and also their performance does greatly vary with

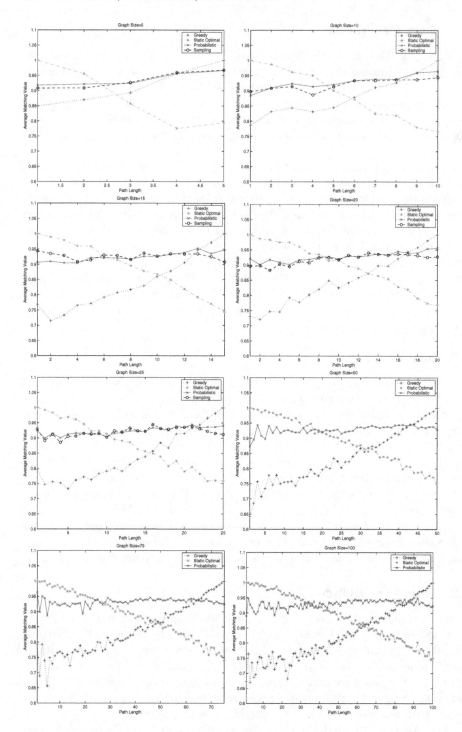

Fig. 2. Normalized Average Matching Values of Heuristics for Various Graph Sizes

the path length. Their performance seems very good, specially as it is scaled with respect to the post facto optimal, which is generally higher than the expected optimal matching value that can be realized.

We did not run the sampling heuristic for large graphs (number of source node ≥ 50) as the run time of this heuristic grow very fast with the graph. However, on the smaller graph sizes, the performance of the Probabilistic heuristic is very similar to it and we expect that trend to continue for the larger size graphs as well.

6   Conclusion and Future Work

In this paper, we introduced a new problem and showed a practical e-commerce application of it. We also gave some heuristics that solve the problem well. Some of direction we are planning to explore as our future research are to get some theoritical results and approximation algorithms for this problem and to extend this setting for general (non-bipartite) graphs.

References

1. Allan Borodin and Ran El-Yaniv, Online Computation and Competitive Analysis, *Cambridge University Press*, 1998.
2. Bala Kalyanasundaram and Kirk Pruhs, Online weighted matching, *Journal of Algorithms*, 14: 478 − 488, 1993.
3. Nan Kong and Andrew J. Schaefer, A Factor $\frac{1}{2}$ Approximation Algorithm for Two-Stage Stochastic Matching Problems, to appear in *European Journal of Operational Research*.
4. H.W.Kuhn, The Hungarian Method for the assignment problem, *Naval Research Logistics Quarterly*,i2: 83 − 97, 1955.
5. Natwar Modani, Parul A Mittal, Amit A Nanavati and Biplav Srivastava, Series of dynamic targetted recommendations, *EC-Web 2002*: 262 − 272.
6. G. Adomavicius and A. Tuzhilin, "Extending Recommender Systems: A Multidimensional Approach", IJCAI Workshop on Intelligent Techniques for Web Personalization, 2001.
7. C. Basu, H. Hirsh and W. W. Cohen, "Recommendation as classification: Using social and content-based information in recommendation", Proc. of AAAI 1998, pp 714–720.
8. M. Deshpande and G. Karypis, "Selective Markov Models for Predicting Web-Page Access", Univ. of Minnesota Tech. Report 00-056, Oct 2000.
9. J. B. Schafer, J.A.Konstan and J. Riedl, "E-commerce recommendation applications", Journal of Data Mining and Knowledge Discovery, 5(1/2), 115-153, 2001.
10. J. Srivastava, R. Cooley, M. Deshpande and P. Tan, "Web Usage Mining: Discovery and Applications of Usage Patterns from Web Data", Proc. of ACM SIGKDD Vol 1, Issue 2, 2000.
11. D. B. West, "Introduction to Graph Theory", Prentice-Hall Inc., NJ, 1996.

Automatic Knowledge Recommending System Using E-Mail

DooHyun Kim, WonHyuck Choi, BurmSuk Seo, JungGoo Seo,
and ByoungWon Hwang

School of Electronics, Telecommunication and Computer Engineering,
Hankuk Aviation University,
200-1, Hwajon-Dong, Deokyang-Gu,
Goyang-City, Gyeonggi-Do, 412-791, Korea
kdh_r2@yahoo.com, rbooo@korea.com, avi97@dreamwiz.com,
bsmanse@hanmail.net, bwhwang@mail.hangkong.ac.kr
http://www.hau.ac.kr

Abstract. This paper suggests Knowledge Management System(KMS) using E-mail. When KMS is constructed through E-mail, the cost of service construction and the education of users are almost unnecessary. We use user profile in order to provide Automatic Knowledge Recommending System(AKRS) based on user's preference. In addition, this paper proposes E-mail classification method and automatic knowledge recommending method. We conducted an experiment to evaluate AKRS effectiveness of these methods. From the result of the experiment, we draw conclusions that user can use easily knowledge without special search.

1 Introduction

According to the generalization of internet and the formation of digital information, enormous amount of documents gets constantly created and shared[1]. Such created documents hold diverse information, thus, various information Systems have developed for its better and effective administration. E-mail, Groupware, Document Management System(DMS) are the most well-know examples for such information System[14].

The information Systems like above classify information in order for users to access to it hierarchically based on its stored subject, and enable users to share information they want through search function[2, 14]. KMS offers effective methods for group members to share and apply knowledge in any organization[3, 4]. However, the current information systems have several shortcomings.

First of all, it requires too much cost and time to construct the KMS in an organization. Because it is constructed for high capacity, the KMS is very expensive and also takes much time for previously used system to be converted and fitted into a new system after its construction. Second of all, the practical application plan for the KMS is still insignificant. In many organizations, they invested a great amount of money and constructed the Knowledge Management System; however, important information is hardly sharable and making practical use of such shareable information is

K. Bauknecht et al. (Eds.): EC-Web 2005, LNCS 3590, pp. 118–127, 2005.

feeble. It is because sharing information effectively is somewhat hard and information is managed exclusively by system administrators.

Therefore, this paper proposes KMS using E-mail. E-mail is used to reduce construction cost and time of KMS. Almost every organization has set up E-mail system and it provides familiar interface to users. Also, the data structure of E-mail is standardized so that it is easy to be used for the KMS. Thus, it is possible to use the System without investing construction cost and user education when the management system is built by using E-mail.

In addition, it uses user profile in order to provide Automatic Knowledge Recommending Service(AKRS) based on user's preference. The AKRS recommends automatically knowledge that is related to users by systems without special search. Also, this paper proposes E-mail classification method and automatic knowledge recommending method.

This paper is organized as follow. The second Section introduces KMS with related study, the Section 3 addresses the AKRS that the paper proposes, the Section 4 shows result of actualization of the system, classification of E-mail, and Automatic Recommending Service. And as for the last, the Section 5 concludes and suggests future plans for the study.

2   Related Study

Many organizations implement KMS to efficiently capture, organize and disseminate their most critical organizational resource knowledge. A KMS is a class of information knowledge. One common objective of KMS is to enable employees to enhance learning, improve performance and produce long-term sustainable competitive advantage[3].

For enhancement of competition in every organization, knowledge, which is incorporeal assets, has become prominent figure recently[6, 7]. It is because knowledge reduces possible mistakes and repetition in work by utilizing created information through working and mastering at given fields in organization, thus, it enables people to solve problems more rapidly that have been being dealt in the real world. Especially, the KMS has studied actively and systematically to enhance competitive power of organizations as it provides a way to share individual knowledge that is accumulate in every human resource[2, 8].

Such KMS can be formed through 4 steps; Creation, Storing, Sharing, and Application of Knowledge. Since today, many studies for sharing plan have made progress especially in the Creation of Knowledge step[1, 2, 4], and many good studies' result have been made public[3, 5].

However, the study for knowledge application is still insignificant. The members of organizations share the gained knowledge through work only within their belonged group and content of the sharing knowledge is limited to more general subject. It shows that the currently suggesting knowledge application plans of the KMS are still weak to be more practical.

For this reason, we propose the KMS that provides AKRS using User Profiles. Through the measurement of User Profile and Similarity between knowledge, users' preference concerned AKRS method is studied.

3 Automatic Knowledge Recommending System

Currently, many organizations are using E-mail for management of work and communication of information for their business. Thus when KMS is built through E-mail, construction of additional software gets easier, the expression of structural information becomes convenient, and administration of data gets manageable. The constructed KMS with use of E-mail in the paper is pictorialzed in the Fig. 1 and the function of each step is as the follow.

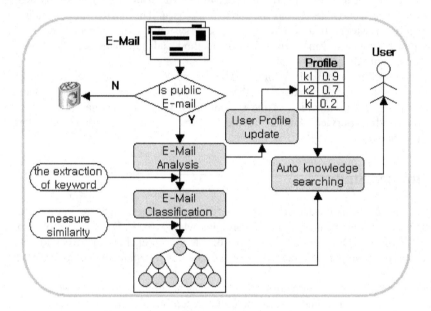

Fig. 1. KMS by using E-mail

E-mail analysis. A user decides whether to share the delivered E-mail. In this step, only representing data from the shared E-mail is extracted. If the occurrence frequency of E-mail title and certain terms in E-mail content get higher, it means the terms express content of the E-mail well. Key words are extracted by using the frequency of the extracted words with morphemic analyzer.

E-mail classification. Similar E-mails are classified based on contents. Strongly related E-mails are put together so that it reduces overload of system and makes the best use of information.

User Profile. It consists of extracted key words from Morphemic Analyzer, which is to know users' area of interest and its value.

Automatic knowledge search. It provides searched result through the User Profile from the stored documents or query languages of users.

3.1 E-Mail Analysis

E-mail has standardized data structure. The Fig. 2 shows documental structure of E-mail. From the head of E-mail, necessary information like an information creating group, a creator, a title, date, form of information, and so on can be extracted automatically from E-mail in order to administer the information.

The Fig. 2 classifies the original message structure of E-mail into head and body, and if you take a careful look, it is obvious that it contains enough information to construct its own KMS.

HEAD	Received: from mail.newslinx.co.kr From: postmaster@korea.internet.com To: stop8@gasystem.co.kr Subject: easy integration method of process Date: Wed, 24 Nov 2004 10:41:53 +0900 Content-Type: multipart/alternative
BODY	This document provides a method overview, practice and use description, and language reference for the IDEF3 Process Description Capture Method develop Under the Information Integration for Concurrent...

Fig. 2. The structure of E-mail

The information of E-mail can be classified into standardized information - Data, Content-Type, Received, From, and To - and non-standardized information - subject and content - as the Table 1 shows.

Table 1. The form of E-mail information.

Standardized information		Non-Standardized information
Date type	String type	String type
Date	Content-type, Received, From, To	Subject, Content

It is possible to administer or classify information of the standardized one only through query languages because of its clarity on expression. However, the non-standardized information requires transformation into the standardized one in order to grasp given information.

3.2 E-Mail Classification

In order to classify E-mail according to its content, similarity between E-mails is measured in the paper by adopting clustering technology. The clustering technology regards assigned key words to E-mail or technically extracted key words as a discerning element of E-mail content, thus, a cluster is created when similarity between E-mails becomes standard.

The key words that are extracted through a morphemic analyzer are an important element to represent E-mail content. It is considered to have high similarity between E-mails if there are as many key words as possible between them.

To measure level of similarity between E-mails, the extracted key words from E-mail title and content are used and occurrence frequency of key words is applied as its weight. When occurrence frequency is applied as its weight, certain key words are expected to occur more frequently as if there is more content of E-mail and it is simply because of size difference between E-mails. Therefore, the formula for Similarity measurement that applied different weight to the occurrence frequency of key words according to the size of E-mail content is demonstrated below.

The set of extracted key words from two different E-mails X and Y

$X = \{T_{x1}, T_{x2}, ..., T_{xn}\}, Y = \{T_{y1}, T_{y2}, ..., T_{yn}\},$

The set of occurrence frequency according to key words

$X = \{W_{x1}, W_{x2}, ..., W_{xn}\}, Y = \{W_{y1}, W_{y2}, ..., W_{yn}\},$

The sum of sets of key words for X and Y

When $X Y = \{T_1, T_2, ..., T_n\},$

$$Similarity = \frac{\sum_{n=1}^{n}(T_n * W_{xn} * D_x) * (T_n * W_{yn} * D_y)}{\sqrt{\sum_{n=1}^{n}(T_{xn} * W_{xn} * D_x)^2} * \sqrt{\sum_{n=1}^{n}(T_{yn} * W_{yn} * D_y)^2}} \tag{1}$$

At this point, D: the weight according to size of E-mail content.

3.3 User Profile

The User Profile is one of ways to show each user's preference and interest. When it is used, it is possible to extract appropriate information that users concern the most among various kind of information. The paper uses User Profile in order to suggest suitable information automatically to users.

The using User Profile in the paper is constituted like in the Fig. 3. It contains user's ID, terms for users' interest areas, and the value of the terms between 0 and 1. Also, T consists of extracted key words from E-mail title and content.

User ID	
Subject	
T_1	V_1
⋮	
T_n	V_n

User ID: Distinguish User Profile
Subject: User's interest area
T: User's preferred terms
V: Value of the terms

Fig. 3. The structure of User Profile

The renewal of User Profile occurs when a user shares E-mail or searches information through query language, and two cases exist for the renewal like below.

When key words exist in user's preferred terms

$$V_{nij} = V_{nij} + \frac{1}{N} \sum_{i=1}^{n} V_{nj} * C \qquad (2)$$

When key words do not exist in user's preferred terms

$$V_{nij} = C * 0.01 \qquad (3)$$

But, the number of n : T, C: Number of time for repetition
V_{nij} : The value for i times of subject for n times
V_{nj} : The existing value to subject k
To indicate value between 0 to 1, the total value is multiplied by weight, which becomes its value as 1 if value of user's certain preferred terms gets bigger than 1.

3.4 Automatic Knowledge Search

In the KMS that shares and administers knowledge of an organization, a great amount of knowledge is accumulated. In order for a user to use such abundant knowledge effectively, it has to automatically provide highly related knowledge to users after the evaluation of newly created knowledge according to each user's interest level. The Automatic Knowledge Recommending method that the paper suggests is like below.

Once a user logs in to the KMS, it searches created knowledge after the person's most recent access. Then it extracts key words and occurrence frequency from respective knowledge. The User Profile and Similarity of the knowledge are calculated by the numerical formula (**1**). Finally, it provides knowledge list to the user, whose Similarity is more than critical value.

4 Experimentation and Performance Evaluation

For the paper' experimentation of AKRS using E-mail, 12,981 E-mails have extracted for 12 days from an E-mail server of KMS developing organization. Except for junk mail, 2,491 E-mails are used for the experiment. Also, operating System used Windows 2000 Server, and programming development language used ASP.NET(C#), and database used MS_SQL 2000.

4.1 Result and Analysis of Experimentation

The E-mail used KMS that is realized in the paper is demonstrated in the Fig. 4. The KMS is constituted to be possible to add-in to Web-Mail. Therefore, it provides familiar interface to users without spending additional constructing fee and education. Also, previously stored E-mails can share it knowledge without extra work for data transformation.

Because it is difficult to make standard that estimate precision for E-mail classification, we do not evaluate it. Instead, we are two experiments about algorithm A and algorithm B.

Fig. 4. The E-mail used KMS

Algorithm A : that size of document is not considered.
Algorithm B : that size of document is considered

The first experiment measures knowledge group about critical value. Fig. 5 is result of the first experiment. The proposed algorithm appeared that knowledge group is smaller than general algorithm. By this result, we proved that the proposed algorithm is more efficient than general algorithm.

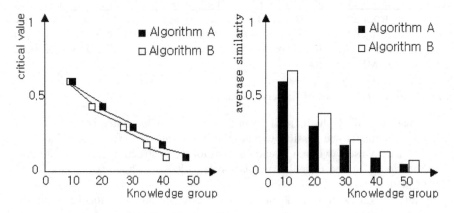

Fig. 5. A first experiment graph   **Fig. 6.** A second experiment graph

The second experiment measures similarity average value of each knowledge group. Fig. 6 is result of the second experiment. The proposed algorithm appeared that similarity average is high than general algorithm.

The following is an experiment about Automatic Knowledge Recommending Service. Let's assume a user's profile is like the Table 2 and take a careful look for Knowledge Automatic Recommending Service.

Table 2. User Profile

user = kdh_r2			
Term	Value	Term	Value
knowledge	0.571	news	0.26
distribute	0.415	model	0.252
network	0.4	planning	0.211
development	0.381	windows	0.102

Fig. 7. Screen of the Knowledge Automatic Recommending Service

Through User Profile and Similarity calculation of E-mail, the documents that reflect the user's interest is recommended as the Fig. 7 shows. The critical value is 0.3 in this case.

If user approaches to KMS, because knowledge that User Profile is considered automatically is recommended, user can use easily knowledge with own without special search.

5   Conclusion

In this paper, KMS that uses E-mail to provide Knowledge Automatic Recommending System, which concerns users' interest, was proposed. In order to boost up the users concerned KMS, profiles are constructed to indicate users' preference, and the profiles are renewed by using extracted key words from E-mails. Also by using an algorithm that classifies similar knowledge and User Profile according to the level of similarity between E-mails, it suggested an algorithm, which searches appropriate knowledge to users based on their preference.

We conducted an experiment to evaluate AKRS effectiveness of these methods. From the result of the experiment, we draw conclusions that user can use easily knowledge without special search.

The proposed KMS uses already established E-mail System, thus, no additional hardware or software is necessary. In addition, the system suggests related knowledge to users automatically. For this reason, users can utilize knowledge easily without extra steps for data search.

We do not consider any attached file in E-mail and the E-mail may indicate important information. Therefore, further study is expected to explore the classification and administering method for attached files of E-mail as knowledge.

References

1. Sandra M. Richardson, James F. Courtney. : A Churchmanian Theory of Knowledge Management System Design, in IEEE Proceddings of the 37nd Hawaii International Conference on System Sciences, Track8. (2004) p.80246a
2. Spender, J.C. : Making Knowledge the Basis of a Dynamic Theory of the Firm, Strategic Management Journal, 17, Winter/Spring Issue. (1996) 45-62
3. Dong-Gil Ko, Alan R. Dennis. : Who Profits from Knowledge Management?: A Case of Experience versus Expertise, in IEEE Proceddings of the 37nd Hawaii International Conference on System Sciences, Track8. (2004) p.80239c
4. Alavi, M. and Leidner, D. Review: knowledge management and knowledge management systems: conceptual foundations and research issues. MIS Quarterly, v.25, no1, (2001) p.107-36
5. Yogesh Malhotra, Dennis F. Galletta. : Role of Commitment and Motivation in Knowledge Management Systems Implementation: Theory, Conceptualization, and Measurement of Antecedents of Success, in IEEE Proceddings of the 36nd Hawaii International Conference on System Sciences, - Track 4, (2003) p.115a
6. Dyer, G. and McDonough, B. : The State of KM, Knowledge Management, v. 4, no. 5, May (2001)

7. KPMG Consulting. Knowledge Management Research Report, Netherlands: KPMG, (2000)
8. Maryam A, Dorothy L. : Knowledge Management System:Emerging Views and Practices from the Field, in IEEE Proceddings of the 32nd Hawaii International Conference on System Sciences, (1999) pp.1-11
9. Michael J. Pazzani. : Representation of Electronic Mail Filtering Profiles, Association for Computing Machinery, (2000) 202–206
10. Bracha Shapira, et al., : Information Filtering: A New Two-Phase Model using Stereotypic User Profiling, Journal of Intelligent Information Systems, Vol. 8, (1997)
11. Budi Yuwono, Dik L. Lee, : Search and Ranking Algorithms for Locating Resources on the World Wide Web, Proc. of the 12th Int'l Conf. on Data Engineering, New Orleans, Louisiana, Feb, (1996) pp.164-171
12. Sima C. Newekk, : User Models and Filtering Agents for Improved Internet Information Retrieval, User Modeling and User-Adapted Interaction, Vol. 7, (1997) pp. 223-237
13. Woo, Sunmi, Lee, Gihyung, Yoo Chunshick, Kim, Sungyong, : User-Centered Filtering and Document Ranking, ICAI 99, (1999)
14. Lee, Sangjin, : Implementation of Dynamic Folder for the Effective Knowledge Share, Master's Thesis of Seoul National University, 2000, 2

Narrowing the Gap Between Humans and Agents in e-Commerce: 3D Electronic Institutions

Anton Bogdanovych[1], Helmut Berger[2], Simeon Simoff[1], and Carles Sierra[3]

[1] Faculty of Information Technology,
University of Technology Sydney,
Sydney, NSW, Australia
{anton, simeon}@it.uts.edu.au
[2] Electronic Commerce Competence Center – ec3,
Donau-City-Strasse 1, A-1220 Wien, Austria,
helmut.berger@ec3.at
[3] Artificial Intelligence Research Institute (IIIA-CSIC),
Barcelona, Catalonia, Spain
sierra@iiia.csic.es

Abstract. Electronic Institution are regulated environments populated by autonomous software agents that perform tasks on behalf of users. Users, however, are reluctant in delegating full control of critical decisions to agents and prefer to make them on their own. In order to increase trust in agents we propose 3D Electronic Institutions as an environment inhabited by a heterogenous society of humans and agents. We present a novel approach that introduces humans to Electronic Institutions via 3D Virtual Worlds. Such a 3D Virtual World provides an immersive user interface that allows humans to observe the behavior of their agents as well as the intervention in the agents' decision process if necessary. We step beyond the agents view on Electronic Institutions, take a human-centered perspective and concentrate on the relation between humans and agents in the amalgamation of 3D Electronic Institutions.

1   Introduction

Nowadays individuals are the product of a particularly mobile and entrepreneurial society. As a result, individuals are socially constituted and socially situated in everyday business activities. Preece et al. criticize that the satisfaction of social needs, despite of its great importance, is widely neglected in nowadays systems [1]. A truly feasible e-Commerce system that supports business activities can hardly be obtained without taking care of the social issues behind these activities [2]. Most system analysts, however, perceive e-Commerce systems from a purely technical viewpoint without trying to establish the social and business norms that companies and consumers comply with.

Immersive environments such as 3D Virtual Worlds address the satisfaction of users' social needs and are complemented with a realistic experience. Virtual Worlds support to a certain extent the way humans act and communicate in real

K. Bauknecht et al. (Eds.): EC-Web 2005, LNCS 3590, pp. 128–137, 2005.

life and offer an environment to "meet" people. Such interfaces go beyond the form-based approaches dominating the World Wide Web and graphically represent the user in terms of an "avatar" [3]. Users are literally "in" the World Wide Web rather than "on" it. Overall, the design and development of Virtual Worlds has emerged as a phenomenon shaped by the home computer user rather than by research and development activities at universities or companies. As a result, Virtual Worlds are more or less unregulated environments. In order to exploit the benefits of Virtual Worlds interfacing e-Commerce systems, strong methodologies for reliable interactions need to be applied. Electronic Institutions, for instance, focus on controlling these aspects. In particular, an Electronic Institution is an environment populated by autonomous software agents that interact according to predefined conventions. Furthermore, Electronic Institutions guarantee that certain norms of behavior are enforced. This view permits that agents behave autonomously and make their decisions freely up to the limits imposed by the set of norms of the institution [4]. However, not much attention has been paid to the relationship between an autonomous agent and its principal. Users are rather reluctant in delegating full control of critical decisions to agents and prefer to make them on their own. A better modeling and, above all, understanding of this relationship is needed.

In this paper we present a novel approach that addresses this issue and introduces humans to Electronic Institutions (EI) via 3D Virtual Worlds. Such a 3D Virtual World provides an immersive user interface that allows humans to observe the behavior of their agents as well as the intervention in the agents' decision process if necessary. The major objective of this approach is to take a human-centered perspective on Electronic Institutions and concentrate on the relation between humans and agents in the new metaphor of *3D Electronic Institutions*. We expect that this new metaphor will reveal new insights about the relationship between humans and agents and, moreover, increase trust in agents inhabiting such e-Commerce environments.

This paper is structured as follows. In Section 2, applications of Multi-Agent Systems in e-Commerce are reviewed and related work in the area of human-computer interaction is presented. In Section 3, design considerations for 3D Electronic Institutions are outlined and the relation between humans and software agents in this environment is described. The architecture of 3D Electronic Institutions is presented in Section 4. Finally, a conclusion is given in Section 5.

2   Related Work

Multi-Agent Systems (MAS) have proven to be a perfect paradigm for modeling environments that are composed of many autonomous individuals. In order to develop complex MAS, sophisticated methodologies supporting the entire development life cycle including design, analysis and deployment are needed [5]. Methodologies that distinguish between the social (macro-level) and agent (micro-level) aspects of the system are preferable. However, considerable research efforts take an agent-centered view while ignoring social aspects of individual participants.

So, most research concentrates on the development of theories, languages and methodologies whereof Gaia [6], Madkit [7] and Electronic Institutions [8] are prominent representatives. Moreover, not much attention has been paid to applications of Multi-Agent Systems. One among the few is the recently completed MASFIT project [9]. MASFIT is a Multi-Agent Systems that enables participants to delegate the task of fish trading to autonomous agents. So, users are able to participate in multiple fish markets at the same time while ensuring traditional auctioning of goods. This project was designed as an EI and was deployed at the markets of Vilanova and Tarragona, Spain.

Another interesting application of Multi-Agent Systems is the air-traffic management system OASIS (Optimal Aircraft Sequencing using Intelligent Scheduling). OASIS combines artificial intelligence, software agents and conventional software [10]. Its purpose is to calculate estimated landing times, determine the sequence in which aircrafts are supposed to land and advise air traffic controllers on appropriate control actions. The system was successfully trialed at Sydney airport during the late nineties.

Social interaction plays an important role in real world commerce and are an important issue for the future of e-Commerce [1] as well. Some operators of e-Commerce Web sites even believe that online communities supporting social interactions serve the same purpose as the "sweet smell of baking cakes" does in a pastry shop. Both evoke images of comfort, warmth, happiness and probably even trust. An e-Commerce environment fostering social interactions was implemented by [11]. It incorporates a novel, spatially-organized and interactive site map that provides visibility of people, activities and mechanisms for social interactions. 3D Virtual Worlds implicitly address the issue of social interactions since location awareness, presence as well as direct communication are intrinsic elements. Inspired by the success of 3D graphical user interfaces in application domains such as computer games, CAD as well as medical and scientific visualization, researchers applied this emerging technology to new domains including e-Commerce. In [12] a 3D e-Commerce environment is proposed featuring animated products, which act as navigational aids, and guide users through the 3D representation of the online shop. 3D product visualizations literally "move around" and assist users in finding the appropriate section within the shop.

Another interesting representative, even though in the area of cultural heritage, is the reconstruction of Leonardo da Vinci's "Ideal City" [13]. Based on original sketches the city was realized as a 3D Virtual World. The main objective was to provide an immersive virtual experience of da Vinci's ideas and concepts and to offer users the possibility to explore the city in a collaborative fashion.

3   Design Considerations for 3D Electronic Institutions

The design of Virtual Worlds has been governed by different principles. Bricken identified in [14] the shift from the user role to a participant in the actual design, the move from interface towards inclusion (i.e. embedding participants in the design process within the environment), and the change from visual to multimodal interaction. It is argued that the design of Virtual Worlds changes from using familiar metaphors towards applying appearances that are completely arbitrary. However, in Virtual Worlds designs related to human everyday experiences have been predominant. The emphasis has been placed on the design of the *static* visual spaces. The development and research in distributed gaming environments as well as in computer-mediated collaborative design identified the need of dynamic generation of Virtual Worlds out of design specifications. For example, Smith et al. changed static 3D Virtual Worlds into adaptable worlds by incorporating agents as the basis for representing the world's elements [15]. The emphasis, however, was placed on the software side, i.e. the "society of agents" rather than on the *heterogenous society* of humans and agents. Contrary, we concentrate on this issue and describe main design considerations for 3D Electronic Institutions in order to address heterogenous societies.

Firstly, appropriate user interface design is crucial for sophisticated human-computer interaction, which especially applies to 3D Virtual Worlds, as such interfaces are designed with the goal in mind to emulate the way humans operate and interact in the real world. More precisely, 3D Virtual Worlds aim at combining the use of space with an immersive experience in order to construct a useable virtual representation of a particular domain. Space and objects in space are used to model different impressions. Social power, for instance, might be expressed in terms of "height". Proximity of things could indicate that they belong to the same group or are of a similar type. Humans live in a well structured environment following different metaphors. Metaphors such as buildings or streets might be used in Virtual Worlds as well [16]. Considering an Electronic Institution, a possible 3D visualization might be the metaphor of a town. Each building identifies an institution, different institutions are accessed via public transport and rooms refer to different activities that can be performed.

Virtual Worlds visualized in 3D are environments where people "meet". Such environments provide a consistent and immersive user interface that facilitates awareness of other participants. Communication and interaction between participants are main issues in these environments. Smith et al. point out in [15] that these environments have to provide appropriate mechanisms which enable users to communicate and encourage social interactions. Satisfying social needs of users is regarded a key issue in nowadays virtual communities but, however, remains mostly neglected [1]. 3D Virtual Worlds stimulate social interactions just by simple "visual presence" of other visitors. Being aware of other users constitutes an implicit and integral feature of this user interface and offers communication possibilities at any time detached from any physical place.

Another important issue in user interface design is the avoidance of overloaded interfaces. Traditional web pages overloaded with form elements such as input fields or checkboxes overwhelm and distract users. This issue is addressed in 3D Virtual Worlds by taking "distance" into account. More precisely, the detail level increases or decreases according to the avatar's distance to a particular object, i.e. the closer an avatar is to an object the more information is visible and presented to the user. This reduces the information overload known from conventional interfaces while still conveying a basic impression of the context.

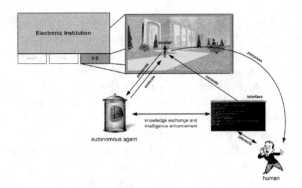

Fig. 1. Relation between agents and humans in 3D Electronic Institutions

Secondly, beside humans, other types of participants might be present in e-Commerce environments. Users delegate activities to autonomous (software) agents that act on their behalf in such environments. Our view on the relation between humans and software agents in 3D Electronic Institutions is illustrated in Figure 1. The couple agent/principal is represented in a Virtual World as an *avatar*. Either a human or an agent may control the avatar through the *interface*. Metaphorically speaking, the interface is a "glove puppet" that translates all actions of its "puppeteer" into an institutional and machine-understandable language. Agent and human cooperate during the accomplishment of tasks the human has to deal with. Representing autonomous agents as avatars allows humans to perceive agent's actions in a transparent way that assists in deciding whether the human should intervene or not. It is envisioned to provide additional interaction possibilities between humans and agents. Consider a human issuing instructions to an agent or an agent suggesting solutions to the human like an "expanded intelligence" mechanism similar to "expanded reality" offered by state-of-the-art virtual reality tools.

The duality, agent/principal, introduces the possibility of co-learning between humans and their agents. On the one hand, the agent learns to make proper decisions from its principal and on the other hand the agent assists the human in learning the rules that apply in the environment. Additionally, a human might be advised by its agents about the consequences of certain actions by compiling information gathered from external information sources. Behaviour patterns of other participants in specific situations might be observed in order to derive solutions for current tasks.

4   3D Electronic Institutions

3D Electronic Institutions combine the two metaphors of *Electronic Institutions* and *3D Virtual Worlds* while retaining the features and advantages of both. Originally, an Electronic Institution is an environment populated by autonomous software agents that interact according to predefined conventions on language and protocol. Furthermore, Electronic Institutions guarantee that certain norms

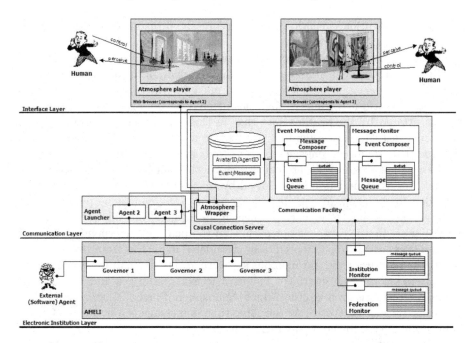

Fig. 2. System architecture of 3D Electronic Institutions

of behavior are enforced. This view permits that agents behave autonomously and make their decisions freely up to the limits imposed by the set of norms of the institution [4]. 3D Electronic Institutions broaden this view and are environments that enable humans to participate in a heterogenous society of individuals. The essence is to step beyond the agents view on Electronic Institutions, take a *human centered* perspective and concentrate on the relation between humans and agents in the amalgamation of the two metaphors.

Basically, 3D Electronic Institutions are built according to a three-layered framework [17]. The system architecture following this framework is depicted in Figure 2. The bottom layer hosts the runtime environment AMELI for arbitrary Electronic Institutions that are designed with ISLANDER [18], a graphical specification tool. Both, AMELI and ISLANDER, are part of the Electronic Institution Development Environment, EIDE [19]. AMELI loads an institution specification and mediates agents interactions while enforcing institutional rules and norms. To execute an Electronic Institution, AMELI is launched up-front and agents join the institution by connecting to the runtime environment.

The second layer contains the *Causal Connection Server* that *causally* connects the Electronic Institutions runtime environment AMELI with the 3D Virtual World at the top layer. As Maes et al. point out in [20], is a system "causally connected" to its representation when the following aspects are taken into account: First, whenever the representation of a system is changed, the system itself has to change as well. Second, whenever the system evolves, its representations has to be modified in order to maintain a consistent relationship. The

Electronic Institution execution itself is represented in terms of a 3D Virtual World consisting of rooms, avatars, doors and other graphical elements. So, the causal connection needs to materialize in two directions. First, messages uttered by the agent in the institution have immediate impact on the 3D representation. Movements between scenes, for instance, must let the avatar "move" within the Virtual World accordingly. Messages uttered by the agent must be considered as uttered by the avatar. Note that in this exposition the terminology of Electronic Institutions is adopted. *Scenes*, are activities following a structured dialogue that agents can engage in. *Transitions* synchronize and re-route agents between scenes. Second, events caused by the human via the interface in the Virtual World are understood as caused by the agent. This implies that actions forbidden to the agent at the current execution state, cannot be performed by the user via the interface. For instance, if an agent is not allowed to leave a particular scene, the avatar is not permitted to open the corresponding door.

Two types of participants need to be considered in 3D Electronic Institutions, namely human users and autonomous software agents. Human users connect to the system via the web interface. The user access is validated and if admission to the institution is granted, the Adobe Atmosphere Player [21] starts and visualizes the 3D Virtual World. At the same time, a message is sent via the Causal Connection Server to the *Agent Launcher* that, in turn, spawns a new software agent. This software agent represents the human user at the Electronic Institution level (cf. Figure 2, the left browser window corresponds to *Agent 2*, the right to *Agent 3*). Each agent participating in an Electronic Institution communicates via a *Governor*. The Governor serves the purpose of "safe-guarding" the institution, i.e. it checks whether a particular message is allowed to be uttered at the current stage or not. The second type of participants are autonomous agents, i.e. software programs, that contact AMELI directly. Each software agent requests access and, if granted, communicates via a Governor as well.

An arbitrary event, e.g. a mouse click on a door handle, caused by a human user leads to a sequence of processing steps. First, the event is caught by the Atmosphere Player and transmitted in terms of a 2–tuple <AvatarID, Event> to the Causal Connection Server. Then the event tuple is stored in the *Event Queue* which is observed by the *Event Monitor*. As soon as the Event Monitor notices the arrival, it translates the event by means of the *Event/Message* mapping table into the corresponding message. In analogy to that, the *AvatarID* is mapped onto the *AgentID*, this time though, by means of the *AvatarID/AgentID* mapping table. A 2–tuple <AgentID, Message> is composed and stored in the *Message Queue*. This time the *Message Monitor* detects the arrival and sends it to the corresponding agent using the *Communication Facility*. Finally, the agent actually utters the message and the state of the Electronic Institution evolves. AMELI validates whether the received message adheres to the institutional rules and generates an adequate response. Messages, however, originating from AMELI need to be reflected in the Virtual World and are processed in exactly the opposite way.

Fig. 3. The user interface of a 3D Electronic Institution exemplified by means of a graffiti poster shop

The *Institution Monitor*, which offers an interface to AMELI, allows the observation of all messages within a single Electronic Institution. More precisely, the Causal Connection Server is connected to a socket provided by the Institution Monitor, and collects available messages. These messages assist in maintaining the synchronized and consistent relation between the 3D Virtual World and the Electronic Institution. Consider, for example an autonomous software agent that intends to enter the EI (cf. external agent in Figure 2). This particular software agent is not driven by a human user, i.e. it is not required to visually represent the agent for its own sake. However, taking the presence of human participants into account this software agent needs to be visualized as well. So, the Causal Connection Server generates such a representation and assembles it based on the messages obtained via the Institution Monitor. However, since more than one EI might be executed at one time, the *Federation Monitor* notifies about newly launched Electronic Institution. This is rather feasible since movements between Electronic Institutions are possible indeed.

Technically speaking, the user interface comprises the Adobe Atmosphere Player, embedded in a HTML page, accessible via web browsers. Events caused by users within the 3D Virtual World are caught and processed with JavaScript. Conceptually, the embodiment of participants in the 3D Virtual World creates additional opportunities to involve people in social interactions just by the fact of their presence. Being aware of someone's position or her/his line of sight allows observing the environmental context of each particular user. The presence of others creates a more open and a less formal environment. People are more likely to engage in conversations if they perceive the social context as well.

The specification of an Electronic Institution is used to obtain a 3D representation. However, this specification does not contain explicit information related to the visualization of Electronic Institutions. Nevertheless, it is possible to generate a simple 3D Virtual World by exploiting available data. In a straightforward approach, scenes are mapped onto rooms, transitions between scenes are represented as corridors and doors limit the access between scenes. The maximum number of participants per scene determines the size of each room. Doors are positioned in order to connect adjacent rooms. Such an institution is already fully functional, i.e. all security issues are imposed, agents are free to join the environment, interact and engage in conversations.

Figure 3 exemplifies a possible visualization of a 3D Electronic Institution. This particular example features a virtual poster shop that imitates the atmosphere of a real-world art gallery. The gallery's visitors are embodied as avatars. Visitors communicate with each other via the chat window at the bottom of the interface. A transparent institution map, i.e. the layout of the gallery, overlays the Virtual World and is placed at the top right corner of the interface. The large cuboids in the map represent rooms and smaller ones correspond to connections between these rooms. The avatar's position within the institution is symbolized by means of a highlighted figure having an arrow pointing at it. All other figures identify avatars controlled by software agents. These avatars act on behalf of the user and try to fulfill specified tasks. However, only one avatar is actually controlled and driven by the human at one time. This example illustrates the heterogeneity of 3D Electronic Institutions since the two possible types of participants are present. The artist, for instance, is engaged in a conversation with a potential (human) buyer while the software agent (buyer) keeps observing.

5   Conclusion and Future Work

In this paper we presented a novel approach enabling human participation in a Multi-Agent System, namely Electronic Institutions, by means of a 3D Virtual World that materialized in 3D Electronic Institutions. This new environment opens a perfect research playground for heterogenous societies comprising humans and software agents and to examine their relationship in domains such as e-Commerce. Due to the fact that social interaction is crucial in e-Commerce but, however, widely neglected we took up this issue and enabled users to act within the socially augmented context of 3D Virtual Worlds. Since 3D Electronic Institutions allow the specification of arbitrary scenarios, we exemplified its application in terms of an online graffiti poster shop. In this environment users interact with other participants and are able to observe the behavior of their agents as well as to intervene in the agents' decision process if necessary.

We are about to complete the implementation of the system and aim at investigating in detail the co-learning aspects between software agents and their principals. Additionally, we plan to conduct an extensive usability study that evaluates the acceptance and feasibility of this new environment. We expect to obtain new insights about the relationship between humans and agents that assist in future developments.

References

1. Preece, J., Maloney-Krichmar, D.: Online Communities. In: The Human-Computer Interaction Handbook. Lawrence Erlbaum Associates Inc. (2003) 596–620
2. Wyckoff, A., Colecchia, A.: The Economic and Social Impacts of Electronic Commerce: Preliminary Findings and Research Agenda. Organization for Economic Cooperation and Development (OECD) (1999)
3. Damer, B.: Avatars: Exploring and Building Virtual Worlds on the Internet. (1998)
4. Esteva, M., Rodriguez-Aguilar, J., Sierra, C., Garcia, P., Arcos, J.: On the formal specifications of electronic institutions. In: Agent Mediated Electronic Commerce, The European AgentLink Perspective, Springer-Verlag (2001) 126–147
5. Jennings, N., Sycara, K., Wooldridge, M.: A roadmap of agent research and development. In: Autonomous agents and Multiagent Systems. (1998) 275–306
6. Wooldridge, M., Jennings, N., Kinny, D.: The Gaia Methodology for Agent-Oriented Analysis and Design. Autonomous Agents and Multi-Agent Systems **3** (2000) 285–312
7. MADKIT: A multi-agent development kit. http://www.madkit.org/ (2005)
8. Esteva, M.: Electronic Institutions: From Specification to Development. PhD thesis, Institut d'Investigació en Intel.ligència Artificial (IIIA), Spain (2003)
9. Cuní, G., Esteva, M., Garcia, P., Puertas, E., Sierra, C., Solchaga, T.: MASFIT: Multi-agent systems for fish trading. In: Proceedings of the 16th European Conference on Artificial Intelligence, ECAI04, Valencia, Spain (2004)
10. Ljunberg, A., Lucas, A.: The oasis air traffic management system. In: Proceedings of the 2nd Pacific Rim International Conference on AI (PRICAI-92), Korea (1992)
11. Girgensohn, A., Lee, A.: Making web sites be places for social interaction. In: Proc. of the 2002 ACM Conf. on Computer Supported Cooperative Work, ACM Press (2002) 136–145
12. Chittaro, L., Coppola, P.: Animated products as a navigation aid for e-commerce. In: CHI '00 Extended Abstracts on Human Factors in Computing Systems, ACM Press (2000) 107–108
13. Barbieri, T., Paolini, P.: Reconstructing Leonardo's Ideal City from Handwritten Codexes to Webtalk II: A 3D Collaborative Virtual Environment System. In: Proceedings of the Conference on Virtual Reality, Archeology, and Cultural Heritage, Greece (2001) 61–66
14. Bricken, M.: Virtual worlds: No interface to design. In: Proceedings of First International Conference on Cyberspace. (1990)
15. Smith, G.J., Maher, M.L., Gero, J.S.: Designing 3D Virtual Worlds as a Society of Agents. In: Proceedings of CAADFutures. (2003)
16. Russo Dos Santos, C., Gros, P., Abel, P., Loisel, D., Trichaud, N., Paris, J.P.: Mapping Information onto 3D Virtual Worlds. In: Proceedings of the International Conference on Information Visualization. (2000) 379–
17. Bogdanovych, A., Berger, H., Simoff, S., Sierra, C.: E-Commerce Environments as 3D Electronic Institutions. In: Proc. of IADIS e-Commerce 2004, Portugal (2004)
18. Esteva, M., de la Cruz, D., Sierra, C.: ISLANDER: An Electronic Institutions Editor. In: First Int'l Conf. on Autonomous Agents and Multiagent Systems, Bologna, ACM Press (2002) 1045–1052
19. Electronic Institution Development Environment: Web site. http://e-institutor.iiia.csic.es/ (2005)
20. Maes, P., Nardi, D.: Meta-Level Architectures and Reflection. Elsevier Science Inc., NY, USA (1988)
21. Adobe Atmosphere: Web site. http://www.adobe.com/ (2005)

Standard K-Languages as a Powerful and Flexible Tool for Building Contracts and Representing Contents of Arbitrary E-Negotiations

Vladimir A. Fomichov

Faculty of Applied Mathematics,
Moscow State Institute of Electronics and Mathematics (Technical University),
109028 Moscow, Russia, and
Department of Information Technologies,
K.E.Tsiolkovsky Russian State Technological University - "MATI",
121552 Moscow, Russia
vdrfom@aha.ru

Abstract. The paper discusses a new class of formal languages called standard K-languages (SK-languages) as a powerful tool for building contracts concluded by computer intelligent agents and representing contents of arbitrary e-negotiations. The definition of SK-languages is a part of a mathematical model describing a system consisting of such 10 operations on structured meanings (SMs) of natural language texts (NL-texts) that, using primitive conceptual items as "blocks", it is possible to build SMs of, probably, arbitrary NL-texts. This means that a class of languages is determined being convenient for building semantic descriptions of arbitrary goods, services, and contracts. The principal advantages of SK-languages in comparison with first-order logic, Discourse Representation Theory, Theory of Conceptual Graphs, and Episodic Logic concern representing complicated goals and destinations of things, definitions of concepts, compound definitions of sets, and meanings of discourses with the references to the meaning of a phrase or larger part of discourse.

1 Introduction

During several last years in the fields of E-commerce two interrelated fields of researches have emerged called e-negotiations and electronic contracting. The birth of these fields was formally denoted by means of the organization at the beginning of the 2000s of several international conferences and workshops.

The collection of central problems faced by the researchers in these fields includes the creation of formal languages for representing contents of the records of negotiations conducted by computer intelligent agents (CIAs) and for forming contracts concluded in the course of such negotiations. These tasks can be considered as important particular cases of the problem of constructing general-purpose formal languages for business communication [1, 2].

Hasselberg and Weigand underline in [1] that if the messages in the field of E-commerce are to be processed automatically, the meaning must be formalized. This

K. Bauknecht et al. (Eds.): EC-Web 2005, LNCS 3590, pp. 138–147, 2005.

idea coincides with the opinion of Kimbrough and Moore [2] about the necessity of developing logical-semantic foundations of constructing formal languages for business communication (FLBC).

It is suggested in [2] to use first-order logic insofar as possible and reasonable for expressions in any FLBC. However, the expressive possibilities of the class of first-order logic languages are very restricted as concerns describing semantic structure of arbitrary business documents.

The analysis shows that the records of commercial negotiations and contracts can be formed with the help of expressive means of natural language (NL) used for the construction of arbitrary NL-texts pertaining to medicine, technology, law, etc. In particular, the texts from such documents may include: (a) the infinitives with dependent words expressing goals, offers ("to sell 30 boxes with apples"), promises, commitments, or destinations of things; (b) constructions formed out of infinitives with dependent words by means of the logical connectives "and", "or", "not" and expressing compound designations of goals, offers, promises, commitments or destinations of things; (c) complicated designations of sets ("a consignment consisting of 50 boxes with apples");   (d) fragments where the logical connectives "and", "or" join not the designations of assertions but the designations of objects; (e) fragments containing the references to the meanings of phrases or larger fragments of a discourse ("this proposal", "that order", "this promise", etc.); (f) the designations of the functions whose arguments and/or values may be the sets of objects ("the staff of the firm A", "the suppliers of the firm A", "the number of the suppliers of the firm A"), (g) questions with the answer "Yes" or No", (h) questions with interrogative words.

Meanwhile, the first-order predicate logic provides no possibility to build formal analogues (on the semantic level) of the texts from business documents where the NL phenomena listed in items (a) – (g) are manifested.

That is why the problem of developing formal languages allowing for representing contents of the records of commercial e-negotiations carried out by CIAs and for forming contracts concluded in the course of such negotiations is very complicated. Hence it seems to be reasonable to use for solving this problem the most broadly applicable theories (ideally, universal) of representing meanings of NL-texts provided by mathematical linguistics and mathematical computer science.

The papers [6-9] describe two slightly different versions of the basic mathematical model of the theory of K-calculuses and K-languages (the KCL-theory); it considerably expanded the stock of formal tools destined for representing in a formal way the meanings (or contents, or semantic structure) of NL-texts. This basic model described in [7, 8] includes the definition of a new class of formal languages called standard knowledge languages (standard K-languages, SK-languages).

The goal of this paper continuing the line of [10, 11] is to ground the broad prospects of using the theory of SK-languages for building the records of commercial e-negotiations in arbitrary application domains conducted by CIAs and for forming the contracts concluded in the course of such negotiations.

2   A Short Description of the Class of Standard K-Languages

During last decade, the most popular approaches to building formal representations of the meanings of NL-texts have been Discourse Representation Theory (DRT) [3],

Theory of Conceptual Graphs (TCG), represented, in particular, in [4], and Episodic Logic (EL) [5]. In fact, DRT and TCG are oriented at describing the semantic structure of only sentences and short simple discourses. EL studies the structure of only a part of discourses, more exactly, of discourses where the time and causal relationships between the situations (called episodes) are realized.

The authors of DRT, TCG, EL don't pose the problem of representing by formal means the structured meanings of arbitrary texts pertaining to arbitrary fields of human professional activity: medicine, technology, business, etc. The reason is that, in particular, the expressive possibilities of these theoretical approaches are restricted from the standpoint of modeling the semantic structure of NL-texts of the kinds (a) – (h) listed above.

On the contrary, the definition of the class of SK-languages became an answer to the following question: how it would be possible to describe in a mathematical way a system of operations on conceptual structures allowing for building (after a finite number of steps) semantic representations (SRs) of arbitrarily complicated sentences and discourses from arbitrary application domains, starting from primary informational items.

In other words, an attempt was undertaken to elaborate a new theoretical approach enabling us effectively describe structured meanings (or contents, or semantic structure, or conceptual structure) of real sentences and arbitrarily complicated discourses pertaining to technology, medicine, business, etc.

As a result, a mathematical model was created describing a system of 10 partial operations on structured meanings (SMs) of NL-texts and, in particular, determining the class of SK-languages. The following hypothesis was put forward: using primitive conceptual items as "blocks", we are able to build SMs of arbitrary NL-texts (including articles, textbooks, etc.) and arbitrary pieces of knowledge about the world by means of these 10 partial operations. The substantial advantages of SK-languages in comparison with DRT, TCG, and EL are discussed in [6, 9].

Let's consider the main ideas of determining a new class of formal languages called SK-languages. The exact mathematical definitions can be found in [7, 8] and their preliminary versions – in [6].

At the first step (consisting of a rather long sequence of auxiliary steps), a class of formal objects called *conceptual bases (c.b)* is defined. Each c.b. B is a system of the form $((c_1, c_2, c_3, c_4), (c_5, ..., c_8), (c_9,..., c_{15}))$ with the components $c_1,..., c_{15}$ being mainly finite or countable sets of symbols and distinguished elements of such sets. In particular, $c_1 = St$ is a finite set of symbols called sorts and designating the most general considered concepts; $c_2 = P$ is a distinguished sort "sense of proposition"; $c_5 = X$ is a countable set of strings used as elementary blocks for building knowledge modules and SRs of texts; X is called a primary informational universe; $c_6 = V$ is a countable set of variables; $c_8 = F$ is a subset of X whose elements are called functional symbols.

Each c.b. B determines three classes of formulas, the first class $Ls(B)$ being considered as the principal one and being called *the standard K-language in the c..b. B*. Its strings (they are called K-strings) are convenient for building SRs of NL-texts. We'll consider below only the formulas from the first class $Ls(B)$.

In order to determine for arbitrary c.b. B three classes of formulas, a collection of inference rules P[0], P[1],..., P[10] is defined. The rule P[0] provides an initial stock of formulas from the first class. E.g., there is such a c.b. B_1 that, according to P[0], $Ls(B_1)$ includes the elements   *box1, green, city, set, India, 7, all, any, Weight, Distance, Staff, Suppliers, Quantity, x1, x2, P5.*

Let's regard (ignoring many details) the structure of strings which can be obtained by applying any of the rules P[1],..., P[10] at the last step of inferring the formulas. The rule P[1] enables us to build K-strings of the form *Quant Conc* where *Quant* is a semantic item corresponding to the meanings of such words and expressions as "certain", "any", "arbitrary", "each", "all", "several", etc. (such semantic items will be called *intensional quantifiers*), and *Conc* is a designation (simple or compound) of a concept. The examples of K-strings for P[1] as the last applied rule are as follows: *certn box1, all box1, certn consignment, certn box1 * (Content1, ceramics)*, where the last expression is built with the help of both the rules P[0], P[1] and the rule with the number 4, the symbol *'certn'* is to be interpreted as the informational item corresponding to the word "certain" in cases when this word is associated with singular.

The rule P[2] allows for constructing the strings of the form $f(a_1,..., a_n)$, where f is a designation of a function, $n \geq 1$, $a_1,..., a_n$ are K-strings built with the help of any rules from the list P[0],..., P[10]. The examples of K-strings built with the help of P[2]:

$$\textit{Distance(Moscow, Tokyo),}$$
$$\textit{Weight(certn box1 * (Colour, green)(Content1, ceramics))}\ .$$

Using the rule P[3], we can build the strings of the form $(a1 \equiv a2)$, where $a1$ and $a2$ are K-strings formed with the help of any rules from P[0],..., P[10], and $a1$ and $a2$ represent the entities being homogeneous in some sense. Examples of K-strings for P[3]:

$$\textit{(Distance(Moscow, Tokyo)} \equiv \textit{x1), (y1} \equiv \textit{y3) ,(Weight(certn box1)} \equiv \textit{8/ kg)}\ .$$

The rule P[4] is destined, in particular, for constructing K-strings of the form $rel(a_1,..., a_n)$, where *rel* is a designation of n-ary relation, $n >= 1$, $a_1,..., a_n$ are the K-strings formed with the aid of some rules from P[0],..., P[10]. The examples of K-strings for P[4]: *Belong(Bonn, Cities(Germany)), Subset(certn series1 * (Name-origin, tetracyclin), all antibiotic).*

The rule P[5] enables us to construct the K-strings of the form *Expr: v* , where *Expr* is a K-string not including *v*, *v* is a variable, and some other conditions are satisfied. Using P[5], one can mark by variables in the SR of any NL-text: (a) the descriptions of diverse entities mentioned in the text (physical objects, events, concepts, etc.), (b) the SRs of sentences and of larger texts' fragments to which a reference is given in any part of a text. Examples of K-strings for P[5]: *certn box1 : x3 , Higher(certn box1 : x3, certn box1 : x5) : P1* .   The rule P[5] provides the possibility to form SRs of texts in such a manner that these SRs reflect the referential structure of NL-texts.

The rule P[6] provides the possibility to build the K-strings of the form $\neg$ *Expr* , where *Expr* is a K-string satisfying a number of conditions. The examples of K-strings for P[6]: $\neg$ *antibiotic,*

$$\neg \textit{Belong(penicillin, certn series1 * (Name-origin, tetracyclin))}\ .$$

Using the rule P[7], one can build the K-strings of the forms $(a_1 \wedge a_2 \wedge ... \wedge a_n)$ or $(a_1 \vee a_2 \vee ... \vee a_n)$, where $n > 1$, $a_1,...., a_n$ are K-strings designating the entities which are homogeneous in some sense. In particular, $a_1,..., a_n$ may be SRs of assertions (or propositions), descriptions of physical things, descriptions of sets consisting of things of the same kind, descriptions of concepts. The following strings are examples of K-strings for P[7]:

> (*streptococcus* ∨ *staphylococcus*), (*Belong((Bonn* ∧ *Hamburg* ∧ *Stuttgart*),
> *Cities(Germany))* ∧ ¬ *Belong(Bonn, Cities((Finland* ∨ *Norway* ∨ *Sweden))))*.

The rule P[8] allows us to build, in particular, K-strings of the form c * $(rel_1, val_1),..., (rel_n, val_n)$, where c is an informational item from the primary universe X designating a concept, for $i=1,...,n$, rel_i is the name of a function with one argument or of a binary relation, val_i designates a possible value of rel_i for objects characterized by the concept c. The following expressions are examples of K-strings for P[8]:

> *box1* * *(Content1,ceramics)*, *consignment* * *(Quantity, 12)(Compos1, box1* *
> *(Content1, ceramics))*.

The rule P[9] permits to build, in particular, the K-strings of the forms ∀*v (conc)* D and ∃*v (conc)* D, where ∀ is the universal quantifier, ∃ is the existential quantifier, *conc* and D are K-strings, *conc* is a designation of a primary concept ("person", "city", "integer", etc.) or of a compound concept ("integer greater than 200", etc.). D may be interpreted as a SR of an assertion with the variable v about any entity qualified by the concept *conc*. The examples of K-strings for P[9] are as follows:

> ∀*n1 (integer)* ∃*n2 (integer) Less(n1,n2)*,

> ∃*y (country* * *(Location, Europe)) Greater(Quantity(Cities(y)),15)*.

The rule P[10] is destined for constructing, in particular, the K-strings of the form $<a_1,..., a_n>$, where $n>1$, $a_1,..., a_n$ are K-strings. The strings obtained with the help of P[10] at the last step of inference are interpreted as designations of n-tuples. The components of such n-tuples may be not only designations of numbers, things, but also SRs of assertions, designations of sets, concepts, etc.

3   Studying the Possibilities of Forming Contracts and Records of E-Negotiations by Means of SK-Languages

The analysis shows that the SK-languages posses the expressive possibilities being necessary and sufficient for representing in a formal way the contents of contracts and of the records of commercial negotiations.

For illustrating an important part of such possibilities, let's consider a multi-partner scenario of the interaction of business partners in the course of handling a car damage claim by an insurance company (called AGFIL). The names of the involved parties are Europ Assist, Lee Consulting Services (Lee C.S.), Garages, and Assessors. Europ Assist offers a 24-hour emergency call answering service to the policyholders. Lee C.S. coordinates and manages the operation of the emergency service on a day-to-day level on behalf of AGFIL. Garages are responsible for car repair. Assessors conduct the physical inspections of damaged vehicles and agree repair upon figures with the garages [12, 13].

The process of a car insurance case can be described as follows. The policyholder phones Europ Assist using a free-phone number to notify a new claim. Europ Assist will register the information, suggest an appropriate garage, and notify AGFIL which will check whether the policy is valid and covers this claim. After AGFIL receives this claim, AGFIL sends the claims details to Lee C.S. AGFIL will send a letter to the policyholder for a completed claim form. Lee C.S. will agree upon repair costs if an assessor is not required for small damages, otherwise an assessor will be assigned. The assessor will check the damaged vehicle and agree upon repair costs with the garage. After receiving an agreement of repairing car from Lee C.S., the garage will then commence repairs. After finishing repairs, the garage will issue an invoice to the Lee C.S., which will check the invoice against the original estimate. Lee C.S. returns all invoices to AGFIL. This firm process the payment. In the whole process, if the claim is found invalid, all contractual parties will be contacted and the process will be stopped.

This scenario provides the possibility to illustrate some properties of SK-languages making them a convenient tool for formally describing contracts. We'll use in the examples below restricted SK-languages determined in [6].

Property 1. The possibility to build compound designations of goals.

Example. Let T1 = "The policyholder phones Europ Assist to inform about a car damage". Then T1 may have the following K-representation (KR), i.e. a semantic representation being an expression of some SK-language:

*Situation(e1, phone-communic * (Agent1, certn person * (Hold1, certn policy1 : x1) : x2)(Object2, certn firm1 * (Name1, "Europ Assist") : x3) (Purpose, inform-transfer * (Theme1, certn damage1 * (Object1, certn car1) : x4))).*

Property 2. The existence of the means allowing for representing in a compact way the time and causal relations between the situations.

Property 3. The possibility to construct compact semantic representations of such fragments of sentences which are obtained by means of joining the designations of things, events, concepts or goals with the help of logical connectives AND, OR.

Example. Let T2 = "After receiving a repair invoice from the firm "Lee C.S." and a claim from the policyholder, the company "AGFIL" pays the car repair to the garage". Then a KR of T2 can be the expression

*(Situation (e1, (receiving1 * (Agent2, certn firm1* (Name1, "AFGIL") : x1)(Object1, certn invoice * (Theme, certn repair : e2) : x2)(Sender1, certn firm1* (Name1, "Lee C.S.") : x3) ∧ receiving1 * (Agent2, x1)(Object1, certn claim1 : x4) (Sender1, certn person * (Hold1, certn policy1 : x5) : x6))) ∧ Situation (e2, payment1* (Agent2,   x1)(Addressee1, certn garage : x7)(Sum, Cost (e2))) ∧ Before (e1, e2)) .*

Property 4. The existence of the formal means allowing for representing structured meanings of the discourses with the references to the meanings of sentences and larger fragments of the texts.

Example. Let T3 = "The firm "Europ Assist" provides a policyholder with a telephone service; in particular, assigns a garage for repair and informs the company "AGFIL" about a claim of a policyholder". Then T3 may have KR

(Situation (e1, service1 * (Agent2, certn firm1* (Name1, "Europ Assist") : x1)(Instrument, certn telephone : x2)(Object1, arbitrary person ** (Hold1, certn policy1: x3) : x4) : P1 ∧ Concretization (P1, ((Situation (e2, assigning1 * (Agent2, x1)(Addressee1, x4))(Object3, certn garage * (Destination1, repair) : x5)) ∧ Situation (e3, inform-transfer * (Agent2, x1)(Addressee1, certn firm1* (Name1, "AFGIL") : x6)(Content1, certn claim1 * (Authors, x4) : x7))))) .

The variable *P1* in the constructed formula is a mark of the semantic representation (SR) of the sentence S1 = "The firm "Europ Assist" provides a policyholder with a telephone service". In the second part of the discourse T3 this mark is used for representing in a compact way the reference to the meaning of the sentence S1.

Property 5. The possibility to formally represent the meanings of contractual obligations depending on conditions.

Example. Let T4 = " The firm "Lee C.S." assigns an expert for investigating a car during 41 hours after receiving a claim about a car damage if the repair cost doesn't exceed 500 USD". Then a KR of the text T4 can be the expression

Implies(Greater1 (Cost1 (certn repair1 * (Object1, certn car : x1) : e1), 500/USD) , (Situation (e2, assigning1 * (Agent2, certn firm1* (Name1, "Lee C.S.") : x2)(Person1, certn expert : x3)(Goal1, certn investigation1 * (Object1, x1) : e3)(Moment, t1)) ∧ Greater1 (Difference (t1, t0), 41/ hour) ∧ Situation (e4, receiving1 * (Agent2, x2)(Object1, certn claim1 * (Theme, certn damage1 * (Object1, x1) : e5))(Time, t0)))) .

Going beyond the scope of the scenario of business interaction discussed above, let's formulate two additional important properties of SK-languages.

Property 6. The existence of formal means allowing for constructing compound designations of sets as components of semantic representations of NL-texts being records of negotiations or contracts. For instance, the set consisting of 12 single rooms in the three-star hotels of Vienna may have a K-representation of the form

certn set * (Number, 12) (Qualitative-composition, room * (Kind1, single)(Location, any hotel * (Kind2, three-star)(Loc, Vienna)))   .

Property 7. The possibility to build object-oriented semantic representations of the records of negotiations or contracts, i.e. the expressions of the form

certn inform-object * (Kind, concept)(Content1, cont)(r1 , u1)...(rn , un) ,

where *concept* is the designation of the notion "negotiation record" or "contract", *cont* is a K-representation of a document, r_1, ..., r_n are the designa-tions of the external characteristics of a document (expressing its metadata, for instance, the data about the authors, date, language, etc.), and u_1, ..., u_n are the strings interpreted as the designations of the data associated with a document.

The additional useful properties of SK-languages from the standpoint of building SRs of contracts and records of negotiations are the possibilities (a) to explicitly indicate thematic roles (or conceptual cases, or semantic cases) in the structure of SRs of NL-texts, (b) to reflect the meanings of the phrases with direct and indirect speech, with the word "a concept", (c) to consider the functions with the arguments and/or values being the sets of objects or concepts (Suppliers, Staff, etc.).

The author of this paper carried out a comparative analysis of the expressive possibilities of SK-languages and of the natural language phenomena reflected in the structure of commercial contracts and the records of negotiations. A number of the results of this analysis is set forth above. The fulfilled analysis allows for formulating the assumption that the expressive possibilities of SK-languages are sufficient for building with their help the formal representations of contracts and records of commercial negotiations.

On the other hand, the expressive possibilities of another known approaches to formally representing the contents of NL-texts are insufficient for building semantic representations of arbitrary contracts and records of negotiations. In particular, it applies to first-order logic, Discourse Representation Theory, Theory of Conceptual Graphs, and Episodic Logic.

The advantages of the theory of SK-languages in comparison with first-order logic, Discourse Representation Theory (DRT) [3] and Episodic Logic (EL) [5] are, in particular, the possibilities: (1) to distinguish in a formal way objects (physical things, events, etc.) and concepts qualifying these objects; (2) to build compound representations of concepts; (3) to distinguish in a formal manner objects and sets of objects, concepts and sets of concepts; (4) to build complicated representations of sets, sets of sets, etc.; (5) to describe set-theoretical relationships; (6) to effectively describe structured meanings (SMs) of discourses with references to the meanings of phrases and larger parts of discourses; (7) to describe SMs of sentences with the words "concept", "notion"; (8) to describe SMs of sentences where the logical connective "and" or "or" joins not the expressions-assertions but designations of things, sets, or concepts; (9) to build complicated designations of objects and sets; (10) to consider non-traditional functions with arguments or/and values being sets of objects, of concepts, of texts' semantic representations, etc.; (11) to construct formal analogues of the meanings of infinitives with dependent words and, as a consequence, to represent proposals, goals, obligations, commitments.

The items (3) – (8), (10), (11) indicate the principal advantages of the theory of SK-languages in comparison with the Theory of Conceptual Graphs (TCG) [4]. Besides, the expressive possibilities of the new theory are much higher than the possibilities of TCG as concerns the items (1), (2), (9). In particular, TCG doesn't allow for building an analogue of the constructed above semantic description of a set consisting of 12 single rooms in the three-star hotels of Vienna and doesn't possess the Property 7.

Thus, the theory of SK-languages opens new prospects of building formal representations of contracts and records of commercial negotiations.

Besides, it follows from the fulfilled study that SK-languages provide a unique spectrum of possibilities for representing the results of semantic-syntactic analysis by linguistic processors of the discourses being contracts or the records of commercial negotiations. Additional information on this subject can be found, in particular, in [9, 14-16].

It is stressed in [1] that it is particular interesting for e-commerce that one format can be used both for electronic messages (to be processed by computers) and for human interfaces. A many-year experience of using SK-languages for the design of NL-interfaces reflected, in particular, in [14-16], shows that SK-languages possess this precious feature.

One of other possible applications of the new formal theory in E-commerce can be the elaboration of feedback languages for knowledge acquisition computer intelligent agents, i.e. the use of SK-languages for representing in a formal (but readable for the end users) way the meanings of NL descriptions of knowledge fragments inputted into computer by the end user.

4   Conclusions

The paper grounds the possibility of using the theory of SK-languages for reflecting the contents of the records of commercial negotiations conducted by computer intelligent agents (CIAs) and for building the contracts concluded by CIAs. In fact, the elaboration of the definition of the class of SK-languages means that a class of formal languages is determined being convenient for building semantic descriptions of arbitrary goods, services, and contracts. It seems that now the theory of SK-languages is the only formal theory allowing for constructing semantic analogues of arbitrary complicated goals and, as a consequence, of offers, promises, commitments. That is why its potential of developing general-purpose formal languages of business communication exceeds the potential of first-order logic, DRT, TCG, and EL.

References

1. Hasselbring, W., Weigand, H.: Languages for Electronic Business Communication: State of the Art. Industrial Management and Data Systems, 101 (2001) 217-226
2. Kimbrough, S.O., Moore, S.A.: On Automated Message Processing in E-Commerce and Work Support Systems: Speech Act Theory and Expressive Felicity. ACM Transactions on Information Theory, 15 (1997) 321-367
3. Kamp, H., Reyle, U.: A Calculus for First Order Discourse Representation Structures. Journal for Logic, Language and Information (JOLLI), 5 (1996) 297-348.
4. Sowa, J.F.: Knowledge Representation: Logical, Philosophical, and Computational Foundations. Pacific Grove, CA: Brooks/Cole (2000) 594 pp.
5. Schubert, L.K., Hwang, C.H.: Episodic Logic Meets Little Red Riding Hood: A Comprehensive, Natural Representation for Language Understanding. In: Iwanska, L., Shapiro, S.C (eds.): Natural Language Processing and Knowledge Representation: Language for Knowledge and Knowledge for Language. MIT/AAAI Press, Menlo Park, CA, and Cambridge, MA (2000) 111-174
6. Fomichov, V.A.: A Mathematical Model for Describing Structured Items of Conceptual Level. Informatica An Intern. J. of Computing and Informatics (Slovenia) 20 (1996) 5-32
7. Fomichov, V.A.: Mathematical Foundations of Representing Meanings of Texts for the Elaboration of Linguistic Informational Technologies. Part 1. A Model of the System of Primary Units of Conceptual Level. Informational Technologies (2002), No. 10, 16-25 (in Russian)

8. Fomichov, V.A.: Mathematical Foundations of Representing Meanings of Texts for the Elaboration of Linguistic Informational Technologies. Part 2. A System of the Rules for Building Semantic Representations of Phrases and Complicated Discourses. Informational Technologies (2002) No. 11, 34-45 (in Russian)

9. Fomichov, V.A.: Theory of K-calculuses as a Powerful and Flexible Mathematical Framework for Building Ontologies and Designing Natural Language Processing Systems. In: Andreasen, T., Motro, A., Christiansen, H., Larsen, H.L. (Eds.), Flexible Query Answering Systems. 5th International Conference, FQAS 2002, Copenhagen, Denmark, October 27 - 29, 2002. Proceedings; LNAI 2522 (Lecture Notes in Artificial Intelligence, Vol. 2522), Springer Verlag (2002) 183-196

10. Fomichov, V.A.: Theory of Restricted K-calculuses as a Comprehensive Framework for Constructing Agent Communication Languages. In: Fomichov, V.A., Zeleznikar, A.P. (eds.): Special Issue on NLP and Multi-Agent Systems. Informatica. An Intern. J. of Computing and Informatics (Slovenia), 22 (1998) 451-463

11. Fomichov, V.A.: An Ontological Mathematical Framework for Electronic Commerce and Semantically-structured Web. In: Zhang, Y., Fomichov, V.A., Zeleznikar, A.P. (eds.): Special Issue on Database, Web, and Cooperative Systems. Informatica (Slovenia), 24 (2000) 39-49

12. CrossFlow Project. Insurance Requirements. CrossFlow Consortium, 1999; http://www.crossflow.org/public/pubdel/D1b.pdf.

13. Xu, L., Jeusfeld, M.A.: A Concept for Monitoring of Electronic Contracts. Tilburg University, The Netherlands, 2003 (http://infolab.uvt.nl/research/itrs/itrs010.pdf). 19 p.

14. Fomichov, V.A.: K-calculuses and K-languages as Powerful Formal Means to Design Intelligent Systems Processing Medical Texts. Cybernetica (Belgium), XXXVI (1993) 161-182

15. Fomichov, V.A.: Integral Formal Semantics and the Design of Legal Full-Text Databases. Cybernetica (Belgium), XXXVII (1994), 145-177

16. Fomichov, V.A.: The Method of Constructing the Linguistic Processor of the Animation System AVIAROBOT. In: Pohl, J. (ed.): Proceedings of the Focus Symposium on Collaborative Decision-Support Systems; InterSymp-2002, the 14th International Conference on Systems Research, Informatics and Cybernetics, July 29 – August 3, 2002, Baden-Baden, Germany. CAD Research Center, Cal Poly, San Luis Obispo, CA, USA (2002) 91 – 102

Automated Negotiation Based on Contract Net and Petri Net

Fu-Shiung Hsieh

Department of Computer Science and Information Engineering,
Da-Yeh University,
Taiwan, R.O.C.
apistech@ms14.hinet.net

Abstract. In agent-mediated electronic markets, an agent may delegate part of the assigned tasks to other agents to achieve the business objectives via establishment of contracts. Electronic contracting relies on an effective model to automate the negotiation processes and analyze the feasibility of the resulting contracts. In this paper, we concentrated on automated negotiation mechanism in contract manufacturing supply chains. Contract manufacturing has been widely accepted in many industries. Time and cost are two significant factors to be negotiated in contract manufacturing. Formation of contract manufacturing supply chain networks is based on the contract orders and tends to be more dynamic than ever to accommodate the fast changing innovative technologies, products and customers' preference. Optimization of such contract manufacturing supply chain networks usually relies on coordination among the trading partners and is much more difficult than traditional production networks. The objectives of this paper are to propose a framework to model the negotiation processes in contract manufacturing, analyze the feasibility of the contracts and optimize contract awarding based on the proposed model.

1 Introduction

Agent-mediated electronic markets have been a growing area in intelligent agent research and development in the last decade [1]-[6]. A lot of agent-mediated electronic commerce systems have been developed based on intelligent agent technologies [7]-[8]. In agent-mediated electronic markets, an agent may delegate part of the assigned tasks to other agents to achieve the business objectives via establishment of contracts. Electronic contracting is a hot research topic in agent-mediated electronic markets. A contract is an agreement between two or more parties to create mutual business relations or legal obligations. A contract defines a set of activities to be performed by different parties satisfying a set of terms and conditions. Electronic contract (e-contract) is a contract modeled, specified, executed and enacted (controlled and monitored) by a software system (such as a workflow system) [9]. The issues of electronic contracting include collaborative contract drafting, automated contract negotiation with trading partners, modeling of contracts, contract monitoring and execution. In existing literature, some of the above research issues have been studied. For example, in [10] the author concentrates on the representation of the legal relations obtained between parties once they have entered a contractual agreement and

K. Bauknecht et al. (Eds.): EC-Web 2005, LNCS 3590, pp. 148–157, 2005.
© Springer-Verlag Berlin Heidelberg 2005

their evolution as the agreement progresses through time. Contracts are regarded as process and they are analyzed in terms of the obligations that are active at various points during their life span. In [11], the authors presented a prototype system for supporting contract-based problem solving based on the Workflow-Contract-Solution model (WCS model) [12]. In [13], the authors presented a solution for designing and implementing a contract monitoring facility as part of a larger cross-organizational contract management architecture. In [14], Milosevic et al. attempted to identify the scope for automated management of e-contracts, including contract drafting, negotiation and monitoring. Despite the above studies on electronic contracting, there is still a lack of research on electronic contracting in the context of contract manufacturing. Contract manufacturing has been widely accepted in many industries. Formation of contract manufacturing supply chain networks is based on the contract orders and tends to be more dynamic than ever to accommodate the fast changing innovative technologies, products and customers' preference. Optimization of such contract manufacturing supply chain networks usually relies on coordination [15]-[17] among the trading partners and is much more difficult than traditional production networks. The objectives of this paper are to propose a framework to model the negotiation processes in contract manufacturing, analyze the feasibility of the contracts and optimize contract awarding based on the proposed model.

Multi-agent system (MAS) theories [18]-[19] are suitable for modeling and analysis of contract manufacturing systems in agent-mediated electronic markets. In MAS, contract net protocol [20] is a distributed task distribution and resource allocation mechanism for multi-agent systems based on a negotiation process involving a mutual selection by both contractee and contractor. Although contract net was originally proposed as a negotiation protocol to distribute tasks and allocate resources in multi-agent systems, it can be tailored to automate electronic contract negotiation among multiple parties. However, as contract net only specifies a framework for problem solving, care should be taken to evaluate the bids from the bidders. The lack of a formal model in contract net makes it hard to analyze the feasibility and performance of the resulting contracts. To analyze the feasibility of contracts, a mathematical model is required to describe the requirements of the task to be accomplished by the manager. The model should be able to fully capture the task requirements, including the workflow to describe the precedence constraints among the operations in the task, resource requirements, time constraints and costs. In existing literature, Petri net has been demonstrated as an effective tool for modeling of complex processes. A promising approach to model and analyze contract net is based on Petri net theory. In [21], we have proposed a Petri net model to analyze contract net. In this paper, we will extend the results presented in [21] to complex processes. To model the interactions between the bidders and the managers in contract net, we first proposed Petri nets to model the state transition of the bidder and the manager. We then proposed Petri net models to automate the processes of request for tender, evaluation of contracts and awarding of contracts. We used Petri nets to model the task workflow. Based on this task workflow, we proposed Petri net models for request for tender, evaluation of contracts and awarding of contracts. By combining the modeling and analysis capability of Petri nets with the robust contract net protocol, the negotiation results can be analyzed before execution. Our framework offers a foundation to support the automated negotiation mechanism based on the contract net protocol.

The remainder of this paper is organized as follows. In Section 2, we proposed the Petri net to model the state transition of contract net protocol. In Section 3, we proposed a Petri net model based on the task workflow to facilitate request for tender in contract net. We then proposed a Petri net model for evaluating and awarding contracts in Section 4. Finally, we concluded this paper.

2   Contract Net Protocol for Electronic Negotiation

In contract net protocol, there are two types of agents, managers and bidders, that interact with one another to find a solution for a problem through negotiation processes. The four-stage negotiation processes in contract net protocol are similar to those in electronic contracting. Step1: Request for tender: The manager announces a task to all potential bidders. Step2: Submission of proposals: On receiving the tender announcement, bidders capable of performing the task draw up proposals and submit to the manager. Step3: Awarding of contract: On receiving and evaluating the submitted proposal, the manager awards the contract to the best bidder. Step4: Establishment of contract: If the awarded bidder commits itself to carry out the required task, it will send a message to the manager and become a contractor. Otherwise, the awarded bidder might refuse to accept the contract by notifying the manager. The manager will reevaluate the bids and award the contract(s) to another bidder(s). Figure 1 (a) illustrates a scenario where a manager negotiates with N bidders to process a task w with time and cost constraints. We use d_w to denote the due date and c_w to denote the maximum cost of task w, respectively. We assume that the task consists of a set of inter-dependent operations and it takes time and costs to perform each operation. We also assume that only the manager has the full knowledge of the workflow W of the task w. The objectives of this paper are to propose a framework to automate the execution of contract net and optimize the awarding of contracts based on Petri net model. To achieve these objectives, we proposed Petri net models to capture the interactions between a manager and the bidders, a Petri net model to generate request for tender messages, a Petri net model for evaluating the submitted proposals and a Petri net model to award contracts.

We adopt Petri net to model the negotiation process. The advantages of applying Petri nets formalism can be summarized as follows. First of all, the graphical nature of Petri nets can visualize sequences of transition firing via token passing over the net. Second, Petri nets have well-established formal mechanisms for modeling and property checking of systems with concurrent, synchronous and/or asynchronous structures. Third, the mathematical foundation of Petri nets can analyze structural and dynamic behaviors of a system. These advantages make Petri nets a suitable modeling and analysis tool to model contract net negotiation processes.

A Petri Net (PN) G is a five-tuple $G = (P, T, I, O, m_0)$, where P is a finite set of places with cardinality $|P|$, T is a finite set of transitions, $I : P \times T \to \{0,1\}$ is the input function that specifies input places of transitions, $O : P \times T \to \{0,1\}$ is the output function that specifies output places of transitions, and $m_0 : P \to Z^{|P|}$ is the initial marking of the PN with Z as the set of nonnegative integers. The marking of G is a vector $m \in Z^{|P|}$ that indicates the number of tokens in each place and is a state of the system. In Petri Net theory, $^\bullet t$ denotes the set of input places of transition t and $t^\bullet$ denotes the set of output places of transition t. A transition t is enabled and can be fired under a marking m if and only if $m(p) \geq I(p,t)\ \forall p \in\ ^\bullet t$. Firing a transition removes one token from each of its input places and adds one token to each of its output places. A marking m' is reachable from m iff there exists a firing sequence s of transitions from m to m'. Reader may refer to [22] for a tutorial on Petri nets.

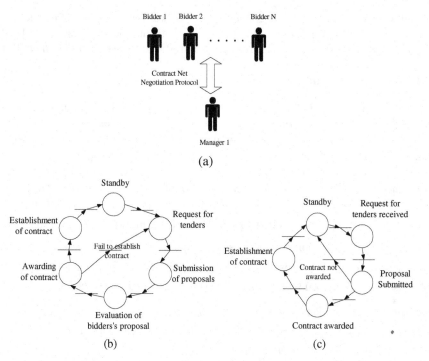

Fig. 1. (a) Contract Net Negotiation, (b) State Transition of a Manager, (c) State Transition of a Bidder.

A formal model of the contract net protocol consists of two parts: a manager's Petri net and a bidder's Petri net to describe the state transition of the manager and the bidder. A manager's Petri net model is depicted in Figure 1 (b) while a bidder's Petri net is depicted in Figure 1(c). Remark that the Petri net models in Figure 1 (b) and (c) only describes the state transition in the execution of contract net protocol. Although the Petri nets enjoy the liveness properties, which implies the contract net protocol can be executed infinitely many times, it does not imply the established contracts are feasible or guarantee the task can be completed by executing the established contracts. A set of contracts is said to be feasible if all the operations in the given task can be completed by executing the contracts. On the contrary, if a set of contracts cannot grant sufficient resources required for performing all the operations in a given task, the set of contracts is infeasible. Even if there are sufficient resources to complete a task, a set of contracts may also be infeasible if the time constraint cannot be met. Remark that the outcomes of the contract net negotiation processes are not represented in the state transition models. Therefore, the state transition models cannot be used to analyze the feasibility of the contracts. To analyze the feasibility of contracts, we proposed several Petri nets based on the task workflow.

3   Automatic Request for Tender Based on Workflow Petri Nets

To automate the contract net negotiation process, we first proposed a Petri net model to facilitate the request for tender process. The Petri net model is based on the Petri net workflow model of a task. Therefore, we introduce the task workflow model first.

3.1 Petri Net Workflow

A task w is executed by performing a set of operations. The set of operations in task w satisfies the precedence constraints. To perform an operation, a number of different types of resources may be required. The manager of task w must assign the required operations to the proper bidder with the required resources to perform the operations. To model a task w in Petri net, we use a transition to represent an operation whereas a place to represent a state. The set of transitions and the set of places in a task w are represented by T_w and P_w, respectively. Each transition $t \in T_w$ has only one input place and only one output place. The firing time of each transition $t \in T_w$ is characterized by a mapping f_w. We use p_w^f to denote the final state of task w. Assume that there is no job in process under initial marking m_{w0}. The precedence constraints of a task w are described by a connected acyclic Petri net as follows.

Definition 3.1: The Petri net $W = (P_w, T_w, I_w, O_w, m_{w0}, f_w)$ of task w is a connected acyclic Petri net and there is at least one directed path from each transition t to p_w^f $\forall t \in T_w$, where $m_{w0}(p) = 0$ $\forall p \in P_w$.

Figure 2(a) illustrates a Petri Net workflow model.

Let P_w^{in} denote the subset of places in P_w without input transitions and let P_w^{out} denote the subset of places in P_w without output transitions. A token in place $p_i \in P_w^{in}$ represents an established contract with the corresponding bidder. The Petri net W only models the workflow of a task. To represent the event to establish a contract associated with place $p_i \in P_w^{in}$, we augment W with a transition t_i^c by adding a directed arc from t_i^c to p_i. The set of all contracts the bidders establish with the manager are denoted by $T_w^c = \{t_i^c\}$. We use t_w^f to denote the operation that consumes the completed task. The augmented Petri net is denoted by W^c. Figure 2(b) illustrates the augmented Petri net corresponding to Figure 2(a). In Figure 2(b), $P_w^{in} = \{p_1, p_2, p_3, p_4, p_5\}$, $P_w^{out} = \{p_{14}\}$, $T_w^c = \{t_1^c, t_2^c, t_3^c, t_4^c, t_5^c\}$ and $t_w^f = t_{11}$.

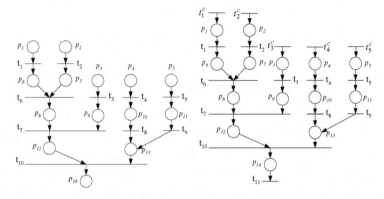

Fig. 2. (a) Petri Net Workflow W , (b) Representation of Contracts by a Petri Net W^c .

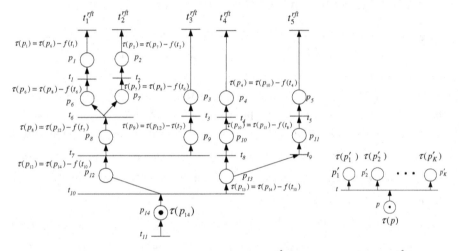

Fig. 3. (a) The token value for each place in W^{rft} , (b) A transition t in W^{rft} .

3.2 Due Date Calculation

To facilitate the calculation of the due date for each subtask in W , we proposed a request for tender Petri net model W^{rft} . The Petri net model W^{rft} is constructed by reversing the direction of each directed arc in the Petri net workflow model W^c , rename t_i^c with t_i^{rft} for each $t_i^c \in T_w^c$ and rename t_w^f with t_w^{rft} , where t_w^{rft} denotes the event that starts the "request for tender" process and t_i^{rft} denotes the event that issues a "request for tender" message for place p_i . The request for tender Petri net model W^{rft} corresponding to the workflow model W^c in Figure 2(b) is shown in Figure 3(a). A request for tender message consists of the due date for each subtask in task w . The due date for each subtask in task w can be calculated by firing each transition in W^{rft} once, starting with t_w^{rft}. Each token generated in W^{rft} is assigned a token values $\tau(p)$, where p denotes the place where the token resides. To compute the due date for each subtask in w, we fire each transition in W^{rft} once. Let t be a transition in W^{rft} with ${}^\bullet t = \{ p \}$ and $t^\bullet = \{ p_1', p_2', ..., p_K' \}$ as shown in Figure 3(b). Once transition t is fired, the token value $\tau(p)$ is updated as follows: $\tau(p_k') = \tau(p) - f(t)$. For the example in Figure 3(a), transition t_{11} is fired first. A token with token value $\tau(p_{14})$ is brought to place p_{14}. The token in place p_{14} enables transition t_{10}. By firing t_{10}, one token is generated in place p_{12} while the other token is generated in p_{13}. The token values in place p_{12} and place p_{13} are updated as follows: $\tau(p_{12}) = \tau(p_{14}) - f(t_{10})$, $\tau(p_{13}) = \tau(p_{14}) - f(t_{10})$. The tokens in places p_{12} and p_{13} enable transition t_7 and t_8 or t_9.

4 Petri Net Model for Evaluating and Awarding Contracts

After receiving the request for tender messages, the potential bidders submit their bids. We use a transition t_i^{sop} to represent the arrival of a submitted proposal for associated with place p_i. Let $T_w^a = \{ t_i^{sop} \}$ denote the set of all such transitions. Note that W only models a task workflow. The proposals submitted by the bidders are not represented in W. To evaluate the proposals submitted by the bidders, we augment the workflow model W with the set T_w^a of transitions to facilitate the contract awarding decisions. The augmented Petri net model W^a is constructed by adding the input transition t_i^{sop} to place p_i. The resulting augmented Petri net is defined as follows.

Definition 4.1: The Petri net $W^a = (P_w, T_w \cup T_w^a, I_w^a, O_w^a, m_{w0}, \tau_w, c_w)$.

To evaluate the proposals submitted by the bidders, each transition in W^a is fired exactly once. Firing transition t_i^{sop} generates a token in place p_i. The token carries a token value $c(t_i^{sop})$ that denotes the cost of the submitted proposal. We calculate the cost for each token generated in each place by firing each transition exactly once. The token value for a token in place p is calculated by finding the cost to fire each of its input transitions first and then taking the minimum to minimize the costs. Let p be a place in W^a. Suppose ${}^\bullet p = \{ t_1, t_2, ..., t_J \}$. Let ${}^\bullet t_j = \{ p_1^j, p_2^j, p_3^j, ..., p_{K_j}^j \}$ and $t_j^\bullet = \{ p \}$. The token value $c(p)$ is updated by $c(p) = \min\limits_{j \in \{1,2,...,J\}} \sum\limits_{k \in \{1,2,3,...,K\}} c(p_k^j) + c(t_j)$.

The set of submitted proposals is feasible if $c(p_w^f) \le$ the maximum allowed cost c_w. To optimize contract awarding, the subnet corresponding to non-minimal cost proposal(s) should be removed from W^a. Consider Figure 4(a). Suppose $c(t_{10}) + c(t_8) > c(t_{11}) + c(t_9)$. Then the subnet consisting of t_4^{sop}, p_4, t_4, p_{10} and t_8 should be removed from W^a. The resulting Petri net is shown in Figure 4(b).

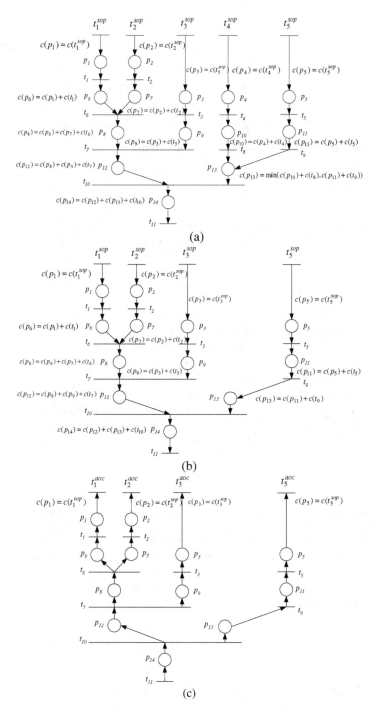

Fig. 4. (a) Petri Net Model W^a for Evaluating Contracts, (b) $W^{a'}$ is obtained by removing non-minimal cost proposal from W^a, (c) Petri Net Model W^{aoc} for Awarding Contracts.

Let $W^{a\,\prime}$ denote the Petri net by removing the non-minimal cost proposal(s) from W^a. To automate contract awarding, we construct a contract-awarding Petri net W^{aoc} by reversing the direction of each arc in $W^{a\,\prime}$ and replacing t_i^{sop} by t_i^{aoc}. Figure 4(c) shows the contract awarding Petri net corresponding to Figure 4(b). If $c(p_{14}) < c_w$, the contracts are awarded to the corresponding bidders. Contract awarding is conducted by firing each transition in W^{aoc} once starting from t_w^f. The bidder associated with t_i^{aoc} will be awarded the contract if t_i^{aoc} is fired.

5 Conclusion

Contract manufacturing has been widely adopted in many industries to form supply chain networks based on the contracts. A supply chain may involve tens to hundred of partners depending on the products to be produced. To improve the efficiency of contract negotiation, the negotiation processes needs to be automated. The feasibility of the resulting contracts should also be analyzed in the negotiation processes. Moreover, the contracts should also be optimized in the processes of contract negotiation to reduce the overall costs involved. To achieve these objectives, contract net is adopted as the underlying negotiation protocol. To capture the transition of states in the negotiation processes, we proposed Petri nets for contract net protocol, one for the manager and the other for each bidder. To automate the negotiation processes, we propose a Petri net for request for tender, a Petri net for evaluating contracts and a Petri net for awarding contracts. The Petri net for request for tender calculates the due date for each subtask required for a given task. The Petri net for evaluating contracts is used to access the feasibility of the contracts and optimizes the contracts. Our work provides a formal model to automate the negotiation processes.

References

1. A. Chavez, P. Maes, Kasbah: An agent marketplace for buying and selling goods, in: Proceedings of the first International Conference and Exhibition on The Practical Application of Intelligent Agents and Multi-Agents, pp. 75–90 (1996)
2. R.H. Guttman, A.G. Moukas, P. Maes, Agent-mediated electronic commerce: a survey, The Knowledge Engineering Review 13 (2) 147–159 (1998)
3. R.H. Guttman, P. Maes, Agent-mediated integrative negotiation for retail electronic commerce, in: Proceedings of the 2nd International Workshop on Cooperative Information Agents (CIA98) (1998)
4. J.A. Rodriguez, P. Noriega, C. Sierra, J. Padget, A Java-based electronic auction house, in: Proceedings of the 2nd International Conference on the Practical Application of Intelligent Agents and Multi-Agent Technology (PAAM97) (1997)
5. T. Sandholm, eMediator: A next generation electronic commerce server, in: Proceedings of the Sixteenth National Conference on Artificial Intelligence (AAAI99), AAAI Press, pp. 923–924 (1999)

6. P.R. Wurman, M.P. Wellman, W.E. Walsh, The Michigan Internet auctionbot: a configurable auction server for human and software agents, in: Proceedings of the 2nd International Conference on Autonomous Agents (Agents-98) (1998)

7. K. Sycara, Multiagent systems, AI Magazine 19 (2) pp.79–92 (1998)

8. E. Turban, J.E. Aronson, Decision Support Systems and Intelligent Systems, 5th Edition, Prentice-Hall International, Inc. (1998)

9. P. Radha Krishna, K. Karlapalem, D.K.W. Chiu, "An EREC framework for e-contract modeling, enactment and monitoring," Data & Knowledge Engineering vol. 51, pp. 31–58 (2004)

10. Aspassia Daskalopulu, "Modelling Legal Contracts as Processes," In Proceedings of the 11th International Workshop on Database and Expert Systems Applications (DEXA'00) (2000)

11. Mizuho Iwaihara, Haiying Jiang, Yahiko Kambayashi, "An Integrated System for Supporting Problem Solution in e-Contract Execution," Proceedings of the First International Workshop on Electronic Contracting (WEC'04) (2004)

12. M. Iwaihara, H. Jiang, and Y. Kambayashi, "An Integrated Model of Workflows, e-Contracts and Solution Implementation," Proc. ACM Symp. Applied Computing, Organizational Engineering Track, Nicosia, pp. 1390-1395, Mar. (2004)

13. Z. Milosevic, S. Gibson, P. F. Linington, J. Cole, S. Kulkarni,"On design and implementation of a contract monitoring facility," Proceedings of the First International Workshop on Electronic Contracting (WEC'04) (2004).

14. O. Marjanovic and Z. Milosevic, "Towards Formal Modelling of e-Contracts," In Fifth IEEE International Enterprise Distributed Object Computing Conference, Seattle, USA, September (2001)

15. Beck, J.C. & Fox, M.S. "Supply Chain Coordination via Mediated Constraint Relaxation" Proceedings of the First Canadian Workshop on Distributed Artificial Intelligence, Banff, AB, May 15 (1994)

16. M.Barbuceanu, and M.S.Fox, "Coordinating Multiple Agents in the Supply Chain," In: Proceedings of the Fifth Workshops on Enabling Technology for Collaborative Enterprises, WET ICE'96, *IEEE Computer Society Press*, pp. 134-141 (1996)

17. Fu-Shiung. Hsieh, "An Evolutionary Approach for Self-Organization of Contract Manufacturing Supply Chains", Proceedings of the 2001 IEEE International Conference on System, Man and Cybernetics, pp. 1058-1063, Tucson, Arizona, Oct. 7-10 (2001)

18. Nilsson N.J., *Artificial Intelligence*: A New Synthesis, Morgan Kaufmann Publishers, Inc. San Francisco, California. (1998)

19. Ferber J., Multi-Agent Systems, An Introduction to Distributed Artificial Intelligence, Addison Wesley (1999).

20. Smith R.G.: The Contract Net Protocol: High-Level Communication and Control in a Distributed Problem Solver, IEEE Trans. On Computers, vol. 29 pp.1104-1113 (1980)

21. Fu-Shiung Hsieh, "Modeling and Analysis of Contract Net Protocol", Lecture Notes in Computer Science, vol. 3140, p.p142-146 (2004)

22. Tadao Murata: Petri Nets: Properties, Analysis and Applications, Proceedings of the IEEE, vol. 77, no. 4, pp.541-580 (1989)

Linking the Balanced Scorecard to Business Models for Value-Based Strategic Management in e-Business

Chien-Chih Yu

National ChengChi University,
Taipei, Taiwan, ROC 11623
ccyu@mis.nccu.edu.tw

Abstract. Values have been noted as integral elements of an electronic business model (BM) while value creation has been considered as a central strategic task in e-business planning. It has also been suggested that performance measurement and strategic management should focus on the value creation process. In recent years, the balanced scorecard (BSC) has evolved to become a dominant strategic management mechanism and has been widely adopted in business sectors. However, a gap between BM and the BSC still hinders the usefulness and effectiveness of applying the BSC to the e-business domain. This paper aims at providing an integrated framework for linking the BSC to e-business models through identified values and strategies to facilitate strategic management activities. Value dimensions identified include market, supply chain, customer, enterprise, and product and service, and therefore the adapted value-based BSC framework contains market, supply chain, customer, as well as business structure and process as balanced perspectives.

1 Introduction

Due to the fast blooming of Internet and web-based applications, new business models (BM) have quickly emerged in the electronic commerce (EC) and electronic business (EB) environments. How to design and implement suitable e-business models has become a critical success factor for gaining business profitability and sustainability. Developing right EB strategies in correspondence with the business models is crucial for creating business values and is definitely a major challenge to the top management. In the literature, values have been circled as integral elements of e-business models while value proposition and value creation (VC) have been noted as central tasks in the EB strategic planning process [5,6,16,19,26]. The literature also points out that performance measurement (PM) is a prerequisite to strategic management (SM) and should focus on the value creation process [7,13]. In other words, without proper value creation and performance measurement, it would be difficult to adequately evaluate and control the effectiveness of EB strategies. It seems clear that BM, VC, PM, and SM are inter-related issues and thus require an ontology-based framework to constructively illustrate the integrated structure and cause-effect relationships of these key EB factors. Nevertheless, collected literature results related to the development of BM-oriented and value-based performance measurement systems for measuring EB strategies are still very limited. On the other hand, the balanced scorecard (BSC), introduced in 1992 by

K. Bauknecht et al. (Eds.): EC-Web 2005, LNCS 3590, pp. 158–167, 2005.

Kaplan and Norton, has evolved from a performance measurement tool to a strategic management mechanism and has been widely adopted in both the private and public sectors [8,9]. The BSC has been reported as the dominant concept in the business performance measurement field. It has also been considered as an effective method to link measurement with strategy as well as to translate values into metrics. It seems quite likely that the BSC could be an appropriate tool for successfully linking values, strategies, and performance measures. But still, how to adapt the BSC concept to fit the e-business model and subsequent value creation, strategic planning, and effectiveness evaluation processes remains as a less-touched issue waiting for further research exploration. This paper aims at providing a structured framework for linking the BSC to e-business models through value identification and strategy development. The goals are to enhance the usability and usefulness of the BSC method, as well as to achieve the efficiency and effectiveness of the performance measurement and strategic management activities in EB applications. Values from various aspects such as market, supply chain, enterprise, product and service, and customer views will be identified within a generic e-business model. Corresponding value-based EB strategies and performance measures will be developed and described based on an adapted value-based BSC framework that consists of four aligned perspectives, namely, market, supply chain, business structure and process, and customer. In the following sections, a brief review regarding related research issues and methodologies will be provided in section 2. In section 3, an e-business model framework will be proposed with identified value dimensions. A modified BSC in which identified values, strategies, and associated performance indicators in all four perspectives will be presented in section 4, followed by a conclusion in the final section.

2   Literature Review

In this section, previous research works related to business models, value creation, and strategic planning issues, as well as the concept and application of the BSC are briefly described.

2.1   Business Models, Value Creation, and Strategic Management

A business model is often defined as an architecture for the product, service and information flows, including business actors, potential benefits, and sources of revenues, or as a method for managing resources to provide better customer values and make money [1,21]. Earlier research on the BM issue focuses on model type classification. For example, relationship-oriented BM types are business-to-consumer (B2C), business-to-business (B2B), and consumer-to-consumer (C2C), and market-oriented BM types include e-shop, e-mall, e-procurement, e-marketplace, e-auction, e-broker, virtual communities, value chain integrator, and trust service provider etc [21,25]. Since then, different researchers used different classification schemes and presented a variety of BM types. In recent years, one quickly emerging research stream of BM is to develop a component structure or ontology-based framework for explicitly representing structured BM constructs with their causality relationships. Among this category of research, Afuah and Tucci (2001) present a BM component structure that is composed of value, scope, revenue sources, price, connected activities, implementation, capabilities, sustainability, as well as linkages and dynamics [1]. Yu (2001) propose an integrated BM framework that consists of markets, customers, competitors, products and services, assets and costs structures, promotion and distribution, pricing and billing methods, revenues and profits sources, marketing strategies and competitive advantages, market shares and economic scales etc as major model components [25]. Osterwalder and Pigneur (2003) present an e-business model ontology that includes four model elements, i.e. production innovation, customer relationship, infrastructure management, and financials [16].

In addition to the BM issues, research topics with respect to proposition, creation, assessment, and management of values in the EB domain have also increasingly attracted attentions. As mentioned, value is recognized as a major component of the BM and also a measurement construct of the BM effectiveness. In the literature, value proposition and creation issues have been addressed from various perspectives including business value, customer value, supplier value, and relationship value such as buyer-seller value or manufacturer-supplier value. Other types of values classified include product value, process value, shareholder value, supply chain value, and information technology (IT)/information system (IS) values etc [3,4,5,11,14,19,22]. Frequently, business values have been measured by financial profits involving cost reduction and market revenues, whereas they have also been considered as non-monetary benefits such as brand awareness, competitive gains, social relationships, and management capabilities. Kirchhoff et al. (2001) suggest a group of strategy-based value metrics for measuring and managing the R&D portfolio to create shareholder values in the communication industry. In their value creation model, two quantitative metrics are portfolio value and risks, while four qualitative categories include strategic initiatives, market categories, intellectual property classes, and business units designations [11]. Walter et al. (2001) indicate profit, volume, safeguard, innovation, resource-access, scout, and market-signaling as the direct and indirect value functions in a buyer-supplier relationship [24]. Ulaga (2003) points out eight dimensions of value creation in manufacturer-supplier relationships, namely, product quality, service support, delivery, supplier know-how, time-to-market, personal interaction, direct product costs, and process costs [22]. Yu (2004) identifies five value types including market value, supply chain value, enterprise value, product and service value, and customer value from an e-business model framework [26]. He also specifies a set of associated value-based EB strategies including market strategy, supply chain/value chain strategy, organization strategy, product and service strategy, and customer strategy. It has been realized from the recent literature that value proposition and creation are central strategic tasks in EB planning and management, and have a strong relation to the business model constructs. Therefore, a strategic framework for identifying and assessing EB values from an integrated BM perspective is needed to direct the development of effective EB strategies, as well as to facilitate the measurement and management of strategy performances.

2.2 The Balanced Scorecard

As mentioned in the previous section, the BSC is a management instrument to measure business performance from four perspectives, namely, the financial, the internal process, the customer, and the learning and growth perspectives [8]. From these perspectives, visions and strategic objectives are defined, and measurement metrics and performance indicators are specified. The basic intent of the BSC is to maintain a balanced view of performance measurement between financial and non-financial measures, between performance outcomes (lagging indicators) and performance drivers (leading indicators), between internal and external perspectives, as well as between short-term and long-term objectives. For the past decade, the concept and model of the BSC has been adopted to a variety of business and public domains such as information and communication industries, as well as governments and libraries to facilitate organizational strategic management [2,10,13,15,17,18,23]. Among the enormous amount of previous BSC researches, Martinsons et al. (1999) propose a framework for evaluating IT and IS activities based on the BSC concept [13]. In the BSC-for-IS framework, four aligned perspectives include user orientation, business value, internal processes, and future readiness. They reinforce the need and benefit of a standard BSC-IS framework due to the fact that the specifics of a BSC for IS differ from company to company. Hasan and Tibbits (2000) take into account the BSC-IS approach presented by Martinsons et al. and modified the BSC model to fit the strategic management of EC [7]. Their resulting four EC scorecard perspectives are value of the business, relationships, internal process and structures, and human and intellectual capital. They argue that for applying the BSC to the EC strategic management, there is a need to constructively adapt and enhance the original BSC to suit the emerging EC business models. van Grembergen and Amelinckx (2002) present a generic e-business BSC for measuring and managing EB projects [23]. Four perspectives taken by the proposed EB-BSC include customer orientation, operational excellence, business contribution, and future orientation. Furthermore, they indicate that the operational excellence and the future orientation measures act as enablers of respectively the business contribution and the customer orientation goals. Terano and Naitoh (2004), in their work of agent-based modeling of investment decisions in a television set market, adopt the BSC principle to value proposition strategies for customers [20]. Four selected value-associated strategic objectives are benefit, market share, cash flow, and borrowing. Seven attributes of the value proposition used in their experiment process include price, quality, time, function, services, relationship, and brand image. Ritter (2003), in his study of applying the BSC to corporate communications, emphasizes the importance of identifying key success factors to meet the company's strategic objectives [17]. He argues that a company's business models can be defined during the creation process of the BSC as long as the key success factors are organized according to the four BSC perspectives and the cause-and-effect relations are set among these factors. In a citation analysis conducted by Marr and Schiuma (2003), the BSC is the most influential concept in the business performance measurement field, besides that, about 60% of Fortune 1000 companies have experimented with the BSC in recent years [12]. Nevertheless, they also report that there is a significant lack of theoretical foundation as well as body of knowledge in the research areas of the BSC and business performance measurement.

Summarizing findings from the research literature, it becomes clear that (1) the business model is considered as the foundation of value creation and strategic management, (2) value should be addressed as an integral part of the business model, and value creation should be placed as a central strategic task, (3) performance measurement and strategic management should focus on the value creation process, (4) the BSC is a dominant method that translates values into metrics for facilitating performance measurement and strategic management, (5) the BSC must be adapted and enhanced to suit the business models emerged in the EC and EB domains, as well as to support organizations in taking advantages from extracted values, (6) previous research efforts related to BM, VC, PM, SM, and the BSC methods take inconsistent views and produce diversified outcomes, and (7) the literature provides no integrated framework for guiding the entire process of building e-business models, identifying and creating values, planning and managing strategies, as well as measuring and controlling performances.

Although there seems to exist strong linkages between the BM and the BSC through value creation and strategic management, it has never been sufficiently explored and explicitly discussed yet. As a result, the need of an integrated framework for structurally representing e-business models, values, strategies, and performance measures, as well as for linking values, strategies, and metrics to the BSC perspectives is significant. We believe that using the generic BM as the foundation for adapting the BSC and implementing the adapted BSC as the measurement and control system of the BM associated values and strategies, efficiency and effectiveness of developing and using both the BM and BSC can be assured, in addition, the expected values and strategy performances can be attained.

3 The BM-Based BSC Framework

To fill the literature gap by developing a BM-based BSC framework, we first adapt Yu's integrated framework of e-business models as the foundation for building the BSC [25,26]. The e-business model framework with value dimensions and associated model components is illustrated in Figure 1. Five identified value dimensions are market, supply chain, enterprise, product and service, and customer. Products and services are main value objects to be exchanged in the market between business companies and their customers, and are developed, sold, and distributed with the

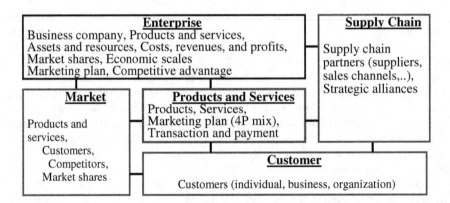

Fig. 1. A business model with value dimensions

support of the supply chain. Proposing product and service values to customers for capturing customer values can eventually create internal business values and external market values. With the creating and sharing of supply chain values, profit and value gains associated with all participants in the entire value chain can be assured. Consequently, a company's EB strategies should focus on market, supply chain, and customer strategies, and enterprise-level strategies regarding organization structure, business processes, as well as product and service design and marketing. Therefore, to facilitate the strategic management based on the value-oriented BM framework, we specify market, supply chain, customer, and business structure and process as the four aligned BSC strategic perspectives. Key model components, values, strategies, and performance indicators within each BSC perspective are described below.

3.1 The Market Perspective

Markets are trading environments for buyers and sellers to make transactions and exchange values. Markets can be classified in terms of scope, customer types, transaction functions and processes, and product and service categories. Markets provide opportunities for business to make profits but also fill with risks to loss. The mission in this aspect is to create market value and deliver value to shareholders. Market values refer to the external view of business values that is perceived by the market and stakeholders. Market values are created when a company properly allocates assets and resources to targeted markets, provides value-added products and services to meet customers' needs, creates competitive advantages to make profits, and leverages market capitalization to deliver shareholder values and sustain business continuity. Objectives of the value-based market strategy are to clarify success factors of market selection and segmentation, to identify market opportunities and risks, and to specify goals on market shares, profit gains, and other market values. Value metrics and performance indicators of the market strategy include level of market competitiveness, market revenues and profits, market share, market capitalization, market-oriented return on investment, earning per share, and their increasing rates.

3.2 The Supply Chain Perspective

Supply chain partners and strategy alliances are market players that include direct and indirect materials suppliers, sales channel and marketplace providers, distribution and delivery services providers, as well as payment and related financial services providers. Supply chain partners and strategic alliances coordinate closely in production and transaction cycles to gain values of operational efficiency and effectiveness in terms of cost and time reductions and profit gains. The mission in this perspective is to create and share supply chain-related information and values through established network relationships. Supply chain values are created from sharing market, customer, and production information, as well as integrating production, selling, payment, and distribution cycles.

Objectives of the supply chain/value chain strategy are to direct the partner selection and supply chain establishment and management processes, as well as to develop information and value sharing policies. Value metrics and performance indicators of the supply chain strategy include cost and time reductions in information, production and transaction processing, time reduction in response to market demand and integration of production and distribution cycles, revenue and profit increases for all supply chain participants, as well as the level of customer satisfaction with respect to time and location conveniences attained from the supply chain.

3.3 The Customer Perspective

Customers are buyers of products and services in the markets and can be categorized into individual, business, organization, or community types. The mission of the EB company with respect to the customer perspective is to create customer values and gain customer shares by satisfying their needs with better quality levels than competitors. Customer value is generally defined as the trade-off between costs and benefits in the market exchange process of products and services. Focusing on customer's perception, customer values can be interpreted as the product and process values that are proposed to the customers to activate actual buying transactions with lower costs and higher satisfaction. From the business viewpoint, customer values refer to the benefits derived from business efforts in attracting and retaining customers, as well as managing and utilizing customer relationships.

Strategic objectives of the value-based customer strategy include specifying customer clustering and classification rules, enforcing personalization and customization products and services, as well as generating customer shares and values from business process improvement and customer relationship management. Value metrics and performance indicators related to customer strategy include number of registered customers, customer profitability levels (current and future profit gains), customer shares, customer satisfaction levels, and associated increasing rates.

3.4 The Business Structure and Process Perspective

The business structure and process refer to the organizational structure, product and service classes, IT/IS infrastructure, as well as internal and business operating processes that are established by the EB companies for conducting business in the targeted markets. Business companies are providers/sellers of products and services to customers in specific markets. They set up and execute EB operations by allocating budgets and human resources, developing and delivering products and services, designing and implementing enterprise information systems and EB web sites, establishing supply chain and strategic alliances, planning and launching marketing mixed actions, as well as handling security transactions and payments. The mission in this perspective is to create business values including product and service values and process values for sustaining competitive advantages and continuous business operations. Enterprise-oriented business values refer to organization capabilities, resources, and deliveries to sustain business, create excellence, and capture opportunities. Business values reside in assets, human resources, organization culture and structure, IT/IS infrastructure, domain knowledge and intellectual property, brand name and publicity, as well as organizational capabilities in learning and innovation, management and control, marketing and process improvement. Business values are created through asset allocation and financial management, business operation and process improvement; human resources and knowledge management, IS development and operation, technology and product innovation; and marketing plan implementation and control. In particular, product and service values refer to specific features and qualities of the products and services to win over customers' purchasing and satisfaction. Competitive features include content and functions, prices and supports, quality and warranty, as well as customization and personalization flexibilities. Product and service values are generated when the proposed product and service features get higher level of matchability to customers' needs than that of competitors, and eventually stimulate their desire to activate the transaction and payment processes.

Table 1. The BSC with value-based strategic objectives and performance indicators

Market Perspective	Supply Chain Perspective
Mission: To create market value and deliver value to shareholders. **Objectives:** To clarify success factors of market selection and segmentation, To identify market opportunities and risks, To specify goals on market shares, profit gains, and other market values. **Performance indicators** Level of market competitiveness, Market revenues and profits, Market share, Return on investment (ROI), Market capitalization, Earning per share, Increasing rates of these indicators.	**Mission:** To create and share supply chain-related information and values. **Objectives:** To direct the partner selection and supply chain establishment, management and operation processes, To develop information and value sharing policies. **Performance indicators** Cost and time reductions in information and production processing, market response, and production/distribution cycles integration, Revenue/profit increases for the entire chain, Customer satisfaction level in time and location conveniences.
EB Structure&Process Perspective	**Customer Perspective**
Mission: To create business values including product, service, and process values etc. **Objectives:** To leverage organizational capabilities, To achieve decision effectiveness, To improve internal processes, To create business image and brand names, To develop value-added products/services, To provide transaction system and process, To create business values and make profits. **Performance indicators** Return on asset, Asset utilization measures, Cash flow ratios, Profitability ratios, Operating efficiency metrics, HR skill levels and productivity ratios, IT/IS ROI, IT/IS usability measures, Innovation effectiveness metrics, Incr. rates.	**Mission:** To create customer values and to gain customer shares. **Objectives:** To specify customer clustering and classification rules, To enforce personalization and customization products and services, To generate customer shares and values from business process improvement and customer relationship management. **Performance indicators** Number of registered customers, Customer profitability levels (current gains and future potential), Customer shares, Customer satisfaction levels, Increasing rates of these measurement items.

The enterprise-level strategic objectives are to leverage organizational capabilities in productivity and innovation, to achieve efficiency and effectiveness of business decisions and operations, to improve internal communications and processes, to create business image and brand awareness, to develop value-added products and services, to provide transaction systems and processes, and ultimately to create business values and make profits. The global enterprise strategy may be further decomposed into intra-organizational sub-strategies such as the asset and financial strategy, the innovation and competition strategy, the product and service strategy, the IS and web site strategy, the business process and operation strategy, the marketing strategy, as well as the profit strategy. Business value metrics and performance indicators related to the enterprise strategy include return on asset (ROA), asset utilization measures, cash flow ratios, operating efficiency metrics, HR skill levels and productivity ratios, return on IT/IS investments, IT/IS usability measures, innovation effectiveness metrics, profitability ratios, and related increasing rates. In addition, specific product and service value indicators include function level, price level, quality level, as well as levels of supports, customization and personalization, and customer satisfaction.

Table 1 shows a generic BM-BSC with 4 perspectives and associated value-based strategic objectives and performance indicators.

4   Conclusion

In this paper, we present a BM-based BSC for facilitating performance measurement and strategic management in EB. Starting from identifying value types out of a BM framework, value-based strategies and performance indicators are then systematically illustrated and structurally categorized into four adapted BSC perspectives including market, supply chain, customer, and business structure and process. We believe that this is the first research attempt in the EB domain to bridge the gap between the BM and the BSC, and to provide guidance for developing the BSC from BM through value identification, strategy formation, and performance indicator selection. Future research works will focus on validating the proposed BSC model and associated value metrics and performance indicators, as well as on implementing the BSC to EB companies to test the effectiveness of this BM-BSC strategic management approach.

References

1. Afuah, A. and Tucci, C. L.: Internet Business Models and Strategies: Text and Cases. McGraw-Hill, (2001).
2. Banker, R. D., Chang, H., Janakiraman, S. N. and Konstans, C. A.: Balanced Scorecard Analysis of Performance Metrics. European Journal of Operational Research, 154 (2004) 423-436.
3. Favaro, J.: Value Based Management and Methods. XP2003, Lecture Notes in Computer Science, Vol. 2675, (2003) 16-25.
4. Garbi, E.: Alternative Measures of Performance for E-Companies: A Comparison of Approaches. Journal of Business Strategies, 19(1) (2002) 1-17.
5. Grey, W. et al.: An Analytic Approach for Quantifying the Value of e-Business Initiatives. IBM Systems Journal, 42(3) (2003) 484-497.
6. Hackney, R., Burn, J., and Salazar, A.: Strategies for Value Creation in Electronic Markets: Towards a Framework for Managing Evolutionary Change. Strategic Information Systems, 13(2) (2004) 91-103.

7. Hasan, H. and Tibbits, H.: Strategic Management of Electronic Commerce: An Adaptation of the Balanced Scorecard. Internet Research: Electronic Networking Applications and Policy, 10(5) (2000) 439-450.

8. Kaplan, R. S. and Norton, D. P.: Using the Balanced Scorecard as a Strategic Management System. Harvard Business Review, 74(1) (1996) 75-85.

9. Kaplan, R. S. and Norton, D. P.: Strategy Maps Converting Intangible Assets into Tangible Outcomes. Harvard Business School Press, (2003).

10. Kim, J., Suh, E., and Hwang, H.: A Model for Evaluating the Effectiveness of CRM Using the Balanced Scorecard. Journal of Interactive Marketing, 17(2) (2003) 5-19.

11. Kirchhoff, B. A., Merges, M. J., and Morabito, J. A.: Value Creation Model for Measuring and Managing the R&D Portfolio. Engineering Management Journal, 13(1) (2001) 19-22.

12. Marr, B. and Schiuma, G.: Business Performance Measurement – Past, Present and Future. Management Decision, 41(8) (2003) 680-687.

13. Martinsons, M., Davison, R., and Tse, D.: The Balanced Scorecard: A Foundation for the Strategic Management of Information Systems. Decision Support Systems, 25(1) (1999) 71-88.

14. Moller, K. E. K. and Torronen, P.: Business Suppliers' Value Creation Potential: A Capability-Based Analysis. Industrial Marketing Management, 32(2) (2003) 109-118.

15. Niven, P. R.: Balanced Scorecard Step-by-Step, for Government and Nonprofit Agencies. John Wiley & Sons, (2003).

16. Osterwalder, A. and Pigneur, Y.: Modeling Value Propositions in E-Business. Proceedings of the 5th International Conference on Electronic Commerce, (2003) 430-437.

17. Ritter, M.: The Use of Balanced Scorecards in the Strategic Management of Corporate Communication. Corporate Communications: An International Journal, 8(1) (2003) 44-59.

18. Self, F.: From Values to Metrics: Implementation of the Balanced Scorecard at a University Library. Performance Measurement and Metrics, 4(2) (2003) 57-63.

19. Sharma, A., Krishnan, R., and Grewal, D.: Value Creation in Markets: A Critical Area of Focus for Business-to-Business Markets. Industrial Marketing Management, 30(4) (2001) 391-402.

20. Terano, T. and Naitoh, K.: Agent-Based Modeling for Competing Firms: From Balanced Scorecards to Multi-Objective Strategies. Proceedings of the 37th Hawaii International Conference on Systems Sciences, (2004) 8p.

21. Timmers, P.: Business Models for Electronic Markets. Electronic Markets, 8(2) (1998) 3-8.

22. Ulaga, W.: Capturing Value Creation in Business Relationships: A Customer Perspective. Industrial Marketing Management, 32(8) (2003) 677-693.

23. Van Grembrergen, W. and Amelinckx, I.: Measuring and Managing E-Business Projects Through the Balanced Scorecard. Proceedings of the 35th Hawaii International Conference on Systems Sciences, (2002) 9p.

24. Walter, A., Ritter, T., and Gemunden, H. G.: Value Creation in Buyer-Seller Relationships. Industrial Marketing Management, 30(4) (2001) 365-377.

25. Yu, C. C.: An Integrated Framework of Business Models for Guiding Electronic Commerce Applications and Case Studies. EC-Web01, Lecture Notes in Computer Science, Vol. 2115, (2001) 111-120.

26. Yu, C. C.: Value Based Management and Strategic Planning in E-Business. EC-Web04, Lecture Notes in Computer Science, Vol. 3182, (2004). 357-367.

The Framework of Web-Based Voice of the Customers Management for Business Process Management in Service Industry

Chong Un Pyon[1], SungMin Bae[2], Ji Young Woo[1], and Sang Chan Park[1]

[1] Department of Industrial Engineering, KAIST,
373-1 Kusong-Dong, Yusong-Gu, Taejon, Korea 305-701
{pcu, jywoo}@major.kaist.ac.kr, sangchanpark@kaist.ac.kr
[2] Department of Industrial & Management Engineering, HANBAT National Univ.,
SAN 16-1, Duckmyung-Dong, Yusong-Gu, Taejon, Korea 305-719
loveiris@hanbat.ac.kr

Abstract. To manage the quality of services, internal business processes should be managed as like the intermediate products are controlled for quality of final products in the manufacturing industry. The business process management (BPM) with the aim of improving processes requires both analysis and evaluation of practices. Till now, while the transactional data such as total sales are sufficiently analyzed, Customers' responses on the business processes are not considered. In this paper, we introduce the voice of the customers (VOC) as a data source for BPM in the service industry. We suggest a VOC management framework that acquires data about business processes performance and quality of services. A consequent data model and business process model are followed.

1 Introduction

While companies try to find and improve key business processes to maximize the company's own value, business processes are mostly managed based on experts' or leaders' experiences in business practice. Non-value added processes are sometimes over-controlled. In this environment, a simple and structured framework for a systematic business process management (BPM) is required.

But, there is a surprising lack of the overall frameworks to support continuous improvement based on the data about the performance of each business process.

In the service industry such as financial, hotel, etc., the significance of BPM is greater than any other industries such as the manufacturing industry. The process of acquiring and receiving the services is a product itself in service industry. There are some difficulties to apply BPM in service industry [1]. First, it is difficult to define processes and their flows. The flowcharts and process maps are hardly used in the service industry. Secondly, it is hard to measure process performance. Third, some noisy or uncontrollable factors such as customer behaviors influence service processes.

Although the processes management with the aim of improving processes necessarily requires both analysis and critical evaluation of practices, most of existing packages for BPM focus mainly on process design, configuration or a process aware

K. Bauknecht et al. (Eds.): EC-Web 2005, LNCS 3590, pp. 168–177, 2005.

information system, and process enactment. Although they report the simple statistical summaries about the workflow status, they do not support sufficiently diagnoses [2]. Because non-measurable factors such as customer responses are not considered, the analysis results are not enough to find effective process improvement methods. The limited competency of analysis is basically caused by the poor data model.

To overcome these shortcomings, we propose Voice of the Customer (VOC) as the new data source for BPM in service industry. The VOC is all kinds of messages from customers including asking, claiming, complaining and commending or praising. The VOC tells what customers think about companies' current offerings. Companies' offerings are highly related to business processes. It is possible to detect problematic internal business processes through the VOC analysis. However, VOC itself is not suitable for analysis purpose from the viewpoint of knowledge discovery in databases (KDD). As VOC represents what customers think, it is expressed by customers' words. VOC should be conversioned from the customer-side view to the company-side view.

In this paper, we propose a new framework for BPM using VOC in service industry. The VOC will be converted to enhance the data quality, and the practical methodology for analysis will be presented with managerial implications. We propose the family of measurements (FOM) as the performance of businesses processes. To demonstrate application results, we will apply the framework to financial industry. We gather the VOC from call centers of a credit card company and build a web-based system embedding the proposed methodology.

2 Literature Review

2.1 Business Process Management

While many people consider business process management to be the 'next step' after the workflow wave of 1990s, BPM is above workflow management. Figure 1 shows the relationship between workflow management and business process management using the BPM life cycle [2]. First, processes are designed. Second, designs are implemented by configuring a process aware information system (e.g., a workflow management system). Third, operational business processes are executed using the configured system in the enactment phase. Finally, the operational processes are analyzed to identify problems and find possible improvements in the diagnosis phase. As these four phases iterate, processes are redesigned.

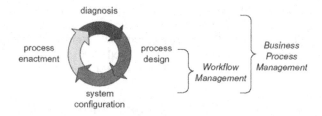

Fig. 1. BPM life cycle to compare WFM and BPM

The traditional workflow management system focuses the lower half of the BPM life cycle. As results, there is a little support for the diagnosis phase. Few systems support the collection and interpretation of real-time data. The Gartner group expects the BPM market to grow and also identifies Business Process Analysis (BPA) as an important aspect [3].

3 Methodology

3.1 VOC Management for Business Process Management

Companies set up customer supporting centers, which manage VOC all together over the diverse VOC receipt channels such as ARS, call centers, the internet homepages, and so on. Some of VOC cannot be directly handled on contact points. CSRs (Customer Support Representative) can not handle the complicate VOC that requires approvals of the other departments or inquiries to the other institutes. In this case, the VOC is transferred to the responsible person (or department) on the back office.

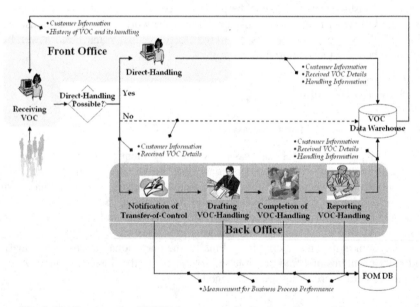

Fig. 2. The Framework of VOC Management for Business Process Management

There are problems on handling of transferred VOC; transfers to inappropriate persons, failures to notices, non-sharing of transferred VOC, and so on. Therefore, we suggest the framework of VOC management for BPM as depicted in Figure 2. It has following features.

– According to the type of VOC, required posterior processes and responsible persons should be mapped.
– Notices of transferred VOC should be systematically performed in enterprise-wide operating systems that should be integrated on both back office and front office.

- We construct a data warehouse, in which customer information, received VOC details, and handling information is recorded, to share the status of VOC handling or any feedbacks.
- From the initial transfer to the end of the VOC-handling, every intermediate processes, from drafting a plan to completion, should be monitored. We record business performance measurements on the FOM (Family of Measurements) database.
- Companies analyze the data on both VOC data warehouse and FOM database, and get knowledge about bottleneck processes and value-added processes.

VOC itself is not suitable for analysis of business process because it is expressed by customers' words who don't care about internal business processes. After, we present requisite VOC conversion viewpoints and an analysis framework for BPM.

3.2 Data Enrichment by VOC Conversion

Companies have their own code-structures to record received VOC details on the data base. This code structure represents the topic that the received VOC is related with. The existing VOC code-structures are poor for models because they are for transaction processing rather than for analysis. Companies focus on issues such as database storage efficiency, but do not include a plan for how the data will eventually be used and analyzed.

In order to produce reasonable and valuable analysis results for decision making, we suggest the code-structure that describes the substance of customer complaints. It reflects requisite analysis viewpoints about VOC by conversion. To comprehend descriptions, we present a case of credit card company of financial industry.

3.2.1 Business Processes Mapping

For business process management based on VOC, business processes should be mapped to VOC. The internal business processes may not be the same with customer-perceived external processes. Because customers do not care about internal business processes, the actual processes and their flows should be identified through conversion. In conversion, we use Process Classification Framework (PCF) as a basis. PCF has been developed by the APQC International Benchmarking Clearinghouse, with the assistance of several major international corporations. PCF is a high-level, generic enterprise model. Many organizations have used PCF in practical ways to understand their processes better. PCF serves as a common reference about business processes [4].

Through business process mapping, companies can get direct feedback of customers' evaluation on external processes. Also, they assess the adequacy and performance of current approaches for fulfilling customer needs, and identify their strengths and weakness. Eventually, companies could detect the critical processes that affect customer satisfaction.

3.2.2 VOC Primary-Cause Identification

In order to find the remedies for problematic processes, companies should understand what causes customer complaints on the process. To discover the causes, we adapt the concept of the Cause and Effect Diagram from Total Quality Management (TQM).

The cause and effect diagram is also known as the fishbone diagram or Ishikawa Diagram. It helps to search for root causes, identify problems, and compare the relative importance of different causes [5].

Possible causes should be defined in advance for instant detection of causes and efficient derivation of improvement directions. Causes can be pre-defined based on 4M which classifies the process affecting factors from quality management perspective. While these categories can be anything, 4M such as manpower, methods, materials, and machinery is often used. We modify 4M into 5M that are customized to the credit card case as shown in Table 1. Once companies define and apply 5M according to their industrial characteristics, it is useful to prioritize resources for process improvement.

3.2.3 VOC Characteristics Identification
To differentiate the necessity of process improvement, we identify the characteristics of VOC by applying the Failure Modes and Effect Analysis (FMEA). FMEA is a

Table 1. Customized 5M of the Cause and Effect Diagram

5M	Description
Man-customer	The VOC originated from customers' peculiarity, so cannot be easily solved
Man-Employee	Employees' mistakes cause the VOC. The employee training or education is required.
Materials	The characteristics of goods or services cause the VOC. The examination for initial design or adjustment is required.
Methods	The processes themselves cause the VOC. So the process improvement or process innovation is required.
Machinery	Machinery means the affiliations or support agencies. Companies should clear up their authorities and responsibilities.

Table 2. The types of failure mode error in FMEA and the examples of the credit card case

Type of error	Description
Information Validation Omission	There are no checks to catch incorrect or incomplete information items. ex) inquiries, confirmations
Process Validation Omission	There is no mechanism for catching or correcting an incorrectly applied process. ex) erroneous notices, insufficient notices
Reception Omission	There is no mechanism for checking that an information item is received by a process after being sent by another process. ex) application errors, application omissions
Transmission Omission	There is no mechanism for checking that an information item required by a process has been sent by another process. ex) transaction delay
Process Exception	A process is not designed to handle a possible situation within its scope. ex) discontents

series of systematic activities intended to recognize and evaluate the potential failure modes of goods or services and their effects. Because the FMEA classifies the types of failure modes, which are reasons of VOC occurrence, companies could reduce the chance of potential failure modes occurring [5], [6]. The identification of characteristics of VOC enables to prioritize the VOC seriousness. For example, the seriousness of inquiries cannot be the same with the seriousness of complaints caused by transaction delay.

3.3 Data Mining: VOC Analysis

3.3.1 Business Process Performance Data: Family of Measurements (FOM)

In addition to the status of VOC receiving, it is also important to handle the received VOC. Companies should manage the operational processes by which VOC is handled and customers recovered on back office. Therefore, they should gather the outputs (or performance) of business processes to find key business processes and bottleneck processes. To follow up VOC handling, we apply the Family of Measurements (FOM) concept from USAA case as summarized in table 3 [7].

Table 3. Family of Measurements in service industry

FOM	Description
Quantity	- The number of the VOC occurrence - Both the absolute quantity and the relative quantity should be considered. The relative quantity is estimated by normalization. According to the managerial analysis purpose, companies can select the various bases, for example, the number of subscribers per product, the number of subscribers per district.
Quality	- The degree of contribution to customer satisfaction - It means how the VOC handling affects customer satisfaction. Companies can differentiate the VOC that is directly related with customer satisfaction according to its contribution. Because it cannot be estimated only by VOC handling, the surveys such as the customer satisfaction index survey or the focus group interview should be combined with the VOC handling.
Timeliness	- The speed of the VOC handling - Usually companies measure only the time elapsed from the VOC receiving to the VOC handling completion. However, the intermediary processes should be measured; receiving, notification of transfer-of-control (if the VOC is transferred), drafting VOC-Handling, and completion of VOC –handling should be measured.
Cost	- The amount of money to handle the VOC - Because some of VOC arouses the loss such as the compensation payment, companies should reduce the occurrence of VOC with heavy cost.

3.3.2 VOC Analysis Framework

The VOC analysis model consists of four phases: entity construction, summary, exception, and comparison as depicted in Figure 3. The entity means the analysis viewpoint that is the criteria to read VOC data from the VOC data warehouse and make a
data subset. We use the viewpoints of VOC conversion as entity. Also, we use the
combination of two entities (two-dimensional).

In the summary phase, we derive a summary of a VOC data subset for the FOM.
After we find the problems with one dimensional entity vs. FOM, we take a drill-
down analysis by two-dimensional entity vs. FOM. We identify the root causes and
the characteristics per processes. We examine whether the distribution of FOM is
biased by a specific entity. The ANOVA test exhibits the significant interaction between VOC and the entity. The summary phase is the basis for the following exception and comparison phase.

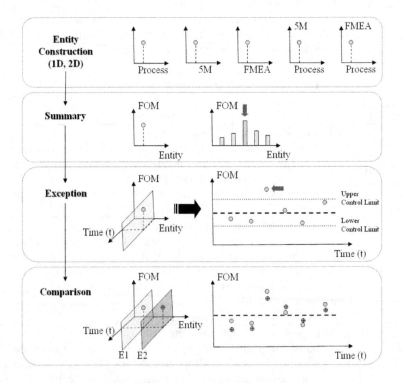

Fig. 3. The framework of VOC analysis

In exception phase, we examine whether the temporal factor affects business processes and finds the exceptional processes' performance using the control chart. Control limits are established based on domain knowledge and displayed in the control
chart. Usually, companies set control limits to 3σ according to the Six Sigma philosophy. If an exceptional case occurs, we examine the occurrence reason and detect key
events that provoke the process troubles. Key events can be new good or service
launching, strategy changes, regulation changes, novice employments and so on.

In the comparison phase, we compare discovered patterns in terms of shapes of fluctuation and time by F-test. We induce temporal rules and use them for forecasting. Common patterns are detected from inter entities or intra entities. Within a group, cycle time can be derived from accumulated patterns. Between groups, time gap can be detected. For example, if the VOC of process A and B occur together in time lag of two weeks, and if the VOC of process A increases, we expect that the VOC of process B increase as well. The comparison helps to cluster similar processes, and the clustering suggests the hints for process improvement.

4   Application (Case of a Credit Card Company)

We applied our VOC management framework in a credit card company in South Korea. It is one of the largest credit card companies in South Korea, and receives principally through call centers. There are problems on VOC management. On the contact points, if the responsibility for the VOC is not clearly defined, some VOC are transferred to the inappropriate person. Although the number of VOC per month is around 4,000,000, the VOC is transferred by the telephone without documented notice system. Because CSRs cannot know the handling of transferred VOC, they cannot reply to the customers' requests for confirmations. There is no process improvements based on VOC, a repetition of the same VOC transfer impedes the entire business processes.

We developed the web-based VOC Management System (VMS) that enables the VOC registration, handling, and sharing enterprise-widely on web. All of information related with the VOC, such as customer data, the past business transaction data and the history of VOC per customer, is presented from the VOC data warehouse. When a responsible person logs in VMS, he or she is informed of the lists of VOC that are not handled. VMS automatically puts on records of cost and time for VOC handling, such as initial recognition time, the time of remedy establishment, and the duration of overall treatment. All of required information, such as customer data, attached files, and payment information, is offered. Figure 4 shows the registration screen of VMS.

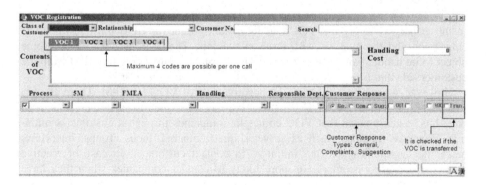

Fig. 4. The registration screen in VMS

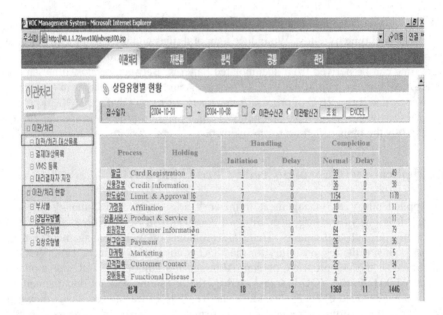

Fig. 5. The inquiry screen for status of transferred VOC handling in VMS. The click on the upper rectangle on left side displays the list of transferred VOC and handling-completed VOC. The click on the lower rectangle on left side displays the status of transfer/handling per departments, and per processes.

Figure 5 shows the screen to inquire the status of transferred VOC handling according to the processes. The VOC managers can drill down the specific process by clicking the process name, and then the 5M and FMEA are displayed in Pareto Charts. When CSRs want to know the status of the VOC, they use the 'The list of transferred VOC/Handling Completed VOC' menu on the left side.

5 Conclusion

In this paper, we apply the VOC and its handling data for BPM through the VOC conversion and the analysis with three viewpoints. The VOC is not a troublesome object to be handled any more. It is a valuable information source for BPM from the customer side that is one of four sides of BSC (Balanced Score Card)

However, we consider the only the negative side of VOC for BPM. There are two basic ways to gather the VOC [8]. Reactive methods, such as customer calls, web page hits, e-mails mean that VOC comes to companies through a customer's initiative. Proactive methods, such as surveys, questionnaires, focus groups, interviews mean that companies take the initiative to contact customers. In case of reactive methods, because customers are more likely to contact companies when they have problems, the majorities of reactive VOC are complaints (negative side). Therefore, the methodology to consider the positive side of VOC through proactive methods is required.

References

1. Jiju Antony : Six Sigma in the UK service organisations: results from a pilot survey. Managerial Auditing Journal, Vol. 19 No. 8 Emerald Group (2004) 1006-1013
2. M. Weske, W.M.P. van der Aalst, H.M.W. Verbeek : Advances in business process management. Data & Knowledge Engineering, Vol. 50. No.1 Elsevier (2004) 1-8
3. Gartner : The BPA Market Cathes another Major Updraft. Gartner's Application Development and Maintenance Research Note M-16-8153, (2002) http://www.gartner.com
4. APQC's International Benchmarking Clearinghouse. www.apqc.org
5. Bob : Better Desing in Half the Time. GOAL/QPC, Methuen, MA. (1989)
6. Gavin, David A., Managing Quality : The Strategic and Competitive Edge. New York: The Free Press (1988)
7. Robert F. McDermott : Service Comes First : An Interview with USAA. Harvard Business Review September-October (1991)
8. Michael L. George : Lean Six Sigma for Service. McGraw-Hill (2003)

E-Business Perceptions Versus Reality: A Longitudinal Analysis of Corporate Websites

Niels Bjørn-Andersen[1] and Steve Elliot[2]

[1] Copenhagen Business School,
Copenhagen, Denmark
nba@cbs.dk
[2] School of Business,
University of Sydney, Australia
S.Elliot@econ.usyd.edu.au

Abstract. Commonly held perceptions (including the ones reflected in the Call for Papers for this EC-Web 2005 Conference) are 1) that the Internet is changing the way companies and organizations are working, 2) that the amount of innovation and change seems to accelerate, and 3) that further development is constrained by numerous technical issues that still need to be resolved.

Preliminary analysis of developments in the websites of 120 companies from 8 industry sectors across two countries over a period of five years from 2000 – 2004 challenges these perceptions. The websites were analysed by means of a framework with 30 evaluation criteria developed from theory and leading examples of web-applications across a broad range of web-sites in Asia-Pacific, Europe and North-America.

This major international study suggests that: the impact of e-business on companies and organizations differs between sectors; the rate of innovation and change does not reflect constant improvement but in some cases exhibits degraded web-capabilities over time; and that the major challenges constraining further development may be more managerial than technical.

1 Introduction

Industry has embraced the concept of Electronic Business with the expectation that the Internet will transform the global marketplace (Economist 1999, OECD 2001, Mullaney *et al* 2003). Forrester Research calculates that in the US alone, the business-to-business e-commerce transactions in 2003 was $2.4 trillion, and the business-to-consumer e-commerce reached $95 billion. Furthermore, productivity gains from e-commerce where businesses use the Internet for forecasting, inventory control and increased integration with suppliers were expected to reach $450 billion a year by 2005 (quoted in Mullaney *et al* 2003). With such impressive figures, it is not surprising that international surveys have identified the challenges of transforming business through Internet-enabled innovation and of maximising the return to business from this innovation as being the highest priority for Chief Information Officers (CIO) irrespective of whether their organization is large, medium or small or located in Asia, Europe or North America [CSC 2003, CIO 2004a, CIO 2004b].

This paper seeks to assist organizations in better managing these challenges of transforming current practice through a longitudinal, cross-sectoral, international

K. Bauknecht et al. (Eds.): EC-Web 2005, LNCS 3590, pp. 178–187, 2005.

study of corporate websites. The website evaluations were achieved through application of a previously developed framework identifying key features and facilities of B2C web sites. This framework enabled an assessment of a firm's current Internet provision against a standard set of key characteristics. The initial intent, to provide a means of benchmarking a firm's web site against others, was extended to assist firms in identifying a potential path for development of a consumer-oriented web site from their current implementation. In addition, the framework serves as a mechanism for clearly identifying options, opportunities and their implications for web site development, in order to place it on the agenda for senior management.

Any framework intended for evaluation of commercial web sites is destined for criticism not only from those companies whose sites are evaluated less positively but also from scientific sources. In designing an evaluation framework, decisions must be made as to the purpose or outcomes intended from the evaluation process. Is it merely to identify who is doing what; to determine who is doing it best at present; to compare sites with best business practice at the time of the evaluation; or to help identify a path for future development of a firm's Internet presence? The potentially subjective nature of the evaluation process may be criticised as well.

In developing and utilizing a web site evaluation framework we acknowledge all of these issues. The aims of this framework were clearly stated, and steps were taken to address the issue of subjectivity. This paper examines a range of design details (both theoretical and empirical) relevant to evaluations of web sites and explores the rationale of these features. The resulting draft framework was tested against 100 sites and then revised. The outcome of this process - the so-called Centre for Electronic Commerce (CEC) Web site Evaluation Framework – was used to evaluate the corporate websites (Elliot, *et al* 2000).

2   Literature Review – Theory and Practice

Since the area of Internet retailing is relatively new and theoretical development is at an early stage, our examination of potentially relevant theoretical contributions to successful web site design also included more general issues relating to consumer adoption of innovations. The factors are initially presented with related research issues and then grouped into evaluation categories.

Early work by Bell *et al* (1975) suggests that the customer needs to be attracted to an innovation and that 'attraction may be a function of the seller's advertising expenditure, the effectiveness of the advertising, the price of the product, the reputation of the company, the service given during and after purchase, the location of retail stores and much more' (Bell *et al* 1975).

Boyd and Mason (1999) conducted a US study of consumer evaluations of innovative consumer electronic products that confirms Bell *et al*'s (1975) finding of the importance of attractiveness as an antecedent of adoption and the implications of attractiveness for firms:

'Managers can improve an innovation's chances of success by influencing the level of the factors they can change and knowing the implications of the factors they cannot change.' (Boyd and Mason, 1999).

An indication that theory relating to adoption of innovations may be applicable to web site design is partly through recognition of the characteristics of sites as extremely dependent on the 'look and feel' and partly through recognition of the changing nature of innovations over their life:

> 'A shortcoming of much research studying innovations is that the innovation is assumed to remain unchanged over its life. It is more realistic to recognise that the innovation changes over time and that, as a result, consumer perceptions and evaluations can also change.' (Boyd and Mason, 1999).

The limited academic literature specifically dealing with Internet retailing is generally consistent with adoption studies, but with the addition of specific features, e.g. interactivity and home page presentation. In a study of online banking, Krishnan *et al*, (1999) find,

> 'Customers seem to be receptive to the potential benefits offered by an electronic system, such as speed and convenience, provided it addressed all their trading needs and was easy to use.'

Farquhar *et al* (1998) identify 20 generic consumer requirements, including: ease of use, consistency in user interfaces, privacy, security, cost transparency, reliability, error tolerance, design for different types customers, order confirmation and system status information. Conversely, problems with web sites that may alienate customers include: out of date information, inconsistent navigation, slow loading pages, virtual company with no physical address or contact numbers, poor responsiveness to email or other queries, poor transaction processing, poor ease of use and lack of integration of Internet services with the rest of the organisation (Alsop 1999, Elliot and Fowell 1999, Kirsner 1999, LSE / Novell 1999).

In addition to consumer factors, organisation-level characteristics have been identified. A 1996 study of 137 Internet sites selling women's apparel identified the following attributes that influence store traffic and sales: merchandise, service (FAQ, policies), product promotion, convenience (help functions, navigation, shopping cart, ease of use), checkout processes (carts, ease of use, full transaction pricing), as well as store navigation (product search function, site maps, consistent navigation, no broken links) (Lohse and Spiller, 1998).

Behavioural studies present an alternate view of consumer adoption factors. Concerned that much research into Internet shopping has been based on the demographic characteristics of consumers, Ramaswami *et al* (1998) took a consumer behaviour perspective explaining Internet usage for shopping using an ability-motivation-opportunity (AMO) framework. The authors suggest that the major determinants of on-line buying are: the consumer's ability to purchase on-line, their motivation to do so, and their opportunity to access on-line markets.

To be effective, a framework for reviews and evaluations of web sites should not be narrowly focused on individual perspectives and current implementations but should methodologically be more broadly based. Prior experience in relevant areas, often incorporated in theoretical models, may be considered, e.g. Information Systems as a discipline has a considerable body of knowledge on successful development of user interfaces. Recognising the overwhelming amounts of information available to firms, suppliers and consumers, IS development experience suggests that unless the design of an information systems user interface is inviting, encouraging, timely, informative and user friendly then it is unlikely to be successful (Taylor, 1986). However, many web sites appear to have been developed without regard to such lessons. Similarly, the necessity for integration of IS systems and their alignment with corporate strategies has been (belatedly) acknowledged as being applicable also to Internet activities (Blodgett, 1999).

Since the Internet is anticipated to transform markets and industries (Benjamin and Wigand 1995, Economist 1999) it is inevitable that a level of uncertainty exists in retailers as to how it can be utilised (Andersen 1999, Brown and Chen 1999, Nambisan and Wang 1999). Uncertainties include a lack of knowledge of: Internet technologies, resources required to develop and implement web sites, specific business objectives, web site features and the value of web site features to the business (Nambisan and Wang 1999).

3   Research Approach

The overall objective of the research was to assist corporations unsure about the effectiveness and competitiveness of their Internet strategies and implementations by longitudinal analysis of the website developments of 120 companies from 8 industry sectors in Australia and Denmark over five years.

The initial study was undertaken in 2000 in Denmark. The ten largest companies by revenue within each of ten major Danish business sectors were selected. The firms ranged in size from medium to large. Diversity in size and industrial sector was sought to test the capability of the framework and to reflect a variety of levels of web site activity across different companies and industries. It is important to note that there were no 'pure-players' among the companies initially selected in Denmark nor subsequently selected in Australia. Firms were selected in order to examine the extent to which traditional companies are meeting the requirements of the e-economy.

While it was intended that the 10 largest companies in 10 sectors would be compared across the two countries, this level of comparative analysis proved problematic. The standard industry classification scheme in each country was utilised but on detailed examination across countries, the composition of two industry sectors, consumer goods and supplies, was so different that international comparisons became meaningless. Re-alignment of national industry classification schemes was considered but discounted since it would exclude the future capacity for analysis of nationally published data on the sector that might be required to clarify or explain the research findings. The industry sectors examined throughout the study were automobile; financial services; food industries; pharmaceutical; printed media; retail; telecommunications; and transport and travel.

Reduction in the number and type of observations occurred due to fatigue in the sample members over the period, typically as a result of mergers, acquisitions and implementation apparent policies to consolidate websites globally rather than maintaining websites locally.

The websites were analysed by means of a Website Evaluation Framework (see Appendix) previously developed from theory and leading practice that has been applied successfully across a broad range of industries in Europe, North America and Asia-Pacific (Elliot *et al* 2000, Elliot 2002). The Framework consists of 30 evaluative elements grouped into six categories: company information, product/service information, buy / sell transactions, customer services, ease-of-use, and innovation (in website application). Details are shown in the Appendix.

The Website Evaluation Framework was previously found to be an effective means of longitudinal monitoring of developments in websites over time.

A multiphase approach was adopted that comprised the following stages/elements:

Firstly, about 60 companies in Denmark in eight industry sectors had five sets of observations in 2000, 2001, 2002, 2003 and 2004.

Secondly, about 60 companies in Australia in eight corresponding industry sectors had four sets of observations in 2001, 2002, 2003 and 2004.

The method was for all website analyses to be performed by a single researcher in each country with interaction between researchers to establish consistency of application. Initially, two independent reviews were conducted of each website with verification across reviewers. Subsequently, single reviewers were undertaken for 2001 and 2002 in both countries with the reviewers sampling sites in each country to ensure consistency of evaluation. In 2003 and 2004 different reviewers were utilised but these remained the same in each country for both years. The principal researchers ensured consistency across the complete period in both countries through training, cross evaluation, sampling and standardisation to ensure consistency of the Framework's application across the years.

4   Research Findings

Evaluation of 120 firms over eight sectors in each of two countries across four-five years with each evaluation consisting of ratings in 30 elements, all represents a wealth of detail that is beyond the scope of this paper to examine. The focus of this paper is, therefore, on challenging or supporting three commonly held but critical perceptions:

- o   the Internet is changing the way companies and organizations are working;
- o   the amount of innovation and change seems to accelerate; and
- o   further development is constrained by numerous technical issues that still need to be resolved.

4.1   Transforming Work Practices

Although this perception does not distinguish between industry sectors, Table 1 shows that some industries, notably automobile and food, have not changed their practices as a whole while others, e.g., financial services, have enthusiastically adopted Internet-based transaction processing. The nature of the industry could be seen to dictate industry practice, e.g., food is a regulated product for health and safety reasons. However, within the industries there is some variation. One of the ten auto manufacturers, BMW, supports online purchasing of life-style products branded with the corporate name. Similarly, even in the highly regulated food industry, an industry leader (Fosters) sells its branded lifestyle products as well. Note that the CEC scale is from 0–5, where 5 means that full transaction functionality is available on all websites, as assessed using the CEC Web Evaluation Framework. The low average rating across all industries suggests that the level of transformation of work practice, as indicated by adoption of online transaction processing capabilities, remains modest. Since processing of buy/sell transactions is a core business activity, evaluation of the extent to which this is conducted online indicates the level of transformation of industry practice resulting from the Internet.

Table 1. Australian online transaction capabilities for selected industries [Source: Elliot & Bjørn-Andersen 2004]

	2001	2002	2003	2004
Automobile	0.3	0.0	0.3	0.4
Financial Services	3.0	4.0	4.0	4.0
Food Industries	0.0	0.0	0.5	0.5
Av. All Industries	1.2	1.5	1.4	1.7

4.2 Accelerating Rates of Innovation and Change

Table 2 shows that the ratings for innovation in use of the Internet to support customer services have not accelerated for all firms over the period 2000 – 2004. In some cases the ratings have actually decreased. As can be seen in the Appendix, this category in the Website Evaluation Framework examines the extent to which websites reflect enhanced customers services for orders, feedback, communities or customization and any novel AND effective use of multimedia. These services are not expensive to implement nor are they technically challenging. Websites across both countries in several different sectors were rated highly in this category (4 to 5 / 5). The low ratings for all firms appear to reflect a widespread lack of interest in exploring website capabilities for core business activities that is remarkable.

Table 2. Denmark Customer Services & Innovation capabilities for all industries [Source: Elliot & Bjørn-Andersen 2004]

	2000	2001	2002	2003	2004
Innovation	0.9	1.7	1.9	1.9	1.6
Customer services	2.0	2.3	2.5	3.2	2.8

4.3 Technical Constraints on Future Development

Table 2 also shows the ratings for customer services. This category rates websites for provision of basic services including sales assistance (e.g., FAQs); customer policies (e.g., privacy, warranties); after sales procedures (e.g., returns, repairs, help); membership clubs/loyalty schemes; and on whether there is an extended/broader view of customer services, e.g., links to other relevant sites. As with 4.2 above, these services are not unreasonable or extreme, they are not expensive to implement, nor are they technically challenging. It appears that the management commitment to provide such services beyond a basic level is lacking.

5 Conclusion

This paper reports on preliminary longitudinal analysis of the website developments of 120 companies in 8 industry sectors over a period of four-five years, with 60 of the largest companies in Australia and Denmark. These two countries are frequently rated at the highest level in international comparisons of adoption and use of the Internet. While it is believed the findings may have broader significance, these limitations of firm size, industry sector and country of origin should be noted. It should also be noted that organisations update their websites infrequently, and that an evaluation could occur just before or just after an upgrade. But over the period of time this will be taken into account since the basis of the analysis (i.e., the evaluation framework) is constant.

The assessment of the corporate websites applied a Website Evaluation Framework (Elliot, *et al* 2000) based on theoretical and empirical sources that identified key elements for retail web sites, including types of information presented, levels of functionality provided and degrees of alignment with consumers' requirements. The framework was piloted and tested through application of the framework to the web sites of 100 traditional firms in a range of industries and subsequently applied internationally and longitudinally (Elliot, 2002). The research method was specifically designed to minimise any potential variance due to researcher bias. Training, sampling and independent verification of ratings were used to ensure consistency of evaluation.

The complexity of the research findings from this study cannot be adequately presented here in 10 pages so this paper considers how the data collected might address three common perceptions, that:

- the Internet is changing the way companies and organizations are working;
- the amount of innovation and change seems to increase if not accelerate; and
- further development is constrained by numerous technical issues that still need to be resolved.

This analysis is based on an aggregation of more than 500 website ratings of 120 firms in different industry sectors in two countries over time. A reasonable query may be raised as to the appropriateness of drawing conclusions based on aggregated results from such a diversity of sources. Since the objective of this analysis is to consider common perceptions relating to changes in work practises; patterns of innovation and possible constraints on future developments across a diversity of industries, such an aggregated data source appears appropriate.

This study suggests that: the impact of e-business on the work practises of companies and organizations differs between sectors; that the rate of innovation and change does not reflect constant improvement but may exhibit degraded website functionality over time; and that the major challenges constraining further development may be more managerial than technical.

Table 1 above shows in 2004 the average Website Evaluation Framework rating for online transaction processing across all industries was 1.7, having risen slowly and unevenly from 1.2 in 2001. An average of 5.0 would that indicate that the Internet had made a transformative impact on all companies in all industries. The common perception is, therefore, not supported, although specific industries (e.g., Financial Services) have high ratings that indicate transformation has been affected.

The second common perception is of a consistently increasing rate of innovation and change. Table 2 shows that use of the Internet for innovation in online services increased steadily between 2000 and 2002, was static in 2003 and declined in 2004. Drilling down to further details (not presented due to space constraints) shows that two sectors with low ratings increased their ratings from 2003-4 while three of the four highest rating sectors declined. The common perception of consistent innovation is not supported. Further examination is warranted to determine conditions.

The third common perception is that major constraints to future development of Internet use are predominantly technical in origin. Table 2 also shows that use of the Internet for provision of essential customer services (e.g., sales assistance, customer policies and after sales service) increased steadily between 2000 and 2003 but declined in 2004. Drilling down to further details (not presented due to space constraints) shows that sectors as a whole either remained static or declined with the ratings of four sectors declining substantially, one in excess of 30%. One sector (Financial Services) showed an increased rating in online provision of customer services from 2003 to 2004. It is difficult to conclude that the cause of a reduction in provision of online services across several sectors concurrent with an increase in another sector could be attributed to technical causes. An alternate explanation may be possible; that a major constraint on website development is lack of customer demand. While assessment of mitigating demand-side constraints on website development and implementation, e.g, consumer resistance, remains outside the scope of this study, drilling down in the worst case industry sector shows a market leader actively engaging in website innovation. This would suggest that any customer resistance is not sector wide. Managerial rather than technical or demand issues appear to be the major constraint on Internet use and further development.

The contribution of this paper is also as a means of assistance to practitioners who recognise the critical importance of the Internet but remain unsure of how best to implement corporate strategies using the Internet. The framework is intended to enable clear identification of options, opportunities, and their implications for web site development. Researchers with a broad range of interests from organisational transformation to web site design may also benefit from our web site evaluation framework, and may want to test other common but possibly equally invalid perceptions of the nature of Internet-enabled business.

References

Alsop S. (1999) 'How I judge if a web site deserves my business' Fortune, New York, August 16, Vol. 140, No. 4, pp 167-8.

Andersen (1999) 'eEurope Takes Off'. Executive Summary. Andersen Consulting September. London. Executive Summary reports results of survey of 410 senior executives in major European firms, their experiences & expectations of Electronic Commerce.

Bell D.E., Keeney R.L. and Little J.D.C. (1975) 'A Market Share Theorem', Journal of Marketing Research. May, pp 136-141.

Benjamin, R. and Wigand, R. (1995) Electronic Markets and Virtual Value Chains on the Information Superhighway. Sloan Management Review, Winter, pp62-72.

Blodgett M. (1999) 'The bigger picture'. CIO, Section 1, October 15 pp 69 – 75

Boyd T.C. and Mason C.H. (1999) 'The link between attractiveness of 'extrabrand' attributes and the adoption of innovations'. Academy of Marketing Science Journal, Greenvale. Vol 27, No. 3, pp 306-319

Brown E. and Chen C. (1999) 'Big business meets the E-World' Fortune Vol. 140 No. 9 August pp 88-94

CIO (2004a) "State of the CIO Survey" CIO Magazine 30 September.

CIO (2004b) "State of the CIO Survey: SMB versus Large Organisations" CIO Magazine. 13 December.

CSC (2003) 16th Annual CIO Survey. Computer Sciences Corporation. El Segundo Calif. USA.

Economist (1999) 'Business and the Internet' June 26, reporting surveys by Economist / Booz, Allen & Hamilton, and Forrester Research. Feature pp 1-34.

Elliot S. and Fowell S. (1999) 'Expectations versus Reality: A snapshot of consumer experiences with Internet shopping' University of New South Wales, School of Information Systems, Technology and Management Working Paper Series number: 99_001.

Elliot S, Morup-Petersen A, Bjørn-Andersen N. 'Towards a framework for Web site evaluation' In Klein S, O'Keefe B, (eds) (2000) *Proceedings of 13th International Conference on Electronic Commerce* Bled, Slovenia, June 19-21.

Elliot S. And Bjørn-Andersen N. (2004) A comparative international and longitudinal study of corporate websites: Preliminary analysis. BIS Working Paper Series, University of Sydney.

Farquhar B., Langmann G. and Balfour A. (1998) 'Consumer needs in Global Electronic Commerce' Electronic Markets. Vol 8, No. 2. Pp 9-12.

Gomez web site (www.gomez.com)

Hamel G. and Sampler J. (1998) 'The E-Corporation' Fortune, Vol. 138, No. 11 December 7.

Kirsner S. (1999) 'The dirty dozen' CIO Web Business, September 1. Pp 22 – 25.

Krishnan M.S., Ramaswamy V., Meyer M.C. and Damien P. (1999) 'Customer Satisfaction for Financial Services: The Role of Products, Services and Information Technology' Management Science, Vol. 45, No. 9, September, pp 1194-1209.

Lohse G.L. and Spiller P. (1998) 'Electronic shopping' Communications of the ACM, July, Vol. 41, No. 7, pp 81-87

LSE / Novell (1999) 'The 1999 Worldwide Web 100 – ranking the world's largest 100 firms on the web.'

Moore G.A.(1995) Inside the Tornado. Harper Business, New York.

Mullaney T., Green H., Arndt M., Hof R. and Himelstein L. (2003) The E-Biz Surprise. Business Week 12 May, USA.

Nambisan S. and Wang Y.M. (1999) 'Roadblocks to Web technology adoption?' Communications of the ACM. January, Vol. 42, No. 1, pp 98-101.

OECD, (2001) 'The Internet and Business Performance', OECD Paris, p.7

O'Neill H.M., Pouder R.W. and Buchholtz A.K. (1998) ' Patterns in the diffusion of strategies across organisations: Insights from the innovation diffusion literature.' Academy of Management Review, Vol. 23, No. 1, January, pp 98-114.

Ramaswami S.R., Strader T. and Brett K. (1998) 'Electronic Channel Customers for Financial Products: Test of Ability-Motivation-Opportunity Model' Proceedings of the Association of Information Systems, Americas Conference, August pp 328-300.

Rogers, E.M. (1983, 1995) Diffusion of innovations. The Free Press, New York.

Roth A.V. and Jackson W.E. (1995) 'Strategic determinants of service quality and performance: evidence from the banking industry.' Management Science, Vol. 41. No. 11, pp 1720-1733.

Taylor R.S. (1986) 'Value-added processes in information systems'. Norwood, NJ: Ablex.

Tyler G. (1999) 'Lets go Internet shopping' Management Services, Institute of Management Services Enfield UK, January, pp 26-29

Appendix - Web site evaluation framework Evaluation overview:

	Company info + functions	Product / service information and promotion	Buy / sell – transactions	Customer services	Ease of use	Innovation in services and technology
1	Ownership, company mission statement, Financial performance	General product / service groups	Supports on-line purchasing	Sales assistance, e.g. FAQ's	Layout and design (easy to read, consistent, not distracting, intuitive easy to understand, creative design)	Enhanced customer services – orders (e.g. decision support, order status, delivery tracking, flexibility in delivery after order…)
2	Operations & product / service areas	More detailed product / service specifications - e.g. quality, performance etc	Security (policy/lock on transaction data not just on credit cards)	Customer policies e.g. privacy, warranties, purchase exchanges	Site map or search engine	Enhanced customer services – feedback (e.g. customer input/ reviews)
3	Image building, e.g. company news, press releases (must be less than one month old).	Pricing	Simplified processes e.g. shopping trolley, 2-click purchasing	After sales procedures (e.g. returns/repair/ exchange/help/ problem FAQ's)	Navigation, intuitively easy to find what one needs from the web site	Enhanced customer services – communities (development of communities with users e.g. games, quizzes, prizes but also chat)
4	Contact details or list of distributors	Promotions on special products / services	Online payment + capacity for alternative payments	Customised services, e.g. loyalty scheme, memberships or user "clubs"	Site information easily accessible, and identified from general search engines	Enhanced customer services – web site customisation for individual customers
5	Richer set of company relevant functions, e.g. recruitment etc	Details on new or future products / services	Details of full transaction costs + order confirmation + delivery time / mode + trust assurance.	Broader approach to customer services e.g. links to other relevant sites	Caters for a range of users, e.g. graphics / text, novice / experienced, business / consumer, and different languages	Novel and effective use of multimedia (e.g. audio / video / animations)

Knowledge Discovery in Web-Directories: Finding Term-Relations to Build a Business Ontology

Sandip Debnath[1], Tracy Mullen[3], Arun Upneja[2], and C. Lee Giles[1,3]

[1] Department of Computer Sciences and Engineering
[2] School of Hotel, Restaurant and Recreation Management
[3] School of Information Sciences and Technology,
The Pennsylvania State University, University Park, PA 16802 USA
debnath@cse.psu.edu, tmullen@ist.psu.edu, aupneja@psu.edu,
giles@ist.psu.edu

Abstract. The Web continues to grow at a tremendous rate. Search engines find it increasingly difficult to provide useful results. To manage this explosively large number of Web documents, automatic clustering of documents and organising them into domain dependent directories became very popular. In most cases, these directories represent a hierarchical structure of categories and sub-categories for domains and sub-domains. To fill up these directories with instances, individual documents are automatically analysed and placed into them according to their relevance. Though individual documents in these collections may not be ranked efficiently, combinedly they provide an excellent knowledge source for facilitating ontology construction in that domain. In (mainly automatic) ontology construction steps, we need to find and use relevant knowledge for a particular subject or term. News documents provide excellent relevant and up-to-date knowledge source. In this paper, we focus our attention in building business ontologies. To do that we use news documents from business domains to get an up-to-date knowledge about a particular company. To extract this knowledge in the form of important "terms" related to the company, we apply a novel method to find "related terms" given the company name. We show by examples that our technique can be successfully used to find "related terms" in similar cases.

1 Introduction

With the number of documents on the Web in trillions, less time to search for the right document, and inefficiencies or limitations of search engine technologies, Web-directories are an important way of organising Web documents. Examples include Yahoo directories, Google directories or DMOZ directories, MSN directories and other similar (mostly) hierarchical clusters or taxonomies of documents on the Web. Web-directories are nowadays becoming more valuable for several reasons. First of all, novice or first-time users sometimes may not necessarily know what keyword to search with to get documents in certain area of interest. Lack of proper keyword in certain specific domain can hinder the possibility of getting valuable documents. Secondly for even expert users, it is always helpful to filter valuable documents and arrange them in some fashion to save their time. These taxonomies help the users by filtering valuable documents and arranging them in some fashion to save their time.

K. Bauknecht et al. (Eds.): EC-Web 2005, LNCS 3590, pp. 188–197, 2005.

Learning term-relationships is considered one of the most useful steps in the context of knowledge discovery, construction of knowledge-bases (e.g. domain ontologies) or knowledge management issues. Our main goal is to build business ontologies for major public companies listed in Forbes list. These ontologies will be part of our business knowledge-base, which will be used for analysing textual information (such as corporate news sources, whitepapers or annual reports etc.) for individual companies.

To construct these ontologies for individual companies, we needed up-to-date information, in the form of useful terms e.g. from news articles available in business Web-sites. We can learn useful terms from these sources, which in the later stages, can be incorporated into the ontology with human assistance. We use OWL-Lite for creating the ontology. Although this part is relevant, however in this paper, due to space constraints, we mainly focus on the pre-processing of documents so that we can have all related terms for a company (in this case) extracted from the corresponding news document set.

Though we do not have enough space for the details of the ontology construction process here (we give a block-diagram in Figure 1), however, in this paper, we present the learning model (shown as a dotted rectangle surrounding "Related Term-vector Generator") involved in this work. The model is used to retrieve important terms to be included in the ontology.

Our approach of finding useful terms borrows ideas from query expansion or query term re-weighting. We basically are looking for "related term-vector" (defined later) for a particular company. This is an on-line learning process, where we do not rely on dictionary, thesaurus, or word-net to generate the "related term-vector", which can be thought of as query-expansion. We use news articles to learn the term co-occurrences for the companies and we used company names as query terms. This knowledge is used to build the "related term-vector" and the corresponding ontology. As new news articles are introduced we do the analysis on-the-fly to update the *ontology*.

2   Related Work

Building ontology is a complex process. Though large-scale ontologies exist, they may not be appropriate for specific purpose. According to Noy [17], ontologies should be built for specific purpose or reason. To elaborate on that she advised ontology-builders to follow yet we need to build ontology for a particular domain, such as business domain. Moreover we need to keep it relevant and up-to-date. Building ontologies completely manually is time-consuming, and erroneous. It is also difficult to modify ontologies manually. Automatic ontology building is a hard problem.

Ontology building process can be top-down, bottom-up or middle-out. Uschold et.al. proposed a manual ontology building process, parts of which can be made automatic. According to them the manual process consist of (1) identifying the key concepts and relationships between them, (2) committing to the basic terms such as class, entity, relation etc., (3) choosing a representation language, (4) integrating existing ontologies. Our method of discovering the knowledge by way of finding related terms for a company name falls under the first step. Though discovering relationships between terms is a whole different subject of research and out of scope for a discussion here, we mainly focus here on the prelude, which is finding the related terms. We believe that automating each individual sub-process of the ontology building process is the only way to automatise it as a whole.

Learning term-term relationships has its root in Information Retrieval (IR) research in the context of relevance feedback and is used mainly for query modification. The two main trends in this research is query term re-weighting and query expansion.

Harman [8,9,11,10] examined these two trends in a probabilistic model. There he discussed the question of adding best possible terms [8] with the query. Term re-weighting is an essential part of relevance feedback process, which has been investigated by Salton et. al. [23,12] in addition to their experiments with variations of probabilistic and vector space model [22]. Smeaton and van Rijsbergen [25] investigated query expansion and term re-weighting using term-relationships. The results from these experiments are largely negative. Query expansion via Maximum Spanning Tree shows poor performance for unexpected query. The same happened using Nearest Neighbour approach too. They cited the reason behind this as the difficulty in estimating the probability. We introduced a simple way of estimating the probability for a set of documents. Two words are associated if they co-occur in a sentence or nearby-sentences. In our belief, this is more realistic and reasonable approach and this can be viewed as learning the relationships from a set of documents.

User specific information has been used to expand the query [1]. Personal construct theory has been used in this [13] paper. We analyse the document set to find out the probability of co-occurrence and use that instead of user-preference. A user-centric evaluation of ranking algorithms can be found in [5]. In [15] Ramesh worked with Sen-Tree model to find term-dependencies. In [21] researchers used a logical approach to describe the relationship between a term and a document. They used a *probabilistic argumentation system* and claimed after Rijsbergen that IR systems are a form of uncertain inference. In order to be relevant to a term, a document must imply the term. Our approach can be seen from this angle, that each term must imply the occurrence of the related term with a certain probability. Our idea of term-relationship is somewhat similar to term co-occurrence [19]. In that work Peat and Willett explained the limitations of using term co-occurrence. But they used a more generic calculation of similar terms by three similarity measures, *cosine*, *dice*, and *tanimoto*. They used the whole document to find the term co-occurrence instead of a small region. We believe that the way the similarity measures are formed and the way term co-occurrences are identified are too generic in nature to find any useful result. Instead of completely relying on the document statistics, if we can exploit the usual constructs of natural language sentence formation and use a smaller region of terms rather than the whole document, we can achieve better result.

Other researchers such as Turtle and Croft [26], Fung et. al. [6], Haines and Croft [7], Neto [16], Pearl [18] and Silva [24] also contributed in this area of research. Some of the researchers viewed the document as a sample of the collection of terms. Terms occur randomly in the document with some probability distribution and these distributions are not always known. Even if we do not know the real distribution, document-term-relationship or term-term relationship can play a major role.

3 Our Approach

We introduce a new way to look into term co-occurrences. Natural language documents are not just arbitrary array of words. Words co-occurring in sentences or nearby sentences, relate to each other more closely that in two distant sentences. As described above, the reason behind the failure of term co-occurrences as studied in [19] can possibly be improved. We introduce "Weighted-Sentence" (*WS*) based term co-occurrence.

The system architecture is shown in Figure 1 for a category. The document collection is pre-filtered but not ranked. In taxonomies or Web-directories, candidate documents for a category are already organised using shallow filtering techniques, as explained above. This means that we have got the preliminary document set for a company or category. We use this document set to generate the related-term vectors for the query (category/company name).

For the rest of the discussion, it will be easier to think of the company or category name as the keyword in question. Actually, not only just for the sake of discussion, but sometimes documents are clustered in the same way in reality too. For example we will see that in financial news domain of Yahoo [1], news articles are filtered according to the occurrence of the ticker symbol in those articles. Even if it is not the case, for the sake of generality we can assume that the set of documents are pre-filtered for the keyword in question.

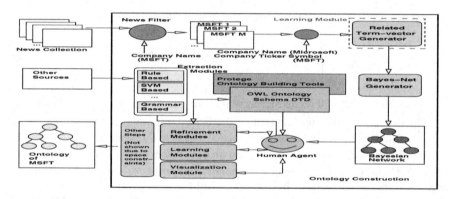

Fig. 1. The architecture of our system describing the ontology building process. We collect up-to-date and useful information from several different sources including financial news documents. News filter filters news for a specific company (e.g. MSFT or Microsoft). We describe the theory behind the "Related Term-vector Generator" in this paper.

Let us assume that in a category C there are in total M documents $D_1, D_2, \ldots, D_M$ pre-filtered for the query w. This constitutes the document collection C. So

$$C = \{D_1, D_2, \ldots D_M\} \tag{1}$$

Each of these documents can be thought of as a set of sentences. Therefore, if document D_d has N_d number of sentences in it, then we can write

$$D_d = \{S^d_1, S^d_2, \ldots S^d_{N_d}\} \text{ where } S^d_j : j^{th} \text{ sentence in document } D_d \tag{2}$$

---

[1] http://finance.yahoo.com

Similarly we can also imagine each individual sentences as a set of words and extend the same notation. Hereafter we removed the superscript of S_i to reduce the notational clumsiness. So if S_i contains P_i number of words in it then

$$S_i = \{w^i{}_1, w^i{}_2, \ldots w^i{}_{P_i}\} \text{ where } w^i{}_k \text{ represents the } k^{th} \text{ word in sentence } S_i \quad (3)$$

3.1   Related-Term Vector

Related-term vector of a query w is a vector of all the words which co-occur with w and are important (ranked higher than a given threshold). Basically it is the set of terms for which the term co-occurrence measure between them and the query is higher than a threshold. The difference between conventional co-occurring terms [19] and our approach is that we consider words in the same sentence or neighbouring sentences (will be explained in section 4.1) as probable candidates for related-term vector. We will come to the implementation part of it, (where this concept will be made clearer) where we took another assumption that no "verb", "preposition" or so-called stop-words are included in the related word-set. So according to this definition, if a sentence does not contain the query keyword w, then the related word-set of w for that sentence is a null-vector.

At this point, we assume that we have a function Ψ which generates all the related-terms of w when it is applied to a sentence S_j containing w. Therefore,

$$\overrightarrow{\Psi}(w, S_i) = \begin{cases} \overrightarrow{\langle w^r{}_1, w^r{}_2, w^r{}_3, \ldots w^r{}_{r_i}\rangle}, & w\mathcal{R}w^r{}_j \text{ and } w \in S_i \\ \overrightarrow{\phi}, & otherwise \end{cases} \quad (4)$$

Ψ generates a vector of related-terms of the query w. Considering the fact that function Ψ generates a vector, we can write $\Psi(w, S_i)$ as $\overrightarrow{\Psi}(w, S_i)$. $\mathcal{R}$ implies that w and $w^r{}_j$ are related. r_i is the total number of related words in this sentence S_i.

An example would be useful here. In a sentence *"Microsoft (MSFT) CEO Bill Gates announced today about the upcoming version of windows operating system, codenamed longhorn"* , the words/phrases like "CEO", "Bill Gates", "today", "upcoming", "version", "windows", "longhorn" etc. could be all related to the keyword "Microsoft". Given this sentence and the keyword "Microsoft", the function Ψ will generate the related-term vector which may include the above words depending on the threshold used.

Similar to the above derivation (3) we can see that in case of a whole document D_j and for the whole document collection C in category C,

$$\overrightarrow{\Psi}(w, D_j) = \sum_{k}^{N_j} \overrightarrow{\Psi}(w, S_k) \text{ and } \overrightarrow{\Psi}(w, G) = \sum_{j}^{M} \overrightarrow{\Psi}(w, D_j) \quad (5)$$

where the summation indicates a vector addition.

We describe the algorithm to implement the Ψ function and the related-term vector generating process in subsection 4.1.

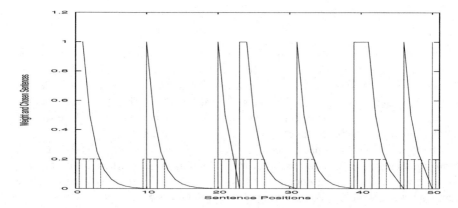

Fig. 2. The weighting function $W(j)$ and the set of sentences included in $N(S_i)$ as shown by the bar graphs. Each bar indicates a sentence. The preliminary sentence set was 1, 10, 20, 23, 24, 31, 39, 40, 41, 46, and 50 and the final extended sentence set is 1-3, 10-12, 20-26, 31-33, 39-43, 46-48, and 50.

4   Theory and Implementation

Here we elaborate our theory behind related-term vector.

4.1   Weighted Sentence Based Related-Term Vector

We introduce a novel concept of finding related-term vectors based on weighted sentences. On-line publishable natural language texts are almost always written in a coherent way. That means once a topic is mentioned, a few consecutive sentences are devoted to describe the topic. We exploit this this editing style to extract related-term vector by using our weighted sentence (WS) based method.

As mentioned earlier, related-term vector basically depends on the concept of term co-occurrences. From equation (4)

$$\overrightarrow{\Psi}(w, S_i) = \begin{cases} \langle \overrightarrow{w^r{}_1, w^r{}_2, w^r{}_3, \ldots w^r{}_{r_i}} \rangle, & w \mathcal{R} w^r{}_j \ and \ w \in N(S_i) \\ \overrightarrow{\phi}, & otherwise \end{cases} \tag{6}$$

Let us proceed step-by-step assembling all the concepts necessary to get the generating function for related-term vector. Let us first modify the concept of "sentences" to an "extended sentence-set". This will also help us define the weighted sentence (WS) based method. We introduce a function $N(S_i)$ which takes the position of a sentence S_i and generates the extended sentence-set. First we define the following function to get the weighting factor.

$$W(w, j) = e^{(j-i)log(\tau)} \text{ where } w \in S_i, j \geq i, \tau = \text{ threshold} \tag{7}$$

Here $W(w, j)$ is a weighting factor for all consecutive sentences at position j after the sentence i containing the query w. In our implementation, $\tau = 0.5$. With this definition we define $N(S_i)$ as

$$N(S_i) = \{S_k | k \geq i, W(w, k) \geq \epsilon\} \tag{8}$$

In our implementation $\epsilon = 0.2$. Figure 2 shows the $W(w, j)$ for a sample document where sentences at positions position 1, 10, 20, 23, 24, 31, 39, 40, 41, 46, and 50 contain the query term. In this particular case sentences at positions 1-3, 10-12, 20-26, 31-33, 39-43, 46-48, and 50 will be included in corresponding $N(S_j)$s. This idea is the result of an empirical study about the effect of sentences in document relevance and we showed that this technique can be useful to increase document relevance.

The idea behind is that natural language sentences cluster together based on topic. Term-significance is calculated using a formula similar to [20], where term-term significance was calculated per document basis. We calculate it per collection-basis. The significance of a word w_m co-occurring with w in sentence S_j is

$$\sigma_{w_m} = \frac{pt f_m}{\sqrt{\sum_r pt f_r^2}} \times \log \Phi \tag{9}$$

where $pt f_m = (\frac{t f_m}{max_r t f_r})$ and where $\Phi = \frac{N}{n_m}$ where

$$t f_m = n t f^j{}_m \times W(w, j | S_j \in N(S_i)) \text{ (from (8))} \tag{10}$$

where $n t f^j{}_i =$ term-frequency of term w_i in sentence S_j. N is the number of total sentences in the document collection C which is (from (1) and (2))

$$N = \sum_k^M N_k \tag{11}$$

$$n_m = \sum_{S_k \notin N(S_i), w_m \in Nouns(S_k)}^M N_k \tag{12}$$

which in simple term is the number of sentences outside the set $N(S_i)$ where the term w_m appears. $Nouns(S_k)$ is an NLP function which gives the set of all nouns of a sentence, taken as its input.

Now $\mathcal{R}$ represents the relatedness between two terms. It is a defined as a relation between w and w_m which produces the candidacy of w_m to be included in the related-term vector depending on some conditions.

$$\mathcal{R} \equiv \{f : w \rightarrow w_m | \sigma_{w_m} > \zeta, w_m \in Nouns(N(S_i))\} \tag{13}$$

Here $Nouns(N(S_i))$ gives the whole set of nouns from the extended WS set of S_i. ζ is a threshold.

5   Evaluation

Experimenting and evaluating the processes responsible for automatic ontology construction is a hard problem. First of all the process consists of several sub-process and each has separate goals. Secondly it is hard to quantify the betterness of an ontology over other ontologies. The reason lies in the basics of ontology construction. As Noy [17] said, ontologies are build for specific purposes. Therefor our business ontology for business document analysis can not be compared with another business ontology, constructed for a different goal. For these reasons we decided to provide the experimental results in the form of the related term-set generated by our technique. In future we would like to concentrate on finding out the use of these terms in the context of relevance or some other purpose and can compare the usefulness and betterness of our approach over others.

Table 1. Details of the dataset. We have 112 companies/categories in total but due to the enormous size of the latex table all of them are not shown. Number of pages taken from individual categories are shown in the third column, followed by related-term sets as found by our method.

Symbol	Company	Number of documents	Related terms
AAPL	Apple	86	AAPL, Apple, Computer, Music, MSFT, Lehman, Steve Jobs, Cowen, etc.
DELL	Dell Inc.	169	DELL, Computer, www.dell.com, Michael Dell, HP, Server, IBM, Storage,
EBAY	eBay	108	EBAY, Paypal, Amazon, AspenTech, Andale, Auction, Bid, etc.
GE	General Electric	238	GE, Finance, General Electric, Schwarzenegger, Capital, China, Aegon, Medical, etc.
IBM	IBM	387	IBM, Sco, Linux, Services, Unix, Lego, Equifax, Lotus, eServer, HP, Tivoli, etc.
JNJ	Johnson and Jonhson	74	JNJ, Johnson, Merrill, Centocor, Medtronic, etc.
JPM	JPMorgan Chase and Co	88	JPM, JPMorgan, Chase, Risk, Equity, Metropoulas, etc.
MSFT	Microsoft	492	MSFT, Microsoft, Security, AOL, Apple, Sco, Caldera, Macintosh, Wi-Fi, etc.

5.1   Data Set

We crawled Yahoo's financial news page [2] starting from summer 2003 and cached individual news articles as appeared in Yahoo web-pages in respective company ticker symbol. We selected 112 stock symbols for this experiment. We converted the HTML pages into text using a combination of our own extraction algorithms *ContentExtractor* and *FeatureExtractor* [4,3,2].

In short they are based on HTML features and information content blocks. We divided the HTML pages into several different blocks, based table, page or other type of boundaries. These blocks are then analysed for the required feature or based on their similarity over a collection. We got over 95% of F-measure in this part. Due to space

---

[2] http://finance.yahoo.com

constraints we are not showing the results here. The details of the dataset is shown in Table 1 for 8 companies. Due to space constraints we could not show all 112 categories. The total number of documents we analysed for this paper is 2333.

5.2 Experiment

We implemented our algorithms in Perl on Unix platform. We used Alembic workbench [14] (for the $Noun$ function), which is one of the best natural language processing softwares available. From the Table 1 we can see that our approach can be used to extract very useful terms for all these companies.

6 Conclusion and Future Work

We came up with a novel technique of discovering knowledge from web-directories by finding term-term relations in news article collections available from these web-directories. From our approach and the formula used, we claim that our approach is flexible and it can be applied to any document collection for any query term, if we just replace the company names with the desired query term. In future we would like to create a Bayesian Network from these term-relations which can play a major role in assisting humans to populate the company ontology instances. The formation of Bayesian Network and the proper use of it can also help us quantify the usefulness and to do performance comparison of our approach over others in the context of document relevance.

References

1. Sanjiv K. Bhatia. Selection of search terms based on user profile. In *Proceedings of the ACM/SIGAPP Symposium on Applied computing*, pages 224–233, 1992.
2. Sandip Debnath, Prasenjit Mitra, and C Lee Giles. Automatic extraction of informative blocks from webpages. In *Proceedings of the ACM SAC 2005*, pages 1722–1726, 2005.
3. Sandip Debnath, Prasenjit Mitra, and C Lee Giles. Identifying content blocks from web documents. In *Proceedings of the 15th ISMIS 2005 Conference*, pages 285–293, 2005.
4. Sandip Debnath, Prasenjit Mitra, Nirmal Pal, and C Lee Giles. Automatic identification of informative sections from webpages. In *Upcoming journal of IEEE Transactions on Knowledge and Data Engineering*, 2005.
5. Efthimis N. Efthimiadis. A user-centred evaluation of ranking algorithms for interactive query expansion. In *Proceedings of the 16th ACM SIGIR*, pages 146–159, 1993.
6. Robert Fung and Brendan Del Favero. Applying bayesian networks to information retrieval. In *Communications of the ACM*, volume 38(3), pages 42–ff, 1995.
7. David Haines and W. Bruce Croft. Relevance feedback and inference networks. In *Proceedings of the 16th ACM SIGIR*, pages 2–11, 1993.
8. Donna Harman. Towards interactive query expansion. In *Proceedings of the 11th ACM SIGIR*, pages 321–331, 1988.
9. Donna Harman. Ranking algorithms. In *Information Retrieval: Data Structures and Algorithms*, pages 363–392. Englewood Cliffs: Prentice Hall, 1992.
10. Donna Harman. Relevance feedback and other query modification techniques. In *Information Retrieval: Data Structures and Algorithms*, pages 241–263. Englewood Cliffs: Prentice Hall, 1992.

11. Donna Harman. Relevance feedback revisited. In *Proceedings of the 15th ACM SIGIR*, pages 1–10, 1992.
12. Wu Harry and Gerard Salton. A comparison of search term weighting: term relevance vs. inverse document frequency. In *Proceedings of the 4th ACM SIGIR*, pages 30–39, 1981.
13. George A. Kelly. A mathematical approach to psychology. In *B. Maher, Ed. Clinical Psychology and Personality: The Selected Papers of George Kelly*, pages 94–112. John Wiley and Sons, 1969.
14. MITRE. Alembic workbench - http://www.mitre.org/tech/alembic-workbench/.
15. R. Nallapati and J. Allan. Capturing term dependencies using a language model based in sentence tree. In *Proceedings of CIKM 2002*, 2002.
16. Berthier Ribeiro Neto and Richard Muntz. A belief network model for ir. In *Proceedings of the 19th ACM SIGIR*, pages 253–260, 1996.
17. N.F. Noy and C. Hafner. The state of the art in ontology design: A survey and comparative review. In *AI Magazine*, volume 18, pages 53–74, 1997.
18. Judea Pearl. *Probabilistic reasoning in intelligent systems: networks of plausible inference*. Morgan Kaufmann Publishers Inc., San Francisco, CA, 1988.
19. Helen J. Peat and Peter Willett. The limitations of term co-occurrence data for query expansion in document retrieval systems. In *Journal of the American Society for Information Science*, volume 42(5), pages 378–383, 1991.
20. Ulrich Pfeifer, Norbert Fuhr, and Tung Huynh. Searching structured documents with the enhanced retrieval functionality of freewais-sf and sfgate. In *Computer Networks and ISDN Systems*, volume 27(6), pages 1027–1036, 1995.
21. Justin Picard and Rolf Haenni. Modeling information retrieval with probabilistic argumentation systems. In *20th Annual BCS-IRSG Colloquium on IR*, 1998.
22. Gerard Salton. *Automatic Information Organization and Retrieval*. McGraw-Hill, 1968.
23. Gerard Salton and C. Buckley. Improving retrieval performance by relevance feedback. In *Journal of the American Society for Information Science*, volume 41, pages 288–297, 1990.
24. I. R. Silva. Bayesian networks for information retrieval systems. In *PhD thesis, Universidad Federal de Minas Gerais*, 2000.
25. A. Smeaton and C. J. van Rijsbergen. The retrieval effects of query expansion on a feedback document retrieval system. In *Computer Journal*, volume 26(3), pages 239–246, 1983.
26. H. Turtle and W. B. Croft. Inference networks for document retrieval. In *Proceedings of the 13th ACM SIGIR*, pages 1–24, 1990.

Music Rights Clearance Business Analysis and Delivery

Carlos Pedrinaci[1], Ziv Baida[2], Hans Akkermans[2], Amaia Bernaras[3],
Jaap Gordijn[2], and Tim Smithers[1]

[1] Parque Tecnológico de San Sebastián, Mikeletegi 53, 20009 San Sebastián, Spain
cpedrinaci@miramon.net, tsmithers@miramon.net
[2] Free University, FEW/Business Informatics, De Boelelaan 1081a, 1081 HV
Amsterdam, The Netherlands
{ziv, elly, gordijn}@cs.vu.nl
[3] Idom, Paseo de los Olmos, 14 Bidebieta I, 20009 San Sebastián, Spain
abernaras@idom.es

Abstract. Semantic Web Services can be seen as remote Problem Solving Methods offered via the Web through platform and language independent interfaces. They can be seamlessly integrated to achieve more
complex functionality by composing pre-existing software components.
Despite technical advantages surrounding Semantic Web Services technologies, their perspective overlooks the commercial aspects of services
in the real – non-IT – world, and is therefore incomplete and limiting. Real-world services – business activities such as insurances, medical
services, ADSL etc – have nowadays an increasing social and economic
importance. Important trends are the bundling of services and a growing customer-need orientation. Thus, there is a need for a computational
background for describing real-world services and applying knowledge-
based technologies for reasoning about them: configuring composite services and analysing them from a business perspective. We have developed
ontologies and software tools to fill this gap, and applied them to industrial case studies. We present here a case study from the music industry,
going from the analysis of a new business scenario to the development of
an application called Xena that coordinates IT infrastructures in order
to provide a profitable service that reflects major business principles. As
opposed to currently proposed solutions in the Semantic Web Services
community, our system is an automated implementation of a real-world
service where important business decisions can be traced back.

1 Introduction

Reasoning about business value, economic feasibility of businesses and other business logics has traditionally been performed within business science [8,9,10,11].
The rise of Internet and Web service technology presents businesses with the opportunity to integrate business activities into a value constellation [10,9]. Businesses bundle forces and use automated processes to offer the best solution for
customer needs: a bundle of goods and services that together offer a higher added

K. Bauknecht et al. (Eds.): EC-Web 2005, LNCS 3590, pp. 198–207, 2005.
© Springer-Verlag Berlin Heidelberg 2005

value than single services/goods. In spite of this strong intertwining of business and IT, the wealth of Web service research is dominated by a technical perspective, not taking into consideration the business logics that drive business transactions, eventually executed by Web services.

The use of Web services, like other technologies, should be justified by their support of strategic business goals. Hence, transactions they execute must adhere to business logic, as dictated by the business domain, including issues such as competition, legislation and an understanding of the market. Consequently, a first step in Web service implementation should be understanding the business environment. A (possibly inter-organisational) bundle of services – business activities – has to be defined that provides a solution for customer needs. The next step is to define a business process model to carry out this service bundle. And subsequently, based on the process model and driven by business logics, it is possible to implement and select Web services that distribute the computation of the earlier described business activities (e-services). Thus, decisions made on the business perspective propagate to the system implementation.

In this paper we cross the boarders of research disciplines, and present an exploratory case study, where we investigate and implement e-service offerings, starting with a business analysis, and ending with a Web service based implementation of a scenario sketched by the business analysis. Important business decisions, made during the business analysis, are reflected in the system implementation. Our prototype application adheres to these business decisions, and coordinates the execution of distributed Web Services for the actual offering of e-services over the Internet. Our Web service based system differs from other work by the Semantic Web Services community in its business grounding, originating from a business analysis that can be traced back in the system implementation.

This paper is organised as follows. In Section 2 we present the case study domain, followed by an analysis from a business perspective. This analysis is the business-grounding of the system implementation, presented in Section 3. Finally, in Section 4 we present our conclusions and discuss important issues for future research on what we refer to as *business-value driven Web services*.

2 A Business Perspective on Music Rights Clearance

2.1 Case Study: Music Rights Clearance and Repartitioning

Conventional and Internet radio stations broadcast music to attract audience, and sell this audience to their advertisers. Commercial music use is bound by several rights reserved by right holders (e.g. artists and producers). Specifically, a radio station has to pay right holders for the right to broadcast music.

The process of charging radio stations for music use and of distributing the money among artists, producers and other right holders is supported by organisations called *rights societies*. These may be government-appointed organisations (as is the case in the EU) or commercial companies (as is the case in the US and is intended to be in the EU in the future). They collect fees from radio stations (an activity referred to as *rights clearance*), and distribute the fees among right holders (an activity referred to as *repartitioning*). With respect to the right to communicate music to the public, rights societies provide Internet radio stations with the service of *clearing* this right, and right holders with the service of benefiting from this clearance: *repartitioning*.

Due to the liberalisation of the market for rights societies in the EU, the way of doing business in this industry may change dramatically. New rights societies may appear, and will start competing on customers: radio stations (customers for the clearance service) and right holders (customers for the repartitioning service). Currently the Dutch law determines which rights societies clear certain rights and repartition fees. A radio station has no flexibility in choosing a rights society to work with. Market liberalisation will bring an end to this situation, causing a collapse of the power structures within the industry. Our case study aims at analysing new ways of doing business in a liberalised market, concentrating on clearing rights for Internet radio stations, where the whole process can be supported by e-services. We present our case analysis, gradually going from a business analysis (Section 2) to Web service implementation (Section 3). The analysis process (Figure 1) includes the following steps: (1) analysis of network value constellations of enterprises; (2) specification of elementary commercial services and opportunities to bundle them; (3) description of inter- and intra-organisational processes for service delivery; and (4) implementation of an inter-organisational information system, based on ontologies and web-services, and supporting the business process/service description and business model.

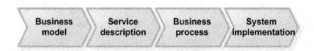

Fig. 1. Analysis process: from a business perspective to an IT implementation

2.2   Business Analysis

Business analyses are studies that result in an understanding of how actors can profitably do business. The way of doing business can be conceptualised in so-called *business models* that show (1) the actors involved, (2) the activities performed by these actors, and (3) the objects of economic value that these actors exchange in their business activities. Business models for networked enterprises typically show multi-party dependencies, rather than a bi-lateral alignment of activities. The reader is referred to [3] for an ontology-based method to perform a business analysis, and to [7] for a detailed business analysis of our case study domain. Here we only discuss the most relevant issues for the current case study.

Market liberalisation means that new rights societies may emerge, that radio stations are no longer obliged to clear rights with a specific rights society, and that rights societies will compete on representing artists. This could be a nightmare for radio stations. A typical Dutch Internet radio station plays a large number of music tracks every month. Nowadays all the rights are cleared with the same two rights societies, as determined by Dutch law. But in the liberalised market an Internet radio station would have to find out which (not necessarily Dutch) rights societies represent the artists of every track, and clear rights with all these rights societies. Radio stations may have to do business with a large number of rights societies, rather than just two. Two scenarios may solve this problem, by introducing new actors:

1. A *clearing organisation* is introduced; it takes over rights societies' role to interact with Internet radio stations. It offers a rights clearance service to Internet radio stations, and in fact acts as a proxy, and forwards individual clearing requests to the appropriate rights society. Consequently, rights societies no longer need IT to perform the inter-organisational clearing process themselves. Although a single organization interacts with radio stations, liberalisation implies that *any* rights society may represent *any* right holder, as opposed to the current situation.
2. Instead of a clearing organisation we introduce a *clearing coordinator*. Internet radio stations continue interacting with a rights society of their choice. This rights society cannot clear all the rights itself. Instead, it uses the services of a clearing coordinator to find out through which other rights societies it can clear rights for a customer (this information is not publicly available). Yet, the clearing coordinator does not interact with radio stations.

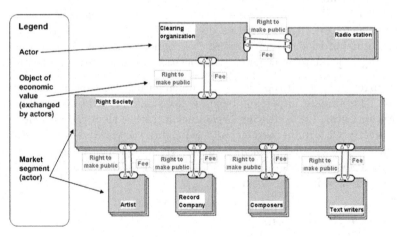

Fig. 2. Clearing organisation business model

The two scenarios, for which business models are depicted in Figure 2 and Figure 3, encapsulate important strategic business decisions:

1. Which actors are involved? Both scenarios involve rights societies and right holders, as in the current situation. However, both scenarios introduce a new actor: a clearing organisation and a clearing coordinator.
2. Which actor interacts with customers? In the first scenario, rights societies give up some power: they no longer interact with radio stations, making it

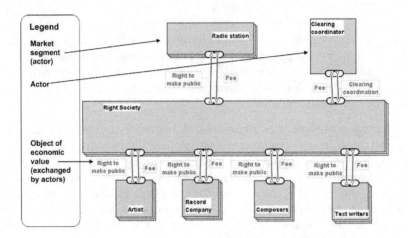

Fig. 3. Clearing coordinator business model

hard to build a strong relationship with radio stations and to create customer loyalty. In the second scenario rights societies maintain their traditional position, maintaining direct interaction with radio stations.

3. Who determines fees? The party that interacts with radio stations can eventually determine the fees that radio stations have to pay. As long as another entity stands between rights societies and radio stations (clearing organisation scenario), rights societies do not determine the final clearance fee, making it hard for them to compete on radio stations as customers. In the clearing coordinator scenario rights societies continue determining the fees.

In the current paper we report about implementing the clearing organisation scenario. This implies important business decisions: (1) introducing a clearing organisation actor, (2) a clearing organisation, rather than rights societies, interact directly with radio stations, and (3) rights societies no longer determine the final fee. We created a business model [7] with which financial feasibility can be analysed for all actors involved. The clearing coordinator scenario was implemented as well, as reported in [7].

2.3 Service Description

The clearing organisation scenario includes two services: clearance and repartitioning. These services can be offered by multiple rights societies; each may require somewhat different fees. Consequently, rights societies need to describe their services in a way that attracts customers, from a business perspective: describe what the e-service provides to the customer, and what the customer gives in return. Hence, business activities identified in the business model (see Figure 2) are now described as *services*, using a service ontology [2]. Based on such a description, a customer can choose the e-services – being business activities – that he or she wishes to consume. A discussion on using the service ontology to describe and bundle services based on business logics is presented in [2].

2.4   Business Process

The clearing organisation's business process for rights clearance consists of the activities of identifying the tracks being reported and the rights societies that can clear rights for these tracks, calculating fees (by rights societies), collecting fees (by the clearing organisation), and distributing the fees among rights societies. Repartitioning (distributing collected fees among right holders) involves identifying right holders, calculating their commission and distributing fees (either to right holders or to other rights societies that represent these right holders). Each activity operationalises a value-exchange, expressed by higher-level ontologies; it does not include pure technical activities, such as upload a play report to a database. In the next section we go another step further and we describe how, based on the business analysis performed, we have developed a clearing organisation prototype that provides the music rights clearance e-service to Internet radio stations by coordinating the interaction with distributed rights societies.

3   Xena: Web-Service Based Music Rights Clearance

The clearing organisation business model relies on establishing a new actor (i.e. the clearing organisation) that merely acts as a proxy between Internet radio stations and rights societies. Driven by this business model, we have developed Xena, a clearing organisation prototype. It is supported by our *E-Services Delivery Architecture* and relies on Semantic Web and Web Services technologies in order to actually deliver the music rights clearance e-service over the Internet. In this section we describe how we have reconciled business and technical aspects to implement our prototype. We first present the underlying software architecture that provides the structural framework for its development. We then present how business studies were applied to determine the activities to perform as well as their coordination. Finally, we review our prototype in the light of the main business decisions that were initially adopted.

3.1   E-Services Delivery Architecture

For a system to satisfy the business model proposed, it has to be the realisation of the business offering. This involves, applying the business logics captured in the business model during the system design and development and, most importantly, maintaining them at runtime. As a consequence, the system needs to support the service delivery process informed by the business knowledge. Moreover, because we are delivering an e-service that involves several actors, the system needs to be able to coordinate and seamlessly integrate distributed and heterogeneous systems. Finally, the system needs to be scalable; after all, there are thousands of radio stations in the Web.

   These highly demanding requirements pose the need for supporting runtime reasoning over an inter-organisational process where highly heterogeneous systems need to be coordinated. For this, Xena is developed on top of our E-Services Delivery Architecture. The core of the architecture which has previously been applied for supporting designing events, such as conferences or meetings [1], is an adaptation for the Internet of a what is usually referred to as a *Blackboard Framework* [5], a task independent architecture for implementing the blackboard problem-solving model. The blackboard problem-solving model [5] is a highly structured opportunistic-reasoning model where pieces of knowledge are applied at the most *opportune* time: either reasoning from data towards a solution; or from a possible solution towards needed data. The fundamental philosophy of this problem-solving model establishes that experts, also known as *knowledge sources*(KSs) in the blackboard literature, do not communicate with each other directly; instead, all the interactions strictly happen through modifications over a shared data structure called *blackboard.*

In order to adapt the Blackboard Framework to the Internet, our framework "externalises" knowledge sources thus enabling the use of their expertise to improve the interaction with the different business actors. In fact, given that KSs encapsulate expertise, we apply this knowledge to improve and direct the interaction with remote systems (such as web services from other companies). In order to streamline the collaboration among the business actors, we identify as part of our software architecture, ontologies as a means for representing the domain knowledge of the application (e.g. the music rights management ontology), and Semantic Web Services as the vehicle for a seamless but effective communication.

3.2   A Real-World Service Oriented Approach

Web Services have been proposed as a standard means for supporting interoperation between different systems independently from their platform or language. The power of Web Services lays in the fact that they can be seamlessly composed to achieve more complex operations, thanks to the use of so-called orchestration languages. The Semantic Web Services initiative couples Web Services with semantic annotations in order to establish the computational ground for a higher automation of the discovery, composition and execution processes. In spite of the technical advantages of (Semantic) Web Services technologies, their perspective overlooks commercial aspects and is therefore unnecessarily limiting.

In Section 2 we have presented the real-world services involved in the clearing organisation scenario and how they are composed in the final e-service offering. These services, are understood from a business perspective and are therefore different from (Semantic) Web Services some IT systems could provide. Still, we need to fill the gap between the e-services definitions and their Web Services based execution, in order to automate the provisioning of the music rights clearance service over the Web. Informed by the real-world services identified and the business process model obtained, we have followed what we call a *Real-World Services Oriented Approach* as opposed to (IT) service-oriented approaches. In our prototype, each of the real-world services identified are provided by a particular knowledge source. The KSs encapsulate the expertise for delivering these real-world services and hence allow us to bring IT services to their e-services executable form.

Based on the activities the business process model identifies, we have developed three KSs. The first one, the *Main KS*, is derived from the first business activity and it is in charge of interacting with Internet radio stations and determining the rights societies to deal with, based on the different tracks being reported. The second KS, namely the *Clearing KS*, encapsulates the expertise for contacting rights societies, and executing the fee calculation service. Finally, the third activity, which is related to money transfers (collecting and distributing fees), is handled by the *Accounting KS*. See Figure 4 for a general overview of the system implementation.

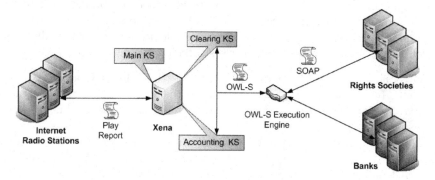

Fig. 4. Xena Architecture

3.3   E-Services Delivery Process

In addition to determining the e-services involved in the service delivery, the business process model establishes how the different business activities need to be coordinated. Therefore, the process model roughly specifies how the different KSs need to be coordinated and even establishes the activities they have to perform by identifying the actors they need to interact with and the expected results. In Xena we can distinguish two different levels where the delivery process is defined. On the first level, we determine how the different e-services must be composed for the final delivery as specified by the business process model. On the second level, we define workflows for mapping e-services into Web Services executions.

The e-services composition is supported by the opportunistic-reasoning platform. The KSs are informed by a music rights management ontology we have modelled in OWL and a set of inference rules. These rules determine the activities to be performed under certain conditions. In some cases, the action will result in rather simple tasks such as calculating the commission, but in other cases they will trigger the execution of remote services, such as the clearing or the bank transfer services. The need to match real-world services into IT services, leads to the need for specifying and executing workflows that map business services into a composition of IT services. In order to be able to execute these (real-world) services we describe them using OWL-S[4], their groundings being linked to Web Services offered by the different actors identified in the business analysis. For example, the clearing service has been modelled in OWL-S as a sequence of Web Service methods offered by Rights Societies IT systems. In runtime, knowledge sources trigger the execution of the OWL-S services making use of an OWL-S execution engine[1] and the results of the executions are placed into the blackboard for further processing (see Figure 4).

3.4   Reviewing Our Approach

Having a business understanding of the scenario allows us to examine the system developed from a business perspective, to check whether the IT implementation faithfully composes the e-services that were identified. Comming back to the main business decisions that were adopted, it is then possible to check whether the implemented system adheres to the business logics dictated by the business model. In Section 2.2 we identified three strategic business decisions:

1. Introduce a new actor, the clearing organisation: this new actor is represented by our prototype, Xena. The rest of the actors, that is, Internet radio stations, rights societies and right holders, still remain involved in the business process.
2. The actor in charge of dealing with Internet radio stations is the clearing organisation: in our IT implementation Xena is charged of dealing with Internet radio stations and is therefore directly offering them the music rights clearance e-service (see Figure 4).
3. Final fees are determined by the clearing organisation: Xena contacts rights societies for calculating the fees and eventually adds its own commission to the final fee. Thus, the final fee is indeed determined by the clearing organisation.

Therefore, Xena implements the main strategic business decisions adopted during the business and services modelling phases. For this, the system is built on top of three important blocks: (1) the E-Services Delivery Architecture; (2) ontologies to model the domain and business knowledge; and (3) Semantic Web Services for a seamless integration of distributed and heterogeneous systems. This has shown to be a good solution for an automated implementation of a real-world service offering where important business decisions can be traced back.

4   Conclusions

The European music industry will have to face a new business environment with the forthcoming liberalisation of the market for the music rights clearance and repartitioning. Using knowledge-based technologies for *business modelling* [6] and *service modelling* [2], we have analysed this business scenario and obtained a profitable solution. A resulting business model relies on establishing a clearing organisation that merely acts as a proxy between Internet radio stations and rights societies. Driven by this business model, we have developed a

---

[1] http://www.mindswap.org/2004/owl-s/api/

prototype of a clearing organisation. The prototype, named Xena, is supported by our E-Services Delivery Architecture and relies on Semantic Web and Web Services technologies in order to actually deliver e-services over the Internet. Our business-value driven approach is an interdisciplinary approach where business and technical aspects are combined in order to actually deliver profitable e-services over the Web. There still remain, however, important issues we expect to tackle in the future. For instance, further case studies will be required in order to better establish the rules and guidelines that lead from the business analysis to the business process to the actual implementation. Finally, we intend to profit from the business knowledge and the flexibility of the E-Services Delivery Architecture in order to support business practitioners in the task of declaratively defining the delivery process.

References

1. J. Aguado, C. Pedrinaci, A. Bernaras, T. Smithers, H. Calderón, and J. Tellería. Online design of events application trial, version 2, September 2004. OBELIX IST-2001-33144 DELIVERABLE 7.8.
2. Hans Akkermans, Ziv Baida, Jaap Gordijn, Nieves Peña, Ander Altuna, and Iñaki Laresgoiti. Value webs: Using ontologies to bundle real-world services. *IEEE Intelligent Systems - Semantic Web Services*, 19(4):57–66, 2004.
3. Ziv Baida, Jaap Gordijn, Andrei Z. Morch, Hanne Sæle, and Hans Akkermans. Ontology-based analysis of e-service bundles for networked enterprises. In *Proceedings of The 17th Bled eCommerce Conference (Bled 2004)*, Bled, Slovenia, 2004.
4. The OWL Services Coalition. Owl-s: Semantic markup for web services, 2003. http://www.daml.org/services/owl-s/1.0/.
5. R. Engelmore and T. Morgan. *Blackboard Systems*. The Insight Series in Aritificial Intelligence. Addison-Wesley, 1988. ISBN: 0-201-17431-6.
6. Jaap Gordijn and Hans Akkermans. Value based requirements engineering: Exploring innovative e-commerce ideas. *Requirements Engineering Journal*, 8(2):114–134, 2003.
7. Jaap Gordijn, Patrick Sweet, Borys Omelayenko, and Bert Hazelaar. *D7.4 Digital Music Value Chain Application*. Obelix consortium, Amsterdam, NL, 2004. Available from http://obelix.e3value.com.
8. Morris B. Holbrook. *Consumer Value: A Framework for Analysis and Research*. Routledge, New York, NY, 1999.
9. Richard Normann and Rafael Ramirez. *Designing Interactive Strategy: From Value Chain to Value Constellation*. John Wiley & Sons, Chichester, UK, 1994.
10. Michael E. Porter. *Competitive Advantage: Creating and Sustaining Superior Performance*. The Free Press, New York, NY, 1985.
11. Don Tapscott, David Ticoll, and Alex Lowy. *Digital Capital: Harnessing the Power of Business Webs*. Harvard Business School Press, Boston, 2000.

RDF Schema Based Ubiquitous Healthcare Service Composition

Wookey Lee[1], Mye M. Sohn[2], Ji-Hong Kim[3], Byung-Hyun Ha[3], and Suk-Ho Kang[3]

[1] Department of Computer Science, Sungkyul University,
wook@sungkyul.edu
[2] Department of Industrial Engineering, SungKyunKwan University,
myesohn@skku.edu
[3] Department of Industrial Engineering, Seoul National University,
{valentine@ara, pepper@netopia, shkang@}snu.ac.kr

Abstract. We suggest a service framework and algorithms of provisioning healthcare services in a ubiquitous computing environment. In order to meet customers' need we translate the need into relevant goal and repeatedly refine the goal into sub-goals through commonsense knowledge until there are appropriate services for sub-goals and after, employ the services. The results of this research enable integration and interconnection of devices, applications, and functions within the healthcare services. By RDFSs and their interoperability, a ubiquitous healthcare service composition is achieved, and the hidden semantic distances can be measured dynamically.

1 Introduction

When healthcare services are provided in a ubiquitous computing environment, the tailor-made services are easily employed in everyday life and enterprises can realize commercial in-house services by minimizing the medical experts' intervention accompanying high costs. To put it concretely, possible healthcare services that enterprises can provide according to the health state of an individual are as follows: health improvement for normal people, early diagnosis of disease, improvement of life quality for elderly people, healthcare for chronic invalids and prognoses, management of medical conditions like pregnant women and athletes, and so on. With ubiquitous computing the quality of human life can be improved by interoperation among various devices and services [8]. However when the needs are indirect and the tasks that fulfill the needs are complex, we need the ingenious mechanism that coordinates a variety of objects including the users themselves [4, 7].

When services are modeled for the functionalities of devices, the services need to be combined dynamically according to the situation using knowledge base in other to achieve high-level requirements of users. The reasons for dynamic composition of services can be stated with three perspectives of users, devices, and domains. First, at user perspective, the needs of users in reality seem too diverse to define all possible schemes of services in advance. If we define every service scheme statically, it will be have limited scalability. This is because almost all services need to be redefined, even when the details of user's needs change slightly. At the device perspective, the

K. Bauknecht et al. (Eds.): EC-Web 2005, LNCS 3590, pp. 208–217, 2005.
© Springer-Verlag Berlin Heidelberg 2005

availability of devices and applications making up ubiquitous environment changes according to time and place. Therefore the services that they can provide are impossible to predict and it is not applicable to assume fixed conditions. Lastly, in order to apply one successful system in a certain domain to anther domain, the system requires to be designed in a generic form. If a system is implemented using generic rules and domain-specific knowledge to meet the needs of users, the system can be easily applicable in another domain only after modifying the domain-specific knowledge. As a result, it is important to compose services dynamically based on predefined knowledge to build successful ubiquitous computing.

In this research we suggest a service framework and algorithms of provisioning healthcare services in a ubiquitous computing environment. The framework is composed of atomic services, user's goals, goal-based agents, dynamic service composition algorithm, and knowledge bases. Currently most researches of composing services dynamically depend on the conventional planning methods of Artificial Intelligence domain. This approach stands on the Mikrokosmos ontology [6] which enables querying and answering based on shared knowledge base and on the HowNet [2] for causality inference based on the set of lexical knowledge bases. All these show that the network of concepts is used for extracting more refined knowledge.

2 Motivating Example for Ubiquitous Health Service

Mike currently has registered to uHealthInsurenceNet Inc. In the past winter, Mike has met with accident at ski resort. No sooner had met accident to him than his smart watch on a wrist checked his heart beat, body temperature, and so on. This information is forwarded to Mike's agent. Mike's agent collects to other information in its DB about Mike's clinical history and then the agent forwards this information to uHealthInsurenceNet. The expert system at uHealthInsurenceNet then noticed that Mike's ankle is sprain. The agent at uHealthInsurenceNet then searches for an appropriate orthopedic surgery doctor for Mike's ankle in the company's database. After an appropriate orthopedic doctor has been selected, Mike's data is sent to the doctor's agent through the agent. Upon reviewing Mike's current condition and medical history, the orthopedic doctor, Annie, realizes that Mike's ankle ligament is pulled. Annie can now tell the agent to notify Mike that he needs to take a medical treatment and therapy. The uHealthInsurenceNet agent forwards this information to Mike's agent. Mike's agent checks the Mike's schedule and interacts with doctor's agent to make an appointment with doctor. Doctor recommended Mike to treat a therapy after Mike was treated for ankle ligament. Doctor's agent forwards medical treatment result and recommendation to the uHealthInsurenceNet agent. The uHealthInsurenceNet agent prepares list of therapy centers that are located within a 5 miles from Mike's home, and then forwards to Mike's agent. Mike's agent checks the Mike's schedule and interacts with therapies' agent to make an appointment with therapist. If therapist who satisfies Mike's constraints exists, Mike's agent makes an appointment with therapist's agent. If therapist who satisfies Mike's constraints doesn't exist, Mike's agent proposes schedule alteration (or constraint relaxation) to Mike.

We refer to the example, and provide a knowledge-base. Knowledge base consists of four elements. First is the semantic part, that is, ontology and logic is the second part. Third is the participant part and the last part is service. In this section we explain these elements in detail.

In the state of incompletion, a plan needs to be determined in order to complete the goal. The pending state is when the service is actually in motion to complete the goal. In this state, service is continually in motion until the goal is completed or an outside event interferes with the current state. While the goal is in a pending state it can end in terminated state before reaching a completed or incomplete state. The goal in its pending state alters into incomplete state again, either when achieving the goal ends in failure due to an exception, or when new opportunities appear to attain the goal in a more appropriate way. And whenever a goal turns into an incomplete state, an agent builds plans to complete the goal as soon as possible. Likewise, when an agent decides the goal in the complete state is invalid because of outside events, the goal turns into an incomplete state. When a one time applicable goal is completed or when a certain goal is no longer preferable by a user any more, the goal is altered into terminated state.

3   RDFS Based Service Composition

To compose services dynamically conventional approach directly connect user's goal to unit service's output. So the goal is achieved by using only the combination of unit services. This approach has many limits as we refer to above. In order to overcome limits, we will fill the missing link between services using approach that refine the goal. We grasp the meaning of a goal that is complex, various and user-centric by reasoning through knowledge-base, and refine the goal using methods that refine the goal. Because of this, the meaning of goal can be more precise and explicit. Through this, we can achieve to provide a more flexible service by using an appropriate service.

3.1   Semantic Agent and Algorithm

In this paper, we adopt Resource Description Framework (RDF) Schema to represent light weight ontology. The RDF is a data model that can identify relationships among web resources at instance level. To illustrate, let's consider the statement, "Annie has a title orthopedic doctor." We can express this statement within several forms such as triple (Annie, title, orthopedic doctor), the semantic net for a human being, and RDF for the software agent. We know that the data model of the RDF uses its own terms like, Annie, title, orthopedic doctor, etc. It obstructs data interchanging and sharing on the Web because of a lack of mutual understanding. The RDF Schema (RDFS) is proposed to overcome the limitation of the RDF [5, 11]. The RDFS describes the relationship between objects and defines vocabulary which is used in the RDF. In this sense, the RDFS is called lightweight ontology.

The schema in Fig 1 is itself written in a forma language RDF Schema that can express its components: subClassOf, Property, subPropertyOf, Resource, and so on. Fig. 1 represents semantic part that is constructed for our research, and we describe this semantic part based on orthopedics diseases. Our semantic part also contains various services, medical knowledge, and etc. that enable to execute our scenario in section 3.2. In this example, we illustrate the RDF statement

Smart watch belongs to Mike. Mike is suffered by ankle pain. Ankle pain is perceived by Smart watch and diagnosed by orthopedic doctor Annie. Mike is treated by physical therapist Bill.

The statement of this statement may classes such as hospital staff, diseases, unit, patient, therapist and properties such as isTreatedBy, isPrescribedBy, isPerformedBy, etc. The following is brief description about each part. Fig. 1 illustrates the layers of RDF and RDF Schema for this example. In this example boxes are properties, oval above dashed line are classes, and oval above solid lines are instances.

We describe the language of RDF Schema in more detail in next section. Let us make a few descriptions about class Hospital Staff. First the namespace mechanism of XML is used.

```
<rdf:RDF xmlns:rdf="http://www.w3.org/1999/02/22-rdf-syntax-ns#"
xmlns:rdfs=http://www.w3.org/2000/01/rdf-schema#> </rdf:RDF>
```

Second, a class `HospitalStaff` can be defined as follows. The `rdf:ID` attribute of element `rdfs:Class` defines a name of the class. Element `rdfs:Class` that defines `orthopedics_dr` is subclass of `rdf:resource`. The `rdfs:subClassOf` is adopted to represent the relationship.

```
<rdfs:Class rdf:ID="radiotherapist">
<rdfs:subClassOf rdf:resource="doctor"/>
</rdfs:Class>
<rdfs:Class rdf:ID="doctor">
<rdfs:subClassOf rdf:resource="hospitalstaff"/>
</rdfs:Class>
```

Let us make a few descriptions about class Hospital Staff. First the namespace mechanism of XML is used.

```
<rdf:RDF xmlns:rdf="http://www.w3.org/1999/02/22-rdf-syntax-ns#"
  xmlns:rdfs=http://www.w3.org/2000/01/rdf-schema#
  xmlns:medi=http://medicalservice.org#>
</rdf:RDF>
```

Second, a class `HospitalStaff` can be defined as follows. The `rdf:ID` attribute of element `rdfs:Class` defines a name of the class. Element `rdfs:Class` that defines `orthopedics_dr` is subclass of `rdf:resource`. The `rdfs:subClassOf` is adopted to represent the relationship.

```
<rdfs:Class rdf:ID="&medi;orthopedics_dr">
<rdfs:subClassOf rdf:resource="&medi;doctor"/>
</rdfs:Class>
```

Finally, a class `hospitalstaff` has properties such as `id`, and `name`. The domain and range of properties is specified with `rdfs:domain` and `rdfs:range`.

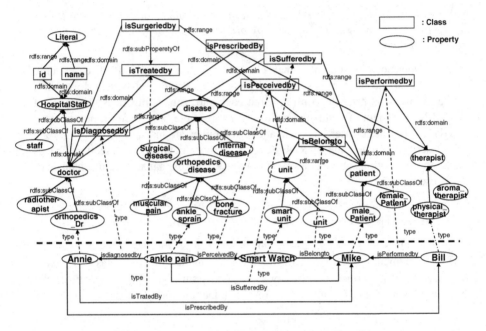

Fig. 1. RDF and RDFS part about orthopedics disease

3.2 Agents and Their Interaction

Through the example, we know that Mike's personal agent may interact with other agents to achieve goals; for example, synthetic judge diagnostics about Mike's symptoms, an appointment with a doctor, and an appropriate therapist; to do so, RDF data should be transported among agents based on pre-defined procedure in the instance level. It is called a serialization with RDF/XML [5, 11]. We can try serialization for interaction between agents. For instance, the patient, Mike, has a name and email and interacts with an insurance agent, Jenny. Jenny has a name and email, too. RDFS ontology for intelligent agents and interaction models are depicted in Fig. 2.

```
<rdfs:Class rdf:ID="altered_schedule">
<rdfs:subClassOf rdf:resource="schedule"/>
</rdfs:Class>
<rdfs:Property rdf:ID="isInteractWith">
<rdfs:domain rdf:resource="#intelligent_agent"/>
<rdfs:range rdf:resource="#intelligent_agent"/>
</rdfs:Property>
<rdfs:Property rdf:about="isNegotiatedWith">
<rdfs:subPropertyOf rdf:resource="#isInteractWith"/>
</rdfs:Property>
```

```
<rdfs:Property rdf:about="isCoordinatedWith">
<rdfs:subPropertyOf rdf:resource="#isInteractWith">
</rdfs:Property>
```

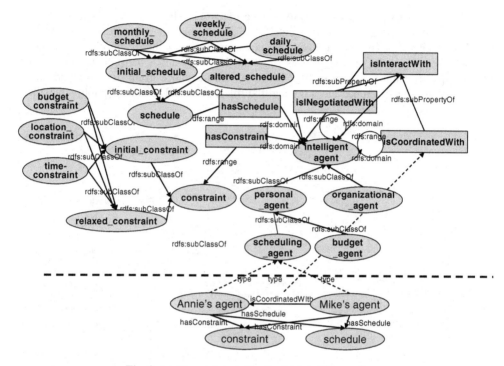

Fig. 2. Intelligent Agent Class and related Properties

Based on Fig. 2 and RDF Schema document, we know that Mike's agent and Annie's agent may have some constraints, for instance, appointment time because they may have daily, weekly, and monthly schedule in advance. Annie's agent say to Mike's agent on appointment time when Mike's agent request treatment for Mike. Then Mike's agent tries to match available appointment times with Mike's schedule. In a few minutes, Mike's agent finds that there is not exist exact matching between Annie's available appointment time and Mike's schedule. Mike's agent informs a Mike of the situation and requests alteration of schedule. Mike tries to postponement or cancellation of his trivial things. Mike's agent makes appointment with Annie's agent and notifies to Mike about appointment.

3.3 The Procedural Steps

Step 1: Setting a goal. As soon as some abnormal symptoms of human beings are detected by the smart unit, a personal agent first sets new goals that select adequate services to treat the person's disease. The personal agent first receives some message about abnormal symptoms from a smart unit. If a goal is set, it first searches services whose index matches the predicate of the goal. Simultaneously, it searches services whose index matches the object of the goal. And finally it searches the synonyms of the predicate and the object. The personal agent interprets the information and transmits a message to the insurance agent to achieve its goal.

Step 2: Discovering an adequate service provider. The insurance agent sets a new goal that selects an adequate doctor based on the patient's symptoms and medical insurance status. First of all, the insurance agent searches the member's DB to check whether or not the precondition is satisfied. In this context, the precondition means the qualification for membership. To do so, the insurance agent may draw an inference based on reference ontology and the rules. A partial ontology graph is depicted in Fig. 3.

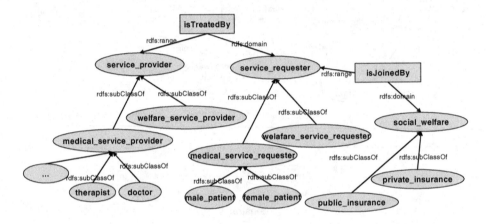

Fig. 3. Partial ontology graph

The inference agent should cope with a difficult situation such as the heterogeneity of the subject, predicate, and the object of the goal. To do so, we propose lightweight ontology based on RDFS and on the semantic similarity measure. In this process, personal agents, however, may encounter difficult situations such like deadlock, thrashing, and resource poaching [Klein, 2000]. This is why a process monitoring agent is proposed. The role of a process monitoring agent is to detect, diagnose, and resolve difficult situations that are unexpectedly met with by a personal agent. To detect some dysfunction in the coordination process, we set the logic and corresponding rules. The logic part defines and represents the principle, rule, and knowledge between facts. The logic part enables one to refine the user's goal and sub-goal into a more precise and explicit goal. Furthermore, it enables to detect some dysfunction of coordination process. In Mike's example, if Mike receives some medical treatment, he gets membership before the injury and treatment a member of a medical insurance provider. If the process is halted, the monitoring agent checks his medical insurance membership. If Mike's membership is retained, it checks other issues. Fig. 4 represents the partial logic component and the RDFS document in Mike's case. If an appropriate service is discovered by the insurance agent, it notifies the doctor's agent and the patient's agent. From now on, two agents' interaction is initiated on behalf of the person in question.

Logic Part

($\forall$x: patient) ($\forall$y: medical insurance)

Request (x, y)————— PRECONDITION —————▶ Membership (x, y)

"**Patient X requests to medical insurance to search an adequate doctor**" **has precondition** "**X has pain**" **and** "**X is medical service requester**"

($\forall$x: patient) ($\forall$y: medical insurance) ($\forall$z: medical service requester)

Act (x, Z) ————— PRECONDITION —————▶   Membership (x, y)

"**Patient X acts medical service requester**" **has precondition** "**X retain a membership of medical insurance**"

($\forall$x: patient) ($\forall$y: medical insurance) ($\forall$d: doctor)

————— PRECONDITION —————▶ propose (y, d)

Treat (x, d)   AND

————— PRECONDITION —————▶ accept (x, d)

"**Patient X treats from Doctor d**" **has precondition** "**Medical insurance propose to patient X as an adequate doctor**" **and patient X accepts an offer from medical insurance**"

```
<rdfs:Class rdf:ID="&medi;medical_insurance">
<rdfs:subClassOf rdf:resource="&medi;public_insurance"/>
</rdfs:Class>

<rdfs:Class rdf:ID="&medi;patient">
<rdfs:subClassOf
rdf:resource="&medi;medical_service_requester"/>
</rdfs:Class>

<rdfs:Class rdf:ID="&medi;medical_service_requester">
<rdfs:subClassOf rdf:resource="&medi;service_requester"/>
</rdfs:Class>

<rdfs:Class rdf:ID="&medi;doctor">
<rdfs:subClassOf
rdf:resource="&medi;medical_service_provider"/>
</rdfs:Class>

<rdfs:Class rdf:ID="&medi;service_provider"/>
<rdfs:Class rdf:ID="&medi;service_requester"/>
```

Fig. 4. Logic part and RDFS ontology for monitoring agent

Step 3: Coordination between two agents for constraint relaxation. In this step, coordination between doctor's agent and patient's agent is the critical issue. The two agents have their own time schedule and constraints. First of all, the two agents try to match available times for both doctor and patient. If exact matching is achieved by two agents, then they make an appointment. Two agents may use forward chaining and fact base. Otherwise, the patient's agent should try to relax the patient's schedule. We assume that the patient's schedule has some priority. The patient's agent requests the immediate reschedule to the patient. The patient tries to alter his/her schedule based on a given order of priority. The order of priority is excluded from our paper because it is too subjective.

Step 4: Medical Service Execution. If coordination is completed in step 3, the patient will be treated with some medical service from an appropriate doctor. Furthermore, if physical therapy is required in the full recovery of the patient, then the doctor consults with the therapist. Coordination between the patient's agent and the therapist's agent will occur. This process is similar to step 3.

Mike's agent explores entire ontology with RDF Schema that is a language for defining the semantics of particular domains [10]. Furthermore, Mike's agent should negotiate and coordinate with other agents to achieve its goals. In this process, Mike's personal agent rapidly and accurately, executes overall business for Mike. In ubiquitous environment, Mike receives appropriate medical service with the personal agent's support. Ultimately, human being's quality of life can be improved.

3.4 Semantic Distance Measure

We obtain the value of similarity distance between services as the weighted sum of similarities between entities – subject, object and predicate that consist of service.

$$D(A, B) = W_{sub} \times D_{sub}(A_{sub}, B_{sub}) + W_{obj} \times D_{obj}(A_{obj}, B_{obj}) + W_{pre} \times D_{pre}(A_{pre}, B_{pre}) \qquad (1)$$

$D(A, B)$ represents the similarity between service A and B . W_i represents the weight of each entity. $D_i(A_i, B_i)$ represents the similarity between each entity of services.

$$D_x(A_x, B_x) = 1 - \underset{\substack{Z_0, Z_1, \dots, Z_{r+1} \in \Sigma \\ Z_0 = X, Z_{r+1} = Y}}{MIN} (1 - \prod_{i=0}^{r} (1 - d'(Z_i, Z_{i+1}))) \quad x \in \{sub, obj, pre\} \qquad (2)$$

We obtain the value of the similarity of each entity, using the semantic distance measure [3]. In Equation 2, A_x and B_x represent entities, $D_x(A_x, B_x)$ represents semantic similarity between A_x and B_x, and $d'(Z_i, Z_{i+1})$ represents direct distance between the entities. We obtain value of $d'(Z_i, Z_{i+1})$ using the entity matching algorithm in [1].

4 Conclusions and Future Works

We construct domain ontology that is related to orthopedics and minimum common sense ontology for service composition using the RDF Schema, and knowledge-base is represented according to this RDF Schema as RDF. We simulated company's back-end function to provide healthcare service through the use of simple expert systems. Components communicate with each other using RDF messages. Experiments with limited number of services in virtual environment show that the approach of our research is feasible. We expect that our research will provide a foundation that realizes these efforts faster and provide better quality of service in ubiquitous healthcare.

Acknowledgement

This work was supported by the Korea Science and Engineering Foundation (KOSEF) through the Advanced Information Technology Research Center (AITrc).

References

1. Aversano, L., Canfora, G., Ciampi, A.: An algorithm for Web service discovery through their composition. In: Proc. IEEE ICWS, (2004) 332-339
2. Choi, K.-S., Kim, J.-H., Miyazaki, M., Goto, J., Kim, Y.-B.: Question-Answering Based on Virtually Integrated Lexical Knowledge Base. In: Proc. Int'l Workshop on Information Retrieval with Asian Languages, (2003) 168-175
3. Cooper, M.C.: Semantic Distance Measures. Computational Intelligence. 16 (2000) 79-94
4. Fujii, K., Suda, T.: Dynamic Service Composition Using Semantic Information. In: Proc. Int'l Conf. Service Oriented Computing, (2004) 39-48
5. Alesso H. P., and Craig F. S.: Developing Semantic Web Services, A K Peters, Ltd. 2004.
6. Shin, H., Koehler, S.: A Knowledge-Based Fact Database: Acquisition to Application. Lecture Notes in Computer Science, Vol. 1886, (2000) 828
7. Lee, Wookey, Kim, J.: Structuring the Web to Cope with Dynamic Changes. In: Proc. Int'l Conf. Web Services, Orland, Florida (2005)
8. Weiser, M.: The Computer for 21st Century. Scientific American. 265 (1991) 94-104
9. Klein M, and Chrysanthos D.: A Knowledge-based Approach to Handling Exception in Workflow Systems, Computer Supported Cooperative Work, Vol. 9, pp. 399-412, 2000.
10. Antonius G. and Harman v. F.: A Semantic Web Primer, The MIT Press, 2004.
11. W3C: RDF/XML Syntax Specification (Revised), 2004.

An Integrated Supply Chain Management System: A Case Study in Healthcare Sector

Dongsoo Kim

Graduate School of Healthcare Management and Policy,
The Catholic University of Korea,
505 Banpo-Dong, Seocho-Gu, Seoul 137-701, Republic of Korea
dskim@catholic.ac.kr

Abstract. This research has designed and developed an integrated supply chain management (SCM) system for optimizing inventory control and reducing material handling costs of pharmaceutical products in healthcare sector. The supply chain in this work is composed of pharmaceutical companies, a wholesaler, and hospitals. At first, we have analyzed hospital's business processes and reviewed system requirements for the efficient supply chain management. VMI (Vendor-Managed Inventory), which is one of important applications of SCM, has been adopted and implemented to improve material handling efficiency. Online procurement system is also developed for the departments that consume drugs and place orders. Besides, real time information sharing functionalities are provided for optimizing inventory control of pharmaceuticals. The developed SCM system enables hospitals to improve the procurement processes and inventory control of pharmaceutical products, which results in decreasing total inventory more than 30%. By sharing information with hospitals, the wholesaler can gather more timely and exact data about inventory status and drug usage volumes of hospitals, so it can forecast the demand more accurately, which enables needed products to be supplied timely and cost-effectively. With the SCM system, total supply chain cost of pharmaceutical products has been decreased significantly.

1 Introduction

Many large-sized hospitals have adopted advanced management methods widely used in other industries to cope with changes in healthcare environment, and to manage hospitals efficiently. Hospital information systems (HIS) became one of the most important infrastructures of hospital management and information technology (IT) plays an increasingly significant role in the healthcare industry. Therefore, IT investments of hospitals are growing exponentially [14].

As competition among hospitals grows intense, there is an urgent need to improve the quality of healthcare services and reduce operational costs. For this purpose, a variety of information systems for managing clinical processes and administrative activities of hospitals have been implemented at a number of hospitals. Clinical information systems include CPOE (Computerized Physician Order Entry), EMR (Electronic Medical Record), and PACS (Picture Archiving and Communication System) and so on. Furthermore, ERP (Enterprise Resource Planning), SCM (Supply Chain

K. Bauknecht et al. (Eds.): EC-Web 2005, LNCS 3590, pp. 218–227, 2005.

Management), and CRM (Customer Relationship Management) for optimizing hospital management are being adopted rapidly. Hospital information systems can be regarded as the memory and nervous system of a hospital [12].

The Internet, WWW (World Wide Web) and the evolution of related information technologies enable easier information sharing among heterogeneous organizations and systems. A lot of organizations regard inter-organizational collaborations through information sharing as a major strategy for strengthening their competitiveness. SCM is a strategy for optimizing the overall supply chain by sharing information among material suppliers, manufacturers, distributors and retailers.

The key element of SCM is information sharing. Programs like JIT (Just-In-Time), CRP (Continuous Replenishment Process), and QR (Quick Response) in retail rely on the dissemination of scheduling, shipment or manufacturing information to the supply chain [8]. Information sharing improves collaboration among the supply chain to manage material flow efficiently and reduces inventory costs [13]. Software component technology and XML technology facilitates information sharing by providing a means for integrating heterogeneous information systems [7].

In this research, an efficient pharmaceutical supply chain management (SCM) system has been designed and developed to optimize inventory control and reduce material handling costs. The supply chain in this work is composed of pharmaceutical companies, a wholesaler, and hospitals. Especially, this research focuses on the collaboration between a pharmaceutical wholesaler and several university hospitals of a medical center.

At first, we have analyzed hospitals' business processes and reviewed system requirements for the efficient material flow management and inventory control. To meet those requirements, VMI (Vendor Managed Inventory), which is one of important applications of SCM, has been adopted for managing hospital drug warehouses. In addition, online procurement system or CAO (Computer Aided Ordering) system is also developed for the departments that consume drugs and place orders. We have ascertained that information sharing through strong partnership between hospitals and the wholesaler is a key component in achieving the planned goal fully.

The developed SCM system enables hospitals to improve procurement processes and inventory control of pharmaceutical products. By sharing information with hospitals, the wholesaler can acquire exact and current data about inventory status and drug usage volumes so that it can forecast the demand more accurately, which enables needed products to be supplied timely and cost-effectively.

The rest of the paper is organized as follows. Section 2 describes a basic concept of SCM and introduces SCM efforts called EHCR in healthcare sector. Section 3 presents the system requirements of the developed SCM system. Section 4 illustrates the architecture of the SCM system and describes major components of the implemented SCM system. Section 5 summarizes the benefits of the proposed system. Section 6 concludes this paper.

2   SCM in Healthcare Sector

As is illustrated in Figure 1, a supply chain is a value chain network composed of raw material suppliers, manufacturers (pharmaceutical companies in case of our work), distributors (drug wholesalers), retailers (hospitals), and consumers (patients). With the implementation of SCM system, material handling processes can be optimized by integrating the elements of the supply chain and managing the flows of materials, information, and funds in an integrated manner.

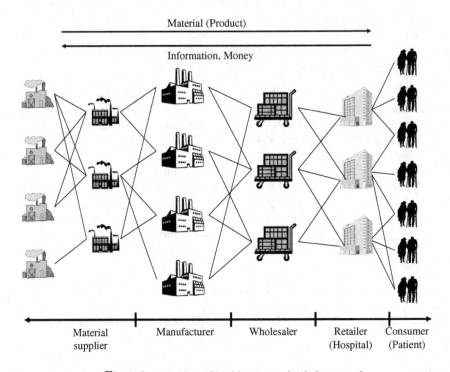

Fig. 1. Composition of healthcare supply chain network

The most important critical success factor of SCM is the efficient and effective information sharing in the supply chain. If the information sharing could not be achieved properly, supply-chain related problems might happen. For example, the bullwhip effect, where a slight variation in demand at the consumer side results in wild swings at the supplier end, might occur without a smooth information sharing. The bullwhip effect is attributed to four causes: demand signal processing, batch ordering, price fluctuation and shortage gaming. More detailed explanations can be found in [11]. To overcome this kind of problems, several core SCM applications have emerged such as consumer direct ordering, computer aided ordering, sharing of point-of-sale capacity and inventory data, vendor-managed inventory, and continuous replenishment program.

The SCM effort in the healthcare sector is called EHCR (Efficient Healthcare Consumer Response). It is an industry-wide effort in which all the players manage the healthcare supply chain in an efficient and effective way so that they can remove unnecessary inefficiency and minimize related costs. The purpose of EHCR is to reduce total healthcare costs and enhance quality by improving the effectiveness of the healthcare product supply chain.

The EHCR Report estimates that the healthcare products industry could significantly improve its ability to deliver quality healthcare products and services to consumers and save as much as $23 billion in supply chain costs in United States [5]. This benefit can be achieved through three foundation strategies: Efficient Product Movement, Efficient Order Management, and Efficient Information Sharing. Enablers of EHCR include partnerships and alliances in supply chains, change management, information technology, and activity-based costing [2].

3   System Requirements

We have designed an efficient pharmaceutical supply chain management system to transform the supply chain to a single, integrated model to improve patient care and customer service, while lowering procurement costs and improving cash flow. Especially, pharmaceutical therapy is very important in the hospital patient care settings. The most appropriate drugs, after an accurate diagnosis is made by a physician, should be delivered to the patient at right time. Pharmaceutical products should be managed in a good way based on pharmaceutical knowledge and basic knowledge about material management.

The validity and safety of drugs has become more important as conditions of drug preservation and usage pattern became more complicated. The number of drug types and high-price drugs used in hospital settings are growing rapidly. Those changes in the healthcare environments require more specialized inventory control and efficient supply chain integration.

We had several problems due to non-existence of efficient and effective inventory control system in hospitals. So, we have decided to implement the pharmaceutical SCM system described in this work. Before the medical center implemented the SCM system, information sharing functionality with the wholesaler was very poor so that there were frequent emergency orders and the average inventory levels were relatively high. And the ordering processes in hospitals were performed by rule of thumb.

To solve these problems, we have analyzed the following system requirements and developed an integrated SCM system to optimize material handling of pharmaceutical products.

3.1   VMI (Vendor-Managed Inventory)

First of all, we have adopted VMI system for efficient inventory control in hospital warehouses. With the VMI system, experts delegated by the wholesaler take the role of inventory control of hospitals' central warehouse. Before the developed SCM system was adopted, pharmacists managed the inventory, which resulted in inefficiencies, high inventory costs and poor services. Therefore, VMI should be applied to inventory control of the drug warehouse to improve work performance of hospital pharmacists.

3.2   Efficient and Effective Inventory Control

With a proper classification scheme, inventory control of hospitals can be improved. It is very inefficient to manage all the pharmaceutical products in hospitals without a classification scheme and control all products in the same way. ABC inventory control mechanism [9] can be applied to make the products be classified by their characteristics and significances. Discriminated inventory control and ordering policies should be applied because there are numerous product types and their importance is different.

3.3 Intelligent Order Management

Instead of rule of thumb, order quantities should be calculated by the computer system based on demand forecasting and safety stock levels. What users should do is only to check the recommended value of order quantities and confirm it. With intelligent order management, the SCM system minimizes user interventions and reduces the time spent in order processing.

3.4 Efficient and Effective Information Sharing

By sharing information about drug usage between hospitals and the wholesaler, it is possible to keep the inventory of the warehouses at a proper level. Besides, item list of contracted drugs, price history of drugs, information about new drugs and insurance codes, and so on can be accessed in real time which is helpful in improving work performances of hospitals and the wholesaler.

3.5 Electronic Order Document Processing

Standardized electronic documents should be exchanged for rapid and accurate order processing. Electronic document exchange through the Internet replaces data exchange using a fax or telephone. The traditional method of exchanging and processing order documents has explicit weakness including time inefficiency and high probability of error occurrences. By exchanging order documents electronically in XML format, order processing of supply chain participants can be enhanced significantly.

3.6 Improving the Efficiency of Material Handling

Barcode technology should be implemented to make material handling in warehouse more efficient. Although, RFID (Radio Frequency Identification) technology can be considered for the identification of products, we did not adopt it due to immaturity of the technology.

Optimized layout planning in hospital warehouses and FCFS (First Come First Served) mechanism in distributing drugs are also required to improve the efficiency of material handling.

4 Pharmaceutical SCM System

4.1 System Architecture

The Pharmaceutical SCM system has been implemented based on the results of requirement analysis summarized in the previous section. The overall architecture of the

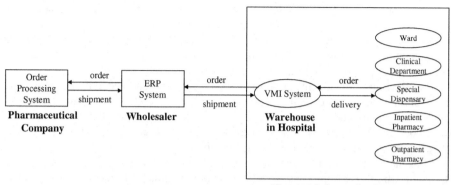

Hospital Information System

Fig. 2. Architecture of the developed SCM system

developed system is shown in Figure 2. The focus of this paper is on the VMI system in the hospital warehouse and information sharing between hospitals and the wholesaler.

Departments consuming drugs like wards, clinical departments, special dispensary, inpatient pharmacy and outpatient pharmacy request necessary items, and then the items are delivered from the central warehouse to the requesting departments. The VMI system in the hospital warehouse manages the overall inventory control system and order processing system.

Order documents, verification of shipping documents and daily drug usage information are transferred from HIS (Hospital Information System) to ERP system of the wholesaler. Invoice documents, tax bills, and price information of drugs are transferred in the opposite direction.

4.2 System Implementation

The project period of the SCM system development was from July 2003 to March 2004. When the system was deployed, there were many problems such as functional errors and data errors in the SCM system, which required continuous refinement and modification of the system.

We have developed the SCM programs using Microsoft .NET framework and C# programming language. C# is a simple, modern, object-oriented, and type-safe programming language that combines the high productivity of rapid application development languages with the raw power of C and C++ [1].

In this section, two important application programs developed to integrate the supply chain are explained.

The first program is used in each department that consumes drugs and it is composed of several functions such as 'Environment setting', 'Sending document', 'Receiving document', and 'Receiving delivery order document'. This program enables online order processing and sharing of information such as inventory levels of hospital warehouse, code lists of pharmaceutical products.

In the 'Sending document' tab, the program shows prepared order documents list. One can select a line from order documents list and send the document by double-clicking the selected line or pushing down 'Send' button. In making an electronic order document, recommended order quantities of each item are provided by the program for rapid preparation of the order document.

The 'Receiving document' tab provides such information needed by hospital users as inventory status of hospital warehouse, a variety of code lists of pharmaceutical products like drug codes, EDI code list, manufacturer's code list, barcode, and ingredient code list. One can select a line item to receive and get the information by double-clicking the selected line or clicking 'Receive' button

After the order from the hospital is received by the wholesaler and the delivery is done, the wholesaler composes the delivery order document. In the 'Receiving delivery order document' tab, delivery order documents prepared by the wholesaler are presented. One can select a line to receive from the data list and get the delivery order document by double-clicking the selected line or pushing down 'Receive' button.

The second important application program of the SCM system is the VMI application program. The hospital warehouse is managed by domain experts delegated from the wholesaler using the VMI application as described in the Section 3.1. The VMI application has several important functions shown in Table 1. The program consists of five major functions; 'Management of item receipt and delivery', 'Information management of item receipt and delivery', 'Management of status of delivery request', 'Base information management', and 'Configuration'.

Table 1. Functions of the VMI application

Functions of VMI	Major roles
Management of item receipt and delivery	- Management of receipt and delivery in each department - Management of receipt and delivery of items shipped from the wholesaler
Information management of item receipt and delivery	- History information management of item receipt and delivery - Inventory management such as physical review of inventory and closing
Management of status of delivery request	- Status tracking of delivery requests from each department
Base information management	- Setting up base information needed for warehouse management
Configuration	- Configuring the environmental parameters

Screenshots of the program are not included due to the space limitation of this paper. Each function has several sub-functions. For example, the menu of 'Management of item receipt and delivery' has several sub-menus such as 'Receipt information', 'Receipt instruction', 'Delivery information', and 'Delivery instruction'. Likewise, other menus have several sub-menus for each function.

5 Benefits of the Developed System

The pharmaceutical SCM system presented in this research has been used by a medical center that is composed of eight university hospitals. At initial stage of system deployment, there was a strong objection to the new SCM system due to the severe change in their work processes of the employees and a little instability of the system.

As an SCM system involves many participants from a variety of organizations, the partnership and collaborations among organizations is a very important factor in implementing the system. With continuous training and system enhancement we have realized the planned purposes.

We have built the SCM system based on the requirement analysis described in the Section 3. Some major benefits of the SCM system, which are results of successful implementation of the system requirements, can be summarized as follows.

First, by applying the VMI application we can relieve the workload of hospital pharmacists who are very busy in doing their specialized jobs. Experts in the field of material handling and inventory management perform the job very well, which results in improvements of inventory management such as reduction of inventory costs, keeping proper inventory level, and decrease of emergency orders.

Second, information integration and optimized supply chain management has been achieved with the information sharing system based on a strong partnership. Instead of exchanging paper documents by mail or fax, online ordering using electronic documents enables speedy order processing and error minimization. In addition, the wholesaler can access information about drug usage in hospitals so that optimized inventory management of the hospital warehouse can be achieved. Also, hospitals can access information provided by the wholesaler such as item list of contracted products, price history, information about new drugs and insurance codes when necessary.

Third, material handling of hospitals has been improved significantly by implementing several applications of SCM. Discriminated management schemes are applied to inventory control of items based on the classifications of items. It is often the case that the inventory amount of items in hospital information systems does not coincide with physical amount of items; nonetheless, the gap between them should be minimized and the reliability of information system should be enhanced. Thanks to the efforts with which the SCM is implemented in the medical center, the reliability of the information system has been improved considerably. Calculated order quantities to replenish items are provided to each department consuming drugs, which simplifies ordering processing of hospitals.

The most significant benefit of the SCM system is the reduction of average inventory amounts and inventory costs. As the new system has stabilized in the hospitals, the total inventory has decreased more than 30%.

To maximize and keep the major benefits described above, it is required to evaluate and improve the developed system continuously. The most significant factor in the successful implementation of the integrated supply chain management system is collaboration between partners and information sharing in the supply chain. Therefore, information needed for supply chain planning should be provided in a timely manner by the hospitals and wholesaler. Especially, information from the hospitals, where the pharmaceuticals are consumed and related data are created, including usage volume of drugs and inventory status, should be provided continuously.

To evaluate the performance of inventory management, various performance indices such as the number and the ratio of returning goods, the number and the ratio of borrowing goods, difference between physical inventory levels and inventory information in computer system, validity of the formula for automated ordering have been developed and maintained.

6 Conclusions

A pharmaceutical supply chain management system to optimize the supply chain has been designed and developed in this research. Although the whole supply chain is composed of raw material suppliers, manufacturers (pharmaceutical companies), distributors (drug wholesalers), retailers (hospitals) and consumers (patients), the focus of this research is on the VMI system in hospital warehouse and information sharing between hospitals and the wholesaler.

We have developed specialized inventory management, called VMI, efficient and effective information sharing system, and computer aided online ordering system. The developed SCM system improves material handling of hospitals, reducing inventory management costs and ultimately improving quality of patient care.

There are lots of efforts still required to improve the efficiency of the total supply chain. To integrate the entire pharmaceutical supply chain, pharmaceutical manufacturers should participate in this kind of collaborative work. A lot of support from the manufacturers was needed during the implementation of the SCM proposed in this research. All participants should share information in the supply chain to fully realize the benefits of supply chain integration.

To extend the benefits presented in this paper, standards for exchanging information electronically must be established and adopted. Since standards associated with barcodes and order documents for pharmaceutical products were not available and easily usable in Korea as of the implementation time, we have developed a temporary ad hoc standard to exchange information between organizations. Standards including formats of information, barcodes, and so on should be established to disseminate the advantages of implementation of efficient healthcare consumer response. At this stage, inter-organizational system integration using Web Services could be incorporated.

As RFID (Radio Frequency Identification) technology evolves rapidly, we can expect that RFID tags will be adopted for the identification of products in SCM system in healthcare sector.

References

1. Anders Hejlsberg, Scott Wiltamuth, Peter Golde: The C# Programming Language, Addison-Wesley Professional (2003)
2. Carl J. McCann: A Supply Chain Revolution: Understanding the Players, Proceedings of HIMSS Annual Conference 2003
3. Cathy Erickson: Managing the Medical Supply Chain; Deliver Smarter, Faster and at a Lower Cost, Proceedings of HIMSS Annual Conference 2005

4. Dona Arbietman, Erez Lirov, Roy Lirov, Yuval Lirov: E-Commerce for Healthcare Supply Procurement, Journal of Healthcare Information Management 15:1 (2001) 61-72
5. EHCR Committee: Improving Supply Chain Management for Better Healthcare, November 2001. Available at http://www.eccc.org/ehcr/ehcr/
6. Efficient Healthcare Consumer Response™ Assessment Study, June 2000
7. Gek Woo Tan, Michael J. Shaw, Bill Fulkerson: Web-based Supply Chain Management, Information Systems Frontiers 2:1 (2000) 41-55
8. Fisher ML, Hammond JH, Obermeyer WR, Raman A: Making Supply Meet Demand in an Uncertain World. Harvard Business Review 1994 May-June 83-93
9. James H. Greene: Production and Inventory Control Handbook (1997) McGraw-Hill
10. Karen Matjucha, Joe Burns, Terrence J. Noetzel, E-Procurement: Energize Your Supply Chain, Proceedings of HIMSS Annual Conference 2002
11. Lee HL, Padmanabhan V, Whang S: The Bullwhip Effect in Supply Chains, Sloan Management Review 38 (1997) 93-102
12. Reinhold Haux, Alfred Winter, Elske Ammenwerth, Birgit Brigl, Strategic Information Management in Hospitals – An Introduction to Hospital Information Systems: Springer-Verlag, New York (2004)
13. Strader TJ, Lin F, Shaw MJ: Information Infrastructure for Electronic Virtual Organization Management, Decision Support Systems 23 (1998) 75-94
14. Wullianallur Raghupathi, Joseph Tan: Strategic IT Applications in Health Care, Communications of The ACM 45:12 (2002) 56-61

Educational Resources as Digital Products

Agnieszka Landowska and Jerzy Kaczmarek

Gdańsk University of Technology,
Faculty of Electronics, Telecommunications and Informatics,
Department of Software Engineering,
Narutowicza Str. 11/12 80-492 Gdańsk, Poland,
nailie@eti.pg.gda.pl

Abstract. In the paper educational resources are treated as regular digital products. The problem of the production, distribution and sale is addressed, especially concentrating on the production effort, cost and price. An original method of estimating development effort of e-learning resources is described and experimental results are presented. The paper presents also two extensions of the existing structure and implementation of learning objects. The structure of a learning object, although flexible, focuses on reuse, which is insufficient for independent learning. Therefore the first extension is the concept of a teaching object that contains all parts of the educational process, from knowledge presentation, through examples and exercises to final examinations. A teaching object is proposed as an independent subject of sale. Addition of data access methods to learning objects is the second proposed extension that creates a learning component. A model of learning object distribution based on Web services and learning components is proposed.

1 Introduction

Education is a part of global and national economy with its products, markets and competition and also with overproduction and pricing problems. The use of Internet in education has resulted in a development and globalisation.

E-learning supports traditional education on the primary, secondary and university levels, while finding its place in some areas like re-education and self-training. The learning process placed in the Internet causes concentration on educational resources, as teacher and learner are distant in time and place. To act as digital products, educational resources must conform to three rules: must be divided into structured units, that can be an independent subject of sale, must have precise calculation of cost and price and must be represented in a technology that allows for effective Internet distribution. The three areas are addressed by the research presented in the article. The use of new Internet technologies is proposed to increase interoperability and usability of educational resources. The presented solutions apply to digital educational resources production, distribution and sale. The paper is organized as follows. Section 2 introduces a model of e-learning market, which allows to define unsolved problems in the addressed area. Section 3 deals with educational resources production. Section 4 concerns educational resources cost and price, while the next one provides a model for distribution.

K. Bauknecht et al. (Eds.): EC-Web 2005, LNCS 3590, pp. 228–237, 2005.

2   Characteristics of Educational Resource Market

The e-learning market is not growing as fast as it was expected to, partly because of payment problems in distance education and other Internet-based domains. The Internet supplies extensive and free of charge data that can be used for education. Unfortunately, the data is often unsuitable in its contents or presentation, which results in the development of chargable educational resources. The learner demands fast and effective methods of education that cope with the changing work market.

Currently, universities are main e-learning centres. Although Internet is used as the learning environment, the education process has not changed. One institution is responsible for resources production, delivery, examination and certification. The evolution of markets usually results in specialization, which can also be expected for e-learning. In the future, the separation of educational resource production, delivery and certification is expected [1]. The vision of future e-learning market is shown in Fig. 1. The Internet based architectures for e-learning commerce introduce the roles of learning services requester, provider and service broker as the intermediator [2].

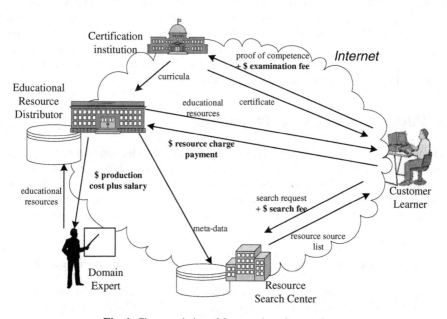

Fig. 1. Characteristics of future e-learning market

Five roles on the e-learning market can be distinguished: the learner, the domain expert, the educational resource distributor, the resource search centre (broker) and the certification institution. The process starts with the domain expert, who produces educational resources and delivers them to a resource distributor. The resource distributor checks the curricula given by the certification institution and calculates the educational resource price. The domain experts are paid for their work.

The learner, who is the final customer, searches for the resource with the help of the search centre and purchases required resource from the distributor. When the learning process is completed, the learner can pass examinations and get a certificate from the certification institution. The search and learning process are assumed to be Internet-based, while examination requires physical presence. The learner pays separately for the course and for the certification, as it is now with language education. In this solution a student selects the best resources from a university in England, learns it with the help of a teacher from Poland and then passes examinations on a university in Spain, that is closest to his place of living. The closest university concerned can be responsible for certification process or just for examination supervising, if appropriate cooperation agreements exist.

In e-learning, the role of universities changes, as they are responsible for curricula definition and certification. Universities can also play a role of educational resources producers because their employees are usually domain experts with pedagogical experience. However, universities are one of the resource offerents, competing with each other and with commercial organizations.

The preparation of high quality resources appropriate for the Internet delivery is difficult and labour-consuming. Therefore, domain experts demand high fees for their work. Additionally, the existence of digital lectures reduces significantly the importance of the lecturer. There is a problem, how to estimate the cost of educational resources production and how much the producer must be paid for it. On the other hand, the learner demands low prices and high quality resources. Apart from pricing problems, copyright violations threat the educational resources sale process. Effective methods of resources protection are highly required.

3   Educational Resources Production

The technological and thematic diversity of information in the Internet causes storage and search problems. One of the most effective ways of knowledge organization is its division into smaller units described with metadata. Many e-learning standards and specifications have been developed to enable the cooperation between different users and systems. A learning object is defined as the primary educational resource unit in e-learning.

3.1   Learning Object Structure According to Standards and Specifications

There are two main learning object specifications: the IEEE/LTSC P1484 standard and the Sharable Content Object Reference Model (SCORM). The IEEE standard defines a learning object as: any entity, digital or non-digital, which can be used, re-used and referenced during technology-supported learning [3]. The definition is very broad and has been criticized for that [4]. The SCORM definition of a learning object is SCO (Sharable Content Object): a collection of one or more assets that include a specific launchable asset that utilizes the SCORM run-time environment to communicate with Learning Management System (LMS) [5]. The definition is narrowed to SCORM-compliant resources. The SCORM describes the data structure for learning objects as a combination of digital contents, metadata and structure description. The basic idea of a learning object and its SCORM representation are shown in Fig. 2.

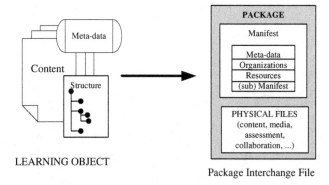

LEARNING OBJECT

Package Interchange File

Fig. 2. Learning object structure according to SCORM specification

The SCO unit consists of assets, which are electronic representation of media, such as text, sound or image (HTML files, XML files, Flash objects etc.). The basic requirement is that an asset is readable by a Web browser. A set of assets is given a manifest file that provides the meta-data, assets organization structure and resources description. The meta-data is the base for an effective search and is the subject of many standards. Manifest file and physical files representing assets are packed into one PIF (Package Interchange File).

3.2 The Concept of Teaching Object

Learning objects can differ significantly in their size and scope taking the form of a single image, a definition, a piece of text, a listing, a lesson, the whole course, an e-book etc. Standards represent a teacher-oriented approach in which re-usability is emphasized. Therefore, fine-grained objects are preferred, e.g., a simple picture or a piece of text. The approach is suitable for teachers, however, it does not fulfil the requirements of learners.

A learner uses e-learning technologies for re-education and self-learning, which requires individualization in courses preparation and precise problem solving (e.g., how to parse XML with Java). The required size of a educational resource piece used for learning is closest to a lesson unit [6,7]. Therefore, in the presented research a new term of teaching object is proposed.

A teaching object is a type of a learning object that represents an interactive knowledge unit of a complete lesson scope on a certain subject dedicated for self-learning. A teaching object provides the lecture together with practice and tests. The idea of a teaching object in comparison with a learning object is shown in Fig. 3.

The teaching object structure is created with the use of educational process theory. The word "teaching" is used to emphasize that it teaches the learners, guides them through a piece of subject.

The teaching object content consists of a Lecture part for reading or watching and interactive Examples, Exercises and Tests. Interactivity of educational resources is necessary, which is supported by IMS Question, Test and Interoperability specification [8]. The Example part is a task made step-by-step with guidelines available if the

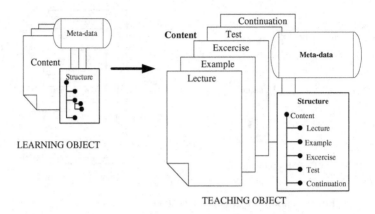

Fig. 3. Learning object compared to teaching object

user does not understand a phase of a solving process. The Exercise part is a task that should be made individually by a student and compared with the final answers, with some hints available, but the entire process not explained. The Test part enables self-testing, while the Continuation part allows to choose the next step in the learning path.

Good e-learning resources must consider psychological and pedagogical issues. Two special problems arise: the lack of teacher and the limited concentration abilities. The first problem causes learning effectiveness to decrease because of low self-discipline of the student. Therefore, the interaction with educational resources, as proposed in teaching objects, is important because it stimulates verification. A traditional face-to-face lesson uses a combination of lecture, example, exercise and test, which is adopted in teaching objects. Not all interactive parts of a teaching object are required, e.g., subject introduction usually does not contain exercises. The Lecture and Test parts are obligatory, while Example and Exercise are strongly recommended for teaching objects. The optimal time of learning with a teaching object should not exceed 25 minutes, because the more time students spend on work, the more likely they are to stop before completing [9]. The teaching object concept does not, however, impose any time constraints.

A teaching object can be represented using standard structures, however, in comparison with a learning object it is more learner-oriented. A lecture together with tasks and a test, makes a complete interactive knowledge unit that can be an independent subject of sale.

4   Effort, Cost and Price in Educational Resources Production

An effective calculation of costs and prices is necessary in all commercial projects. The notion of effort means the amount of work required for the production process. The cost is expressed in financial units and involves the effort, the value of work unit and the value of resources used. The price is the actual amount of money paid for goods.

4.1 Characteristics of Educational Resources as Digital Products

A learning or teaching object is virtually indestructible, easy to modify and almost costless to copy. The cost of design and first-copy production for educational resources is expected to be over 70% of the total cost, as it is for other electronic products [10]. Therefore learning objects can be treated as regular digital products.

Educational resources contain data and interaction definition and are implemented using XML and scripting languages, therefore their physical representation is a combination of application code and text. Human work is the main resource used for production of digital products. Learning object costs result mainly from effort similarly to software. There are many different methods of effort estimation in software engineering. Most widely known methods are parametric models such as COCOMO (Constructive Cost Model) [11,12]. The basic size metric of software code is the standard line of code (SLOC) [13]. The methods are partly applicable to learning object effort estimation.

A learning object is an intellectual product with the author copyrights guaranteed by law. Therefore, it may be compared with art, film or literature. Explicit pricing and effort measurement of such products is difficult. It is impossible to estimate the value of idea with effort estimation methods [14]. But typical XML or HTML code is not so complex and valuable as art and, therefore, may be priced with standard rate.

4.2 Effort Measurement of Learning Object Production

Effort estimations are mainly based on product size and complexity. Learning objects are viewed with Web browsers, which means that one webpage is a good metric of the size of single knowledge unit provided to a learner. In the paper the number of standard pages is proposed as the basic metric of learning object size. Pages differ in resolution, formatting, font sizes and other features, therefore, the standard page is defined as 25 lines, each filled with 60 characters including spaces. The main advantage of the metric is the simplicity (the number of characters including spaces is counted and divided by 60x25). The metric of standard page is not dependent on learning object technology and uses document sizing techniques [10]. Educational resources are often made with tools that generate the XML code automatically, however, the metric measures the final product of the delivery and not its code representation.

The defined metric was used in effort and size calculations of sixty learning objects created by four independent developers. The data come from teaching object production experimet held by the authors at Gdansk University of Technology. Generally, there exists a high correlation between the effort required for the production and the final object size, as shown in Fig. 4.

Figure 4a shows the correlation between learning object production effort and size. The first observation is that learning objects, although standardized, may differ significantly in size. The linear correlation coefficient value is 0.92, which means strong positive correlation between the two variants of size and effort.

Figure 4b shows the effort per standard page for the measurement results. The producers were not experienced in XML learning objects development, which is reflected in a speedup during the development of final pages. The effort of a single page development converges to the average for all producers. The average effort per standard page is 25,58 minutes with the deviation of 36%.

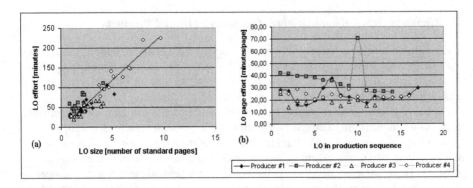

Fig. 4. Effort and size of learning objects production - measurement results

Most of the estimation parametric models transform the size metric to the effort with the use of equation that characterizes size to effort relationship. The metric of standard page is used to estimate the effort of learning object development. The exponential function characteristics bind the code size and effort for software. For the learning objects production, the function characteristics are linear. The effort can be estimated with the Formula (1).

$$\text{Effort}_{LO} = \text{CF} \times \text{E}_{sp} \times \text{Size}_{LO}. \tag{1}$$

where
Effort_{LO} - the effort of learning object production in manminutes,
CF   - the correction factor,
E_{sp} - the effort per standard page rate based on average result,
Size_{LO} - the learning object size in number of standard pages .

The correction factor CF can consider: the use of tools for code generation, the technology difficulty, re-use and producer experience. The effort per standard page rate E_{sp} may vary depending on certain learning object models. The estimation method must be validated on the effort and size data specific for the institution.

4.3   Learning Object Effort Versus Cost and Price

The knowledge about the effort of learning object development is sufficient to calculate the development cost. Cost is obtained by multiplying the effort by the manhour rate. The rate depends on the country the resources are produced in; therefore the metric of effort is more representative for comparisons than cost.

In theory, the price can be based on four factors: natural value of resources used, product usability, production process cost and product rarity. There are almost no resources used in learning object production, so that factor does not influence the real value of a digital product. Learning object production costs result mainly from human work costs, which can be predicted with effort estimation methods. The price of educational resources depends mostly on the usability and rarity. The usability of learning object results from its quality and learner-orientation, while its rarity results from the subject and didactic delivery techniques.

5 Educational Resource Distribution Model

The main idea of the resource distribution model presented in the article is to transform existing learning objects into learning components based on the Web services technology. According to standards a learning object is a set of structured data. The proposed transformation adds an interface to a learning object to create unified and platform-independent data access methods. Getting and setting operations are present in many objects, which allows to manipulate the data encapsulated within it. The methods can be applied to learning objects, what creates a learning component. The idea of learning component is shown in Fig. 5.

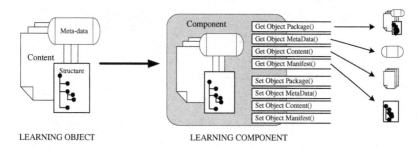

Fig. 5. Learning object representation as learning component

A learning component is equipped with a set of methods. Get_Object_Package() and Set_Object_Package() methods implement the exchange of the whole learning object. The other get methods are used to get a part of a learning component without getting and unpacking the whole package e.g., the price attribute is included in the metadata and can be read with Get_object_metadata() function. The method Get_Object_Content() is used when opening an object with a browser not supported with LMS. Corresponding set operations are also available.

The diversity of learning objects content results in the variety of their behaviour. Other methods can be defined for different learning object types. A teaching object, as one of the types of learning objects, can be also represented as a learning component. Additional methods for a teaching object can be proposed such as Get_one_random_test_question() and Check_test(), which allows to make an examination from teaching objects that create the whole course.

The learning component functionality is implemented as Web services, which makes it independent of technology. The model of learning objects distribution is shown in Fig. 6.

If learning objects are published in the Internet, a protection against illegal copying must be enforced. An access to the whole learning object package by an unauthorized user may result in an easy replication and an unauthorized use. Access rights verification is easy to implement because object data is accessible only through object methods, e.g., Get_Object_Content(). Although one may attempt to reconstruct the whole object from the partial data acquired with object methods, the process is much harder to perform. Method visibility determines, whether methods are publicly or locally

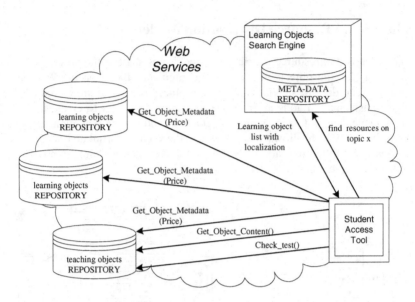

Fig. 6. The model of learning object distribution based on learning component methods

available. Methods that allow an easy search of learning objects such as Get_Object_Metadata() or Get_Object_Method_List() can be public. Methods concerning data with copyrights, e.g., the content, can be restricted, which means that their use will be limited to authorized users. Internal methods can be reserved for the repository owner. The internal methods include set operations and the Get_Object_Package() method that can be used for replication between repositories. The proposed visibility is useful if learning objects will be highly protected. The solution improves the interoperability and simplifies data search and copyright protection.

6   Conclusions

The growing number of commercial resources available in the Internet enforces precise cost/benefit calculations of digital products. Educational resources can be measured with a simple metric of a standard webpage, which enables effort and cost estimations. The presented research has shown, that the effort required to create one standard webpage is constant. Further research has to be done to validate the data and to identify potential factors that influence production costs.

The efficiency of learning objects can be increased with the use of a new concept of teaching object that supports the whole learning process. The distribution of teaching and learning objects is simplified by using learning component concept and Web services. The implementation enables high interoperability and copyright protection.

References

1. Gwozdzinska A., Kaczmarek J.: Virtual University Lifecycle Costs, In: Proceedings of EAEEIE 14th International Conference on Innovations in Education, Gdańsk, Poland (2003) CD-A24
2. Arcelli F., De Santo M.: An Agent based Internet Infrastructure for Learning Commerce, In: Proceedings of the 33rd Hawaii Conference on System Sciences, Hawaii (2000) 10
3. IEEE Learning Technology Standards Committee, IEEE/LTSC P1484 ltsc.ieee.org (2004)
4. Friesen, N.: Three Objections to Learning Objects. In: McGreal, R. (ed.): Online Education Using Learning Objects. London, Routledge (2004) 59-70
5. Advanced Distributed Learning (ADL) Sharable Content Object Reference Model (SCORM) 2nd ed. www.adlnet.org (2004)
6. Redeker G.: An Educational Taxonomy for Learning Objects, In: Proceedings of the IEEE Conference on Advanced Learning Technologies, Sapporo, Japan (2003) 250-251
7. Pitkanen S., Silander P.: Criteria for Pedagogical Reusability of Learning Objects Enabling Adaptation and Individualised Learning Processes, Proceedings of the IEEE International Conference on Advanced Learning Technologies, Padova, Italy (2004) 246-250
8. IMS Global Learning Consortium Question and Test Interoperability (QTI), www.imsproject.org (2003)
9. Thomas P., Paine C.: How students learn to program: Observations of practical tasks completed, Proceedings of the IEEE International Conference on Advanced Learning Technologies, Washington, USA (2001), 170-173
10. Varian, H.: Pricing Information Goods, In: Proceedings of Research Libraries Group Symposium, Boston, USA, www.sims.berkeley.edu/~hal/ (1995)
11. USC COCOMO II Model Definition, University of Southern California, www.cse.usc.edu/cocomoII (1998)
12. Kaczmarek J., Kucharski M.: Size and effort estimation for applications written in Java, Information and Software Technology, 46 (2004) 589-601
13. Park R.E.: Software Size Measurement: A Framework for Counting Source Statements, Software Engineering Institute Technical Report, SEI-92-TR-20 (1992)
14. Gwozdzinska A., Kaczmarek J.: Software Pricing Fair Play Rules, In: Proceedings of International Conference on The Social and Ethical Impacts of Information and Communication Technologies, Gdańsk, Poland (2001) 245-252

Dynamic Load Balancing Method Based on DNS for Distributed Web Systems*

Jong-Bae Moon and Myung-Ho Kim

School of Computing, Soongsil University, Seoul 156-743, Korea
comdoct@ss.ssu.ac.kr, kmh@ssu.ac.kr

Abstract. In most existing distributed Web systems, incoming requests are distributed to servers via Domain Name System (DNS). Although such systems are simple to implement, the address caching mechanism easily results in load unbalancing among servers. Moreover, modification of the DNS is necessary to load balancing considering the server's state. In this paper, we propose a new dynamic load balancing method using dynamic DNS update and round-robin mechanism. The proposed method performs effective load balancing without modification of the DNS. In this method, a server is dynamically added to or removed from the DNS list according to the server's load. By removing the overloaded servers from the DNS list, the response time becomes faster. For dynamic scheduling, the scheduling algorithm consider usage rates of servers' three main resources–CPU, memory, and network. We also implement a GUI-based management tool to manage the system across the network. Experiments show that modules implemented in this paper have a low impact on performance of the proposed system. Furthermore, experiments show that both the response time and the average file transfer rate of the proposed system are faster than those of a pure Round-Robin DNS.

1 Introduction

With the explosive growth of the Internet, online services that require heavy loads such as broadcast, education, gaming, VOD and streaming services have emerged. In addition, the pay-per-service market for Internet content is increasing so rapidly that a plan to provide this type of high-quality, uninterrupted service is required. Currently, a distributed Web system attempts to improve Web performance by delivering Web contents to end-users from servers distributed geographically[1][2][3][4]. The distributed Web system not only guarantees scalability, but also provides the transparency through a single virtual interface. An important factor contributing to the performance improvement, however, is the guarantee of fast response time by allocating user requests to the best server that can handle them quickly.

The distributed Web system typically performs dynamic request routing using the DNS because there is no front-end that is different from a cluster

---

* This work was supported by the Soongsil University Research Fund.

K. Bauknecht et al. (Eds.): EC-Web 2005, LNCS 3590, pp. 238–247, 2005.

system[5]. The DNS server converts the Fully-Qualified Domain Name (FQDN) into IP address(or addresses). Because of the transparent nature of name resolution, the DNS can be exploited to redirect user requests to an appropriate server without requiring any modification to client software, server protocols, or Web applications. In addition, a DNS-based distributed Web system works across any IP-based application, regardless of the transport-layer protocol being used. However, dispatching requests through the DNS has two problems that prevent load balancing among the Web servers. First, since the DNS does not know servers' states, requests can be assigned to an overloaded or nonoperational server. Second, because of the address-caching mechanism, the load distribution under the RR-DNS is unbalanced. To overcome these issues, two potential solutions have been researched. The first approach requires modification of the DNS[7][8]. DNS service also may be stopped during the rebuilding of the DNS. The second approach, which requires no modification of the DNS[1][14][10], integrates a DNS-based dispatching algorithm with some redirection mechanisms. With this approach, the main drawback is increased response time since each redirected request requires a new client-server connection.

In this paper, we propose a new load balancing method based on DNS. The proposed method performs effective load distribution by adding modules without modification of the DNS. A load balancing module, which is implemented using dynamic DNS update defined in RFC2136, dynamically adds or removes a server according to the server's load. By removing the overloaded server from the DNS list, the response time becomes faster. The server's load is measured by applying weight differently to the resource usages of the CPU, memory, and network, according to content type. In addition, the proposed system can manage the DNS easily by using a management tool based on GUI.

The rest of this paper is organized as follows: Section 2 summarizes the existing research regarding the load balancing method based on the DNS. Section 3 proposes a new load balancing system based on round-robin mechanism. Section 4 examines the efficiency of the proposed system. Finally, Section 5 concludes the paper.

2   Related Works

Round-Robin DNS (RR-DNS)[3] can easily scale from locally to geographically distributed Web-server systems and are also used in other related distributed architectures such as CDN. However, the load distribution under the RR-DNS is unbalanced because the address-caching mechanism lets the DNS control only a small fraction of requests[2]. Additional drawbacks result because the algorithm ignores both server capacity and availability. A lot of researches have been conducted to overcome these issues.

IS2-DSI[13] and Distributed Director of Cisco system[7] are examples of Web system architectures based on proximity algorithm. Proximity-based architectures choose a nearby server. The decision is based on the local DNS's identity not the client's, because DNS provides only the IP address of the client's local DNS server to the system rather than the client's IP address. In practice, however, Web service is connected between client and Web server. Therefore, proximity-based architecture assumes that clients are close to their local name-servers. Thus when clients and their local DNS are not proximal, the proximity-based architecture may lead to poor decisions. An additional drawback is that modification of the DNS is required.

TTL-based algorithms are divided into two classes. First, with constant TTL algorithms, the DNS selects servers on the basis of system state information and assigns the same TTL value to all address-mapping requests[12]. Second, with adaptive TTL algorithms, the DNS adapts the TTL values on the basis of dynamic information from servers and clients[8]. Adaptive TTL algorithms are effective, but they do not consider network information in making scheduling decisions. The main drawback of TTL-based algorithms is that modification of the DNS is required.

SWEB[13] and DPR[14] are examples of Web system architectures based on two-level dispatching, where the DNS decision such as round-robin is integrated with some request reassignment mechanism such as HTTP-Redirection or Packet Rewriting. The advantage of this architecture is that no modification is necessary. The user's latency, however, increases because the dispatching of the user requests occurs in more than one step.

3   Proposed DNS-Based Dynamic Load Balancing Method

This section proposes a new dynamic load balancing method based on DNS to overcome the issues of the previous system as described above. The proposed system uses a round-robin mechanism and removes the overloaded server from the DNS list by using a dynamic DNS update mechanism. When the server's load becomes stable, the server is dynamically added back into the DNS list. The user's latency is not delayed since the overloaded server is removed from the DNS list. In addition, scalability is easily guaranteed. The most important advantage is that we do not need to modify the existing DNS.

The architecture of the proposed system is shown in Fig. 1. The proposed system consists of BIND, a monitoring module, a dynamic update module, and a management tool. The monitoring module periodically checks servers' state and collects servers' load information. The dynamic module dynamically updates the DNS list according to the load information collected by the monitoring module. The management tool is provided with a GUI interface that can manage the DNS system across the network easily.

3.1   Design and Implementation of Modules

None of the modules should impact the DNS service. Each module is separated from BIND so that the load of the DNS and the user's latency is prevented from increasing.

The monitoring module periodically collects the load information from servers registered in the DNS list. This module consists of a monitoring daemon and

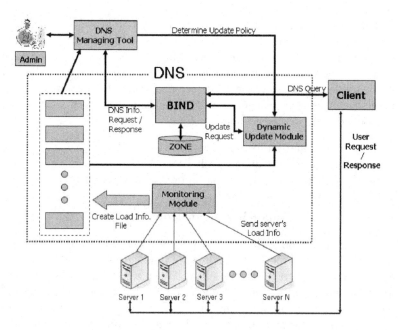

Fig. 1. Proposed architecture for a dynamic load balancing system based on DNS

a monitoring agent. The monitoring daemon resides at the DNS server. The monitoring daemon receives the load information from each server's monitoring agents and creates files that include load information such as CPU, memory and network usage. In addition, the monitoring daemon confirms the servers' states by checking whether the packets with the load information are received. The monitoring daemon assumes the server to be down if the packet is not received from the agent for a given period. If this occurs, the monitoring daemon deletes the load information file to remove the server from the DNS list. A monitoring agent resides at each server. The agent periodically sends UDP packets with the server's IP address and the load information. The packets also act as a heartbeat packet. The packets using UDP decrease network overhead and rapidly inform the monitoring daemon of the load information.

The dynamic update module maintains an optimum server list by measuring the loads of servers that are registered in the DNS. The optimum server list is the list of servers that can quickly handle user requests. The dynamic update module updates the DNS list in real time, according to policies configured by an administrator. At this time, the load information file that is generated by the monitoring daemon is referred to estimate a server's load. Under dynamic changing of a server's load, an update of the DNS list may occur frequently. A threshold should be identified in order to reduce the update frequency. When a server's load is more than the threshold, the module removes the server from the DNS list. When a server's load is less than then threshold, the module adds the server to the DNS list.

The BIND works on Linux and is managed by text-based commands. With growing numbers of servers that must be managed, it is difficult for an administrator to manage the DNS using command-line interface. Thus, a management tool with GUI more efficiently allows an administrator to manage the DNS. It can also be implemented as a network-based program, enabling an administrator to manage the system from a remote site. The main functions provided by the management tool are described below:

- Display the information for all servers.
- Add and remove servers dynamically.
- Set up the policies for maintaining an optimum server list.

3.2 Dynamic Load Balancing Algorithm

The proposed method basically uses round-robin mechanism. For dynamic load balancing, the proposed method dynamically removes an overloaded server from the DNS list according to the server's load. When we estimate the server's load, we need to assign a larger weight to the resource that is more heavily used. For services such as online broadcasting or VOD, which need to transmit a large amount of data files, network usage must be higher than CPU usage or memory usage. For services such as online games, where a higher CPU load is required, CPU usage is obviously more than network usage. In this paper, the following policies are provided for dynamic load balancing:

- CPU-based Policy: removes the server in which the CPU load is greater than the threshold value, and adds the server back to the DNS list when the CPU load is smaller than the threshold value.
- Network-based Policy: removes the server in which the network load is greater than the threshold value, and adds the server back to the DNS list when the network load is smaller than threshold value.
- Memory-based Policy: removes the server in which the memory load is greater than the threshold value, and adds it back to the DNS list when the memory load is smaller than the threshold value.
- Combined Policy: we assume that the sum of load ratio of CPU, memory and network is 100, and then we assign different weights according to the usage of resources.

3.3 DNS Security Issues

Only the administrator should be able to control the DNS because the dynamic update module can modify records remotely without modifying the zone file of BIND directly. For increased security, the DNS adds a securing DNS message called a transaction signature (TSIG) record, which is codified in RFC2845, to the additional data section of a DNS message. The TSIG record signs the DNS message, proving that the message's sender had a cryptographic key shared with the receiver and that the message was not modified after it left the sender.

Upon receipt of a message, the DNS server checks to see if there is a TSIG record. If one exists, then the prerequisite section, which contains a set of record prerequisites that must be satisfied at the time the update packet is received, is checked to determine whether all prerequisites are satisfied by the current state of the zone. For example, if the domain called somewhere.com does not exist, when the server is sent a request to update the record of www.somewhere.com, it will not be permitted to make the update.

The DNS also provides the DNS zone transfer that permits any host to request and receives a full zone transfer for a domain. This also is a security issue, since DNS data can be used to decipher the topology of a company's network. If this information is obtained, it can be used for malicious exploitation such as DNS poisoning or spoofing. The TSIG also allows the DNS to accomplish secure zone transfer.

4 Experiments and Analysis

To estimate performance of the proposed system, we measured the overhead of the DNS. We also conducted an experiment to compare the performance of the proposed system with existing RR-DNS.

In this experiment, the DNS server that services the domain name of ns.grid.or.kr is used. The DNS server has a CPU with P-III 800MHz, 512MB of memory and 100Mbps Ethernet card. In the DNS server, BIND 9 has been installed and TSIG key has been set. Each Web server, which has a CPU with P-IV 3GHz, 1GB of memory and 100Mbps Ethernet card, adopts Linux Operating system and Apache Web server.

4.1 Measurement of the DNS Overhead

To estimate overhead of the proposed system, we measured CPU and network load when the number of servers in the DNS list increased. We also measured the loads depending on the transmission period of load information to estimate the impact of the transmission period on the performance.

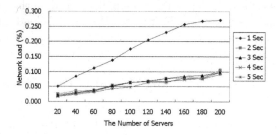

Fig. 2. Network load when the number of servers increases from 20 to 200

Fig. 2 shows network loads according to the transmission periods of load information when the number of servers increased from 20 to 200. The result shows that when the number of servers increases, the network load increases. When the number of servers increases up to 200, and every server is periodically transmitting load information to the DNS, the network load is only about 0.1% of total bandwidth. As the number of servers increases, the load also increases. The load information with UDP packet, however, does not affect the performance of the proposed system. As the transmission period gets longer, the network load decreases. When we measure the load information every second, the load information is more accurate, but more network load occurs. Although the network load reduces when the transmission period gets longer, the load information is unreliable. Therefore, we conclude that measuring the server's load information every 2 seconds can not only get the accurate load information, but also does not have much impact on the proposed system.

Fig. 3. CPU load when the number of servers increases from 20 to 200

Fig. 3 shows the overhead of the dynamic update module when the number of servers increases from 20 to 200. When the number of servers increases, the CPU load also increases. As with the network load, the CPU load is reduced when the transmission period increases, and it increases when the transmission period decreases. When the number of servers is up to 200, the maximum CPU load is 1.3%. Compared to the total performance, this is a small value and does not impact the proposed system. The dynamic update module determines whether each server is to be removed from or added to the optimum server list by estimating the server's load, depending on a policy based on the resources usage. When the dynamic update module estimates the server's load and updates the optimum server list, if heavy overhead occurs, the proposed system may have a very poor performance.

4.2   Impact of a Small TTL Value on the DNS

In DNS-based load balancing systems, large TTL values reduce network load by adopting an address-caching mechanism. The address-caching mechanism, however, leads the DNS to load unbalancing due to allowing the DNS to control only a very small fraction of the user requests. To achieve fine-grained load balancing in the proposed system, the TTL is set to a small value.

To measure the impact of a small TTL value on the DNS, we measured the CPU and network load when the TTL values increase from 0 to 120 seconds.

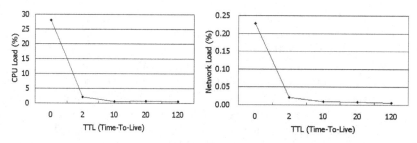

Fig. 4. CPU and Network Loads for various TTL values

In this experiment, we measured the name lookup overhead by timing the geth-ostbyname() system call. We created 1,600 threads on behalf of the clients and estimated an average from the results. Fig. 4 shows the impact of small TTL values on the DNS server. As the TTL value increases, we find that the CPU and network loads on the DNS decrease. The CPU and network loads, however, increase when the TTL value is set to zero in order to disable the address-caching. Compared with a TTL value set at zero, the CPU and network loads decrease considerably when TTL values are more than 2 seconds. Fig. 5 shows the response times for name lookup according to various TTL values when clients increase. We find that the response time is faster when the TTL value is greater than zero because the CPU and network loads on the DNS are reduced as mentioned above. Therefore, we conclude that the proposed system has low impact of a small TTL value when the TTL value is set more than 2 second.

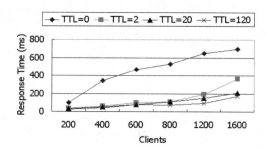

Fig. 5. Response Time for various TTL values

4.3 Performance Comparison

In the next experiment, we measured the average response time and the average file transfer rate when the proposed system and ordinary RR-DNS were used. To evaluate the performance of the proposed DNS-based load balancing system, we used the SIEGE[15], which is an http regression testing and benchmarking utility. In this experiment, clients used SIEGE to request a 3MB media file 125 times from a Web server that was in the DNS list. In this experiment, we registered 4 Web servers in the DNS, and 2 among those servers had a CPU load of 50% ∼ 70%. The other 2 servers had a CPU load of almost 0%. The experiment result is

shown in Fig. 6. We found that both the average response time and the average
file transfer rate of the DLBDNS were about 1.8 times faster than ones of a RR-
DNS. Because a RR-DNS did not consider the server's state, it distributed user
requests equally to servers even though it was overloaded. Therefore, a system
with RR-DNS cannot guarantee a fast response time because the processing
rate of the overloaded servers becomes slow. The DLBDNS, however, removes
overloaded servers from the DNS list, so that the overloaded server does not
handle a lot of user requests. Therefore, we concluded that the DLBDNS does
more effective load balancing than the RR-DNS.

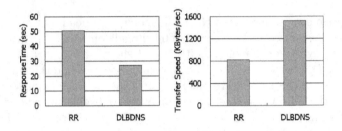

Fig. 6. Comparisons between DLBDNS and RR-DNS

5   Conclusions

In this paper, we proposed a new dynamic load balancing method based on DNS.
This method overcomes the issues of existing RR-DNS. The proposed system can
be implemented without modifying the DNS by adding a load balancing module
to the existing DNS. The proposed system is based on round-robin mechanism
and maintains an optimum server list which contains servers that can handle
user requests quickly. To prevent a user's latency from increasing, the overloaded
server is dynamically removed from the DNS list by using dynamic DNS update.
For dynamic load balancing, the load information of each server is collected
periodically. When the load is estimated, a different weight is assigned depending
on the usage of resources. To manage the DNS easily, a DNS management tool
provides a GUI-based interface.

In the experiments, we evaluated the impact of the modules on the DNS. We
also conducted an experiment comparing the performance of the proposed system
with an existing RR-DNS. In the experiments, we found that the modules implemented in this paper had a low impact on the proposed system. We also found
that the proposed system had better performance than an existing RR-DNS.

References

1. Valerial, Cardellini, Michele, Colajanni, Philip, S., Yu: Geographic Load Balancing
   for Scalable Distributed Web Systems. Proceedings of the International Symposium on Modeling, Analysis and Simulation of Computer and Telecommunication
   Systems (MASCOTS) (2000) 20–28

2. Valleria, Cardellini, Michele, Colajanni, Philip, S., Yu: Dynamic Load Balancing on Web-server Systems. IEEE Internet Computing, Vol. 3, No. 3 (1999) 28–39

3. T., Kwan, R., McGrath, A., Reed: NCSA's World Wide Web Server: Design and Performance. IEEE Computer, Vol. 28, No. 11 (1995) 67–74

4. Balachander, Krishnamurthy, Craig, Wills, Yin, Zhang: On the Use and Performance of Content Distribution Networks. Proceedings of the First ACM SIG-COMM Workshop on Internet Measurement (2001) 169–182

5. Valeria, Cardellini, Emilinano, Casalicchio, Michele, Colajanni, Philip, S., Yu: The State of the Art in Locally Distributed Web-server System. ACM Computing Surveys (CSUR), Vol. 34 (2002) 263–311

6. Anees, Shaikh, Renu, Tewari, Mukesh, Agrawal: On the Effectiveness of DNS-based Server Selection. Proceedings of IEEE INFOCOM (2001)

7. Cisco's DistributedDirector, http://www.cisco.com/

8. Valerial, Cardellini, Michele, Colajanni, Philip, S., Yu: DNS Dispatching Algorithms with State Estimators for Scalable Web-server Clusters. World Wide Web Journal, Baltzer Science, Vol. 2, No. 2 (1999) 101–113

9. Yong, Meng, TEO, Rassul, AYANI: Comparison of Load Balancing Strategies on Cluster-based Web Servers. Transactions of the Society for Modeling and Simulation (2000)

10. Daniel, Andresen, Tao, Yang, Oscar, H., Ibarra: Towards a Scalable WWW Server on Networked Workstations. Journal of Parallel and Distributed Computing, Vol. 42 (1997) 91–100

11. Zhuoqing, Morley, Mao, Charles, D., Cranor, Fred, Douglis, Michael, Rabinovich, Olvier, Spatscheck, Jia, Wang: A Precise and Efficient Evaluation of the Proximity between Web Clients and their Local DNS Servers. Proceedings of USENIX Annual Technical Conference (2002)

12. Michele, Colajanni, Philip, S., Yu: A Performance Study of Robust Load Sharing Strategies for Distributed Heterogeneous Web Server Systems. IEEE Transactions on Knowledge and Data Engineering, Vol. 14, No. 2 (2000) 398-414

13. Micah, Beck, Terry, Moor: The Internet2 Distributed Storage Infrastructure Project: An Architecture for Internet Content Channels. Computer Networking and ISDN Systems (1998) 2141–2148

14. Azer, Bestavros, Mark, Crovella, Jun, Liu, David, Martin: Distributed Packet Rewriting and its Application to Scalable Server Architectures. Proceedings of the 6th International Conference on Network Protocols, Austin Texas (1998) 290–297

15. SIEGE: http://joedog.org/siege/

Performance Based Cost Models for Improving Web Service Efficiency Through Dynamic Relocation

Dennis Pratistha[1], Arkady Zaslavsky[1], Simon Cuce[1], and Martin Dick[2]

[1] School of Computer Science and Software Engineering, Monash University, Australia
{Dennis.Pratistha, Arkady.Zaslavsky,
Simon.Cuce}@csse.monash.edu.au
[2] School of Business Information Technology, RMIT University, Australia
Martin.Dick@rmit.edu.au

Abstract. The performance and quality of a web service are important factors and are expected by parties utilizing the service. This paper proposes and implements a cost efficiency solution to cater for web services in a unique set of situation. The solution is designed for web services that have frequent user groups scattered in various geographic locations, without the existence of access patterns. This optimization solution is developed for the Fluid Infrastructure methodology. Its main emphasis is fundamentally to provide a mechanism that is capable of reacting to various problems (operational and performance related) in an efficient and autonomous manner. Discussions within this paper focus on the algorithms that are used to compute the efficiency metrics and implementation issues of the solution. Further, evaluation of these solutions are also demonstrated and validated.

1 Introduction

Web services present a simple method for creating interoperable applications directed towards the distributed environment. With this paradigm, distributed applications can be implemented through the composition of multiple web service components that are offered by a variety of vendors residing in various geographical locations. Since web services are generally part of an application composition, the preservation of quality and performance of individual services at some efficient level, are essential to limit the possibilities of partial failure and enhance overall application responsiveness [2, 11].

Ideally, this could be achieved through the implementation of performance enhancement procedures catered specifically for the requirements of each web service, and the given environmental situation. However, the implementations of such procedures in existing paradigms are generally complicated. This is due to the lack of facilities to support the development and provide the necessary execution requirements for these additional cost efficiency models.

The drawbacks above, have been resolved by the Fluid Infrastructure [8, 9] methodology, which is the target operating platform of our cost model. Fluid's cost model architecture is flexible in the sense that Cost Model Modules (CMM) can be added and removed, and each web service can select the specific CMM to use. Further, the infrastructure also supports the customization of access to particular

K. Bauknecht et al. (Eds.): EC-Web 2005, LNCS 3590, pp. 248–257, 2005.

environmental information and other specific information necessary for the CMM to make appropriate cost efficiency decisions.

The main emphasis of Fluid is on providing a mechanism that is capable of reacting to various operational and performance related problems by using two approaches: perform structural reconfiguration of utilized components to accommodate current conditions; and relocate the web service to a more suitable hosting environment that fulfils specific requirements. The two are either used as alternative actions or as complementary. For example, a web service is relocated to a different device class, thus requiring structural reconfiguration to be performed as well.

In this paper, we present discussions for the design and development of a cost model. It is proposed for improving efficiency of WS [Fluid 1] applications that exist in situations where the clients frequently utilizing the service reside in a diverse range of geographic locations. The cost model discussed is *Performance-Priority*.

The cost model aims to increase the responsiveness of the WS [Fluid] application by explicitly searching for potential hosts with the greatest processing power, when putting forward potential relocation destinations.

The paper is structured as follows. In Section 2, we provide related work discussions and Section 3 the algorithms that are used within this optimization solution is explained. This section is followed by the design objectives and implementation details of the CMM (Section 4). In Section 5, we provide the evaluation results of our CMM implementation. Finally, we conclude and present future directions of this work in Section 6.

2   Related Work

Several nomadic web service frameworks have been proposed, with variations in their main objectives and the techniques used for relocations. Pratistha [7] and Elkarra [3] implemented a lightweight web service architecture to allow hosting of web services from a portable device. In this approach the web service itself is not transportable instead the device hosting the web service is the one relocating.

Misfud [6] proposed LAMS (Location and Management Service), a framework that permits web service applications to relocate in real-time. Nevertheless, the primary objective of this framework is as an administrator tool to streamline the packaging and relocation of web service to a selected destination, using peer-to-peer connection. The initiation (timing) and destination for the relocation operation are manually resolved by the web service administrator, as opposed to an autonomous action. This eliminates the need for cost efficiency algorithms to compute the potential and benefit of performing relocation operations.

To the best of our knowledge, since the concept of autonomous web service relocation is relatively new, cost models for assessing the suitability and efficiency outcome of web service relocation operations have not been developed. Although in some aspects similarities could be drawn with the cost model proposed by

---

[1] WS [Fluid] is built upon the Web Service Architecture (WSA) [1], to support the additional features introduced by Fluid.

Krishnaswamy [4, 5], to estimate the response time for performing distributed data mining process using a hybrid approach – integrating client-server and mobile agent paradigms. The similarity is limited to the relocation of mobile agents to a selected destination to retrieve, evaluate and filter gathered information.

3 Cost Model Algorithm

We integrated the foundational cost model previously discussed in paper [10] for the implementation of the Performance-Priority CMM. In this section, we will revisit this algorithm and provide brief explanations of its main features.

3.1 Performance Cost Model

The primary objective of this cost algorithm is to compute the average cost of a call that can be made to each web function available in a web service, within a specified period of time, and based on the current context. This computation is performed for both the Originating Host (OH) and Destination Host (DH). The result is used to determine whether the most beneficial operation is to perform a relocation of the WS ^{Fluid} application to a selected DH, or simply resume at the current host.

The ideal WS ^{Fluid} relocation condition to the selected DH is presented in Equation 1 below:

$$c_{overall\_serv\_iteration\_DH} > (c_{overall\_serv\_iteration\_OH} * \Delta) \qquad (1)$$

where $c_{overall\_serv\_iteration\_*}$ is the cost of the total service execution cycle, for a predefined period T. In order to gain in performing a relocation operation, at least Δ $(0 \leq \Delta \leq 1)$ improvement over running the service at the OH is expected. This is after taking into consideration the relocation operation (inspection and transportation) to DH. For example, $\Delta = .1$ indicates improvement by 10%. Note: the * is replaced with ^{DH} or ^{OH}.

The formula for determining the service execution cycle at the OH is as follows (Equation 2):

$$c_{overall\_serv\_iteration\_OH} = t_{service\_lifetime} / t_{avg\_OH\_service\_runtime} \qquad (2)$$

where $t_{service\_lifetime}$ is a user defined time that is used for determining the total number of times the service can execute at the OH, and $t_{avg\_OH\_service\_runtime}$ is an average value based on the accumulated duration required to execute each web function available in the service at OH.

The formula for determining the service execution cycle at the potential DH is defined in Equation 3:

$$w_{overall\_serv\_iteration\_f} = (t_{service\_lifetime} - t_{service\_reloc}) / t_{avg\_f\_service\_runtime} \qquad (3)$$

where $t_{service\_reloc}$ refers to the total time required for service relocation (including inspection and transportation time) and $t_{avg\_DH\_service\_runtime}$ is an average of the total time required to execute each web function provided in the web service at DH, utilizing the available resources there.

The formula for calculating the average time to execute a web function is defined in Equation 4 below:

$$t_{avg\_DH\_service\_runtime} = \sum_{i=1}^{n} t_{service\_function\_runtime}(i) / n \qquad (4)$$

where $\sum_{i=1}^{n} t_{service\_function\_runtime}(i)$ is the sum of executing the entire web function available in the service, and n refers to the number of functions available.

The formula to calculate the overall service relocation time is defined in the following (Equation 5):

$$t_{service\_reloc} = t_{dest\_host\_insp} + t_{insp\_integration} + t_{service\_trans} \qquad (5)$$

where $t_{dest\_host\_insp}$ refers to the longest DH inspection duration, $t_{insp\_integration}$ is the time taken to process the results of each inspection operation and $t_{service\_trans}$ denotes the time taken to transport the web service.

The cost function to calculate the potential DH inspection duration is defined in Equation 6:

$$i = 1..n$$

$$t_{dest\_host\_insp} = \max\{ t_{insp\_agent(OH, i)} + t_{insp\_process(i)} + t_{insp\_result\_agent(i, OH)}\} \qquad (6)$$

where the inner expression $t_{insp\_agent}(OH, i) + t_{insp\_process}(i) + t_{insp\_result\_agent}(i, OH)$ correspond to the period of the inspection operation to the ith DH, where i ranges from 1..n hosts. Individually the elements of the expression above: $t_{insp\_agent}(OH, i)$ is the transportation of a Scout Agent[2] (SA) from the OH to DH (i), $t_{insp\_process}(i)$ is the time required to perform the actual inspection operation on the DH and $t_{insp\_result\_agent}(i, OH)$ is the transportation of the SA carrying the results from the DH (i) to the OH.

The cost function to calculate the service transportation duration is expressed in Equation 7 as follows:

$$t_{service\_trans} = t_{packaging} + \sum_{c=1}^{n} t_{trans\_agent(OH, i)} + \sum_{c=1}^{n} t_{unpackaging} + t_{construction} \qquad (7)$$

where the term $t_{packaging}$ is the duration for preparing all service elements and the encapsulation of these elements inside individual transport agents, the term $\sum_{c=1}^{n} t_{trans\_agent(OH, i)}$ is the accumulative duration of transporting each Transport Agent (TA) carrying a service component c (where c ranges from 1..n components) from OH to i^{th} DH (selected DH), the term $\sum_{c=1}^{n} t_{unpackaging}$ refers to the extraction of all service components (1..n) from the TA(s), and the term $t_{construction}$ refers to reconstruction and reactivation of the service.

---

[2] ScoutAgents performs the inspection operation of potential DH(s).

4 Cost Model Solution

A cost model module (CMM) is used to govern the types of actions to perform. The implementation of a CMM is generally used to target a particular scenario, with certain objectives. The following sections discuss the implementation of a CMM implementation.

4.1 Performance-Priority Cost Model

The performance-priority cost model solution aims to discover the hosting environment with the best overall computational resources available, from a list of registered hosts. This strategy is employed to optimally increase the processing performance of individual WS ^{Fluid} applications, which will essentially reduce response time in handling incoming client requests.

```
   * The inspected_foreign_context are passed to the method as parameters. It represents the
registered foreign contexts from the Central Registry, which has been inspected. */

   /* Evaluates the suitability of each foreign context inspected. The results returns an array
containing two elements, which represents the two classifications */

1.    Array suitable_foreign_context = Evaluate_foreign_context_suitability(
                                                       inspected_foreign_context)
2.    Array all_higher_threshold_foreign_context = suitable_foreign_context[0]
3.    Array part_higher_threshold_foreign_context = suitable_foreign_context[1]
4.    Integer w highest_iteration = 0
5.    Foreign_Context most_suitable_context

6.    If (length(all_higher_threshold_foreign_context) > 0)
7.        For index=0 to length(all_higher_threshold_foreign_context)
8.            Foreign_Context_Info foreign_temp =
                         all_higher_threshold_foreign_context[index]
   /* The algorithm in line 16 has been abbreviated */

13.            If(w overall_serv_iteration_temp > w highest_iteration)
14.                w highest_iteration = w overall_serv_iteration_temp
15.                most_suitable_context = foreign_temp.Get_Foreign_Context()
               End If
           End For
       Else If (length(part_higher_threshold_foreign_context) > 0)
16.        For index=0 to length(part_higher_threshold_foreign_context)
               /* A similar process is applied from line 11-15 */
           End For
       Else
           Return empty
       End If
17.   Return most_suitable_context
```

Fig. 1. Evaluate_Most_Suitable_Foreign_Context() Psuedocode

Consider a scenario where an application is in high-demand, with frequent user groups scattered in numerous geographical location, without any patterns of accesses either based on time or sequence. To improve responsiveness in these situations requires more than embracing the concept of moving closer to the frequent user's source, without significantly considering performance issues. The reason this is unlikely to make much of a performance improvement, is that the frequent user groups are scattered, and difficult to pin-point a location at the centre of gravity among these groups.

Instead, the most effective process is through the incorporation of a more straightforward technique, by simply looking up the list of available registered hosts, and investigate hosting environments that posses the best overall resources in terms of processing power, and optionally network bandwidth.

Implementation

In implementing this CMM, the cost efficiency process begins with the selection of the most suitable DH(s). This is accomplished by initially retrieving all DH(s) that have been registered with the Fluid *Central Registry*, and individually inspect these hosts to determine their environmental characteristics. Those that are considered suitable for hosting the selected application are returned to the OH (refer to Fig. 1).

Environmental information returned is evaluated and partitioned based on two categories (Line 1-3). The first classification is potential DH(s) that fulfil the higher threshold based on the given values of the WS ^{strategy} module. The second classification is DH(s) that fulfils all the lower thresholds, but only several of the higher thresholds. DH(s) that do not comply with any of these conditions are discarded.

/* This service lifetime is set as an example value of 6 hrs (21600000 millisecond) */

1. $t_{service\_lifetime} = 21600000$

/* Calculates the initial elements for the foreign context required for the weighting algorithm */

2. $t_{service\_reloc} = t_{foreign\_context\_insp} + t_{insp\_integration} + t_{service\_trans}$

3. $t_{avg\_f\_service\_runtime} = \sum_{i=1}^{n} t_{service\_function\_runtime}(i) / n$

4. $W_{overall\_serv\_iteration\_f} = (t_{service\_lifetime} - t_{service\_reloc}) / t_{avg\_f\_service\_runtime}$

/* Calculates the initial elements for the home context required for the weighting algorithm */

5. $t_{avg\_h\_service\_runtime} = \sum_{i=1}^{n} t_{service\_function\_runtime}(i) / n$

6. $W_{overall\_serv\_iteration\_h} = t_{service\_lifetime} / t_{avg\_h\_service\_runtime}$

/* Evaluates whether the selected foreign context is capable of providing a 10% improvements based on the calculated weights when compared to the OH. In both situation the service can be instructed to perform reconfiguration operations, when any of the higher threshold are not met. */

7. If($W_{overall\_serv\_iteration\_f} > W_{overall\_serv\_iteration\_h} + (W_{overall\_serv\_iteration\_h} \cdot 0.1)$)

8.   do relocate(service_id, selected_foreign_context)
    Else
9.   do resume(service_id)
    End If

Fig. 2. Evaluate_Optimization_Potential() Psuedocode

Following the partitioning process, DH(s) part of the first category is evaluated to determine which is capable of producing the best overall weights based on the requirements of the selected WS ^{Fluid} application. In situations where there are no DH(s) existing in the first category, the second category is used instead.

With the most suitable DH selected, we proceed with the computation of potential optimization actions, given the scenario previously discussed. The psuedocode of this operation is illustrated in Fig. 2.

To determine the optimization action to take, as indicated in Line 7-9, the ideal relocation factor is when the total service execution iteration at the selected DH, is at least 10% better than execution on the OH, otherwise the service resume operations on the OH.

Whatever the decision, to relocate or resume, the service can be required to perform structural reconfigurations to adapt with the current situation on the selected context. (Note: structural reconfiguration will not be discussed in this paper.)

5   Evaluation Results

This section demonstrates the effectiveness of the *Performance-Priority* CMM in optimizing the execution of their intended WS ^{Fluid} application. A demonstration is performed that exhibit the corresponding CMM in performing quantitative evaluations to determine the most appropriate efficiency operation (relocate or resume) based on the available information.

Demonstration 1 – *Performance-Priority.*
This demonstration consists of two simulations, with identical scenarios, (1) executing possible optimization methods suggested by the CMM (e.g. relocating the service to another context), and (2) resume existing operations. This was done to present a comparison overview of the actual performance improvement that arises from executing the optimization strategy offered by the CMM. The test environment is detailed in Table 1.

Table 1. Testing Environment Details

	Originating Host	**Destination Host (Network Z)**
O/S	Windows XP Profession (SP 2)	Windows XP Profession (SP 2)
Processor	Intel P3 600 Ghz	Intel P4 1.4 Ghz
Memory	256 MB SDRAM	768 MB SDRAM

Scenario
The '*StockQuoteService*' in Network X is utilized by several clients that are located in numerous geographic locations. In this evaluation a host in Network Z was considered the most suitable potential DH compared to that in Network Y, due to better resource availability.

Although this is clearly a simplified scenario where there are only two potential DH(s) involved (refer to Fig. 3); the computations that are involved in deciding the suitable optimization solutions are identical. Further, we feel that the scenario represents a valid sample to real-world situations, since the aspect that matters most for this CMM is discovering an alternative host that has the most favourable resources.

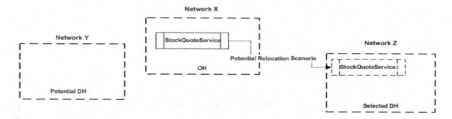

Fig. 3. Relocation Scenario

The scenario illustrated above – service relocating from Network X to Network Y, would theoretically increase the performance in processing client requests, due to the increase in processing power, as indicated in Table 1.

Simulation Data and Results
The variables used in both simulations are shown in Table 2 below. The 'Optimization' variables are not applicable to simulation #2, because no optimization attempts were made. The simulation was performed simply to present a comparison guide that identifies the performance enhancement produced by the CMM, given the scenario.

Table 2. Simulation Variables (Demonstration 1)

	Relocation (#1)	Resume (#2)
General		
Duration	10 mins (600 secs)	10 mins (600 secs)
Total Unique Requests	3	3
Optimization		
Foreign Host Inspection	225th sec	N/A
Service Relocation	250th sec	N/A

The cost efficiency calculation results shown in Table 3, justify the overheads added for relocating the WS ^{Fluid} application to optimize its overall performance. This rationalization is based on the significant advantage of around 36% (or 29% with a 10% safety margin) in the theoretical service performance capabilities between the OH and DH.   The theoretical service performance variable is the result of computations based on the average service processing time (refer to Equation 2-3 in Section 3).

Table 3. Calculated Theoretical Performance Weights (Demonstration 1)

Average Service Processing Time			Home Host	Foreign Host
Home Host	190 ms	**Service Iteration (based on 6 hour lifetime)**	113,684.21	125,052.63
Foreign Host	122 ms	**Difference**	+ 35.79 % (29.37 % w/ 10% safety margin)	

Although the theoretical improvement display significant gains when processing on the selected DH, the actual improvement during our simulation only showed a gain of 7% (refer to the graph in Fig. 4). This amount is based on the total request processed of 574 when relocation is performed, compared with 515 when resuming existing operations.

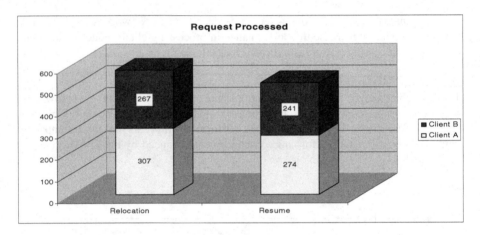

Fig. 4. Requests Processed Graph (Demonstration 1)

This low result is primarily due to the relatively short simulation duration of only 600 seconds, which clearly is not enough time, since: (1) transportation consists of high overheads, and (2) incoming client requests during relocation are queued, thus creating a back-log that needs to be initially processed. Essentially, these relocation costs need to be amortized over a longer period (greater than 600 seconds), before any significant benefit eventuates.

6 Conclusion and Future Work

This paper proposed a cost model solution that can be employed to enhance the performance and also maintain the quality of a WS ^{Fluid} application. This solution is specifically catered for situations where the frequent user groups are scattered in various geographical locations and no particular patterns exists in the requests. The cost formulae utilized in this solution computes the performance for running the service at both the originating host (OH) and destination host (DH) – taking into consideration inspection and relocation costs. The decision to relocate is only made when the DH produce superior results over the OH. We have experimentally validated the use of this cost formulae in our CMM, and our evaluations indicate that the relocation of the web service existing within the above situation, was capable of increasing the responsiveness of processing incoming requests.

The current cost formulae predominantly assess the processing power of the potential host, while placing little emphasis on bandwidth and average load of the host. Future directions of this cost model will assess these issues when performing efficiency measurements. In reviewing the average load, other commitments possessed by the potential DH that may affect the performance of running the relocated web service, over the long term are assessed. For example, this could be achieved by examining other web services registered with the host and determine their specific demands (i.e. frequently or infrequently accessed).

References

1. Booth, D., Haas, H., McCabe, F., Newcomer, E., Champion, M., Ferris, C. and Orchard, D. (2003). Web Services Architecture, W3C.
2. Burghart, T. (1998). Distributed Computing Overview. Cambridge, Massachusetts, Quoin Inc.
3. Elkarra, N. (2003). A Web Services Strategy for Mobile Phones, O'Reilly XML Web Services White Paper.
4. Krishnaswamy, S., Loke, S. and Zaslavsky, A. (2000). Cost Models for Heterogeneous Distributed Data Mining. Twelfth Annual Int. Conference on Software Engineering and Knowledge Engineering, Chicago, Illinois.
5. Krishnaswamy, S., Loke, S. and Zaslavsky, A. (2002). Application Run Time Estimation: A QoS Metric for Web-based Data Mining Service Providers. Seventeenth ACM Symposium on Applied Computing (ACM SAC), Madrid, Spain.
6. Mifsud, T. and Stanski, P. (2002). Peer-2-Peer Nomadic Web Services Migration Framework. Proceedings of the 2nd AMOC, Langkawi, Malaysia.
7. Pratistha, D., Nicoloudis, N. and Cuce, S. (2003). A Micro-Services Framework on Mobile Devices. International Conference on Web Services, Nevada, USA.
8. Pratistha, I. M. and Zaslavsky, A. (2004). Fluid - Supporting a Transportable and Adaptive Web Service. The 19th Annual ACM Symposium on Applied Computing, Nicosia, Cyprus.
9. Pratistha, I. M., Zaslavsky, A., Dick, M. and Cuce, S. (2004). Nomadic and Adaptive Web Services for mBusiness Applications. Third Annual m>Business 2004 Conference, New York City.
10. Pratistha, I. M., Zaslavsky, A., Dick, M. and Cuce, S. (2005). A Generic Cost Model and Infrastructure for Improving Web Service Efficiency through Dynamic Relocation. Technical Paper. Monash University, Australia
11. Waldo, J., Geoff, W., Wollrath, A. and Kendall, S. (1994). A Note on Distributed Computing. Sun Microsystem. SMLI TR-94-29.

Efficient Algorithm for Service Matchmaking in Ubiquitous Environments

Kee-Hyun Choi, Kyu Min Lee, Ho Jin Shin, and Dong-Ryeol Shin

School of Information and Communication Engineering,
Sungkyunkwan University,
300 Cheoncheon-dong, Jangan-gu, Suwon, Gyeonggi-do 440-746, Korea
{gyunee, kmlee, hjshin, drshin}@ece.skku.ac.kr

Abstract. Service discovery middleware allows users to find and use services through service discovery protocols in heterogeneous and ubiquitous environments without previous knowledge of the specific service location or characteristics, and with minimum manual effort. For this reason, in recent years, a number of researchers have studied service discovery middleware and many of papers dealing with this field have been published. However, when a number of service consumers request services from middle agents (e.g. matchmaker, broker, yellow page, blackboard, lookup server, etc) within the service discovery middleware, the middle agents do not guarantee efficient and rapid matching results because they use only a simple matching algorithm based on set theory for match processing. In this paper we address issues of existing matching algorithms, and propose a new matchmaking method adopting the marriage matching algorithm of the ATM network [1] to improve middle agent performance, complementing shortcomings of the existing matching algorithms. Furthermore, we use traffic type (e.g. voice/video applications, data-sharing applications, convenience applications, and so on) priority information for providing application-oriented QoS.

1 Introduction

Service Discovery is becoming increasingly important for ubiquitous networks because Internet services have grown in the past and continues to grow dramatically. As a result, automatic service discovery is becoming a very useful field in network scenarios, for example, in ad hoc networks. Especially, dynamic discovery of services in a foreign network and automatic system configuration will be very significant together with wide utilization of network mobile devices, such as PDAs.

Much work on service discovery is based on centralized registries such as UDDI. It suffers from the traditional problems of centralized systems, namely performance bottlenecks and single points of failure. In addition, they may be more vulnerable to denial of service attacks. Moreover, the possible storage of vast numbers of advertisements on centralized registries prevents the timely update that is happened because changes in the availability and capability of providers occur. In contrast to the traditional 'client/server' architecture of a server-centric design, P2P which stands for "peer-to-peer" architecture can be both a client and a server, i.e. every peer has

K. Bauknecht et al. (Eds.): EC-Web 2005, LNCS 3590, pp. 258 – 266, 2005.

equivalent capabilities and responsibilities. Here, a peer can be any network-aware device such as cell phone, PDA and PC. The focus of P2P networks is how a peer provides services to other peers and also discovers the available services from peers, i.e. the methods of service discovery that are based on different P2P applications.

A variety of papers dealing with service discovery have recently been published. Although theses papers propose efficient and fast searching schemes for service discovery, their schemes do not consider direct matching between service consumers and providers because of device limitations such as power consumption and memory. To be more specific, current matching algorithms have superior functionality but all these frameworks suffer from one common problem, namely lack of the matching algorithm and scheduling in network nodes. We review a few matching algorithms and address their associated issues in ubiquitous environments. In order to mitigate problems associated with current service discovery protocols and matching algorithms, this paper proposes a new matching algorithm, which provides a powerful and adaptive matching scheme using stable marriage matching used in ATM [1]. We present three matching schemes to verify our algorithm. The first is 'Simple Matching' using a simple description advertised by provider and consumer. The second is 'Multiple Matching', which uses more complicated information such as device or IP type, etc. The third is 'Priority based Multiple Matching', which utilizes priority based scheduling policy.

The remainder of the paper is organized as follows. Section 2 describes the basic service discovery protocols and existing matching algorithms. It presents the motivation for this paper, and describes related work. Section 3 presents our proposed scheme in detail. Finally, Section 4 gives conclusions and scope for future work.

2 Related Work

2.1 Service Discovery

Service Location Protocol (SLP) is a product of the Service Location Protocol Working Group (SVRLOC) of the Internet Engineering Task Force (IETF) [3]. SLP is a protocol for automatic resource discovery on Internet Protocol based networks. SLP is a language independent protocol, therefore, the protocol specification can be implemented in any language. It bases its discovery mechanism on service attributes, which are essentially different ways of describing a service.

• **Gnutella** is a pure P2P system because it has no nodes which act as servers [4]. The main concept of Gnutella is that each peer in the Gnutella network can communicate with any other peer. When a computer wants to access Gnutella services, it must connect to a Gnutella network. To do this, each peer only need to know the address of at least one other Gnutella machine on the network.

• **Jini** technology is an architecture that enables developers to construct systems from distributed services over networks [5]. In a Jini system, everything is a service. One of the key components of Jini is the Jini Lookup Service (JLS), which maintains dynamic information regarding the available services in a Jini federation. Every service must discover one or more Jini Lookup Service before it can enter a federation.

• **Universal Plug and Play**(UPnP) [6] is an open standard technology for transparently connecting appliances, PCs, and services by extending Plug and Play to support networks, and peer-to-peer discovery and configuration. UPnP will be implemented for PCs and devices running under the Windows operating systems. Microsoft has made available UPnP specifications, an implementation guideline, and sample source code at WinHEC 99.

The prior mentioned service discovery infrastructures and architectures such as SLP, Jini and UPnP have been developed to explore service discovery issues in the context of distributed systems. While many of the architectures provide good foundations for developing systems with distributed components in the networks, they do not adequately solve all the problems that may arise in a dynamic domain and large-scale network. Thus matching algorithms are to be designed. In the next subsection, we present existing matching algorithms.

2.2 Existing Matching Algorithms

In this subsection, we review three existing matching algorithms, which were suggested by CMU [7, 8], TRASTOUR [9], and LARKS [10, 11], respectively.

The Semantic Matchmaker of the Software Agent Group at CMU operates on OWL-S descriptions. It is strict like exact match, and checks whether the request can give required inputs, or the offer's outputs can satisfy the inputs provided by the requestor. Since the Semantic Matchmaker provides the exact match, in cases of a non-exact match, the offer cannot be used directly and therefore is not flexible.

Another matching algorithm has been developed for service descriptions based on RDF by TRASTOUR et al. The descriptions follow RDF design and rules. To compare a service requestor's description with a service provider's description, the matching algorithm uses a graph matching approach. If both descriptions' root elements are similar, the descriptions are similar. Otherwise, the descriptions are not similar.

The other matcher is for LARKS that was developed by SYCARA et al. In LARKS, services are comprised of functional parameter input, output, inConstraints and outConstraints. The matching engine of the matchmaker agent contains five different filters: context, profile, similarity, signature and constraint filter. The computational costs of these filters are in increasing order. Users can use them, by combining these filters.

The prior mentioned matching algorithms have excellent functionality. However, they are not efficient as fast matching algorithms in ubiquitous computing environments, therefore, we propose a new matching algorithm. This new algorithm provides powerful and adaptive matching algorithms using stable marriage matching used in ATM. We modify this algorithm to be adequate for our environments.

3 Proposed Service Matching Algorithms

In this section, we review a stable marriage matching algorithm [1] briefly and show our proposed algorithm. The motivating example used is the stable marriage problem, which can be defined as follows. A finite set of `men' is given along with a set of `women' of the same cardinality. In addition, each person is assumed to have a ranking of the members of the opposite sex. A matching is a bijection between the two sets. An unstable matching means that between a man X and a woman Y, X ranks Y higher than his spouse and Y ranks X higher than her spouse. In the result of a stable matching, each man has the best partner that he can have in any stable matching. We can see the algorithm of stable marriage matching in Fig. 1.

Function Match_Algorithm

    while there is an unpaired man **do**

        pick an unpaired man **A** and the first woman **a** on his list

        remove **a** from his list so it won't be picked again

        if a i`s engaged then

            if a prefers **A** more than her current partner **B then**

            set **A-a** as married

            set **B-a** as unmarried so now **B** is unpaired

            else

            A is still unpaired since **a** is happier with **B**

            end if

        else

            The woman was not previously paired so accept

            immediately **A-a**, as married

        end if

    end while

Fig. 1. Stable marriage matching algorithm

Applying this algorithm to a switching fabric in high-speed networks, attempts to match inputs to outputs without contention based on the concept of request-grant-arbitrates, or schedules. Its main advantage consists of stable and fast matching. More details of the stable marriage match algorithm are omitted because of space constraints.

We adopt the idea of the stable marriage match algorithm to bind service provider with service consumer promptly. This is different from semantic matching such as OWL-S and LARKS. Our proposed matching algorithm is rather a scheduling scheme in network nodes.

The network is becoming more and more pervasive, ubiquitous, and mobile. There are so many devices able to be attached, and with diverse network communication styles. In a P2P network, a peer works as a relay point or control point, or server just providing services. Thus we need fast algorithms to match provider and consumer because there are a large number of requests.

We assume that most service requests flow into a single point which maybe a device, a peer, or a router in a large-scale and dynamic network. Our proposed algorithm performs well in such dynamic and large-scale networks since it can deal with a large number of requests simultaneously, match optimally, and schedule service requests faster than other matching algorithms.

We use three matching schemes to verify our algorithm. The first is 'Simple Matching' using a simple description advertised by provider and consumer. The second is 'Multiple Matching', which uses more complicated information such as device or IP type, etc. The third is 'Priority based Multiple Matching', which utilizes priority based scheduling policy.

3.1 Simple Matching

Simple matching exploits the basic idea of stable marriage matching. Here we consider only service type and address for simplicity. Table 1 shows descriptions of provider and consumer.

Table 1. Simple descriptions for matching

peer	service	alternation
1	A(95)	C
2	A(90)	B
3	C(80)	E
4	D(75)	A

peer	service	alternation
10	B(80)	.
11	A(100)	C
12	C(70)	.
13	E(60)	B

a. Service consumer   **b. Service provider**

We match each peer using service type. In Table 1, 'peer 1' and 'peer 2' request the same service type (A) concurrently. Preference of 'peer1' regarding A is higher than 'peer2'. In this case, we pair 'peer 1' and 'peer 11' because 'peer 11' has a more similar service. The service type number indicates a service matching factor. Using this factor, we select a service provider. We know that 'peer 11' matches 'peer 1', because the factor value of 'peer 1' is 95. Following this stage 'peer 2' and 'peer 10' are paired because 'peer 2' is an alternative for 'B'.

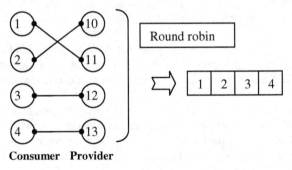

Fig. 2. Packet scheduling after simple matching

3.2 Multiple Matching

We illustrate simple matching using service type shown in the previous subsection. In this subsection, we show more complicated matching using several attributes. Although it takes into consideration other attributes, it performs the same procedure as Simple Matching.

Table 2. Multiple descriptions for matching

Peer	Service	IP	Device	Alternation
1	A(80)	Y	T1	11
2	A(90)	N	T2	12
3	C(70)	N	T3	12
4	D(87)	Y	T4	13

'Service' in the Table 2 indicates service type such as 'Simple Matching', and 'IP' indicates whether a device uses an IP-based address. A value of 'Y' means that a device uses an IP-based address, a value of 'N' means that a device uses a Non-IP based address. The third attribute indicates device type (e.g. PDA, Cell-Phone, Notebook, PC and etc). It matches two peers using these attributes in the gateway or superpeer, control point. At first, 'Multiple Matching' matches two peers similar to 'Simple Matching' and then uses the 'IP', 'Device' and 'Alternation' attributes.

Service consumers may request the same service simultaneously, thus we should schedule which service is selected or which consumer is serviced. While Simple Matching selects a service using consumer attributes, Multiple Matching uses all the attributes of two peers. Thus we can match two peers using the service provider's attributes.

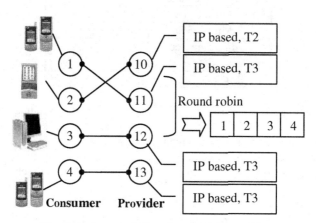

Fig. 3. Packet scheduling after multiple matching

We could add another attribute such as communication protocol (e.g. TCP/ IP (802.3, 802.11), IrDA, Bluetooth and etc) through scheduling polices.

Even though 'Multiple Matching' considers four attributes to schedule which the service provider or consumer service is first, it is insufficient for dynamic network environments utilizing services such as e-commerce, and videoconferencing. In this case, we must define a priority to data type or service type. We propose a new scheme using priority in the next subsection.

3.3   Priority Based Matching

In recent years, there has been exponential growth in purchasing goods online and communicating with each other over the Internet. In ubiquitous networks or P2P ad hoc networks, these services have rapidly increased. To satisfy this need effectively, we use the priority based matching algorithm, appropriate for such dynamic network environments.

The service is classified according to their data type or service type. Table 3 shows the priority associated with each type. We use 8 priority levels in this paper. High priority is allocated into basic traffic in service discovery such as service advertisements, requests, and event messages. Voice traffic, multimedia traffic and E-commerce are allocated into a middle priority level. Light data traffic such as Instance Message is allocated into 7 and bulk data traffic is allocated into a low priority. Using theses information, we can match and then schedule, which traffic service, is first. We can also define first-aid traffic in such an emergency case but we classify this traffic as 'Event Traffic' in this paper.

Table 3. Priority of Services

Services	priority
Service advertisements	1
Service requests	2
Event messages	3
Voice traffic	4
Multimedia	5
E-commerce	6
Light data traffic	7
Bulk data traffic	8

This scheme classifies the traffic according to its property. When a service request arrives at a node (i.e. gateway, router, access point), it classifies the request arrived and then matches the two peers using their associated priorities.

After services are matched, we arrange services according to their priority again. We note that 'Priority based Matching' uses priority twice for scheduling service requests.

Priority based matching uses the same algorithm as the previous ones, except it uses a priority to match consumer and provider (see Fig. 4). It shows that this scheme

---

Function Priority_Match_Algorithm

Arrange all requests according to priority
Save arranged request into consumer list (**CL**)
  while there is an unpaired request **do**

  pick an unpaired request **A** in the **CL** and the first provider **a** on his list

  remove **a** from his list so it won't be picked again

  if a is engaged **then**

    if a prefers **A** more than provider's current partner **B**

    // A's priority is higher than B's priority.

    then

      set **A-a** as married

      set **B-a** as unmarried so now **B** is unpaired

    else

      A is still unpaired since **a** is satisfied with **B**

    end if

  else

    The provider was not previously paired so

    accept immediately **A-a**, as married

  end if

  end while

After all requests matched, rearrange matched pair

according to consumer's priority

Fig. 4. Priority based service matching algorithm

is suitable for dynamic network environments noted prior because it can find services promptly.

The proposed methods could be used in the following applications in order to obtain the dynamic service matching.

- **E-commerce**

Service matching using our proposed scheme can pay bills with less delay. It is useful for a customer who wants to buy daily necessaries in the shopping mall because so many customers exist and also request the same service.

- **VoIP**

In general, a circuit-switched voice connection requires a permanent 64kbps space of bandwidth. Thus we could provide service with less delay.

- **Video Conference**

Like VoIP, videoconferencing requires less delay and also requires more bandwidth. Even though we can't provide enough bandwidth, we can quickly match service providers and service consumers in dynamic environments.

4 Conclusion

As people start using mobile devices such as PDAs, cell-phones and notebooks, the need for connecting these devices to the Internet will become increasingly important. An efficient service discovery infrastructure will play an important role in dynamic environments.

We have reviewed a number of existing service discovery frameworks. We found that all these frameworks suffer from one common problem, namely lack of an efficient matching algorithm and network node scheduling. This paper has introduced three service matching algorithms based on the marriage matching algorithm to resolve these problems.

Performance is a major concern of the matching algorithm in the proposed method especially because it makes every node in the P2P network perform the work of a gateway. It is easy to imagine situations in which the network services would be swamped by large numbers of requests for any type of service. We are currently evaluating tradeoffs between effectiveness and cost in our implementation.

Reference

1. D. Gusfield and R.W. Irving, "The stable marriage problem structure and algorithms", MIT Press, 1989.
2. Service Location Protocol Version 2, Internet Engineering Task Force (IETF), RFC 2608, June 1999.
3. Sumi Helal: Standards for service discovery and delivery, Pervasive Computing, IEEE, Volume: 1, Issue: 3, Pages: 95-100, July-Sept. 2002
4. Overview about Gnutella technology and product application, http://www.gnutella.com/
5. Jini, http://www.sun.com/jini, Sun Microsystems, 1999
6. Universal Plug and Play Specification, v1.0, http://www.upnp.org.
7. M. Paolucci, T. Kawmura, T. Payne and K. Sycara, "Semantic Matching of Web Services Capabilities", First Int. Semantic Web Conference, Sardinia, Italy, 2002
8. OWL-S: Semantic markup for web services, http://www.daml.org/services/owl-s/1.0/
9. David Trastour, Claudio Bartolini and Javier Gonzalez-Castillo, "A semantic web approach to service description for matchmaking of services", Proceedings of the International Semantic Web Working Symposium, Stanford, CA, USA, 2001
10. Kaitia Sycara, Matthias Klusch, Seth Widoff and Jianguo Lu, "Dynamic service matchmaking among agents in open information environments", SIGMOD, Volume: 28, Number: 1, Pages: 47-53, 1999
11. K. Sycara and S. Wido, M. Klusch and J. Lu, "LARKS: Dynamic Matchmaking Among Heterogeneous Software Agents in Cyberspace", Autonomous   Agents and Multi-Agent Systems, Pages: 173-203, 2002

Ontology-Based Filtering Mechanisms for Web Usage Patterns Retrieval

Mariângela Vanzin, Karin Becker, and Duncan Dubugras Alcoba Ruiz

Faculdade de Informática - Pontifícia Universidade Católica do Rio Grande do Sul,
Porto Alegre - Brazil
{mvanzin, kbecker, duncan}@inf.pucrs.br

Abstract. Web Usage Mining (WUM) aims to extract navigation usage patterns from Web server logs. Mining algorithms yield usage patterns, but finding the ones that constitute new and interesting knowledge in the domain remains a challenge. Typically, analysts have to deal with a huge volume of pattern, from which they have to retrieve the potentially interesting one and interpret what they reveal about the domain. In this paper, we discuss the filtering mechanisms of O3R, an environment supporting the retrieval and interpretation of sequential navigation patterns. All O3R functionality is based on the availability of the domain ontology, which dynamically provides meaning to URLs. The analyst uses ontology concepts to define filters, which can be applied according to two filtering mechanisms: equivalence and similarity.

1 Introduction

As the popularity of World Wide Web explodes, a massive amount of data is gathered by Web servers in logs. These are rich sources of information for understanding Web users' behavior. Web Usage Mining (WUM) addresses the application of data mining techniques over web data in order to identify users' navigation patterns [1]. The WUM process includes the execution of specific phases [2], namely data pre-processing (used to select, clean and prepare log raw data), pattern discovery (application of data mining algorithms), and pattern analysis (evaluation of yielded patterns to seek for unknown and useful knowledge).

While WUM techniques are promising, many problems need to be solved for their effective application. Two challenges related to the pattern analysis phase are *pattern retrieval* and *pattern interpretation*. Mining techniques typically yield a huge number of patterns [3]. Hence, users have difficulty on identifying the ones that are new and interesting for the application domain. Thus, pattern retrieval deals with difficulties involved in managing a large set of patterns, and setting focus on a subset of them for further analysis. Pattern interpretation involves analysing the interestingness and relevance of patterns with regard to the domain. For example, the rule "users who purchased in an on-line shop also visited its homepage" is trivial, considering that a homepage is the main entry point of a site. In the context of WUM, the challenges of pattern interpretation refer to understanding what usage patterns reveal in terms of site events, due to the semantic gap between URLs and events performed by users [4]. To

K. Bauknecht et al. (Eds.): EC-Web 2005, LNCS 3590, pp. 267–277, 2005.
© Springer-Verlag Berlin Heidelberg 2005

reduce this gap, recent approaches (e.g. [4, 5,5]) investigate the contributions of do-main ontologies, possibly available in the Semantic Web.

Ontology-based Rules Retrieval and Rummaging (O3R) is an environment targeted at supporting the retrieval and interpretation of sequential navigation patterns during the pattern analysis phase [5]. All O3R functionality is based on the availability of the domain ontology, to which URLs are mapped. Analysts explore pattern semantics interactively during the pattern analysis phase, according to distinct abstraction levels and dimensions of interest. This contrasts with classical approaches (e.g. [7,8]), in which semantic enrichment is performed statically in the pre-processing phase. The ontology-based functionality of O3R allows the retrieval and interpretation of *conceptual patterns*, i.e. patterns formed of concepts in different abstraction levels, in opposition to physical patterns, composed of URLs. The pattern interpretation functionality of O3R is described in [5].

This paper focus on the *pattern retrieval* functionality of O3R, which exploits the domain ontology for defining filters that allow users to manage the volume of rules, and to set focus on a subset of patterns with specific characteristics. Functionality allows users to specify filters that represent their interest in terms of contents, structure, and statistic properties; and to retrieve patterns that either match the specified filter, or are similar to it at some extent.

The remainder of this paper is structured as follows. Section 2 presents related work. Section 3 provides a brief overview the O3R environment, describing the relevant underlying concepts. Section 4 details the filtering functionality. Conclusions and future work are addressed in Section 5.

2 Related Work

Filtering is a very common approach for dealing with issues in pattern retrieval. A filter defines the set of proprieties that patterns must present in order to fit in the analyst's current interest or search space. Filtering mechanisms are responsible for finding the patterns that match these properties. Filtering can be applied both in the pattern discovery and pattern analysis phases [3]. In the first case, the filter is embedded into the mining algorithm, restricting its output. If applied in the analysis phase, the filter is used to focus the search on potentially (un)interesting patterns. The advantage in this case is that new filters can be defined dynamically and interactively, whenever the analyst adopts a new interest focus, without having to re-mine the data.

A filter can express statistic, conceptual and structural proprieties. Statistical proprieties are based on objective and subjective measures [1, 3,9]. Objective measures are generally based upon the inherent structure of mined patterns, i.e. statistics such as support and confidence [9]. Objective measures aim at reducing the number of rules generated by the mining algorithm. For instance, association and sequence mining techniques [9,10] are both based on the support measure, e.g. the fraction of transactions or sequences that contains a specific pattern. However, rules with high support value very seldom are interesting. Most often they represent common sense in the domain. On other hand, when a low support value is defined, many patterns are generated, making the analysis process even more difficult. The authors in [9] discuss the advantages of mining using very low threshold values for objective criteria (e.g.

support, confidence, lift) in order to produce all the potentially interesting rules, combined with a rule filtering mechanism for analyzing the yielded patterns.

Subjective measures depend on prior domain knowledge, and they can be further divided into unexpectedness (if a pattern is "surprising" to the user), or actionable (if the user can do something with it in his advantage). The literature provides techniques supporting pattern retrieval based on subjective interestingness. Most of them compare discovered patterns with some form of belief [1,3] expressing domain knowledge. Thus, any mining result either supporting or contradicting these beliefs is considered interesting. However, the effectiveness of these measures is related to the ability of expressing beliefs for a given domain.

Conceptual properties in WUM are related to domain events, which are represented syntactically by URLs. There is an urge for semantic approaches for providing meaning to these URLs in terms of domain events, i.e. contents and services offered by a site. Most existing work (e.g. [4, 5, 6]) concentrate on exploiting semantics, possibly available in the Semantic Web, for the pattern interpretation task. Structural properties establish constraints on how domain events relate to each other, such as which events should appear in the pattern, possibly in a certain order.

In [8], the authors present the mining language MINT, which allows users to focus on the search of sequential navigation patterns presenting certain structural, conceptual and statistical properties. MINT assumes that the conceptual properties of URLs are stored as metadata, statically provided during the pre-processing phase. [1] uses concept taxonomies to express filters over association rules, which express conceptual and structural properties. Filters are expressed textually using regular expressions. To define the filters, these works assume that the analyst: 1) has a deep knowledge about the domain; and 2) is skilled in the syntax used to specify the filter.

3   O3R Environment Overview

O3R provides support for the retrieval and interpretation of sequential navigation patterns. All O3R functionality is based on the conceptual representation of patterns, which is provided the mapping of URLs into the concepts of the domain ontology. Pattern interpretation functionality allows analysts to rummage around representations of a same pattern according to different dimensions of interest and abstraction levels [5], and is not discussed here due to space limitations. Filtering functionality is detailed in Section 4. In the remainder of this section, we introduce the premises and fundamental concepts upon which O3R was built.

Current implementation of O3R is limited to sequential patterns extracted according to the sequential algorithm described in [10]. It assumes that these patterns were extracted from a dataset resulting from a typical pre-processing phase [2]. No particular data enrichment is assumed for this data set in the pre-processing phase, since patterns are semantically enriched as they are retrieved and interpreted with O3R.

3.1   Domain Events Representation

Events in a web site are roughly categorized as *service* (e.g. buying, finding) and *content* (e.g. Hamlet, television) [4]. O3R assumes the representation of domain events in two levels: conceptual and physical. Physically, events are represented by URLs. The conceptual level is represented by the domain ontology, which is used to dynamically associate meaning to web pages and user actions over pages. We assume a domain expert is responsible for the acquisition and representation of the domain ontology, as well as for the mapping of the physical events into the corresponding conceptual ones.

Fig. 1-a depicts the ontology structure using a UML class diagram. The ontology is composed of concepts, representing either a content of a web page, or a service available through a page. Concepts are related to each other through hierarchical or property relationships. A hierarchical relationship connects a descendant concept to an ascendant one. Two types of hierarchical relationships are considered: *generalization,* in which the generalized concept is ascendant of a specialized one; and *aggregation,* in which the ascendant represents the whole assembly and the descendent represents one of its parts. Every concept has at most one ascendant. Property relationships represent arbitrary associations that connect a subject to an object.

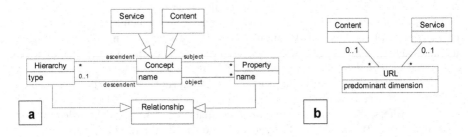

Fig. 1. Ontology structure and URL mapping

URLs are mapped into ontology concepts according to two dimensions: service and content. An URL can be mapped into one service, one content or both. When a URL is mapped into both a service and a content, it means that the URL provides a service that is related to some content. In that case, the mapping also defines the predominant dimension. A same ontology concept can be used in the mapping of various URLs. The above constraints are represented in Fig.1-b.

Fig. 2 illustrates domain events of a hypothetical tourism web site according to the physical and conceptual levels. Services include booking, searching for information, visualizing, etc. Content is related to the subjects available in the site, or related to some services (e.g. a user can book a room in a hotel or search for a restaurant). In Fig. 2, page *URL1* was mapped into the service *Booking*; page *URL2* was mapped to both content *Hotel* and service *Searching* concepts. Page *URL3* is mapped into the content *Indian*. Notice that *URL2* was mapped according to two dimensions, where the content was defined as the predominant dimension.

The domain ontology can be created by hand (quite expensive) or using semi-automatic mechanisms. In the latter approach, machine learning and information retrieval techniques have been employed to improve the ontology engineering process (e.g. [12]). This work does not address the issues related to ontology acquisition and

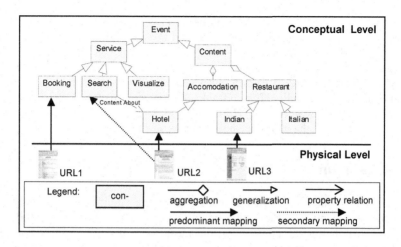

Fig. 2. Domain ontology example

validation. The future semantic web will certainly contribute in reducing this effort [4], in the sense that the creation of the respective ontology layer will be part of any site design.

3.2 Physical and Conceptual Patterns

Since no semantic enrichment is assumed in the pre-processing phase, patterns yielded by the mining algorithm are sequences of URLs. We refer to them as *physical patterns*. O3R uses the mapping between the physical and conceptual representation of events to present these patterns to users as a sequence of the corresponding ontology concepts, i.e. the *conceptual patterns*. Users manipulate this conceptual representation using O3R functionality. For that purpose, users have to set a *dimension of interest*, which can be *content*, *service* or *content/service*.

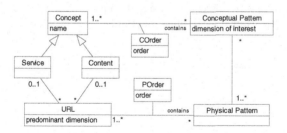

Fig. 3. Physical and conceptual patterns

Fig. 3 shows the relationship between conceptual and physical patterns. Notice that considering the 3 possible dimensions of interest, a same physical pattern can have up to 3 different conceptual representations. By exploring the dimensions of interest, the user is presented with alternative conceptual patterns for the same physical one. Considering the example of Fig. 2, according to the service dimension, the physical pattern *URL1→URL2* is displayed as *Booking→Search*; whereas according to the content/service dimension, it is visualized as *Booking → Hotel*. Conceptual patterns can also be interpreted according to different abstraction levels of the ontology, through the rummaging functionality. For example, the physical pattern *URL1→URL2* can also be interpreted as *Service → Hotel, Service → Accommodation*, or *Service → Content*, by exploring the hierarchical relationships of the ontology.

4 Retrieval Functionality

Retrieval functionality is targeted at managing a large volume of rules, as typically produced by sequential or association mining algorithms [9,11]. The basic idea is to reduce the search space for inspecting the meaning of the rules in the domain, by finding related rules. Two approaches are provided by O3R: rule clustering and rule filtering. Clustering functionality groups related rules in different sets, such that the analyst can set focus for further inspection on a whole set of rules (or discard them all). Presently, we implemented only the maximal sequence criterion of [10] (rules that are subsequences of a maximal sequence rule are grouped in a same cluster), but other criteria are possible. Filtering functionality, detailed in this section, addresses filter definition and filtering mechanisms. By providing filters in the analysis phase, it is possible to focus on part of the result set without requiring to re-mine the data set.

4.1 Filter Definition

A filter in O3R defines conceptual, structural and statistical constraints over sequential patterns. Conceptual constraints are represented by ontology concepts, in order to define the interest on patterns involving specific domain events, at any abstraction level. Structural constraints establish structural rules upon these events, more specifically to start with a specific concept, to end by a specific concept, or that a (immediate or not) subsequence of specified concepts must obey a certain order. Statistical constraints refer to objective measures, such as support in the case of sequence rules. Fig. 4 defines a filter using a UML class diagram.

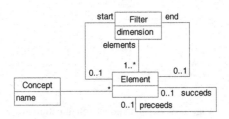

Fig. 4. Filter definition

Fig. 5 shows the filtering interface of O3R. The domain ontology is represented graphically on the leftmost window. It allows the analyst to visualize all concepts and relationships defined for the domain. The upper right window is the area where the user defines the filter, according to some dimension of interest. The filtered patterns appear in the lower right window.To establish conceptual constraints, the user chooses concepts from the ontology and places them at the filter definition area. In the example of Fig. 5, the user is interested in patterns including the concepts *Booking*, *Search* and *Restaurant*. Then he uses the structural operators (buttons at the right of the filter definition area) to establish order between concepts. In the example, the concept *Search* must precede *Restaurant*. He also establishes a statistical constraint (at least 5% of support). Users have the ontology support to understand the domain, and establish interesting filters. They are also not required to learn any complicated syntax, because filters are defined by direct manipulation of domain concepts.

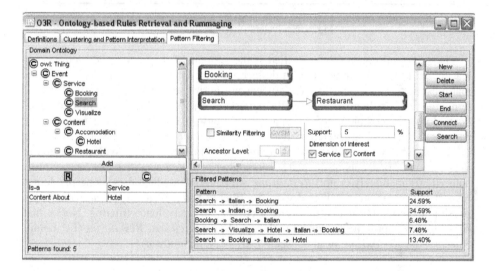

Fig. 5. Pattern filtering interface

4.2 Filtering Mechanisms

Once the filter of interest is defined, the user can choose among two filtering mechanisms, referred to as *equivalence filtering* and *similarity filtering*.

Equivalence Filtering. The pseudo-code for equivalence filtering algorithm is shown in Fig. 6. The inputs of the algorithm are the set of physical patterns (PP), the dimension of interest and the filter. The output is the set of filtered conceptual patterns (FP). First, the algorithm converts PP into the corresponding set of conceptual patterns (CP), according to the dimension of interest. Then, it examines each conceptual pattern of CP, verifying whether it meets the statistical, conceptual and structural constraints of the filter. The functions used in the pseudo-code can be understood from the UML class diagrams of figures 1 and 3.

```
Algorithm: EquivalenceFiltering
Inputs: PP, dimension, filter;
Outputs: FP
CP := PP.convert (dimension);
For each cp in CP
Do  If cp.support() >= filter.minSupport() //* statistical constraint
    Then //* conceptual constraint
           match := true
           For each element in filter.elements() '
           Do  c := element.concept()
               If not cp.contains(c)
               Then match := false;
           If match
           Then    //* structural constraint
                 If cp.start(filter.start())
                 Then  If cp.end (filter.end()
                       Then  Ifcp.order(filter)
                             Then FP.add(cp);
Return(FP);
```

Fig. 6. Equivalent filtering algorithm

The statistical constraint is verified if the support of the conceptual pattern is at least equal to the minimum support defined. A conceptual constraint states concepts that must appear in a rule. In the equivalence filtering, a concept is contained in pattern either if it explicitly composes the pattern, or one of its direct or indirect descendents does. For example, considering the ontology of Fig. 2, if a filter includes the concept *Restaurant*, all patterns containing *Restaurant* or its descendents *Indian* or *Italian*, satisfy the constraint. Checking the structural constraints involves examining the position of concepts in the pattern. The filter of Fig. 5 specifies that *Search* must antecede (immediately or not) *Restaurant*. All patterns in which these concepts do not respect this order are not included in the filtered pattern set. Fig. 5 also illustrates possible patterns that match this filter according to equivalence filtering. Notice that *Booking* can appear in any order with regard to *Search* and *Restaurant* (i.e. before *Search*; after *Restaurant*; or in between *Search* and *Restaurant*).

Similarity Filtering. It extends equivalence filtering by retrieving also patterns that are similar to the filter. Similarity is defined is terms of distance between concepts in the ontology, considering the hierarchical relationships. The adopted similarity function is an adaptation of one proposed in [13], shown in Formula 1, where c1 e c2 are concepts, LCA is the Lowest Common Ancestor of c1 and c2, and depth is the distance of a concept from the root of the hierarchy. The result of the similarity function is a number that ranges from 0 to 1, where Sim(c1, c2) = 1 iff c1 = c2.

$$Sim(c_1, c_2) \quad = \quad \frac{2*depth\ (LCA(c_1, c_2))}{depth\ (c_1) + depth\ (c_2)} \tag{1}$$

To reduce the number of filtered rules, the user has to provide two parameters: the minimum similarity threshold and the Ancestor Scope Level (ASL). The ASL identifies the farthest common ancestor in the hierarchy to be considered for similarity purposes. Consider for instance the ontology of Fig. 2 and the concept *Italian*. If ASL is defined by the user as 1, *Restaurant* is the farthest common ancestor, and therefore, *Indian* is regarded as a similar concept. If it is set to 2, then *Accommodation* and *Hotel* are also assumed as similar, due to the farthest common ancestor *Concept*.

ASL is used to produce a *generalized filter*, a filter in which each element of the user-defined filter is replaced by the respective farthest common ancestor. For instance, consider the filter of Fig. 7, which states that *Booking* must precede *Hotel*. For ASL = 1, the corresponding generalized filter would be *Service* followed by *Content*. Any conceptual pattern containing subsequences of these concepts (or their descendents) would be considered similar to the specified filter. The minimum similarity threshold provided by the user is used to prune the results.

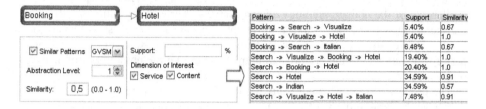

Fig. 7. Example of results yielded by similarity filtering

The pseudo-code of similarity filtering algorithm is presented in Fig. 8. It takes as parameters the set of physical patterns (PP), the dimension of interest, the filter, the minimum similarity threshold, and ASL. It yields a set of conceptual patterns (FP), with the respective similarity measure with regard to the filter, as illustrated in Fig. 7.

```
Algorithm: SimilarityFiltering
Inputs: PP, dimension, filter, similarityThreshold, ASL;
Outputs: FP
//* define generalized filter
generalizedFilter := filter;
For each element in generalizedFilter.elements()
Do  element.setConcept := element.concept().findFarthestAncestor(ASL)
//* find patterns that match the generalized filter
CandidateFP := EquivalenceFiltering(PP, dimension, gf);
//* calculate similarity with regard the user-defined filter
For each candidatecp in candidateFP
Do  If candidatecp.calculateSimilarity (filter) > similarityThreshold
    Then FP.add(cp) ;
Return(FP);
```

Fig. 8. Similarity filtering algorithm

Fig. 7 exemplifies results yielded by similarity filtering. Filtered conceptual patterns with similarity value equal to 1 are totally compliant to the filter. All other patterns are similar to it in some degree. For example the conceptual pattern *Search → Hotel* is similar because concept *Search* is similar to concept *Booking,* since both are services. Comparatively, the pattern *Search → Indian* is less similar because the distance between concepts *Indian* and *Hotel* is greater than the distance between *Search* and *Booking*.

Pattern similarity is based on the similarity of specific concepts composing it, according to the defined structural constraints. These are referred to as *similarity points*. Hence, the similarity of a pattern is the arithmetic average of its similarity points. In case a pattern meets a structural constraint in different ways, the algorithm always considers the highest similarity. In Fig. 8, for instance, the pattern *Search → Booking*

$\rightarrow$ *Hotel* has two possible combinations of similarity points with regard to the defined filter: *Booking* $\rightarrow$ *Hotel* (equal to the filter - 1) and *Search* $\rightarrow$ *Hotel* (similar to the filter - 0.91). This pattern is thus assigned with similarity 1.

5 Conclusions and Future Work

In this paper we focused in the filtering functionality of O3R, an environment targeted at supporting the retrieval and interpretation of sequential navigation patterns. The availability of the domain ontology allows analysts to provide meaning to URLs during the analysis phase, according to different dimensions of interest and abstraction levels. This contrasts with classical approaches, in which semantic enrichment is performed statically in the pre-processing phase, limiting the possibilities of analyses over the mined patterns.

The proposed filtering functionality require less expertise from pattern analysts: 1) they have the support of the ontology to understand the domain, and establish interesting filters, and 2) direct manipulation of domain concepts and structural operators minimize the skills required for defining filters. Filter expressiveness is also a strength, since filters define structural, conceptual and objective statistical constraints. Two filtering mechanisms are provided, in which users are allowed to establish degrees of similarity as convenient. Once patterns are filtered, users use the rummaging functionality [5]to interpret them. Since related patterns are presented to users, they can validate (or discard) several patterns at a time based on similar properties.

O3R is currently under evaluation at PUCRS Virtual, the distance education department of our University. The ontology for a course was created, and sequential patterns revealing students navigation behavior are being analyzed with the support of O3R. Although an empirical validation was not performed, users (domain expert) have expressed a generalized satisfaction towards O3R functionality, particularly in comparison with the difficulties they faced in a previous WUM application [14].

Future work includes, among other topics: empirical validation of O3R at PUCRS Virtual, extension of O3R functionality to other types of patterns (association, other sequential algorithms), adaptation of O3R to ontologies with no constraints, particularly the ones available at the semantic layer of the Semantic Web

References

1. Cooley, R. The use of web structure and content to identify subjectively interesting web usage patterns. *ACM Transactions on Internet Technology*, 3:(2) (2003) 93-116.
2. Cooley, R., Mobasher, B., and Srivastava, J.. Data preparation for mining world wide web browsing patterns. *Journal of Knowledge and Information Systems*, 1 (1999) 5-32.
3. Silberschatz, A., and Tuzhilin, A. What makes patterns interesting in knowledge discovery systems. *IEEE Transactions on Knowledge and Data Engineering 8*, 6 (1996), 970-974.
4. Stumme, G., Hotho, A., and Berendt, B. Usage mining for and on the semantic web. In *National Science Foundation Workshop on Next Generation Data Mining* (Baltimore, USA, 2002).
5. Vanzin, M. and Becker, K. (2004). Exploiting knowledge representation for pattern interpretation. In *Workshop on Knowledge Discovery and Ontologies- KDO 2004*, pages 61-71, Pisa, Italy.

6. Oberle, D., Berendt, B., Hotho, A., and Gonzalez, J. Conceptual user tracking. In *International Atlantic Web Intelligence Conference* (Madrid, 2003), Springer, pp. 142-154.

7. Dai, H. and Mobasher, B. (2002). Using ontologies to discovery domain-level web usage profiles. In *Semantic Web Mining Workshop*.

8. Berendt, B., and Spiliopoulou, M. Analysing navigation behaviour in web sites integrating multiple information systems. *The VLDB Journal 9* (2000), 56-75.

9. Hipp, J., and Guntzer, U. Is pushing constraints deeply into the mining algorithms really what we want?: an alternative approach for association rule mining. *SIGKDD Explor. Newsl. 4*:(1) (2002) 50-55.

10. Agrawal, R. and Srikant, R. Mining sequential patterns. In: *11th International Conference on Data Engineering*. (1995) 3-14.

11. Klemettinen, M., Mannila, H., Ronkainen, P., Toivonen, H., and Verkamo, A. I. Finding interesting rules from large sets of discovered association rules. In *3rd Iinternational Conference on Information and Knowledge Management* (1994) 401-407.

12. Sure, Y., Angele, J., and Staab, S. Ontoedit: Guiding ontology development by methodology and inferencing. In *International Conference on Ontologies, Databases and Applications of SEmantics ODBASE (2002)* 1205-1222.

13. Ganesan, P., Garcia-Molina, H., and Widom, J.. Exploiting hierarchical domain structure to compute similarity. *ACM Transactions on Information Systems*, 21:(1) (2003) 64-93.

14. Machado, L. and Becker, K.. Distance education: a web usage mining case study for the evaluation of learning sites. In: *3rd IEEE International Conference on Advanced Learning Technologies*, (2003) 360-371.

Multimedia Content Preference Using the Moving Average Technique

Sanggil Kang

Department of Computer Science, College of Information Engineering,
The University of Suwon, Whaseong, Gyeonggi-do, Korea
sgkang@suwon.ac.kr

Abstract. In this paper we introduce a new prediction method for multimedia content preference. Unlike typical methods, our method considers the trend of a TV viewer's preference change for estimating the statistical future preference using the moving average technique (MAT). With developing the statistical expression of the MAT based on a Bayesian network, experiments were implemented for predicting the TV genre preference using 2,400 TV viewers' watching history and showed that the performance of our method is better than that of the typical method if the window size in the MAT is large enough to reflect a user's preference changes.

1 Introduction

With the flood of multimedia content over the digital TV channels, the internet, etc., users sometimes have a difficulty in finding their preferred content, spending heavy surfing time to find them, and are even very likely to miss them while searching. By predicting or recommending the user's preferred content, based on her/his usage history in content consumptions, the problems can be solved to some extent.

Various preference recommendation techniques can be classified into three possible categories such as the rule-based, collaborative filtering, and inference method. The rule-based recommendation is usually implemented by a predetermined rule, for instance, if -then rule. Kim et al. [1] proposed a marketing rule extraction technique for personalized recommendation on internet storefronts using tree induction method [2]. As one of representative rule-based techniques, Aggrawall et al. [3, 4] proposed a method to identify frequent item sets from the estimated frequency distribution using association-rule mining algorithm [5]. Collaborative filtering (CF) technique recommends a target user the preferred content of the group whose content consumption mind is similar to that of the user. Because of the mature of the technique, CF has been attractive for predicting various preference problems such as net-news [6, 7], e-commerce [8, 9, 10], digital libraries [11, 12], digital TV [13, 14], etc. In general, rule-based and CF techniques need expensive effort, time, and cost to collect a large number of users' consumption behavior due to the nature of their methodologies. However, inference is the technique that a user's content consumption behavior is predicted based on the history of personal content consumption behaviors. Ciaramita et al. [15] presented a Bayesian network [16], the graphical representation of probabilistic relationship among variables which are encoded as nodes in the

K. Bauknecht et al. (Eds.): EC-Web 2005, LNCS 3590, pp. 278–286, 2005.

network, for verb selectional preference by combining the statistical and knowledge-based approaches. The architecture of the Bayesian network was determined by the lexical hierarchy of Wordnet [17]. Lee [18] designed an interface agent to predict a user's resource usage in the UNIX domain by the probabilistic estimation of behavioral patterns from the user behavior history.

From the literatures mentioned above, there is one thing not to be overlooked, which is that the statistical user preference obtained by their method is not suitable for representing the dynamically changing users' preference because the history of users' preference change is not considered for updating the statistical preference.

In this paper, a new method to predict the preference of the multimedia content is introduced by considering the variations of the past preference changes. It can be done by adding the mean variation of the past statistical preference to the current statistical preference of content.

The remainder of this paper is organized as follows. Section 2 describes Bayesian networks as a framework of our work. Section 3 demonstrates the prediction of users' preference using the moving average technique. In Section 4, we show the experimental results using 2,400 viewers' genre consumption history. We then conclude our paper in Section 5.

2 Bayesian Network

A Bayesian network (BN), as shown in Fig. 1, is an acyclic graphical expression of the causal relationship of variables, which can induce the conditional probability distribution of a random variable with evidences given to other variables directly connected to the variable. The direct connection is called the edge that represents the dependence of variables. A BN can be denoted as $B = \langle G, X \rangle$, here G is the set of edges and X a set of random variables in B.

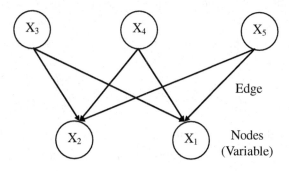

Fig. 1. An example of Bayesian networks

Let's consider a random vector $X = \begin{bmatrix} X_1 & X_2 & \cdots & X_M \end{bmatrix}$, where a variable X_i can have r_i possible attributes (or multimedia content[1] in broadcasting systems) and

---

[1] In this paper, the attribute and the content can be interchangeable for convenience.

can be expressed as $X_i = \lfloor x_{i1} \quad x_{i2} \quad \cdots \quad x_{ij} \quad \cdots \quad x_{ir_i} \rfloor$ where x_{ij} indicates the jth content in X_i. If a variable X_i is arced to another variable X_j, then we say X_i is a parent variable of X_j or X_j is a child variable of X_i. For instance, the parent variables of X_1 and X_2 are X_3, X_4, and X_5 in Fig. 1. The statistical preference $p(X_i = x_{ij} \mid X_{p_i}, B)$ of a state x_{ij} in a variable X_i given X_{P_i} and a BN B can be calculated, with evidence given to the parent variables and can be denoted as:

$$p_{x_{ij}} \equiv p(X_i = x_{ij} \mid E, B) = \frac{n_{ij}}{N_i} \tag{1}$$

where N_i and n_{ij} is the total sample number in X_i and the sample number of x_{ij}, respectively. In equation (1), the conditional probability is calculated by the ratio of the frequency of content x_{ij} to that of the all contents in X_i.

For the statistical prediction models [19, 20], the goal is to obtain the optimal estimate of the conditional probabilities for the future preference. As shown in Equation (1), the typical method does not consider the trend of the preference change so the estimated conditional probabilities cannot be suitable for representing the future preference of the contents, which usually changes in time. In order to compensate the drawback, we apply the moving average technique (MAT) [21] to update the conditional probabilities, which is demonstrated in the following section.

3 Estimation of the Statistical Preference

In order to apply the MAT to the estimation of the future statistical preference of the contents, Equation (1) needs to be modified in a time series. The modification starts with expressing the conditional probabilities in terms of time t. As shown in Fig. 2, the probability of x_{ij} at time t can be computed from the data collected during the data collection interval H between $t - H$ and t with for a given evidence (E) given as viewed in Fig. 2 as follows:

$$p_{x_{ij}}(t) \equiv p(X_i = x_{ij} \mid E, t, H) = \frac{n_{ij,H}(t)}{N_{i,H}(t)} \tag{2}$$

where $N_{i,H}(t)$ and $n_{ij,H}(t)$ are the total sample number of the contents in X_i and the sample number of the content x_{ij} collected during H (window size)in, respectively. The preference change of x_{ij} between two consecutive time steps can be obtained by calculating the probability variation (PV), denoted as $\Delta p_{x_{ij}}(t+1)$ and $t+1$ such as

$$\Delta p_{x_{ij}}(t+1) = p_{x_{ij}}(t+1) - p_{x_{ij}}(t) \tag{3}$$

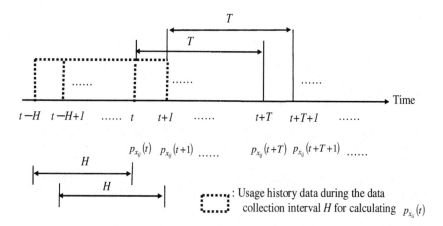

Fig. 2. Schematic representation of the probability update

A set of the successive PVs can be obtained during a predetermined period T from t to $t+T$ such as

$$\Delta p_{x_{ij}}(t,t+1)=[\Delta p_{x_{ij}}(t+1),\Delta p(t+2),\cdots,\Delta p_{x_{ij}}(t+T)] \qquad (4)$$

The set $\Delta p_{x_{ij}}(t,t+1)$ is the history of a user's preference changes of x_{ij} during a time period T from a time t so we use it for predicting the future preference of x_{ij} at time $t+T+1$. If the PVs are normally distributed or similarly normally distributed as shown in Fig. 3, the mean of them can be considered as the maximally likely occurring variation for the one-step-ahead future by the concept of maximum likelihood estimation.

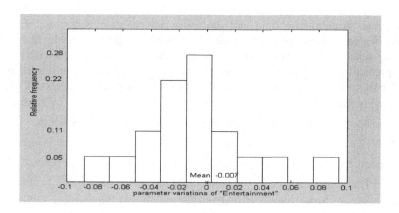

Fig. 3. Empirical distribution of the parameter variations of the genre "Entertainment" in the experiment

Thus, the prediction, denoted as $\hat{p}_{x_{ij}}(t+T+1)$, of the conditional probabilities $p_{x_{ij}}(t+T+1)$ for time $t+T+1$ can be formulated by adding the mean of the PVs, denoted as $\Delta\bar{p}_{x_{ij}}(t,t+T)$, to the probability $p_{x_{ij}}(t+T)$ as shown in Equation (5).

$$\hat{p}_{x_{ij}}(t+T+1)= p_{x_{ij}}(t+T) + \Delta\bar{p}_{x_{ij}}(t,t+T) \qquad (5)$$

where $\Delta\bar{p}_{x_{ij}}(t,t+T)=(1/T)\sum_{k=1}^{T}\Delta p_{x_{ij}}(t+k)$. From Equation (5), the performance of our method depends on $\Delta\bar{p}_{x_{ij}}(t,t+T)$. The larger the value of T, the more accurate the estimated conditional probability can be. For reference, the typical method does not consider $\Delta\bar{p}_{x_{ij}}(t,t+T)$ so the prediction can be expressed as

$$\hat{p}_{x_{ij}}(t+T+1)= p_{x_{ij}}(t+T) \qquad (6)$$

The on-line update of the conditional probability can be feasible by repeating the process from (3) to (5) as moving the window one step forward in time. Thus, the predicted conditional probability of x_{ij} at time $t+T+K-1$ can be calculated as:

$$\hat{p}_{x_{ij}}(t+T+K)= p_{x_{ij}}(t+T+K-1) + \Delta\bar{p}_{x_{ij}}(t+K-1,t+T+K-1) \qquad (7)$$

In the next section, we analyze our method and compare it with the typical method.

4   Experimental Results

The proposed method is applied to predict the statistical preference of a user's TV program genres using 2,400 viewers' watching history collected from December 1, 2002 to May 31, 2003. The data was provided by AC Nielsen Korea, one of the authorized market research company in Korea. A user's TV watching history was collected by a set-top box installed in the user's houses, which can record login and logout time, broadcasting time and day, watched program genre, etc. From the history, we can extract only two parent variables for genre variable such as TV watching time and day. Thus, the structure of the Bayesian network (BN) for TV genre prediction is depicted as in Fig. 4. The watching time we considered is only from 6 p.m. to 12 p.m. in our experiment because the user barely watched TV during other time periods. The watching time variable X_1 has three states by slotting it by every two hours, so X_1 can be expressed as $X_1 = \{6\ \text{p.m.} \sim 8\ \text{p.m.}, 8\ \text{p.m.} \sim 10\ \text{p.m.}, 10\ \text{p.m.} \sim 12\ \text{p.m.}\}$. Also, the watching day variable X_2 includes seven days and it can be expressed as $X_2 = \{$Monday, Tuesday, Wednesday, Thursday, Friday, Saturday, Sunday$\}$. The genre variable X_3 includes eight attributes such as $X_3 = \{$Education, Drama & Movie, News, Sports, Children, Entertainment, Information, Others$\}$. The states in X_1 and X_2 can be considered the evidences (E) for estimating the conditional probabilities of the genres.

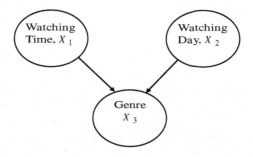

Fig. 4. The BN for TV genre prediction

As varying the values of H and T, the performance of our method is compared with that of the typical method as shown in Equation (6), by calculating the mean error between the estimated probabilities and the true probabilities for 2,400 TV viewers. For each viewer, the error can be calculated as shown in Equation (8).

$$\text{Error} = \left(1/(N \cdot K)\right)\sum_{k=1}^{K}\sum_{j=1}^{M}\left|p_{x_{ij}}\left(t+T+k\right)-\hat{p}_{x_{ij}}\left(t+T+k\right)\right| \tag{8}$$

where M is the number of genres.

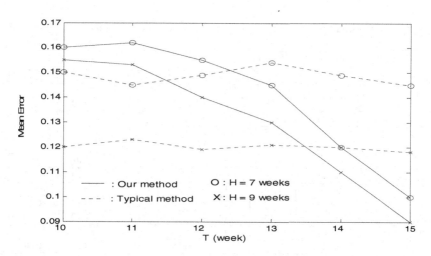

Fig. 5. Performance comparison of our method and the typical method as varying the value of T and H

As shown in Fig. 5, the error of both our method and the typical method depends on the values of H because the reliance of $p_{x_{ij}}(t)$ in Equation (2) places on the population of $N_i(t)$ which depends on the window size H. That is, the larger size of $N_i(t)$, the more representative $p_{x_{ij}}(t)$ is, if a user's preference does not change drastically. For example, the mean error of our method is 0.15 when $H = 9$ (average value of $N_3(t)$ for whole viewers is 70), while 0.16 when $H = 7$ (average value of $N_3(t)$ for whole viewers is 54) with $T = 10$. Also, the mean error of the typical method is 0.12 when $H = 9$, while 0.155 when $H = 7$. The value of T also gives the effect on yielding the optimal performance of our method because the mean value of the PVs depends on the value of T as seen in the equations (4), (5), and (7). For example, as increasing the value of T, the performance for both cases $H = 7$ and $H = 9$ is improved. From Fig. 4, for $H = 7$ and $H = 9$, the performances of our method is superior to those of the typical method as the value of T is larger then 13 and 14, respectively. However, the initialization of our method gets delayed as the values of T and H increase. For example, it is initialized after 18 weeks data collection when $H = 7$ and $T = 10$ but after 25 weeks data collection when $H = 9$ and $T = 15$. For gender and age group of the viewers, we repeated the above experiment and tabulated the mean errors when $H = 9$ with varying T as shown in the table. Each group includes around 220 viewers. From the table, it is shown that the performance of our method is worse than that of the typical method when T is 10 and 11, regardless of age group. However, our method outperforms as T increases. For age groups, 10s (male), 20s (female), 40s (male), 50s (male), the optimal performance was made when T is both 14 and 15, while for age groups 10s (female), 20s (male), T is 14, and for age group 30s (female), 40s (female), 50s (male), T is 15.

Table 1. The mean errors of the typical method and our method by varying the value of T

Age (Gender)	Method	The period of the collection of PVs, T					
		10	11	12	13	14	15
10s (male)	Typical	0.13	0.12	0.13	0.13	0.13	0.12
	Our	0.16	0.15	0.13	0.13	**0.09**	**0.09**
10s (female)	Typical	0.12	0.12	0.13	0.13	0.13	0.12
	Our	0.15	0.14	0.12	0.11	**0.09**	0.1
20s (male)	Typical	0.12	0.13	0.13	0.12	0.12	0.12
	Our	0.14	0.13	0.11	0.1	**0.08**	0.09
20s (female)	Typical	0.13	0.12	0.12	0.13	0.13	0.13
	Our	0.14	0.13	0.11	0.1	**0.12**	**0.12**
30s (male)	Typical	0.12	0.12	0.12	0.11	0.11	0.12
	Our	0.13	0.16	0.15	0.14	0.12	**0.09**
30s (female)	Typical	0.12	0.12	0.13	0.13	0.12	0.12
	Our	0.17	0.16	0.15	0.15	0.1	**0.08**
40s (male)	Typical	0.14	0.13	0.14	0.13	0.13	0.14
	Our	0.17	0.16	0.16	0.14	**0.11**	**0.11**
40s (female)	Typical	0.13	0.13	0.13	0.14	0.13	0.11
	Our	0.15	0.15	0.12	0.1	0.1	**0.08**
50s (male)	Typical	0.12	0.12	0.13	0.13	0.12	0.12
	Our	0.16	0.14	0.13	0.12	**0.09**	**0.09**
50s (female)	Typical	0.1	0.11	0.11	0.11	0.11	0.11
	Our	0.15	0.13	0.12	0.12	0.11	**0.1**

5 Conclusion

In this paper, we presented a new system for estimating the statistical TV user preference by considering the past TV viewers' preference changes. From the experimental results, our method outperforms the typical method if the values of T is large enough to reflect a user's preference changes for predicting the future preference of each TV program genre. However, we determined the optimal values of the parameters from the exhaustive empirical experience using 2,400 TV viewers' watching history. The 2,400 viewers might not be enough for the exhaustive experiment. It is needed to collect more viewers' information. Also, we need to do further study for developing an automatic algorithm to determine the optimal values of parameters T and H for each TV viewer.

References

1. J.W. Kim, B.H. Lee, M.J. Shaw, H.L. Chang, M. Nelson, "Application of decision-tree induction techniques to personalized advertisements on internet storefronts," International Journal of Electronic Commerce, vol. 5, no. 3, pp. 45-62, 2001
2. J.R. Quinlan, Induction of decision trees, *"Machine Learning,"* vol. 1, no. 1, pp. 81-106, 1986
3. R. Aggrawall, T. Imielinski, A. Swami, "Mining association rules between sets of items in large databases," *Proc. ACM SIGMOD Int'l Conference on Management of Data,* pp. 207-216 , 1994
4. R. Aggrawall, R. Srikant, "Fast algorithms for mining association rules," *Proc. 20th Int'l Conference on Very Large Databases,* pp. 478-499, 1994
5. M.Z. Ashrafi, D. Tanizr, K. Smith, "ODAM: An optimized distributed association rule mining algorithm," *IEEE Distributed Systems Online,* vol. 3, no. 3, pp. 1-18, 2004
6. P. Resnick, N. Lacovou, M. Suchak, P. Bergstrom, J. Riedl, "GroupLens: an open architecture for collaborative filtering of netnews," *Internet Research Report,* MIT Center for Coordination Science, 1994, http://www-sloan.mit.edu/ccs/1994wp.html
7. D.A. Maltz, "Distributing information for collaborative filtering on Usenet net news," *SM Thesis,* Massachusetts Institute of Technology, Cambridge, MA, 1994
8. J.B. Schafer, J. Konstan, J. Riedl, "Recommender systems in e-commerce," *ACM Conference on Electronic Commerce,* pp. 158-166, 1999
9. G. Linden, B. Smith, J. York, "Amazon.com recommendations: item-to-item collaborative filtering," *IEEE Internet Computing,* vol. 7, no. 1, pp. 76-80, 2003
10. J.L. Herlocker, J.A. Konstan, L.G. Terveen, J.T. Riedl, "Evaluating collaborative filtering recommender systems, *ACM Transactions on Information Systems,"* vol. 22, no. 1, pp. 5-53, 2004
11. K.D. Bollacker, S. Lawrence, C.L. Giles, "A system for automatic personalized tracking of scientific literature on the web," *Proc. ACM Conference on Digital Libraries,* pp. 105-113, 1999
12. R. Torres, S.M. McNee, M. Abel, J.A. Konstan, J. Riedl, "Enhancing digital libraries with TechLens+", *ACM/IEEE-CS Joint Conference on Digital Libraries,* pp. 228-236, 2004
13. P. Cotter, B. Smyth, "Personalization techniques for the digital TV world," *Proc. European Conference on Artificial Intelligence,* pp. 701-705, 2000

14. W.P. Lee, T.H. Yang, "Personalizing information appliances: a multi-agent framework for TV programme recommendations," *Expert Systems with Applications*, vol. 25, no. 3, pp. 331-341, 2003

15. M. Ciaramita, M. Johnson, "Explaining away ambiguity: Learning verb selectional preference with Bayesian networks," *Proc. Intl. Conference on Computational Linguistics*, pp. 187-193, 2000

16. F. V. Jensen, *Bayesian Networks and Decision Graphs*, Springer, 2001.

17. G. Miller, R. Beckwith, C. Fellbaum, D. Gross, K.J. Miller, "Wordnet: An on-line lexical database," *International Journal of Lexicography*, vol. 3, no. 4, pp. 235-312, 1990

18. J.J. Lee, "Case-based plan recognition in computing domains," *Proc. The Fifth International Conference on User Modeling*, pp. 234-236, 1996

19. H. Akaike, "A new look at the statistical model identification," *IEEE Transactions on Automatic Control*, vol. 19, pp. 716-723, 1974

20. W. Buntine, "A guide to the literature on learning probabilistic networks from data," *IEEE Transactions on Knowledge and Data Engineering*, vol. 8, pp. 195-210, 1996

21. G.E.P. Box, G. Jenkins, *Time Series Analysis, Forecasting and Control*, Holden-Day, 1990

Fuzzy Virtual Card Agent for
Customizing Divisible Card Payments

Soon Ae Chun[1], Yoo Jung An[2], James Geller[2], and Sunju Park[3]

[1] Rutgers University, College of Staten Island, City University of Newyork
[2] New Jersey Institute of Technology
[3] Yonsei University, Korea

Abstract. E-commerce customers may have a problem when paying for the purchase of a major item, if its price is larger than the available credit on their credit card. In the brick and mortar world, this problem would be solved by paying part of the bill with cash or with a second credit card. In e-commerce, however, this has not been an option. Furthermore, even when a customer could pay the whole purchase with one of her credit cards, she may prefer to first max out another card with a lower interest rate. The overall goal of this research is to provide customers with the capability of customizing their payments by splitting an e-commerce payment over multiple cards, while taking into account a set of competing preferences over policies and constraints of various cards in determining which cards to use. This paper presents an intelligent card management agent, called *Fuzzy Virtual Card Agent (f-VA)* that supports the customer's divisible payment decision. By modeling the customer's preferences using weighted fuzzy set memberships, the *f-VA* considers the preferences over the card issuers' policies, such as credit limits, interest rates and many others as well as the policies imposed by the secondary issuers, such as employers, and suggests the best combination of cards to the customer. The customer can take advantage of the suggestion by the *f-VA* or modify it immediately on the Web. Our approach provides customers with a more flexible card payment method for online purchases and can be extended to any types of purchases, such as mobile commerce payments.

1 Introduction

An e-commerce customer may face a problem when paying for the purchase of a major item, if its price is larger than the available credit on each of her credit cards. While the total available credit on all her cards may well exceed the sale price, the merchant would not be able to complete the sale because today's e-commerce systems can only accept a single credit card for a single transaction. In this case, it is in the best interest of the merchant to allow the customer to split the payment over multiple credit cards.

It is also in the interest of the customer to gain the flexibility of splitting a purchase price over several cards. For example, a customer may have a preferred card **A** with a low interest rate and a second card **B** with a high interest rate. Without an option of splitting the purchase price over several cards, the credit limit and prior spending on

K. Bauknecht et al. (Eds.): EC-Web 2005, LNCS 3590, pp. 287–296, 2005.
© Springer-Verlag Berlin Heidelberg 2005

A may leave her to pay the purchase with the higher interest rate card, **B.** The customer, however, would be better off if she could first max out the remaining credit on card **A** and then pay the balance of the purchase price with card **B**, lowering her high interest balance on **B.**

How to split a purchase price over multiple cards, however, is a complex decision to make. Today's typical customer carries a wide variety of cards with a corresponding variety of incentives, such as frequent flyer miles, cash back, introductory low interest rates, promotional gifts, etc. In addition, some credit cards are issued through employer organizations, called secondary card issuers, with company specific policies, such as that the card is allowed only for business expenses or for office supplies, which will further affect the choice of cards. Furthermore, sellers may impose their own constraints such that not every credit card is accepted everywhere. Lastly, the choice of the ideal card (or card combination) often depends on the paying habits of the customer and the calendar date of purchase. Most customers would prefer to pay with a credit card, which will buy them a delay. Thus, all other factors being equal, a customer would prefer to use a card where the closing date is 20 days away over a card where the closing date is only 2 days away. For customers who carry large balances over long periods, the interest rate is an important decision factor. For the customers who pay their bills off every month and do not care about interest rates at all, on the other hand, the closing date might be more important.

Therefore, while it is clearly in the interest of a sophisticated credit card user to be able to split a purchase price over multiple cards, as described above, she may find herself in a state of confusion about how to split the payment exactly. We call this problem of choosing an optimal card or card combination the *divisible payment decision problem.*

Since the criteria for choosing a set of credit cards for payment are diverse and differ from one customer to another, customers need help in keeping track of all their cards and their incentives and constraints. In addition, at the time of making a purchase, customers need help with the complex decision of how to optimally split a purchase over multiple cards. In this paper, we report on a prototype implementation of a *fuzzy virtual card agent,* which allows split credit card payments and helps the customer optimize the distribution of his charges over multiple cards. This paper is organized as follows. The background review of the divisible credit card payment system is provided in Section 2. Section 3 introduces our fuzzy Virtual Card Agent. Experimental results are shown in Section 4. Finally, the conclusions are presented in Section 5.

2   Previous Work and the Divisible Credit Card Payment System

Much research on credit card payments for e-commerce focuses on the security issues [1]. In order to reduce the fraud with the permanent card numbers, the card issuing banks, such as American Express, Discover, and MBNA may issue a one-time use credit-card number instead. A study about payment with single-use credit card numbers appeared in [2]. In our paper, the idea of single-use credit card numbers is applied to divisible card payments. According to the infrastructure presented in [5], the system creates single-use credit card numbers called *virtual card numbers*.

There have been studies on divisible e-cash payment protocols [3, 4]. These studies focus on payment solutions that ensure anonymity while allowing electronic coins to be divisible. That is, each coin can be spent incrementally as long as the total purchases are limited to the monetary value of the coin. These works look at multiple purchases and multiple merchants while this paper is about one purchase with one merchant but with multiple credit card issuers.

Most studies on credit card payment do not focus on the credit card user's practical decision-making problem. However, users may face a complex utility optimization problem during each purchase, namely, which card would be the best one to use among multiple cards for this particular purchase. Most of the early recommender systems are based on simple database queries [11]. Fuzzy logic has been used in modeling market structure since it can handle the uncertainty associated with customer choice [6]. Based on a customer's demographic information, the potential of a visitor as a purchaser of services is classified using fuzzy methods [7]. Fuzzy logic has also been used to cluster customers into several groups based on the customers' data [12]. Miao et al. [13] have conducted a case study on a recommender system regarding automobile purchases. A general introduction to fuzzy set usage can be found in [14].

In the above studies, only the general possibilities of fuzzy technology in e-commerce were discussed. The customer's perspectives on credit-card usage have been addressed in the literature [15,16,17] but not from the perspective of split card payment decisions. In this paper, the fuzzy Virtual Card Agent has been developed not only to obtain the best combination of credit cards with respect to the customer's perspective but also to simplify the complexity of choosing the combination of cards, with many constraints and policies to be considered.

Park et al. [5] has proposed an infrastructure and protocol that support divisible credit-card payments of a single purchase, as shown in Figure 1. In their infrastructure, a *Virtual Card* (V-Card) is created and used each time the customer wants to use a combination of cards. This new infrastructure modifies the existing systems in two ways. First, to support the divisible card payments, the *Virtual Card Manager* (VCM) is added to the merchant side. The VCM handles the V-Card approval process between the merchant and the respective credit card issuers for all the cards in a V-Card. Second, to support the customer's card-usage decisions and to generate a V-Card, the new infrastructure provides the customer with a *V-Card Agent* (VA). As which card(s) to use is a complex decision, an optimization model is built into the VA. Based on the user's preferences, the VA generates a solution that may suggest using multiple cards for a single purchase.

Unfortunately, the optimization model in [5], a linear programming model that maximizes the customer's additive utility function, was rudimentary at best. It considered only a couple of limited card features and provided no details on how to build the utility function (i.e., how to compute the value of the weight for each feature). Our subsequent study suggests the difficulty in creating and maintaining the customer's utility function.

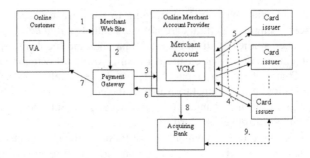

Fig. 1. The Virtual Card Payment Infrastructure (Adopted from [5])

The effectiveness of the VA affects the performance of the whole divisible payment system. Therefore, how to develop an effective and efficient VA that can accommodate numerous card features and policies has remained as an important research issue.

3 Fuzzy Virtual Card Agent

The VA's optimization process requires a computing environment. While one may imagine that in the future a person shopping in a store will be able to use a PDA (a palmtop) to compute an optimal card split and then transfer the solution by Bluetooth or infrared signal to the cash register, this is not currently a viable situation. Therefore, online purchases, which provide a natural computing environment, are our choice for the implementation of the divisible card payment infrastructure. Our approach for the divisible payment decision problem is based on combining fuzzy set theory and user-chosen weights and thresholds with a greedy algorithm, as described below.

Given a set of credit cards $C=\{c_1, c_2, \ldots c_n\}$, and a set of policies or criteria applicable to each card, $P=\{p_1, p_2, \ldots p_m\}$, we can define the customer's preferences for different policies as weights dependent on the policies as shown in (1).

$$\text{Customer's preference for policy } j \text{ on card } i: \ w_i(p_j), \tag{1}$$

where $0 \le w_i(p_j) \le 1$, $1 \le i \le n$, and $1 \le j \le m$. Typically, we assign the same weights of policies to all the n credit cards (i.e., $w_1(p_j) = w_2(p_j) = \cdots = w_n(p_j)$), and use $w(p_j)$ instead of $w_i(p_j)$. For instance, a customer may give a higher weight to interest rate and a lower weight to frequent flyer miles, but she will assign the same weight for a policy to all her cards. Of course, the preference of one policy/criterion over another varies between customers.

The customer may consider a certain value for each policy as favorable. For example, an interest rate below the prime rate or 1000 frequent flyer miles might be viewed as favorable conditions. This is modeled by a threshold value of policy j, $t(p_j)$. Similar to the case with weights, we apply the same threshold value of a policy to all the credit cards.

Each policy j for each credit card i has a "current" value, $v_i(p_j)$. When the policy's value is below the threshold value, there are degrees of goodness of the policy. These degrees of desirable values of a policy are represented by *fuzzy set membership values*. Equation (2) represents the fuzzy value for each policy j on card i, $f_i(p_j)$. The fuzzy membership value is "1" if the current value of the policy/criterion is equal to or greater than the threshold value; otherwise, the membership value will be calculated by the first part of equation (2).

$$
\begin{cases}
f_i(p_j) = \dfrac{v_i(p_j)}{t(p_j)} & \text{,if } v_i(p_j) < t(p_j) \\
\qquad\quad 1 & \text{,otherwise}
\end{cases}
\tag{2}
$$

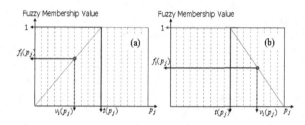

Fig. 2. An example of determining the fuzzy membership value of a certain criterion

The fuzzy membership values are determined for each criterion/policy of each credit card separately. There are two types of criteria. First, the larger the value of the criterion is, the more desired it is by the user, as shown in Figure 2(a). Second, the smaller the value of the criterion is, the more desired it is, as shown in Figure 2(b). To limit the complexity of the user interface and the user friendliness for a population that is not familiar with fuzzy sets, we use the linear shoulder shape fuzzy membership functions [14], as shown in Figure 2. Figures 2(a) and 2(b) show the shapes of a right and a left shoulder, respectively. More complex or user defined fuzzy functions are achievable but require additional computing overhead to implement. Note that the fuzzy membership function is not generated until the user determines the threshold value.

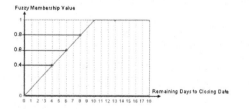

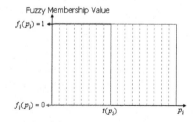

Fig. 3. Fuzzy Membership   **Fig. 4.** Fuzzy Membership for Office Supplies

Figure 3 shows a fuzzy membership function for a policy/criterion of *closing date*. Note that the actual criterion used is the number of days remaining until the closing date. That is, the difference of the closing date and the current date is the parameter of interest. Naturally, most people would prefer to use a credit card for which the closing date is far away. Suppose "10" is the threshold value of this criterion. Then the fuzzy membership values for the numbers of remaining days 4, 6, 8, 13, and 18 are 0.4, 0.6, 0.8, 1, and 1, respectively.

For some credit card usage policies, such as "the credit card can only be used to purchase office supplies," where the criterion is binary, the fuzzy membership function generates either 1 or 0 as shown in Figure 4.

Given the membership function and the preference weights for each card policy, the fuzzy V-Card Agent achieves an optimal card combination through the following steps. First, the user initializes the weights and fuzzy sets, based on her preferences, for multiple criteria (credit card policies). The criteria modeled in this paper include the amount of available credit before reaching the limit, the interest rate, the closing date, and the bonus rate. Secondly, the fuzzy membership value of each criterion of each card is determined by the corresponding fuzzy set, taking into account external factors such as the date of the purchase event. Thirdly, for each card, the *f-VA* sums the weighted fuzzy membership values of all constraints and generates a payment suggestion based on the card with the maximum value. Finally, the *f-VA* proposes to the user to pay the purchase amount with the selected credit card. If the selected credit card does not have enough available credit for the whole payment, the *f-VA* repeatedly performs the above procedure until coming up with a combination of credit cards that covers the total purchase price.

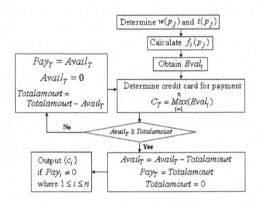

Fig. 5. The flowchart of our fuzzy virtual card agent

Let c_i and $Eval_i$ be the i-th credit card and its evaluation value, respectively. Let $f_i(p_j)$ and $w(p_j)$ be the fuzzy set and the weight of the j-th criterion of the i-th credit card, respectively. Let n and m be the total number of credit cards and the total number of criteria, respectively. Let C_T and *Totalamount* be the selected T-th card for payment and the total purchase amount, respectively. Let $Avail_i$ and Pay_i be the available credit and the payment of the i-th credit card, respectively. Following is our algorithm, and its flowchart is shown in Figure 5.

Fuzzy Virtual Card Agent Optimization Algorithm:

1. The user defines her preferences by initializing the weight, $w(p_j)$, and the threshold value, $t(p_j)$, for each criterion/policy.

2. Calculate the fuzzy membership value, $f_i(p_j)$, for each criterion/policy on each credit card, where $1 \le i \le n$, and $1 \le j \le m$.

3. Obtain the evaluation $Eval_i$ for each credit card c_i by computing

$$Eval_i = \sum_{j=1}^{m} f_i(p_j)*w(p_j) \tag{3}$$

4. Determine the optimal credit card for payment by

$$C_T = \overset{n}{\underset{i=1}{Max}}(Eval_i) \tag{4}$$

5. If $Avail_T \ge Totalamount$ then pay the whole amount with the "best" card T:

$Avail_T = Avail_T - Totalamount$, $Pay_T = Totalamount$, and $Totalamount = 0$.

Else make a partial payment with the best card:

$Pay_T = Avail_T$, $Avail_T = 0$, and $Totalamount = Totalamount - Avail_T$

6. If $Totalamount = 0$ then we are done:

Output Pay_i if $Pay_i \ne 0$ and a corresponding list of cards, $\{C_i\}$ indicating the suggested payment distribution.

Else Repeat steps 3 to 6 until $Totalamount = 0$.

4 Experimental Results

In order to test our fuzzy Virtual Card Agent system, we have considered four policy criteria, available credit limit, interest rate, closing date, and bonus. After all thresholds and weights are determined, the system evaluates each card using Equation

Card No.	Card Nick Name	Account No.	Expiration Date	
card1	yc1	null	null	View Details
card2	yc2	null	null	View Details
card3	yc3	null	null	View Details
card4	yc4	null	null	View Details
card5	yc5	null	null	View Details
card6	yc6	null	null	View Details
card7	yc7	null	null	View Details

Let's Register Another Card in This System CLICK HERE

Fig. 6. List of credit cards of the customer

| Card Nick Name : yc1 |
| Card No. : card1 |
| Account No. : null |
| Expiration Date : null |
| Credit Limit : 1000 |
| Interest Rate : 10 |
| Credit Limit : 1000 |
| Monthly Minimum Payment : null |
| Closing Date : 28 |
| Balance : 0 |
| Available Money: 1000 |
| Balance : 0 |
| Flight Miles : 1 |
| Cash Back : 8 |
| Bonus Coupon : 8 |
| Cash Back : 1 |

Fig. 7. Detailed information

(3). The fuzzy membership function in the system is applied to quantify the user preferences. Figure 6 shows the list of credit cards a user has and Figure 7 shows the detailed information of a credit card that the user wants to view.

Figure 8 shows an example of how the user influences the fuzzy set for the closing date criterion. For example, if a user prefers to make a payment no earlier than 10 days, he will input 10 as the threshold value as shown in Figure 8(a). Figure 8(b) contains the graphical display of the selected fuzzy set for the closing date, based on the desired threshold value, of 10, which was obtained in the step shown in Figure 8(a).

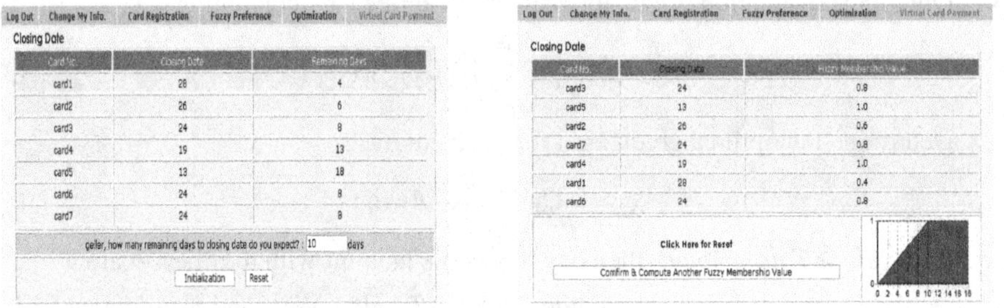

| (a) Entering the threshold value | (b) Graphical display of the fuzzy set for closing date |

Fig. 8. The adjustment of the fuzzy sets

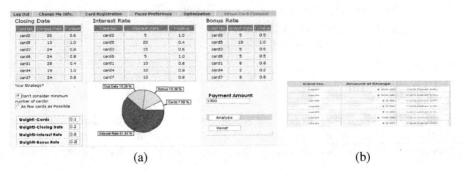

(a)   (b)

Fig. 9. (a) Weight assignment (b) Optimization result when the purchase amount is $1,300

The user may choose between two variations of our implementation. She may ask for a minimal number of cards, or indicate that she does not care about the number of cards being used but is rather concerned about the supported criteria, such as closing date, interest rate, and bonus rate. The interface for the weight assignment of our *f-VA* system is shown in Figure 9(a). The graph located in the center of Figure 9(a) represents the distribution of the weights, which is obtained by the following equation:

$$D_i = \frac{W(P_i)}{\sum_{j=1}^{n} W(P_j)} \qquad (5)$$

where D_i indicates the normalized weight of criterion/policy i relative to the weight sum of all criteria. For example, the normalized weight of the criterion interest is 61.5%, computed as $(0.8/(0.1+0.2+0.8+0.2))$. Figure 9(b) shows the optimization result when the purchase amount is $1,300. The payment is split over three credit cards. After the user has accepted the result of the optimization, the system creates the VC. Combining the numbers of all the cards involved in the payment generates the card number for the VC. The timestamp represents the time when the VC was created.

5 Conclusions and Future Work

We have presented our implementation of a *Virtual Agent* in which a weighted fuzzy set algorithm is used to model user preferences. The use of weights allows users to express relative preferences among criteria. The use of fuzzy sets allows time-dependent and parameter-based computations which determine the evaluation of a card on a daily basis.

We are currently working on the implementation of other modules in Figure 1, including a (simulated) merchant Web site and simulated Web sites for several card-issuing banks. In addition, we are adding functionality to the *f-VA* of inquiring (checking) the available credit limits from issuing banks before generating a VC. This functionality is needed because, although our system can keep track of the purchases done through the *f-VA*, it may not know about the purchases made outside (for example, the card purchases made at a local supermarket).

Several immediate improvements of our implementation and our model are possible. First, the customer could be given the ability to select a fuzzy membership function of his liking by graphically deforming the diagram representing it (see Figure 8). This would allow more complex fuzzy sets without requiring any more knowledge of the user. Other improvements of the user interface are also possible. Secondly, more policy features (in addition to the ones modeled in this paper) should be accommodated. Thirdly, the user should be able to permanently pre-select certain features as irrelevant. For example, a card user who pays off his bill every month would not be interested in the interest rate, so she should not have to say so every time she uses the virtual card system. Fourthly, a more sophisticated optimization model could be possible. Our current model makes a greedy decision at each stage about which card is best, as opposed to trying to achieve an overall optimization. Finally, a split payment system might be of interest in the business-to-business community. This remains a major issue for future work.

References

1. Shankar, U., and Walker, M. "A Survey of Security in Online Credit Card Payments," *UC Berkeley Class Notes*, May, 2001.
2. Rubin, A.D. and Wright, R.N. "Off-Line Generation of Limited-Use Credit Card Numbers." *Financial Cryptography*, pp. 196-209, 2001.

3. Chan, A., Frankel, Y. and Tsiounis, Y. "Easy Come Easy Go Divisible Cash", *Proceedings of Eurocrypt '98 (Lecture Notes in Computer Science)*. Springer-Verlag, 1998. Also available at http://www.ccs.neu.edu/home/yiannis/pubs.html.
4. Nakanishi, T., and Sugiyama, Y. "Unlinkable Divisible Electronic Cash," *Proceedings of Third International Information Security Workshop*, ISW 2000, Australia, 2000, Lecture Notes in Computer Science 1975, pp. 121-134, Springer, 2000.
5. Park, S., Chun, S. A., and Cho, J., An Infrastructure for Customizable and Divisible Card Payments for Online Purchases, ECommerce Track, *Proceedings of the 35th Annual Meeting of the Decision Sciences Institute (DSI 2004)*, Boston, MA, November 20-23, 2004, pp 5091-5096.
6. Jain, V. and Krishnapuram, R., "Applications of Fuzzy Sets in Personalization for e-Commerce", *Proceedings of IFSA-NAFIPS 2001 Conference*, July 2001.
7. Yager, R., "Fuzzy Methods in E-Commerce", *Annual Conference of the North American Fuzzy Information Processing Society - NAFIPS 1999*, p 5-11.
8. Bellman, R. E. and Zadeh, L. A., "Decision-making in a fuzzy environment," Management Science, Vol. 17, No. 4, pp.B141-B164, 1970.
9. Klir. G. J. and Yuan B., Logic Fuzzy Sets and Fuzzy Logic: Theory and Applications, Prentice Hall International, pp.98, 1995.
10. Zadeh, L., "Fuzzy sets," Information and Control, Vol. 8, No. 3, pp.338-353, 1965.
11. Schafer, J. B., Konstan, J. A. and Riedl, J., "E-commerce recommendation applications", Data Mining and Knowledge Discovery. Vol.5, pp115-152, 2001.
12. Zhang, Y., Shteynberg, M., Parasad, S. K. and Sunderraman, R., "Granular Fuzzy Web Intelligence Techniques for Profitable Data Mining", *Proceedings of 2003 IEEE International Conference on Fuzzy Systems*, pp. 1462-1464, May, 2003.
13. Miao, C., Yang, Q., Fang, H. and Goh, A., "Fuzzy Cognitive Agents for Personal Recommendation", *Proceedings of the 3rd International Conference on Web Information Systems Engineering*, 2002.
14. Defining fuzzy sets over Fuzzy variables: http://www.research.ibm.com/able/doc/reference/com/ibm/able/rules/doc-files/arlDefSets.html
15. Juggling Credit card payments: http://www.cardweb.com/cardtrak/pastissues/ct_nov95a.html.
16. Credit Card Debts Balloon: http://www.consumeraffairsjamaica.gov.jm/carddebts.htm
17. Choi, S.-Y. and Whinston, A. B., Smart Cards Enabling Smart Commerce in the Digital Age, http://cism.bus.utexas.edu/works/articles/smartcardswp.html, CREC & KPMG White paper 1998

The New Perspective on Private Cyber Coins in Electronic Commerce: A Korean Case

Seungbong Park[1], Jaemin Han[1], and Jongsoo Yoon[2]

[1] School of Business, Korea University, Seoul, Korea
{sbpark, jaemin}@korea.ac.kr
[2] College of Business Administration, Kangnam University, Gyeonggi-Do, Korea
jongsoo@kangnam.ac.kr

Abstract. This paper examines the importance of 'private cyber coins' to the growth of efficiency in electronic commerce. 'Private cyber coins' such as portal cash, game money, and mileage point are new tokens issued by private companies including Internet portals. It is argued that private cyber coins have encouraged the efficiency in electronic commerce. The paper suggests that monetary freedom theory can be used to inform our understanding of the role of private cyber coins to the growth of efficiency. We suggest that private cyber coins are an essential element to the growth of efficiency through creating value and building relationship between entities.

1 Introduction

With the emergence of Internet as a strong source of doing business, many issues arise from these emerging technologies, which gives more opportunity to electronic commerce. These opportunities via Internet allow for evolution of transaction methods including deployment of new payment media in electronic commerce. The most commonly deployed payment media with expansion of information technology is private tokens such as token, coupon, and mileage point.

This paper looks into the emergence and use of cyber coins as a medium of transactions in electronic commerce. The term 'cyber coins' refers to new tokens that issued by private companies such as Internet portals and other on-offline retail companies and used in limited area for specific purpose. Examples of these purposes include generation of high traffic in portal's community to create more value, promotion medium in marketing area, etc. Increased interest in cyber coins has mainly focused on electronic money supported by central bank. This has resulted in lack of conceptualization of cyber coins issued by private sector such as portal cash, game money, and specific mileage point.

What is Internet? As you know, Internet is defined 'network of network'. The need for this term 'network of network' exists for a number of reasons especially in this paper. First, it is important to suggest new perspectives on cyber coins, which focuses on virtual publics. This in turn suggests that what may be importance is how different features of this new 'virtual public-based' cyber coins. Second, it is also important to understand the meaning of expansion use of these cyber coins in terms of the process for development of money.

K. Bauknecht et al. (Eds.): EC-Web 2005, LNCS 3590, pp. 297–305, 2005.

The purpose of this study is to present rising new role of private cyber coins and their impact on the amount of electronic commerce transactions. Based on theories on characteristics of money established by Matonis [11], Miller et al. [12], and Minskin [13], this paper examines private cyber coins, which are issued by private companies. It shows how these cyber coins strongly pushed monetary freedom to gain much profit from it by presenting both the role of cyber coins in electronic commerce and the relationship between cyber coins and monetary freedom.

The importance of this study lies in its first step towards conceptualizing private cyber coins, which are initially used for gathering customer as new private money (i.e., transaction media). This study is also of great value in that it presents distinction between traditional money and new private cyber coins by presenting concept of consumer-oriented money and it's impact on electronic commerce.

Structure of the manuscripts is constructed as follows. The next section reviews a relevant literature focuses on characteristics of private cyber coins and monetary freedom theory. The following section conducts case study of three types new cyber coins, which have many unique features. This section describes the role of cyber coins, which privately issued by new unit provider (i.e., Internet portal). Finally, we present the main conclusions of our research and delineate future related research.

2 Private Cyber Coins and Monetary Freedom

2.1 Private Cyber Coins

Minskin [13] defines money as anything that is generally accepted in payment for goods and services or in the repayment for debts. Money was introduced as commodity money, which include animal skin, salt, and cattle. Nowadays various forms of electronic money have been adopted and used in many ways with the development of computers and communications technologies.

A development of money is strongly related to two factors, which are forms of money and origin of money. The former one captures that money has been changing and evolving in the forms of money: From commodity money through to electronic money [8]. The latter one captures that money has been developed depending upon whom the issuer of the money is: Public money and private money [11].

Unlike public money, private money is defined as any currency issued by the private sector and accepted as a payment medium that performs monetary functions that include medium of exchange, a unit of account, and store of value to some degree [5].

Cyber coins, sometimes mentioned in the literature as e-money, are defined as 'any form of electronic payment mechanism' [3]. While public cyber coins issued and circulated by the support of central government (or central bank), private cyber coins which include various types of cyber coins such as portal cash, game money, and mileage points are circulated by depending on customers' trust on issuers' willingness. This means that the circulations of private cyber coins are exclusively based on the pattern of modern society especially electronic commerce in which the power comes from customers.

New Unit Provider. In regard to opportunities for providing new value standard, Matonis [11] argue that the greatest advantage goes to the online shopping malls and the large merchant sites on the Internet. In Korea, potential unit providers including Internet portal and online merchant sites are well positioned with the high recognition.

Internet portal is defined as 'a gateway where the user meets the web' [10]. Afuah and Tucci [1] argue that portals main function is to link the information with the user. Internet portal has progressed from giving basic services like email and to retrieving information in the past to giving advanced services like SMS (short message service) and online shopping. Generally, the step-by-step progress of portals is classified in three levels, such as acquiring new users (or new traffic), retaining traffic, and moneterizing traffic. In addition, another analysis on portals progress, Ko and Kim [7] framed three levels such as basic service level, integrated service level, and community-based service. With a wide variety of new services, Internet portals are expanding their way into all businesses. This will give a new definition to the portal site, and expand the traditional definition.

In Korea, several big Internet portals such as Daum Communications and NHN, issue private cyber coins such as portal cash, game money, and mileage point that are basically used for retaining traffic in electronic commerce.

2.2 Monetary Freedom and Efficiency

Matonis [11] argue that monetary freedom is essential to preserve a free-market economy. New transaction media such as private coins that perform one or two of money's general functions could be adopted with little recognition as money in the first place [12]. It suggest that improving public trust and recognition is proposed to be the characteristic most highly associated with acceptance as a true form of transaction instrument [11], [12]. Monetary freedom is highly associated with efficiency of transaction media [11].

The efficient transaction media is defined as a system that settles payments quickly, safely and at reasonable cost [2]. The concept of safety here is related to risk. Risk is composed of legal risk, settlement risk, and operational risk. Legal risk is defined as the risk resulting from uncertainty in agreements and division of responsibility. Meanwhile settlement risk is divided into two categories: credit risk and liquidity risk. Credit risk is created when the bank does not meet his obligation, while liquidity risk emerges when payment obligations are not met on time. Finally, operational risk refers to problems or interruptions in computer systems or communication.

Cost in the payment cycle is defined as payment for using the transaction media and for converting them from one type to another and includes transaction fees and the instability of purchasing power.

In the meantime, Khiaonarong [6] classified efficiency of transaction media into two categories: technological efficiency and economic efficiency. The former is focusing on adoption of computer and communication technologies, while the latter is centering on allocation and management of resources in operation. Technological efficiency can be seen as a measure to achieve economic efficiency. Kvasnička [9] pointed out that this efficiency is closely related to cost in the payment cycle and defined it as the degree of transaction cost. Achieving efficiency is mainly based on financial innovations [2], [6].

To sum up, efficiency in the payment cycle is determined by financial innovation [6], [9]. Financial innovations are largely divided into technological and regulatory ones. Technological innovation includes new payment services that have potential cost-savings arising from computer and communications costs. It also serves as a key factor to determine the degree of cost in payment systems. Meanwhile, regulatory innovation includes changes in regulations or supervision rules that improve the oversight of payment systems and determines the intensity of risk in payment media.

3 Methodologies

This article is an exploratory study that theoretically analyzes practical cases through direct observation, document reviews, and in-depth interviews. To see the role of private cyber coins as a new transaction media, related literatures have been reviewed on economics, electronic commerce, digital cash, and so on.

Following multiple-case design inspired by Yin [14], interviews were conducted with managers during mid to late 2004 at Daum Communications Corp., NHN, and OK Cashabg. In this paper, monetary freedom theory largely drawn on Matonis [11] is used to inform our understanding of the role of private cyber coins to the growth of efficiency. In doing so, we defined transaction media as any tool used to make a payment that was drawn extensively on Kvasnička [9].

4 Findings: A Korean Case

4.1 Portal Cash and Game Money

Daum communications (Daum), the most famous portal site in Korea, provides Daum cash which is used as a transaction media in online content services and Daum shopping, the commercial zone of Daum communications. As of December 1998 the subscribers are over 1 million people, it soon raised to 34 million as of 2003 June. That is 2/3 of total Korean population. Thus making Daum as Asia's largest portal site and third among that World after AOL and Yahoo portals.

Initially Daum provided web mail services named hanmail.net. Then it attracts the customers by using the community Daum café. Based on this community it promoted commerce services. In 1999, Daum issued stocks on its name and collected huge amount of funds. With the help of these funds Daum conducted number of events to attract the customers that further increased the traffic on line. As the traditional steps to the portal development Daum took four steps such as communications, content, community and commerce.

In these four steps Daum cash, private cyber coins, play a major role at community and commerce. Cyber coins thus have indirect relationship with community and direct relationship with the commerce. First it started with relationships indirectly through communities and slowly enters into a direct relationship with the commerce.

Daum cash have the special characters when compare to the mileage such as, mileage is like a reward which is free of charge, whereas Daum cash is which we can get reward and also with payment. In reward we can get Daum cash through using Daum shopping, and writing feedback about the service, and the payment special payment such as server card and enter card. There is one other service we can get Daum cash by payment with using credit card, using cash card and by using Daum certificates. We can use these services as real money for online service and buy goods at Daum shopping on Daum site.

Till now we explained about the Daum cash in the following we will explain Daum cash certificate. In addition, Daum also provides Daum cash certificates. This have two types one is paper type and the other is online type. Paper type is very similar to department store certificate but, the department store certificate can be used only offline stores whereas, the online Daum certificate can be used both online on Daum site and other online companies such as 1318 class and chongnoM.com and also in offline with alliance company which are the famous offline department store such as, Sinseage, Emart and Technomart. If a customer uses 80% of a Daum cash certificate 20% will be added as balance to the Daum cash account. That means Daum cash certificate and Daum cash will have similar exchange services and they can exchange with each other. Daum also have Daum game money, which generally gets free in Daum game site. However, if a customer wants to use for more time the extra time for this he has to pay from the Daum game site.

Meanwhile a few years ago, Naver and Hangame merged to form NHN. This is a classic case for mixing the two core competencies such as Naver's knowledge retrieval ability and Hangame's gaming strategy into one. This synergistic effect they found out new ways of making money. Before they merged they used to issues Hangame money and now they are issuing Han coin. This new Han coins can be used by all Han services such as, buying contents and services related to online transactions. Han coins can be accumulated via credit card and other payments, where as Hangame money is free. These coins can be used for buying online game item, avatar, and various online contents.

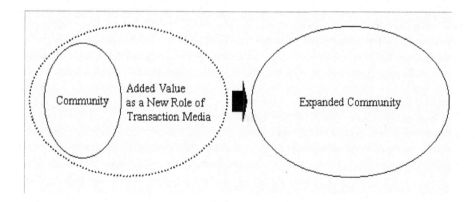

Fig. 1. Added Value and an Expanded Community

It can be explained in simple terms, when a costumer uses Hancoins they receive mileage points and when they receive points more then 10,000 they can also use for buying other contents online. In a broader sense it can be explained that the constant interaction of portal cash and game money that is related through mileage acts as real money. Thus mileage doesn't work in isolation but it is linked with money. In this context, we regard mileage points as new transaction media especially online sites. As, the creation and interaction of these three types of money strongly related to information technology, so in the long run the role of this type of money is on the rise and keeps growing.

In this case, we demonstrated that portal cash and game money could be used as new transaction media that have monetary value. With a technological innovation we can say that the traditional role of private cyber coins is susceptible to challenge. This new role of private cyber coins as transaction media provide more value to the costumer. This value will dramatically increase the traffic on the portal site eventually building a relationship between two entities (i.e., customers) as shown in Fig. 1.

4.2 Mileage Point

Mileage points originally are used only for a discount or substitution of payment to the repurchase [4]. Now mileage data can be shared by allied organizations due to the development of information technology. Different mileage issued by organizations participating to alliance can be exchanged and cleared to be more effectively used for payment.

Mileage as money is different from usual money and digital cash (or so called e-cash) even though it is being used as a payment tool. It is generated only when a transaction is occurred, mileage points are requested to be issued by customers, and membership is authenticated by private companies.

There are websites where mileages issued by different organizations can be exchanged. Furthermore, people can transfer their mileage points to whomever they want to trade. Different ratios can be applied to trading of different types of mileage. A small point of mileage is to be more actively used by trading with the other kind of mileage in need; otherwise to be gone into the discard.

Multiple kinds of mileages can be generated by a single transaction: e.g., a transaction using a credit card can generate mileage point in the membership of an allied airline company as well as mileage points in the membership of the credit card company.

Integrated mileage systems of large allied businesses have been successfully established in Korea. A unique case is already in service. It is called 'OK Cashbag' of SK Corp. that has a number of allied businesses in most of business sectors such as the energy, credit card, mobile telecommunication, restaurants, and so on. All of the allied businesses issue 'OK Cashbag points', an integrated mileage. This integrated mileage point is accepted as the same value at any of these business allied. Consumers can use their point for shopping and paying bills. As of early 2004, the total number of subscribers to OK Cashbag has reached to 24 millions, which accounts for as much as 50% of the whole population in Korea. The number of online and offline allied companies is 300 and 50,000 respectively. Using the current OK Cashbag system, SK Corp. is collecting a huge amount of data on its consumers and consumers' behavior. OK Cashbag service is mutually beneficial to the three parties involved to the ally: end consumers can use their OK Cashbag points at any member stores or branches of allied companies, the allied companies can get easy access to information on the end consumers in addition to customers' royalty, and SK Corp. can just harvest commissions from the allied companies whenever customers generate OK Cashbag points and collect rich data on customers.

The cases mentioned above clearly demonstrate that mileage point works as a medium of exchange and store of value, which are characteristics of the functions of money. The opportunity to launch a mileage point as a alternative transaction media on a grand scale simply has not been available until recently. Although the mileage point is being slowly and gradually adopted with little recognition as money, it is predicted that it is going to be accepted as a more efficient transaction media by constantly improving public trust and recognition.

5 Results and Implications

The results show that the changing the role of private cyber coins in online portals. With respect to the technological innovations in the Internet era, the role of private cyber coins has evolved. As shown in Fig. 2, initially cyber coins which were used only as promotion tool, with the growth and advance of electronic commerce the role is changing to transaction media, which increases the value creation, efficiency in the transaction with the customer, and building relationship. In the long run, this phenomenon increases the efficiency in whole electronic commerce.

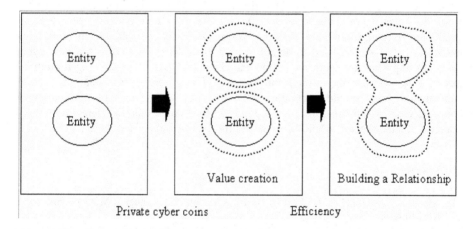

Fig. 2. The New Role of Private Cyber Coins in Electronic Commerce

6 Conclusions

This article focuses on the new role of private cyber coins largely based on monetary freedom theory. This gives several implications to the transactions in the electronic commerce. First, monetary freedom, which means free issuance and circulation of new value standards, is an essential element to electronic commerce growth. Second, the new private cyber coins plays a major role to improve monetary freedom in electronic commerce. Third, these private cyber coins create both new value as a transaction media in limited area such as portals, and increase transaction traffic. This traffic makes to build a new relationship between two entities eventually, growth to affiance in the electronic commerce. Although we presented these implications to a limited area, this article shows that this phenomenon gradually expands to whole of electronic commerce.

This paper further focus on the private cyber coins among several promotion tools in electronic commerce. The view of the future of private cyber coins expressed in this paper was described in terms of changing roles of private cyber coins. This paper tries to demonstrate the progress and expansion of electronic commerce by showing how a promotion tool in Internet portal changes their nature during continuous developments in the information and communication technologies. Until now, most research on cyber coins only focused on marketing perspective mentioning it as a promotion tool. In addition, the term 'private cyber coins' has often been used without precise definitions. This research presents the first step towards building theories that provides insights about the conceptualization of the role of cyber coins in electronic commerce. In addition, this paper highlights the relationship between monetary freedom and the growth of electronic commerce. In this respect, this paper present the direction for future research such as, the relationship of private cyber coins with virtual communities, revenue generation, and social networks.

In Internet era, which is affecting in all ways of human life we should not concentrate our research in a single direction. In most cases, one issue is related to other issue thus, research should focus in various ways and directions making it more dynamic in Internet era. This paper tries to explain the whole concepts of electronic commerce by using monetary freedom theory, which is connected with transaction media. In doing so, we tried to demonstrate not on why cyber coins but how cyber coins are important in electronic commerce. This study has the following limitations that need to be overcome in the future research. First, more solid validations such as confirmatory study should be conducted. Second, our works focused on private cyber coins affected by information technology. Therefore, some other academic references related to finance sector should be reviewed thoroughly.

References

1. Afuah, A., and Tucci, C. L.: Internet Business Models and Strategies, McGraw-Hill Irwin, NY (2000)
2. Bergo, J.: Efficiency in the Norwegian Payment System, Proceedings of Payment System, Norway (2002) 1~10
3. Dias, J., Dias, M. H., and Silva, M. J.: The Demand for Digital Money and its Impact on the Economy, Brazilian Electronic Journal of Economics Vol.2 (1999)
4. Dowling, G., and Uncles, M.: Do Customer Loyalty Program Really Work? Sloan Management Review Vol. 38 (1997) 71~82
5. Good, B. A.: Private Money: Everything Old is New Again? Economic Commentary, Federal Research Bank of Cleveland (1998) 1~4
6. Khiaonarong, T.: Payment Systems Efficiency, Policy Approaches, and the Role of the Central Bank. Bank of Finland (2003)
7. Ko, J., and Kim, Y.: Sense of Virtual Community: A Conceptual Framework and Research Issue, Information Systems Review, Vol.3 (2001) 325~331
8. König, S.: The evolution of money: from commodity money to e-money, UNICERT IV Program (2001), http://www.ww.unimagdeburg.de/fwwdeka/student/arbeiten/009.pdf

9. Kvasnička, M.: Does Electronic Money Increase the Freedom of Choice? In MendelNet 2000 Sborník příspěvkůz konference, Czech Republic (2000) 185~189
10. 10.Ledbetter, J.: Some Pitfalls in Portals, Columbia Journalism Review Vol.38 (1999), 22~23
11. Matonis, J. W.: Digital Cash and Monetary Freedom, Libertarian Alliance, UK (1995)
12. Miller, R. et al.: The Future of Money, Organization for Economic Cooperation and Development, France (2002)
13. Miskin, F. S.: The Economics of Money, Banking, and Financial Markets, Harper Collins Publisher, NY (1992)
14. Yin, R. K.: Case Study Research: Design and Methods, Newbury Park, Sage Publications (1994)

Authentication and Authorisation Infrastructures in b2c e-Commerce

Christian Schlaeger and Guenther Pernul

University of Regensburg, Universitätsstrasse 31, D-93053 Regensburg, Germany
{christian.schlaeger, guenther.pernul}@wiwi.uni-regensburg.de

Abstract. One of the reasons for the failure of PKI in b2c e-commerce might be that too much effort was put in entity authentication. In many applications it is not necessary to know who an entity actually is, but to be sure that he/she possesses the proper rights to perform the desired action. This is exactly the purpose of Authentication and Authorisation Infrastructures (AAIs). Today several proposals and running AAIs are available focusing on different aspects. The purpose of this paper is firstly to introduce common representatives and to discuss their focus, secondly to develop criteria and requirements that any AAI for b2c e-commerce has to fulfil and finally evaluate the proposals against the developed criteria. Candidates for evaluation are Kerberos, SESAME, PERMIS, AKENTI, Microsoft Passport, Shibboleth and the Liberty Framework.

1 Introduction

PKI was thought to be one of the pillars of modern e-commerce. Through its ability to determine the true identity of a user it was supposed to provide missing trust in e-commerce transactions and make the web more secure. Neither have PKI services taken off to be the new gold mine for the internet economy nor is e-commerce faltering because of the lack of a working PKI. Reasons for a non adaption of a large scale PKI lie in its complexity, the problems of large scale deployment and missing interoperability as well as the problem of certificate revocation or the doubtful return on investment [9]. It seems that in b2c e-commerce applications the question of entity authentication has been overrated. The true question to be asked is not "Who are you?" but rather "Are you allowed to perform a certain request?"

The solution of the mentioned problem can be the usage of AAIs – Authentication and Authorisation Infrastructures or PMIs – Privilege Management Infrastructures. The latter is an AAI based on a PKI that authorises users through the usage of Attribute Certificates issued by an Attribute Authority [12]. AAIs provide their services for e-commerce vendors or web service providers allowing them to use authentication and authorisation as a supportive service.

This paper introduces seven infrastructures for authentication and authorisation and matches them against 14 requirements. These 14 requirements are developed based on the generic process of b2c e-commerce.

K. Bauknecht et al. (Eds.): EC-Web 2005, LNCS 3590, pp. 306–315, 2005.
© Springer-Verlag Berlin Heidelberg 2005

2   Generic Architecture and Motivation

Together with integrity and confidentiality especially authentication and authorisation are among the dearest needed security services in b2c e-commerce. To provide authentication and authorisation so called AAIs have been developed. Their aim is to provide these two services (Authentication and Authorisation Services - AAS) in a dynamic, growing, flexible, and heterogeneous environment. AAIs help businesses to use its specialised functions for example for a Single-Sign-On (SSO) over various subsystems.

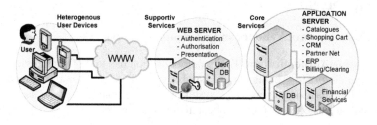

Fig. 1. Generic b2c e-commerce architecture

Fig. 1 shows the generic model of a business architecture with the roles of user and vendor. The user or customer starts the process by requesting a service. These are primarily handled by an application server delivering information services. At the side of the vendor several other institutions may be involved, e.g. shop systems, financial services, trusted third parties, or sub contractors. In between this communication additional, secondary but essential AAS are needed. These can be provided by a third stakeholder, the AAI provider, adding a further role. A specialised AAI generates the following benefits for the identified three groups of stakeholders:

Vendors: AAIs can provide authentication, authorisation and the possibility of a SSO not only over a vendor's own subsystems but over various vendors as well. In such a federation a customer could use services owned by different e-businesses via one single AAI account. The usage of a sophisticated, powerful, and above all known and familiar sign-on-system will increase the usability for customers and prevent drop outs of users before completing an order. To have a standardised directory of users will increase the maintainability and reduce the effort for each single participant. A repository could be organised in a distributed way, which will increase scalability, security, and availability.

Customers: Users tend to use the same credentials for every service risking a misuse if their combination is discovered by an attacker or a bogus merchant. An AAI holds certain benefits to prevent this.

With most services the user, after providing a vendor with his personal data, has to trust the merchant not to misuse his profile. The user finds himself in a situation where he is no longer in control of his personal data. Besides the trust into a vendor a customer also has to trust the technology securing his communication. Studies on technological acceptance have shown that the basis for e-commerce usage is the trust in technology [14]. The usage of a known and well accepted AAI could be one step in this direction.

AAI providers: An outsourced AAI enables the vendor to concentrate on his core business leaving AAS to specialists. This generates a new business model for security experts. In a federation this service could be bundled for various providers reducing costs for each participant and providing the critical customer mass for the provider's business. External accreditation agencies could certify AAI providers with a level of security or trustworthiness. E-businesses could use that seal for their own marketing.

3   Requirements

3.1   Requirements of Vendors and e-Commerce Providers

R1 – Flexible Authentication: Entity authentication has to be flexible with respect to methods and storage (clients should be able to authenticate via username/password, PKI, and biometrical systems). The system should be able to manage user revocation and include a trusted third party in the authentication process.

R2 – Flexible and Effective Authorisation: Authorisation should be flexible and support various techniques such as role based or attribute based access control. It should be independent of the authentication in order to provide modularity.

R3 – Availability: AAIs should avoid single point of failures, bottle necks but rather rely on a distributed architecture.

R4 – Performance: Interactions and communication should be most efficient.

R5 – Development Status: The AAI should have developed from a pure architectural model to a mature product with user experiences and reviews.

R6 – Strong Security: Mutual authentication should be provided. Not only should the user authenticate himself to the AAI but vice versa as well. This is needed against man-in-the-middle attacks and bogus merchants. AAIs should be resistant to replay attacks and sniffing.

3.2   Requirements of e-Commerce Customers

R7 – Privacy and User Control: AAIs have to use a maximum of profile canniness and leave it to the user what profile information is passed on. The AAI should adapt to the user's settings rather than the user to some AAI commands, e.g. he should be able to determine the form of session management. The user should be able to access certain services anonymously or with different roles to eliminate tracking.

R8 – Trust and Openness: To develop trust the AAI should make wide use of standards and open technologies [14]. Its security policy should be published and reviews and field reports publicly available.

R9 – Ease of Use: The AAI should be easy to handle by the client and be able to be reviewed and controlled by non-professional users as well.

3.3 Requirements of Potential AAI Providers

R10 – Outsourcing: AAS should potentially be provided by specialised 3rd parties.

R11 – Single-Sign-On Federation: The AAI should provide secure access to various providers, managing a federation of vendors and the SSO for each one.

R12 – Scalability: AAS have to handle a multi user and multi vendor environment. An increase in the user population must easily be handled by simply scaling up the AAI.

R13 – Communication Security: Secure communication between client, AAI, and all subsystems using common and open standards wherever possible has to be provided. Key distribution has to be secure and usable for numerous entities.

R14 – Resource Awareness: AAS have to respect CPU power, RAM limits, and input functionalities for heterogeneous user devices. AAS have to restrict to build-in browser functionalities and common protocols for their interaction with the user.

4 AAI Usage and Protocols

In the following a short description of seven AAIs is given. Each infrastructure is classified and described by its **general usage**, its **protocol**, and a section dealing with the **client's involvement**.

4.1 Kerberos Like AAIs

Kerberos is a central authentication system for distributed services. It was developed during the Athena project at MIT [2]. A principal orders his client to prove his identity to a verifier. In this communication no data should be transmitted that could potentially allow an attacker to pose as principal. The current version 5 is specified in the RFC 1510. Kerberos uses symmetric encryption, checksum verification, challenge response, and time stamps.

The Kerberos protocol is described in Fig. 2. The shown entities form a Kerberos realm, each realm stands for a complete Kerberos domain with a Key Distribution

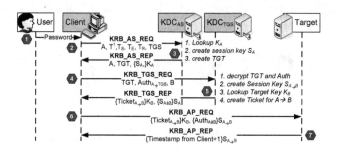

Fig. 2. Kerberos protocol exchange, simplified acc. to [5, 15]

Centre (KDC) and various principals (clients and servers). A KDC is a trusted third party in the domain. It authenticates all principals. Each user or service shares a common secret with the KDC that is used for symmetric encryption. The secret is mostly derived from the user's password and stored encrypted with the KDC master key. The KDC comprises two different but connected services, the Authentication Server (AS) and the Ticket-Granting Server (TGS). The AS authenticates the principal in a session (step 2). He delivers if successful the Ticket Granting Ticket (TGT, see step 3). With the TGT the principal approaches the TGS, which deals with the authorisation and establishes session tickets (steps 4, 5). Tickets can also be established for other realms if a cross-realm authentication is arranged. The client approaches the target with session ticket and key (steps 6, 7).

The user needs a client software installed on his/her device. This client has to be able to compute the symmetric encryption with 3DES or an equivalent. Kerberos version 5 lets you choose the encryption standard. Furthermore the client needs to compute a one-way-hash-function to derive the Master key from the user's password (step 1). An open problem poses the initial key exchange between the user and the Kerberos system. This has to be done offline.

SESAME (Secure European System for Applications in a Multi-Vendor Environment) was developed untpil version 4 and has found entry into several commercial products of Bull SA (Integrated System Management AccessMaster), ICL PLC (Acces Manager), or products of Siemens Nixdorf [1]. SESAME, quite similar to Kerberos, enhances Kerberos through integration of a PKI and the possibility for direct host-to-host interactions. SESAME is compatible with Kerberos.

4.2   Privilege Management Infrastructures

PERMIS realises an X.509 PMI. In PERMIS Attribute Authorities establish attribute certificates (AC) for the users. These bind the distinguished name of the user to a role. An XML policy authorises roles and targets. ACs and their revocation lists are stored in LDAP directories [3]. The ACs are validated by the authority. Figure 3 shows the protocol for access control. If a user wants access to a target the PERMIS access control enforcement function (AEF) will delegate his request to the access control decision function (ADF, step 3) which determines the correctness of the AC and its compliance to the policy (step 4). If access is granted the decision is given back to the enforcement function which grants the access (step 5) or not. Both functions have to be implemented at the target application. The target application is also responsible for user authentication.

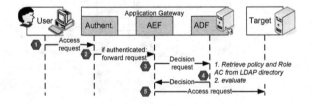

Fig. 3. PERMIS access protocol, adapted from [4]

In PERMIS the client has to pass an application defined authentication to proof his PERMIS distinguished name (steps 1, 2). After that no involvement of the client for authorisation is needed. Ideally the authentication is done with PKI.

AKENTI works similar to PERMIS but with a few differences: It is written in C++ (PERMIS in Java), uses a proprietary XML syntax for its credentials and requires the user to be PKI enabled. Furthermore it concentrates on Discretionary Access Control rather than Role Based Access Control [11].

4.3 Web Focused AAIs

Microsoft Passport was introduced 1999 by Microsoft and should provide an SSO Service for vendors and customers in e-commerce applications. Microsoft wanted to raise customer satisfaction through the advantage of not having to register for every service but only once [10]. The Microsoft passport protocol is shown in Fig. 4.

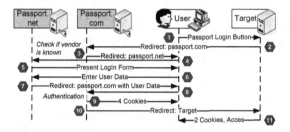

Fig. 4. MS Passport Login procedure

Four parties are involved in the SSO: The user, the vendor and two Passport servers. The user is redirected to a Passport log-in site (steps 1, 2) and the ID of the vendor is submitted via URL-Encoding. The user is referred to passport.com and if the vendor ID is authenticated (step 3) redirected to passport.net (step 4). The connection to passport.net is SSL secured. The user logs in (step 5, 6) and 4 cookies are written to the user's browser cache. MSPSec is a ticket granting cookie with the user ID and his Passport password. According to [10] this information is stored SSL-encoded (!?!¹). A ticket cookie (MSPAuth) with login information and a timestamp, a profile cookie (MSPProf) with profile information as well as a participating sites cookie (MSPVis) with all vendors the user has logged into. The user is redirected to the vendor site and via URL encoding information is transmitted that is read by the Passport Manager, a required software at the vendor's web server. The Manager stores another two cookies this time in the domain of the vendor. Login to other vendors can be accomplished without another manual login from passport.com via its MSPSec and MSPAuth. The Passport logout button at any vendor's site should log out the user from all currently active sites.

The **Liberty Alliance** was founded in 2001 with the aim to provide an open standard with at least the functionality of Microsoft Passport. In Liberty a Circle of Trust (COT) establishes a Liberty system. Each partner provides the authentication

---

¹ SSL is usually only used for securing the communication between client and server using PKI certificates. The information is encrypted with the public key of the other partner.

for his users while they themselves can login to all partners with SSO. In [7] and [8] a framework in which service providers (SP) and Identity Providers (IdP) work together in a COT is defined. In the process of federation a user is made known to all COT members. The user authenticates at his IdP (Fig. 5 step 1) and if he wishes a cookie is stored under a common domain where every member hosts a server so they all can access the cookie (step 2). The user is redirected to the SP.

The SSO works like shown in Fig 5. With a HTTP-Post the user is redirected to his/her IdP with a SAML encoded request for authentication (steps 3, 4). The IdP answers with another HTTP-POST SAML and puts all assertion into a form field (steps 5, 6). The user presents the SAML Attributes (step 7) at the SP and if the SP can evaluate the SAML attributes for the target an access decision is made (step 8).

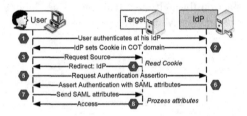

Fig. 5. Liberty SSO procedure [8]

Liberty resembles more a framework than an actual AAI. A COT has to decide on the implementations. Reference installations from SUN can be used as examples. The creation of a COT has to be planned carefully due to its openness. The SAML assertions can carry any attribute the COT agrees upon.

Shibboleth was developed by the Internet2 Organisation, a federation of over 200 universities in the US. Version 1.0 is available since 2003. The project is open source.

Shibboleth is similar to Liberty. Although it has not been developed as a Liberty COT most features comply with the Framework and in the next releases Shibboleth will also be officially Liberty compliant. The difference so far is that Shibboleth provides the SP with a specific assertion and optional SAML attributes. The authorisation has to be done by the SP according to a simple "grant access if authenticated" or according to the SAML attributes [13].

5 Matching AAIs and Requirements

A full AAI with authentication, authorisation, access control decision and access control enforcement is not among the seven candidates. Each of the examined AAIs provides only parts and can be used as a full AAI only in combination with other products or frameworks.

The most flexible **authentication** (R1) might be provided by Liberty as it is open to almost any thinkable entity authentication. The ease of use of Shibboleth, where the user is redirected to his familiar home network for authentication is exemplary. For the **authorisation** (R2) the most potential is shown in the PMI frameworks PERMIS/AKENTI. The usage of attribute certificates with a role based access control is probably the most flexible and interoperable solution. The management of the policy on the other hand should be optimised for a distributed architecture.

The **availability** (R3) of Microsoft Passport is due to the single point of failure and the caused bottle neck at Microsoft.net a matter of criticism. Kormann and Rubin [6] found evidence for a likely Denial of Service attack. The distributed architecture of Liberty and Shibboleth guarantee better availability. However, passport remains the only AAI which is available and in use for several years.

Kerberos and SESAME rank low on the **performance** (R4) scale. This is due to the complex protocol for authentication and ticket granting with large client involvement. Passport makes heavy use of redirects and cookies which decreases user acceptance and performance. For PERMIS and AKENTI much depends on the authentication which is not part of their architecture.

Kerberos is one of the most fully **developed** (R5) and reviewed AAIs in the test. SESAME found its way into several products after the project finished. The considerably younger AAS like PERMIS/AKENTI and Liberty lack thorough testing on real cases or reference implementations. Shibboleth through its adaptation to a specific need is in constant development, heavy usage, and has founded a basis for other national frameworks alike.

Strong security (R6) is provided by Kerberos and SESAME. Replay attacks and sniffing have been addressed. Both can provide mutual authentication. For PERMIS/AKENTI much depends on the establishment of the distinguished name. If the authentication is adequate secure, replay attacks and sniffing are prohibited. The usage of certificates enables strong network encryption. The access control decision is taken based on signed and guaranteed elements only. With Passport the mentioned encryption relies heavily on 3DES. Due to the uniform password used for the encryption of all vendor keys a change to higher encryption is not easy. SSL is used for the user log-in into passport.com.

The user requirement **privacy and user control** (R7) are very questionable with the Passport architecture. The central storage of a profile has been a matter of discussion among privacy groups for long. More self management is granted to users of Shibboleth and Liberty where a user decides what is made public. Kerberos/SESAME force the user into installing a client software and privacy was not a major design goal at the time of invention. As PERMIS and AKENTI are agnostic to the authentication, an implementation might leave free choice to the user. However through the integration of a PKI a user has no anonymity at all.

With an open policy towards documentation or making source code publicly available almost all AAIs have gained **trust**. Passport follows the bad rule of "security through obscurity" and provides neither sufficient nor consistent documentation for its core functionalities. Liberty lacks sufficient reviews. A check is needed confirming the Liberty compliance of an actual implementation.

The **ease of use** is good for most AAIs. However, the user chosen password in Passport is a source of potential weakness. Shibboleth through the login at the familiar home network makes it easy for the user to follow the actions of the protocol. Passport and the PMIs seem like a black box where non-professionals have no idea what is done with their data.

As for the requirements of potential AAI providers, the **outsourcing** factor is of course best addressed in the 3 web focused AAIs as it was a design principle. In Kerberos and SESAME maintenance can be outsourced.

A **Federation** can be best build with the 3 web focused AAIs. Kerberos and SESAME only provide internal SSO. PERMIS and AKENTI with adequate authentication might be able to provide such usage. The LDAP repositories are open and can be accessed by any application.

Best **scalability** is promised again with the 3 web focused AAIs. They can provide services in a multi user and multi vendor environment easily. The policies are a limiting factor in a multi-vendor environment for PERMIS/AKENTI. The problems of key distribution and multi vendors reduce the scalability for Kerberos and SESAME.

The **security of communication** relates with the openness of the AAIs. Except Passport, the AAIs use common standards like SSL, SAML, Challenge Response or PKI. Much depends of course on the actual implementation.

Kerberos and SESAME due to the necessity of client software and heavy encryption on the client rank low on **resource awareness**. The client's involvement with the PMIs is very low – taken into account only the authorisation. Passport with login on the vendor's site, at least six cookies, and URL rewriting makes heavy use of resources and browser functionalities as well. An embedded PKI with a CRL to process will be too resource consuming for most clients.

The evaluated AAIs cannot provide satisfactory answers to our requirements. Very flexible frameworks like Liberty could provide users and vendors with an appropriate AAI. Others like Shibboleth and PERMIS/AKENTI only show parts of the requested functionalities. Missing functionality must be provided by additional tools. Microsoft Passport as an AAI on the retreat[2] is too limited and not open enough. Kerberos and SESAME have been developed for other purposes and provide very good results in the intended environments. However, b2c e-commerce will not be a domain for their implementation. As none of the frameworks was evaluated in working condition but based on desk research and publicly available literature, statements concerning performance have to be dealt with care and will depend on the actual implementation.

6   Conclusion

In this paper it is argued that entity authentication for b2c e-commerce is insufficient and has to be enhanced by authorisation. The combination results in AAIs. AAIs provide customers, vendors, and potential external AAS providers with a list of possible benefits. Fourteen requirements that b2c e-commerce systems have on AAIs are formulated as a guideline to evaluate these infrastructures. Seven candidates have been evaluated against the requirements.

None of the AAIs is perfectly suitable for b2c e-commerce. Frameworks like Liberty show room for improvements and potential to satisfy the requirements while

---

[2] The actual list of customers has been taken from the Microsoft website. Announcements from very prominent user eBay to stop the Passport Service and the rumours that Microsoft will use Passport only internally make the future for Passport doubtable. See TechWeb.com for details: http://www.techweb.com/wire/ebiz/56800077 (accessed 1.3.2005).

others like Kerberos or Sesame are not being intended for b2c e-commerce usage. PERMIS and AKENTI provide sophisticated authorisation services but have to rely on adequate 3rd party authentication to achieve a complete AAI. The security of Microsoft Passport is based on the strategy of security through obscurity which seems at least questionable for providing trusted AAS.

References

1. Ashley, Paul M., Vandenwauver, M.: Practical Intranet Security, Overview of the State of the Art and Available Technologies, Kluwer Academic Publishers (1999)
2. Champine, G., Geer, D. Jr., Ruh, W.: Project Athena as a Distributed Computer System. In: IEEE Computer, Vol. 23, No 9 (1990) 40-51
3. Chadwick, D., Otenko, A.: The PERMIS X.509 role based privilege management infrastructure. In: Proceedings of the 7th ACM Symposium on Access Control Models and Technologies (SACMAT 2002), Monterey, California, USA (2002) 135-140
4. Chadwick, D., Sahalayev, M.: Internet X.509 Public Key Infrastructure LDAP Schema for X.509 Attribute Certificates. In: PKIX WG Internet-Draft Standards Track (2003)
5. Kaufman, C., Perlman, R.; Speciner, M.: Network Security: Private Communication in a Public World. 2nd edn., Prentice Hall PTR (2002)
6. Kormann, P., Rubin, A.: Risks of the Passport single signon protocol. In: Computer Networks, Elsevier Science Press, Netherlands, Vol. 33(1-6) (2000)51-58
7. Liberty ID-FF Bindings and Profiles Specification, Liberty Alliance Project, 2003. http://www.projectliberty.org/specs/liberty-idff-bindings-profiles-v1.2.pdf,   Accessed 2004-10-21
8. Liberty ID-FF Protocols and Schema Specification, Liberty Alliance Project, 2003. http://www.projectliberty.org/specs/liberty-idff-protocols-schema-v1.2.pdf,   Accessed 2004-10-21
9. Lopez, J., Oppliger, R., Pernul, G.: Why have Public Key Infrastructures failed so far? Submitted for publication (2005)
10. Microsoft Passport Review Guide. http://download.microsoft.com/download/a/f/4/ af49b391-086e-4aa2-a84b-ef6d916b2f08/passport_reviewguide.doc, Accessed 2004-11-09.
11. Chadwick, D., Otenko, O.: A Comparison of the Akenti and PERMIS Authorization Infrastructures. In: Ensuring Security in IT Infrastructures, proceedings of the ITI First International Conference on Information and Communications Technology (ICICT 2003) Cairo, Egypt (2003) 5-26
12. Farrell, S., Housley, R.: An Internet Attribute Certificate Profile for Authorization. Request for Comments 3281. IETF PKIX Working Group (2002)
13. Cantor, S.: Shibboleth Architecture Protocols and Profiles Working Draft 05, November 2004, 2004. http://shibboleth.internet2.edu/docs/draft-mace-shibboleth-arch-protocols-05.pdf, Accessed 2004-01-17
14. Salam, A.F., Iyer, L., Palvia, P., Singh, R.: Trust in e-commerce. In: Communications of the ACM, Vol. 48, No 2 February 2005. CACM (2005) 72-77
15. Vandenwauver, M., Govaerts, R., Vandewalle, J.: Security of Client-Server Systems. In: Eloff, J.P.; von Solms, R. (Ed.): Information Security - from Small Systems to Management of Secure Infrastructures. IFIP Press (1997) 39-54

XML-Based Security Acceleration Methods Supporting Fast Mobile Grid

Namje Park[1], Kiyoung Moon[1], Howon Kim[1],
Seungjoo Kim[2], and Dongho Won[2]

[1] Information Security Research Division, ETRI,
161 Gajeong-dong, Yuseong-gu, Daejeon, 305-350, Korea
{namjepark, kymoon, khw}@etri.re.kr
[2] School of Information and Communication Engineering, Sungkyunkwan University,
300 Chunchun-dong, Jangan-gu, Suwon-si, Gyeonggi-do, 440-746, Korea
skim@ece.skku.ac.kr, dhwon@dosan.skku.ac.kr

Abstract. Mobile grid, or wireless grid services refers to value-added grid service by processing in mobile environment. Besides mobile internet the traditional Internet computing is experiencing a conceptual shift from client-server
model to grid and peer-to-peer computing models. As these trends, mobile
internet and the grid, are likely to find each other the resource constraints that
wireless devices pose today affect the level of interoperability between them.
The goal of this paper is to investigate how well the most limited wireless devices can make use of grid security services. This paper describes a novel security approach on fast mobile grid services based on current mobile web services
platform environment using XML signcryption mechanism.

1 Introduction

Grid computing emerges as a technology for coordinated large-scale resource sharing
and problem solving among many autonomous groups. In grid's resource model, the
resource sharing relationships among virtual organizations are dynamic. However,
grid requires a stable quality of service provided by virtual organizations and the
changing of sharing relationship can never happen frequently. This model works for a
conventional distributed environment but is challenged in the highly variational wireless mobile environment[1].

Besides mobile internet the traditional Internet computing is experiencing a conceptual shift from client-server model to grid and peer-to-peer computing models. As
these trends, mobile internet and the grid, are likely to find each other the resource
constraints that Wireless devices pose today affect the level of interoperability between them[2,11].

Grid is the umbrella that covers many of today's distributed computing technologies. grid technology attempts to support flexible, secure, coordinated information
sharing among dynamic collections of individuals, institutions, and resources. This
includes data sharing but also access to computers, software and devices required by
computation and data-rich collaborative problem solving. So far the use of grid services has required a modern workstation, specialized software installed locally and

K. Bauknecht et al. (Eds.): EC-Web 2005, LNCS 3590, pp. 316–326, 2005.
© Springer-Verlag Berlin Heidelberg 2005

expert intervention. In the future these requirements should diminish considerably. One reason is the emergence of grid portals as gateways to the grid. Another reason is the 'web services' boom in the industry. The use of XML as a network protocol and an integration tool will ensure that future grid peer could be a simple wireless device[2,3].

Furthermore, open mobile grid service infrastructure will extend use of the grid technology or services up to business area using web services technology. Therefore differential resource access is a necessary operation for users to share their resources securely and willingly. Therefore, this paper describes a novel security approach on fast mobile grid services based on current mobile web services platform environment using XML signcryption mechanism.

2 The Performance Problem

XML-based messaging is at the heart of the current grid based on web services technology. XML's self-describing nature has significant advantages, but they come at the price of bandwidth and performance. XML-based messages are larger and require more processing than existing protocols such as RMI, RMI/IIOP or CORBA/IIOP: data is represented inefficiently, and binding requires more computation. For example, an RMI service can perform an order of magnitude faster than an equivalent web service-based grid. Use of HTTP as the transport for Web Services messages is not a significant factor when compared to the binding of XML to programmatic objects.

Increased bandwidth usage affects both wired and wireless networks. Often the latter, e.g. mobile telephone network, have bandwidth restrictions allotted for communication by a network device. In addition, larger messages increase the possibility of re-transmission since the smaller the message, the less likely it will be corrupted when in the air.

Increased processing requirements affects network devices communicating using both types of networks (wired and wireless). A server may not be able to handle the throughput the 'network' demands of it. Mobile phone battery life may be reduced as a device uses more memory, performs more processing and spends more time transmitting information. As the scale of Web Services usage increases, these problems are likely to be exacerbated.

Fast grid services attempts to solve these problems by defining binary-based messages that consume less bandwidth and are faster and require less memory to be processed. The price for this is loss of self-description. Fast grid service is not an attempt to replace XML-based messaging. It is designed to be an alternative that can be used when performance is an issue.

3 XML Signcryption

XML signcryption structure and schema has been proposed. Shown below is the XML signcryption XML document.

The root element XML signcryption is the fundamental element of the XML documents. Within the root element are contained various other elements such as signed info and the Signcryptionvalue, Rvalue and Svalue[6,7,10]. The SignedInfo element contains the information about the signcryption methodology used. It described about the implementation details about signcryption. Within the signed info element there are other elements such as Canonicalization Method Algorithm, Signature Method Algorithm, EncryptionMethod Algorithm and Reference URI. The CanonicalizationMethod indicates the method that is used for canonicalization. The canonical method allows the use of different characters in the XML document. For example, if there are white spaces in the xml document, these are removed because of the XML canonicalization method used.

```
<?xml version="1.0" encoding="UTF-8" ?>
< XML_Signcryption >
  <SignedInfo>
    <CanonicalizationMethod Algorithm />
      <SignatureMethod Algorithm />
      <EncryptionMethod Algorithm />
      <Reference URI>
        <DigestMethod1 Algorithm />
        <DigestMethod2 Algorithm />
        <DigestValue />
      </Reference URI>
  </SignedInfo>
  <SigncryptionValue></SigncryptionValue>
  <Rvalue></RValue>
  <Svalue></Svalue>
</ XML_Signcryption>
```

Fig. 1. Proposed XML Signcryption Schema

The signatureMethod element indicates the signature element used in the signcryption process. EncryptionMethod is the encryption method that is used in the signcryption process. In our example, the algorithm used is DES. The element Reference indicates the link of the file that is being signcrypted. It contains the path of the file that is being signcrypted. The reference URI also contains the different Hashing algorithms that are being used in the signcryption process. In our implementation, we are using MD5 and SHA1.

As indicated in sections above, the result of signcryption are three values, namely c, r and s. these three values are required by the system to create the plain text from these messages. When signcryption is performed on a data, the output is a signcryption value. Signcryption requires different digest functions. The description of the hash functions and also the different parameters required for encryption. The encryption method that is used for signcryption is also shown in the XML document. This information is also shown in the canonicalization method is used to embed a document in another document. Using Xpath filtering, an appropriate file is opened so that the file is opened using the application specified.

Signcryption technique has two different variations. These variations are Shortened Digital Signature Standard 1 [6,7] and Shortened Digital Signature Standard 2 [6,7,10]. Using JCE based crypto library, Signcryption will be programmed using verification to [6,7,9].

XML signcryption schema is shown above. The schema is required to validate the received XML message for its integrity. A part of the XML signcryption module is to create a technique where in badly formed XML documents need to be removed. Survey shows that a lot of attacks on XML servers are due to the fact that the XML documents created are not properly formed. The hardware-based solutions perform this additional task. The software-based module also needs to check the validity of the schema before the document is passed onto the next stages for verification.

```
<element name="XML_Signcryption" type="SigncryptionType"/>
  <complexType name="SigncryptionType">
   <sequence>
    <element ref="SignedInfo"/>
        <element ref="SignatuereMethod"/>
        <element ref="EncrptionMethod" />
        <element ref="Reference" minOccurs="0"/>
    </sequence>
        <attribute name="Id" type="ID" use="optional"/>
        <attribute name="MimeType" type="MIME" use="optional"/>
        <attribute name="Mode" type="MODE" use="required"/>
        <attribute name="Type" type="TYPE" use="required"/>
        <attribute name="Encoding" type="CODING" use="optional"/>
  </complexType>
</element>
```

Fig. 2. Signcryption Schema

The schema defines the various attributes and the elements that are required in a XML document. These attributes declare the feature of the XML document. The Id the element possesses and Multipurpose Internet Mail Extensions (MIME) so as to allow non-textual message to be passed can be incorporated into the XML document. The mode in which the signcryption has occurred, Type specifies a built-in data type.

The XML signcryption schema and is being used with Java Crypto Extensions and SAX parser to create a XML signcryption module. As the signcryption algorithm is faster compared to other signature algorithms, because of its reduced computation, the system is faster. This system introduces faster processing and also provides an additional feature of encryption along with the signature. Hence, the XML signcryption not only performs the integrity of the XML document, but also performs the confidentiality of the system. This additional facility is provided to the system with faster execution time.

The proposed XML signcryption test environment, as shown in figure 4, an XML document is parsed and schema is validated using SAX parser. After the XML document is validated, the information is passed to signcryption module. The signcryption components can verify/generate the signature for an XML document.

4   Security Architecture for Open Mobile Grid Middleware

Web services can be used to provide mobile security solutions by standardizing and integrating leading security solutions using XML messaging. XML messaging is referred to as the leading choice for a wireless communication protocol and there are security protocols for mobile applications based upon it. Among them are the follows. SAML is a protocol to transport authentication and authorization information in an XML message. It could be used to provide single sign on web services. XML signatures define how to digitally sign part or all of an XML document to guarantee data integrity. The public key distributed with XML signatures can be wrapped in XKMS (XML Key Management Specification) formats. XML encryption allows applications to encrypt part or all of an XML document using references to pre-agreed symmetric keys. The WS-Security, endorsed by IBM and Microsoft, is a complete solution to provide security to web services. It is based on XML signatures, XML encryption, and an authentication and authorization scheme similar to SAML (Security Assertions Markup Language). When a mobile device client requests access to a back-end application, it sends authentication information to the issuing authority. The issuing authority can then send a positive or negative authentication assertion depending upon the credentials presented by the mobile device client. While the user still has a session with the mobile applications, the issuing authority can use the earlier reference to send an authentication assertion stating that the user was, in fact, authenticated by a particular method at a specific time. As mentioned earlier, location-based authentication can be done at regular time intervals, which means that the issuing authority gives out location-based assertions periodically as long as the user credentials make for a positive authentication.

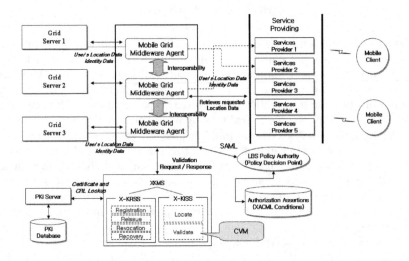

Fig. 3. Security Architecture for Open Mobile Grid Middleware

CVM (Certificate Validation Module) in XKMS system perform path validation on a certificate chain according to the local policy and with local PKI (Public Key Infrastructure) facilities, such as certificate revocation (CRLs) or through an OCSP (Online Certificates Status Protocol). In the CVM, a number of protocols (OCSP, SCVP, and LDAP) are used for the service of certificate validation. For processing the XML client request, certificate validation service from OCSP, LDAP (Lightweight Directory Access Protocol), SCVP (Simple Certificate Validation Protocol) protocols in XKMS based on PKI are used. The XKMS client generates an 'XKMS Validate' request. This is essentially asking the XKMS server to go and find out the status of the server's certificate. The XKMS server receives this request and performs a series of validation tasks e.g. X.509 certificate path validation. Certificate status is determined. XKMS server replies to client application with status of the server's certificate and application acts accordingly. Using the OCSP protocol, the CVM obtained certificate status information from other OCSP responders or other

tained certificate status information from other OCSP responders or other CVMs. Using the LDAP protocol, the CVM fetched CRL (Certificate Revocation List) from the repository. And CA (Certificate Authority) database connection protocol (CVMP;CVM Protocol) is used for the purpose of that the server obtains real-time certificate status information from Cas[3,4,5]. The client uses OCSP and SCVP. With XKMS, all of these functions are performed by the XKMS server component[8,10]. Thus, there is no need for LDAP, OCSP and other registration functionality in the client application itself.

5 Simulation and Results

Components of the grid security are XML security library, service components API, application program. Although message service component is intended to support XML applications, it can also be used in order environments where the same management and deployment benefits are achievable.

The figure for representing testbed system architecture of service component is as follows figure 4. We use testbed system of windows PC environment to simulate the processing of various service protocols. The protocols have been tested on pentium 3 and pentium 4 PCs. It has been tested on windows 2000 server, windows XP.

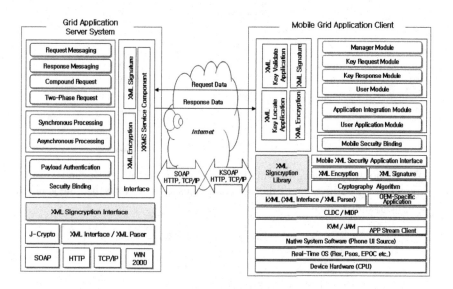

Fig. 4. XML Signcryption Component for Open Mobile Grid Services

Java 2, Micro Edition (J2ME) is a set of technologies and specifications developed for small devices like smart cards, pagers, mobile phones, and set-top boxes. J2ME uses subset of Java 2, Standard Edition (J2SE) components, like smaller virtual machines and leaner APIs. J2ME has categorized wireless devices and their capabilities into profiles: MIDP (Mobile Information Device Profile), PDA and personal. MIDP and PDA profiles are targeted for handhelds and personal profile for networked consumer electronic and embedded devices. As the technology progresses in quantum leaps any strict categorization is under threat to become obsolete. It is already seen that J2ME personal profile are being used in high-end PDAs such as pocketPCs and mobile communicators. We will concentrate on the most limited category of wireless J2ME devices that use MIDP. Applications that these devices understand are Midlets. Typically maximum size of a Midlet varies from 30-50kbs and user can download four to six applications to his mobile phone. Midlet is a JAR-archive conforming to the Midlet content specification[2].

The server is composed server service component of mobile grid platform package. And the message format is based on Specification of W3C (World Wide Web Consortium). XML signcryption based technique that has been under study. Signcryption is a technique that provides both confidentiality and integrity by performing both the techniques of encryption and signature at reduced costs.

As explained in section 3, the signcryption technique has been developed and tested against other signature systems. Table 1 below shows the time taken for the generating signcryption plotted against the number of iterations[12].

Table 1. Total time taken vs. number of iterations for both Signcryption and Unsigncryption

	Signcryption	Unsigncryption
Iterations	Ms	Ms
1	891	1672
10	1157	1906
100	3391	8125
200	6390	13890
300	8219	19109
400	10328	26078
500	12468	31437

Figure 5 shows the plotted information presented in the table 1. It can be seen that the time taken for verification of the signature takes a longer time than the generation of the signcryption value itself.

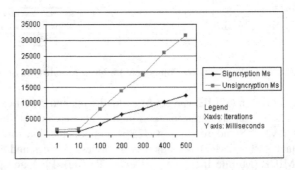

Fig. 5. Time taken plotted against number of iterations for Signcryption and Unsigncryption

Table 2 shows the time taken per iteration versus the number of iterations. Figure 6 shows in the information in a graphical form. It can be noticed that as the number of iterations increase the amount of time taken per iteration decreases significantly.

Table 2. Total time taken vs. Number of iterations for Signcryption and Unsigncryption

	Signcryption	Unsigncryption
Iterations	Ms/iteration	Ms/iteration
1	891	1672
10	115.7	190.6
100	33.91	81.25
200	31.95	69.45
300	27.40	63. 70
400	25.82	65.195
500	24.936	62.874

In the case of Unsigncryption the time taken per iteration is much more than the time taken for signcryption. The process provides both confidentiality and integrity at relatively lesser speed and lesser time as compared to other signature techniques.

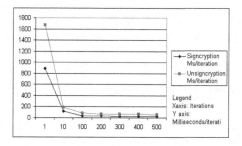

Fig. 6. Time taken plotted against number of iterations for Signcryption and Unsigncryption

5.1 Comparison Among the Signature Techniques

The different techniques discussed above has been tested and compared. The figure 7 shows the time taken per iteration for signature generation. It can be noticed that the time taken for signcryption decreases steadily as the number of iterations are increased. For one iteration, the time taken for signcryption is higher than other signature techniques. But as the number of iterations decrease, the performance of signcryption is comparable with the other techniques. But as the signcryption embodies both signature and encryption, signcryption would be recommended[12].

It can be noted that the best performance in signature verification is performed by SHA1 with DSA. Figure 8 shows the comparison between the time taken per iteration versus number of iterations for signature verification for the signature algorithms discussed. It can be seen that the time taken for Unsigncryption is high for single iteration than compared to others. But as the time increases, the time taken for iteration decreases but is higher than the other techniques.

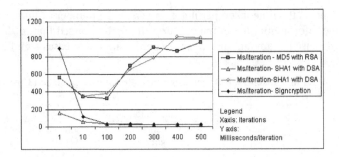

Fig. 7. Comparison between the algorithms for signature generation

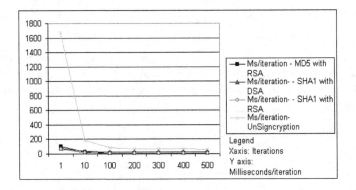

Fig. 8. Showing Comparison between the algorithms for signature verification

The time taken per iteration is not significantly lower in case of verification, but is significant in the case of signature generation except for signcryption. If the primary concern is integrity, then the ideal solution to use would be to use SHA1 with DSA. However if the concern is for both integrity and for confidentiality then signcryption would be an ideal solution to use. This can be demonstrated by figure 9.

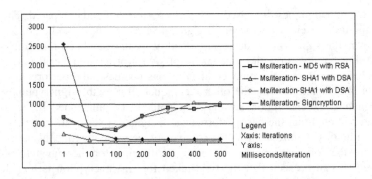

Fig. 9. Showing Comparison between the algorithms for both signature generation and verification

Figure 9 shows the time taken for single iteration of generation and verification plotted against the number of iterations. It can be seen from the graph that the time taken for SHA1 with DSA is the least. But it offers only integrity services. Signcryption offers both confidentiality and integrity and performs well when the numbers of iterations are used.

6 Conclusion

Mobile grid services are so attractive that they can cover all walks of life. However, current grid is growing slower than expected. Many problems like accuracy, privacy, security, customer requirement have to be addressed. It should be understood that there is no single universal solution to grid. Signcryption technique allows simultaneous processing of encryption-decryption and Signature. It has been proved that the use of signcryption decreases the processing time by 58%. Signcryption is being programmed using the field theory. Signcryption technique is very efficient as it uses only a single exponentiation for both encryption and signature.

We propose a novel security approach on fast mobile grid services based on current mobile web services platform environment using XML signcryption mechanism. Our approach can be a model for the future security system that offers security of open mobile grid security.

Acknowledgement

The first author would like to thank Yuliang Zheng, Ph.D. of the University of North Carolina at Charlotte for his encouragement and assistance.

References

1. Mika Tuisku: Wireless Java-enabled MIDP Devices as peers in Grid Infrastructure. Helsinki Institute of Physics. CERN
2. Ye Wen: Mobile Grid Major Area Examination. University of California (2002)
3. E. Faldella and M.Prandini: A Novel Approach to On-Line Status Authentication of Public Key Certificates, in Proc. the 16th Annual Computer Security Applications Conference (2000)
4. Yuichi Nakamur, et. Al.: Toward the Integration of web services security on enterprise environments. IEEE SAINT '02 (2002)
5. Diana Berbecaru, Antonio Lioy: Towards Simplifying PKI Implementation, Client-Server based Validation of Public Key Certificates. IEEE ISSPIT (2002) 277-281
6. Joonsang Baek, et. Al.: Formal Proofs for the security of signcryption, PKC'02 (2002) 80 - 98
7. Y. Zheng: Digital signcryption or How to Achieve Cost(Signature & Encryption) << Cost(Signature) + Cost(Encryption) , Advances in Cryptology -- Crypto'97. Lecture Notes in Computer Science, Vol. 1294. Springer-Verlag (1997) 165-179
8. Jang Hyun Baek, et. Al.: An Efficient Two-Step Paging Strategy Using Base Station Paging Agents in Mobile Communication Networks. ETRI Journal, Vol.26, No.5 (2004) 493-496

9. Proposed Fedral Information Proceeding standard for Digital Signature Standard(DSS), Fedral Register. Vol. 56. (1991)
10. F. Bao and H. Deng: A Signcryption scheme with signature directly verifiable by public key, proceeding of public key cryptography(PKC'98), LNCS Vol. 1431 (1998) 55-59
11. Eung Soon Shin, et. Al.: Determination of the Optimal Access Charge for the Mobile Virtual Network Operator System . ETRI Journal, Vol.26, No.6 (2004) 665-668
12. Yuliang Zheng, et. Al.: Research on Software-based XML Signature Acceleration. Project of ETRI, Vol. 1 (2004) 22-35

Reliably, Securely and Efficiently Distributing Electronic Content Using Multicasting

Indrajit Ray, Eunjong Kim, Ross McConnell, and Dan Massey

Computer Science Department,
Colorado State University,
Fort Collins, CO 80523, USA
{indrajit, kimeu, rmm, massey}@cs.colostate.edu

Abstract. Secure multicasting is one of the most efficient ways of delivering electronic content like streaming mutimedia to a group of users. One of the biggest challenges in secure multicasting is distributing group keys to the multicast group and managing the same. Although researchers have addressed the problem before, none of them address the fact that multicasting is an unreliable process. Thus there is no gurantee that the group key, distributed via multicasting, will be available in its correct form at the receiver. In this paper we propose a reliable and secure content distribution scheme that uses multicasting. The scheme uses an asymmetric multicast group key that is generated using parameters publicly available to all members of the group. The group key is used to encrypt a session key which is then distributed piggybacked on the multicast stream. The encrypted session key is dispersed over the stream in such a manner that receipt of a finite number of fragments of the session key ensures that the session key can be correctly recreated at the receiving end.

1 Introduction

Recently more and more opportunities are becoming available to end users for obtaining goods and services online. Examples of such services include real-time media streams like MP3 music and digital movies. These goods and services are delivered electronically to the consumer over the Internet. A number of these online services are based on paid subscription that imposes certain restrictions on the delivery of the objects – namely (1) consumers who have subscribed to an object should be able to access it, (2) no one other than the subscriber should have access to the object, and (3) the access should be allowed only during the period of validity for the subscription. These objectives can be met with a simple solution: encrypt the data object with a key (either the receiver's public key or a secret key shared between the service provider and the receiver) and transmit the encrypted data. However, if many consumers subscribe to an object then this simple solution becomes ineffcient in terms of computation overhead and bandwidth utilization. Reliable and efficient key distribution and management also pose additional serious challenges.

To overcome these problems researchers have proposed multicasting the object in an encrypted manner and provide an access control mechanism based on cryptographic techniques by which only legitimate subscribers are able to access the content. Since

K. Bauknecht et al. (Eds.): EC-Web 2005, LNCS 3590, pp. 327–336, 2005.

multicasting involves only a single data stream it considerably reduces the problems of computation overhead and bandwidth utilization. This, in turn, has led most researchers to model the problem of securely distributing content as the problem of distributing and managing the keys used in the encryption process. However, none of these works address the fact that multicasting is an inherently unreliable process. They assume that the recipient of a multicast stream will somehow receive the appropriate key(s) correctly. The reason multicasting is acceptable for certain types of transmission nothwithstanding its unrealiable nature, is that for these type of streams (real time audio or video data) some degradation of quality is tolerable but retransmission to rectify the corrupted data is not. Note, however, that no error in transmission is acceptable for keys. If the key is not delivered reliably no portion of the encrypted content will be availble at the receiver. Making multicasting reliable is extremely difficult; currently no practical solution exists. Thus many of these works cannot be implemented efficiently in practice.

In this work we propose a reliable and secure content distribution scheme that is also efficient. The security threat model that we assume in this work is passive eavesdropping and active cryptanalysis. We assume that during multicasting at least some of the packets in the multicast stream will reach the destination in a correct manner and that the error rate is known a-priori. We believe this is a reasonable assumption to make. Such information is often used to determine the quality of service of the network.

The protocol can be divided into two parts. In the first part, paid subscribers of some content generate individual public key / private key pairs and send the public key to the content provider. The public keys are used to generate a group key. The group key technique is based partially on earlier work done by one of the authors (see [3]). A novel property of this group key is that a message encrypted with the group key can be decrypted by any one of the private keys belonging to the subscribers. Thus the group key is never needed to be distributed to the members of the group. In addition, knowledge of the group key does not provide any knowledge about the decryption keys. Changing the group key when group membership changes is simple and efficient. The key change does not need to be propagated to the group members. Thus no change in group membership is visible to the remaining members of the group.

The group key is used in the second part of the scheme to encrypt a session key. The session key is the one that encrypts the content. The encrypted session key is piggybacked over the multicast stream and delivered to the receiver. During piggybacking the encrypted session key is fragmented into pieces and the pieces dispersed uniformly over the stream. The dispersal is done based on Rabin's information dispersal algorithm (IDA) [2]. It ensures that if at least a finite number of fragments of the encrypted session key is available at the receiver, the entire session key can be recovered. We do not need to ensure reliable transmission any more.

The rest of the paper is organized as follows. Section 2 describes our scheme. It begins by establishing the theory on which our group key protocol is based. This is described in Section 2.1. Section 2.3 gives the algorithms for subscriber addition to and deletion from the multicast groups. Section 3 discusses how content is encrypted with the session key which, in turn, is encrypted with the group and dispersed over the encrypted content for distribution. Section 4 concludes the paper.

2   Protocol Description

The proposed secure content distribution system is built around two main protocols. The first is a group key establishment protocol. This protocol generates a group key for secure communication among the members. The protocol is executed as part of the customer subscription process. The second protocol is the content encryption and distribution protocol. In this protocol the content is encrypted with a session key. The session key is encrypted with the group key and distributed to the members piggybacked with the content. The distribution of the session key is such that if a member receives at least some predetermined portions of the encrypted session key, the member is able to regenerate the session key.

   One of the biggest challenges for secure group communication is efficient group re-keying for dynamically mutating groups. Our group key protocol is designed to make re-keying simple and efficient. The group key protocol is based on an extension of RSA keys that we had developed earlier [3]. We briefly discuss the key elements of the theory here. The interested reader is directed to our earlier work [3] for details, in particular the proofs of the various theorems.

2.1   Theory for Group Keys

Definition 1. *The set of messages $\mathcal{M}$ is the set of non negative integers m that are less than an upper bound N, i.e. $\mathcal{M} = \{m | 0 \le m < N\}$*

Definition 2. *A key K is defined to be the ordered pair $< e, N >$, where N is a product of distinct primes, $N \ge M$ and e is relatively prime to $\phi(N)$; e is the* exponent *and N is the* base *of the key K.*

Definition 3. *The* inverse *of a key $K = < e, N >$, denoted by K^{-1}, is an ordered pair $< d, N >$, satisfying $ed \equiv 1 \mod \phi(N)$.*

Definition 4. *The* encryption *of a message* m *with the key $K = < e, N >$, denoted as $[m, K]$, is defined as $[m, < e, N >] = m^e \mod N$*

Theorem 1. *For any message m.*

$$\left[[m, K], K^{-1} \right] = \left[[m, K^{-1}], K \right] = m \tag{1}$$

where $K = < e, N >$ and $K^{-1} = < d, N >$.

Definition 5. *Two keys $K_1 = < e_1, N_1 >$ and $K_2 = < e_2, N_2 >$ are said to be* compatible *if $e_1 = e_2$ and N_1 and N_2 are relatively prime.*

Definition 6. *If two keys $K_1 = < e, N_1 >$ and $K_2 = < e, N_2 >$ are compatible, then the* product key, $K_1 \times K_2$, *is defined as $< e, N_1 N_2 >$.*

Lemma 1. *For positive integers a, N_1 and N_2, $(a \mod N_1 N_2) \equiv a \mod N_1$*

Theorem 2. *For any two messages m and $\hat{m}$, such that $m, \hat{m} < N_1, N_2$,*

$$[m, K_1 \times K_2] \equiv [\hat{m}, K_1] \mod N_1 \ \ if \ and \ only \ if \ \ m = \hat{m} \tag{2}$$

$$[m, K_1 \times K_2] \equiv [\hat{m}, K_2] \mod N_2 \ \ if \ and \ only \ if \ \ m = \hat{m} \tag{3}$$

where K_1 is the key $< e, N_1 >$, K_2 is the key $< e, N_2 >$ and $K_1 \times K_2$ is the product key $< e, N_1 N_2 >$.

Definition 7. *The group key K_g for a group of k members $p_1, \ldots, p_k$, with a member p_i having the public key / private key pair $K_i = < e, N_i > / K_i^{-1} = < d_i, N_i >$, is defined to be the product key $K_1 \times K_2 \times \ldots \times K_k$.*

Corollary 1. *A message $m < N_1 \times N_2 \ldots N_k$ encrypted with a group key $K_g = K_1 \times K_2 \times K_k$ can be decrypted with any one of the private keys K_i^{-1}.*

Proof: The proof follows directly from Lemma 1 and Theorem 2.

2.2   Security and Efficient Implementation Issues

The group key system is as secure as the RSA cryptosystem. The most damaging attack on this scheme would be for an attacker to discover the private key K_i^{-1} corresponding to the key K_i involved in the group key K_g. This will enable the attacker to decrypt all messages encrypted with the group key. The obvious way to do this is to factor the modulus N_i of K_i into its two prime factors. This is a well known hard problem.

Another way to break the group key encryption is to find a technique to compute e^{th} roots $\mod N$. Since the encrypted message is $c = m^e \mod N_1 \times N_2 \times \ldots \times N_k$ and $N = N_1 \times N_2 \times \ldots N_k$ is publicly known, the eth root of $c \mod N_1 \times N_2 \times \ldots \times N_k$ is the message m. This attacks is not known to be equivalent to factoring. However, as pointed out in the discussion related to the security of the RSA scheme in RSA Laboratories' Crypto FAQ [4], there are currently no known technique of doing this.

Care must be taken in choosing the exponent e though. If the exponent e is small and $m^e < N_1 \times N_2 \times \ldots \times N_k$ then $c = m^e \mod N_1 \times N_2 \times \ldots \times N_k = m^e$. Then by simply extracting the eth root of c an attacker can obtain the message m. Choosing large e's makes the encryption process computationally intensive. On ther other hand, choosing an appropriate algorithm for the computation, alleviates the problem considerably. For example, the best time bound for multiplying two n-bit integers is $O(n \log n \log \log n)$ [1]. Finding $m^e \mod p$ where p is an n-bit integer is, thus, $O(\log e \ n \log n \log \log n)$. As will be apparent in the following discussion, encryption using the group key will be done in an off-line manner. Thus, we believe, this computational overhead is within acceptable limits.

2.3   Member Addition and Deletion

We assume that content is distributed in discrete time intervals. We term each such time interval as the *content distribution period*. An end user knows a-priori the beginning and end of the relevant content distribution period in which it is expecting some content. The content is multicast over a pre-advertised multicast channel for the duration of the content distribution period. The end-user listens on this multicast channel for the relevant content.

The subscription based service is provided by the cooperation of two sets of the parties – the **service providers** and the **subscription managers**.

Service Providers. A set M of m entities provide the content to the end users. Each $M_i \in M$ is the source of an object the end user subscribes to. For simplicity we assume that each M_i distributes only one content at a given distribution period. This is not a limitation. Our scheme can be easily modified to accomodate an M_i distributing multiple objects at any given period.

Each M_i lists a set S_i of subscription managers who are responsible for managing the subscription process on behalf of the service provider. Sometime before the beginning of a content distribution period, over a period called the *subscription review period*, a service provider gets lists of subscribers from one or more subscription managers in S_i together with the partial group keys for each list. M_i uses these partial group key to generate the group key for its subscription group.

Subscription Managers. Corresponding to each service provider M_i there is a set S_i of subscription managers. A subscription manager can cater to more than one content provider. Each subscription manager $S_{i,j} \in S_i$ is responsible for managing a subscription zone for the service provider M_i. A subscriber C_k needs to identify the subscription zone closest to itself and subscribe with the subscription manager associated with that zone to access the contents provided by M_i. $S_{i,j}$ is responsible for adding and/or removing subscribers from subscription group and managing the subscriber's accounts. The time interval between two consecutive subscription review periods is when $S_{i,j}$ performs the subscriber addition and/or deletion operations. We call this interval the *subscribing period*. At the beginning of a subscription review period the subscription manager freezes the subsciption process. Any new addition or deletion is effective the next subscribing period.

Figure 1 shows a subscription scenario. Service provider M_1 uses subscription managers $S_1, S_2,$ and S_7; M_2 uses $S_2, S_3, S_4,$ and S_6; M_3 uses $S_4, S_5,$ and S_6. Subscriber C_1 subscribes to M_1 through S_1 and to M_3 through S_4. C_2 subscribes to M_1 via S_2 and to M_2 via S_4. C_6 subscribes to M_2 via S_2, to M_3 via S_6 and to M_1 via S_7. Finally C_9 subscribes to M_2 via S_6.

A *subscription* for a customer is defined by *subscription-content identifier* and a *start-time* and *end-time*. A content provider defines a *subscription subgroup* to be the set of all subscribers that have the same subscription. A subscription subgroup is *active* between the start-time and end-time. Subscription subgroups are managed by subscription managers. A *multicast group* is a collection of one or more subscription subgroups that are current and that identify the same subscription content. Multicast groups are managed by the service provider.

A subscription manager can add a subscriber to an existing subscription subgroup provided the subgroup is not currently active. A subscriber can leave a subscription at

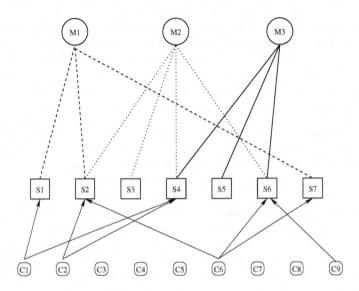

Fig. 1. Relationship between the different entities in the protocol

any point before and till the end-time. At times a subscriber maybe forced to leave a subscription subgroup (for example, if the subscriber fails to adhere to the terms and conditions of the subscription). Algorithm 1. gives the protocol for addition of a member to a subscription subgroup. We use the notation "$X \Rightarrow Y$: M" to describe the event entity X sending a message M to another entity Y.

A major advantage of this protocol is that it does not require any secret channel between the subscriber and the subscription manager for the distribution of the key. Even if the modulus N_i supplied by the subscriber is known to a third party no message that is encrypted with $< e, N_{Skey} >$ (or with a key based on the same modulus e and containing N_{Skey} as a factor) can be decrypted without knowing the decryption key $< d_i, N_i >$. Generating d_i from knowledge of e and N_i or generating a d such that $e.d \equiv 1 \bmod N_{Skey}$ from knowledge of e and N_{Skey} is equivalent to the factoring problem, which is considered a hard problem.

The next algorithm, Algorithm 2., provides the protocol for removing subscribers from subscription groups. There are two sub-protocols – one for removing subscribers when they voluntarily terminate their subscriptions and the other for force removing of subscribers when they fail to adhere to the terms of their subscriptions.

One major advantage of our group key scheme over some other existing group key schemes is that a member revocation operation is transparent to other members of the group. There is no need to redistribute a new group key to other members. They can continue using their original private keys $< d_i, N_i >$ to decrypt subsequent messages. The subscriber who is removed from the group can no-longer use its private key. In fact, a set of subscribers who have been removed from the group cannot collude in any manner to generate decryption keys for future encrypted multicasts. Generating such keys through collusion can be shown to be as hard as breaking RSA cryptography. For lack of space we omit these details here.

Algorithm 1. Add member to subscription subgroup

{We assume that a new subscriber chooses one and only subscription manager to register for the service from a particular service provider. Each service provider M_i defines a unique exponent e for its multicast group key. The exponent is known to all subscription managers for this service provider and is provided to a subscriber as and when required. We also assume the availability of prime number generators with each subscriber that generates large prime numbers at random.

C is the subscriber, S is the subscription manager. CID is the content identifier and *Start* and *End* are the start and end dates for the subscription. N_{Skey} is the modulus for the subscription subgroup key, Skey.}

1. $C \Rightarrow S$: Signup C in CID for $Start, End$
2. If no subscription subgroup corresponding to Skey is currently active then
   $S \Rightarrow C$: Request a public key using exponent e
   else
   $S \Rightarrow C$: Failure to register error message
   (a) C generates key pair $< e, N_i > / < d_i, N_i >$
   (b) C keeps $< d_i, N_i >$ secret; this key will be used for decrypting multicast messages
   (c) $C \Rightarrow S$: $< e, N_i >$
3. If no subscription subgroup exists corresponding to Skey then S performs the following steps:
   (a) $N_{Skey} \leftarrow N_i$
   (b) Skey $\leftarrow < e, N_{Skey} >$
   (c) S creates a database corresponding to Skey and stores a record in it with C's information
4. If no entry corresponding to C exists in the database corresponding to C, then
   (a) S records C's information in the database corresponding to Skey.
   (b) $N_{Skey} \leftarrow N_{Skey} \times N_i$
   (c) SKey $\leftarrow < e, N_{Skey} >$
5. $S \Rightarrow C$: subscription identifier $=$ sid; subscription successful

2.4 Generating Multicast Group Key

During each subscription review period a service provider collects all subscription subgroup keys from the designated subscription managers. (The service provider needs to collect only the modulii corresponding to each subscription subgroup key). There is no need to establish any secure communication channels between the subscription managers. Even if these modulii are known to others messages encrypted with the group key cannot be decrypted without knowing at least one of the private keys of the subscribers. Even the subscription managers cannot decrypt the multicast message. However, the integrity of the subscription subgroup keys need to be ensured. The multicast group key is generated as in algorithm 3..

Note that the service provider utilizes a pull model to gather the subscription subgroup keys; alternately we may follow a push model in which a subscription managers send a subgroup key if and only if the group has changed since last time. This model has the advantage of saving on bandwidth. Computationally, this will not make a major difference at the service provider.

Algorithm 2. Remove subscriber from subscription subgroup

{*C* is the subscriber who is being removed from the subscription group. *S* is the relevant subscription manager. *CID* is the content identifier. A subscriber can be removed for one of two reasons – (a) the subscriber voluntarily cancels its subscription or, (b) the subscriber does not adhere to the terms of the subscription and is forcefully removed. The removal process is the same for both case and involves changing the subscription subgroup key's modulus to exclude *C*'s factor.}

{*Voluntary Termination of Subscription*}

1. $C \Rightarrow S$: Terminate subscription for *C* in CID for subscription identifier sid
2. If subscription for *C* has not yet expired
   (a) Locate *C*'s record in the database
   (b) $N_{Skey} \leftarrow N_{Skey}/N_i$
   (c) Mark *C*'s record as terminated
3. $S \Rightarrow C$: subscription termination successful

{*Forced Termination of Subscription*}

1. Locate *C*'s record in the database
2. $N_{Skey} \leftarrow N_{Skey}/N_i$
3. Mark *C*'s record as terminated
4. $S \Rightarrow C$: subscription terminated; reason for termination

---

3   Content Encryption and Distribution

To distribute content in a secure manner a service provider performs the following steps. It first fragments the content into fixed sized packets suitable for transmission. Next it generates a session key and encrypts each fragment of the content with this key. The service provider then encrypts the session key with the group key generated earlier and disperses the encrypted session over the fragments of the encrypted content using IDA [2]. It then multicasts the encrypted content to a previously announced multicast group address. The intended receiver tunes in to the multicast message to retrieve the content. The encrypted session key dispersal process is described in more detail in the following. We assume the computations are done in $GF(2^8)$.

1. The service provider generates a new session key Q_s. This key is to be used to encrypt the content prior to transmission. The size of this session key is smaller in size than the group key $K_g = < e, N_1 \times N_2 \times \ldots \times N_k >$ generated earlier (see section 2.4).
2. The service provider breaks up the content *M* that is to be multicasted into a number of fixed size packets. The size of each packet needs to be smaller than the MTU of the multicast network. Let the packets be $m_1, m_2, \ldots, m_{\frac{N}{m}}$ (that is $M = m_1 \| m_2 \| \ldots \| m_{\frac{N}{m}}$). Each m_i is encrypted with the key Q_s to generate the encrypted packet p_i; that is, $p_i = E[m_i, Q_s]$.

Algorithm 3. Generate multicast group key

$\{M$ is the service provider, S_i's are the designated subscription managers, N_{Skey_i} is the sub-scription subgroup key modulus for S_i. This process is carried out during q subscription review period. K_g is the multicast group key generated by $M.\}$

1. M accumulates all N_{Skey_i}'s.
2. If no N_{Skey_i} has changed since last time, no need to change K_g; exit
3. $N_g \leftarrow N_{Skey_1} \times N_{Skey_2} \times \ldots N_{Skey_n}$
4. $K_g =< e, N_g >$

---

3. The session key Q_s is encrypted with the group key K_g to produce the encrypted session key Q'_s. That is $Q'_s = Q_s^e \bmod N_1 \times N_2 \times \ldots \times N_k$. Note that since Q_s is smaller in size than K_g, Q'_s will be the same size as Q_s.
4. The encrypted session key Q'_s is divided into N/m blocks such that each block is of length m. The value of m is chosen in a manner such that the encrypted key can be reconstructed from any m of N/m portions but not from some $m-1$ or lesser number of portions, with N/m being the number of packets for the encrypted message. Let $S_i = (b_{(i-1)m+1}, \ldots, b_{im})$, where $1 \leq i \leq N/m$, represent the ith block of the encrypted session key. In this manner the encrypted session key can be viewed as a $N/m \times m$ matrix $\bar{S}$.
5. Choose a set $\bar{A}$ of n vectors; that is $\bar{A} = a_1, a_2, \ldots, a_n$ such that $a_i = (a_{i1}, \ldots, a_{im}), 1 \leq i \leq n$. The vectors are chosen such that every subset of m different vectors are linearly independent.
6. Using the set of n vectors $\bar{A}$ the encrypted session key matrix $\bar{S}$ is transformed into a new matrix $\bar{S}'$ as follows: $\bar{S}' = \bar{A} \odot \bar{S}$, where $\odot$ represent the cross product of the two matrices. The resulting matrix $\bar{S}'$ is an $N/m \times n$ matrix. Each row of $\bar{S}'$ represents a portion of the fragemented encrypted session key that will be appended to each packet of the encrypted message before transmission.

It can be shown quite easily that if at least m packets of the multicast stream are received without errors, then the receiver can reconstruct the encrypted session key. For lack of space we omit the details here. The interested reader is referred to Rabin's work in information dispersal [2]. The parameter m will be chosen based on an estimation of the error rate of the communication channel. The parameter N/m will be chosen depending on the bandwidth of the communication media and the maximum transmission unit allowed and optionally on the buffering capabilities at the receiver (if real-time data is being transmitted).

4   Conclusion

In this work we present a new protocol for distributing electronic content to a group of subscribers in a reliable, efficient and secure manner. At the heart of the protocol is a novel group key scheme. The scheme is based on asymmetric key cryptographic techniques. The scheme generates a new group key everytime the group changes. The group key is used only for encryption purposes and not for decryption. Decryption is performed individually by each group member by using its private key, independent of other members. Thus a basic difference with the major group key schemes is that even if the group key changes the new group key does not have to be re-distributed to the group. The remaining members of the group are not aware of changes in the group. This forms a major advantage of our scheme both in terms of reduced communication overhead and added security. Additionally, our group key scheme is as secure as the RSA cryptographic technique.

Generating the group key is computation intensive. We discuss techniques that can be used to speed up the key generation process. However, encryption using this group key is also computationally more time consuming than symmetric key technology. To alleviate this problem we choose to use a secret session key that is encrypted with the group key and distributed to all members of the group. We argue that distributing the session key in a reliable manner is a very important task that is often overlooked by the research community. This is considerably difficult when an unreliable communication medium like a multicast channel is used. We solve this problem by dispersing the encrypted session key over the packetized multicast message in such a manner that if m out of N fragments of the fragmented session key is received correctly by a member of the group, it can recreate the session key.

At this stage the protocol is in the early stages of development. We plan to undertake real life modeling and simulation studies to determine factors like how often group keys need to be changed, what are the typical sizes of the groups, and what are some good parameters for dispersing the session keys. Our group is also working towards a prototype which we plan to make freely available to the community.

Acknowledgment

The work of Indrajit Ray has been partially supported by the National Science Foundation of the USA under grant IIS-0242258. Any opinion, findings and conclusions or recommendations expressed in this publication are those of the authors and do not necessarily reflect the view of the NSF.

References

1. T.H. Cormen et al. *Introduction to Algorithms*. McGraw Hill, 2nd edition edition, 2001.
2. M. Rabin. Efficient dispersal of information for security, load balancing and fault tolerance. *Journal of the ACM*, 36(2):335–348, April 1989.
3. I. Ray and I. Ray. Anonymous and Secure Multicast Subscription. In E. Gudes and S. Shenoi, editors, *Research Directions in Data and Applications Security, Proceedings of the 16th IFIP TC-11, WG 11.3 Working Conference on Data and Applications Security*, pages 313–327. Kluwer Academic Publishers, 2003.
4. RSA Laboratories, http://www.rsasecurity.com/rsalabs/. *RSA Laboratories' Frequently Asked Questions About Today's Cryptography, Version 4.1*, 2004. Last accessed on December 10, 2004.

MiddLog: A Web Service Approach for Application Logging

Marcelo Pitanga Alves, Paulo F. Pires, Flávia C. Delicato,
and Maria Luiza M. Campos

Departamento de Ciência da Computação, Núcleo de Computação Eletrônica,
Federal University of Rio de Janeiro, P.O. BOX 2324, Rio de Janeiro – RJ – Brasil
mpitanga@domain.com.br
{paulopires, fdelicato, mluiza}@nce.ufrj.br

Abstract. MiddLog is an extensible and configurable logging framework based on middleware technologies that exposes its services as web services, allowing its users to send log information as SOAP messages. It includes a set of components that are deployed on an application server, performing analysis and recordings of application events at a log file, in a dynamic and transparent way. MiddLog extension capability enables developers to augment its services by aggregating new features or creating new components and inserting them into its infrastructure.

1 Introduction

Over the years log has been an important tool for IT professionals to accomplish the task of depurating and documenting several versions of computer systems and monitoring the system life cycle. Both the technological progress and the growing complexity of applications increase application designer concerns about application systems efficiency issues. Therefore, log becomes an important mechanism for capturing application events and details of its behavior.

The implementation of logging mechanisms constitutes a complex task. Logging is usually performed in a proprietary manner and strongly coupled to the application. Statements to create and manage the log are often directly included into the application source code, increasing development time and the complexity of the generated code. Another problem is the lack of standards for the content and the format of the generated log file, which makes its use by log analysis tools very difficult.

Some works have been conducted aiming to facilitate management and standardization of application logging mechanisms. These works propose a development framework [6,7,16] to unburden application developers from the responsibility of developing the complex logging mechanism, allowing them to worry about the business logic of their applications. A logging framework offers a set of classes that the developer can include into the application source code and a set of configuration files that support the generation of log files. Since the logging framework does not act as an external service layer to the application, as it happens, for example, with the transaction control service in application servers [9,15], it

K. Bauknecht et al. (Eds.): EC-Web 2005, LNCS 3590, pp. 337–347, 2005.

requires changes in the source code and recompilation of the application whenever the developer includes or removes log statements from its application code.

This work presents the architecture and the implementation of MiddLog, an extensible and dynamically configurable framework for logging services. MiddLog is a layered framework, which meets the current needs of application developers through a transparent logging mechanism, executing independently from the monitored application and allowing the configuration of log generation in a dynamic way. MiddLog meets such needs through the implementation of the following features: monitoring and transparent capturing of the application information; log data formatting through the use of a canonic data model; removal of log statements from the application code; definition of log statements through configuration files; and minimization of the impact of logging in the applications performance. These features are implemented in MiddLog by using middleware [10,12], Aspect–Oriented Programming (AOP) [2,13] and Web service [18] technologies. In Middlog, logging is offered as a middleware service implemented orthogonally to the application and exposed as a Web service. MiddLog uses interceptors to monitor the application and to capture information about its execution context. Following an AOP approach, it is possible to eliminate logging statements from the application code. In this context, MiddLog infrastructure differs from current logging frameworks [6,7,16], which treats logging as part of the application logics.

This paper has five sections. In Section 2, related works are presented. Section 3 discusses the MiddLog general architecture. In Section 4, a scenario is presented, exploring the infrastructure general operation. Finally, Section 5 concludes this work.

2   Related Work

MiddLog explores features from three research areas: logging frameworks, AOP and Web services. Several works have been proposed in these areas aiming to facilitate the inclusion of a logging process in applications.

Logging Frameworks [6,7,16] provide support to the creation of a logging mechanism for applications through a set of classes that offer basic operations to instantiate, configure, format outputs and send messages to the logging mechanism. However, these frameworks do not offer resources for automatic capturing the application information, leaving this responsibility to the application developer.

AOP [2,13] proposes techniques which allow the inspection of each accessed object, method or field of an application. There are several contributions which provide suitable support to implement aspects with minimum effort. For example, in [11], the author shows how to use AOP techniques for the creation of an aspect, called *interceptor*, which uses a logging framework to record all the execution phases of an application. This is a highly used solution to facilitate information capturing but it leaves formatting of captured data and their dispatching to logging framework in charge of the application developer.

In Web services, few works have been conducted on logging facilities. In [4], the author contemplates the use of intermediaries to provide information about authentication, auditing and management of services through the use of logs, although he does not provide any detail on the log infrastructure. In [1], the authors propose a logging framework also based on intermediaries. In both works, the authors present frameworks for monitoring Web services but their implementations are not focused on middleware services and furthermore they do not expose logging mechanisms as Web services.

3 MiddLog Service Framework

MiddLog architecture (Fig. 1) is composed of several services, organized in 3 basic layers: Integration, Interception and Message Processing layers. The services are implemented as middleware components (Fig. 2), which can be integrated in an application server, facilitating their use by client applications.

The Integration layer is responsible for offering MiddLog basic services to the other layers, providing a higher degree of abstraction and extensibility, since new interception services can be created and incorporated to MiddLog architecture.

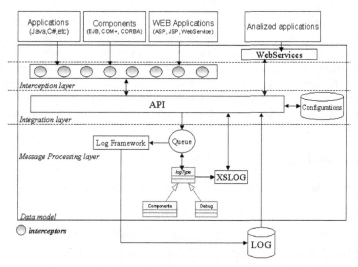

Fig. 1. Architecture layers

The Interception layer comprises components responsible for capturing information on running applications and for sending such information to the Message Processing layer. These components are implemented using AOP advices, which are software modules that are executed when a given application event is started. In MiddLog, advices are implemented through interceptor components [2,8,13]. Interceptors are associated with the application to be monitored through a configuration file, which is managed by the Integration layer. This configuration file contains classes and methods for monitoring. The application information captured by the interceptor are organized according to the data model specified in the proposed framework, generating a message in plain text format or an object which is sent to MiddLog queue in the Message Processing layer.

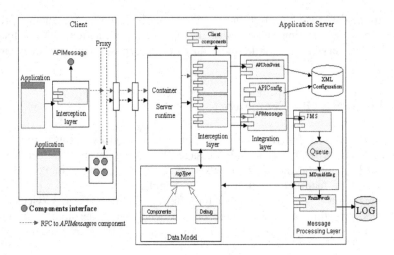

Fig. 2. System architecture

The Message Processing layer is responsible for managing the queue of log messages, generated by the interceptors. When a message is inserted in the queue, a component starts running and removes this message from the queue, extracting and forwarding the data to the log framework, which is the mechanism responsible for physical registering this information in a storage device previously configured. Fig. 2 shows the interaction among these layers, which will be described in detail on the next sections.

3.1 Integration Layer

The Integration layer offers two kinds of services: *Message* service and *Configuration* service.

Message service. The Message service is responsible for offering the interfaces needed so that the interceptor can send data captured from applications to the MiddLog message queue. The message service is implemented by the *APIMessage* component. The function of the APIMessage component is to encapsulate the access to the application server message service, implemented through a high level interface, which is used by interceptor components or directly by client applications, to send captured information to the MiddLog message queue. Fig. 2 shows the APIMessage component invoking the JMS (Java Message Service) component [14], in order to send a message.

Configuration service. The Configuration service offers interfaces needed for accessing the configuration file. It is a runtime service, which allows the developer to include or eliminate applications, classes and methods to be monitored whenever it wants, by simply removing the applications settings from the configuration file. The Configuration service is implemented by the components APIJoinPoint and APIConfig. The APIJoinPoint component is responsible for offering the required service so that interceptors can access the configuration file, which contains applications to be monitored. This configuration file is the connection between the application to be monitored and the interceptors. Interceptors use this service to load the configuration file for the purpose of identifying which classes and methods of an application should be monitored. The APIConfig component is responsible for providing the application developer with the services needed so that he/she can include his/her application to be monitored by MiddLog.

3.2 Interception Layer

The Interception layer, together with the configuration services, is responsible for eliminating the need of including statements inside the application. The application can execute both on the client side and on the server side. Considering the logging process as an aspect [2] enables the use of the AOP technique as the basis for implementing the Interception layer.

The AOP approach treats the application in terms of its *joinpoints*[2], which are points in the application execution where a given aspect can be applied. Thus, it is possible to follow the execution flow of an application when it passes from a method to another. The original application code remains unchanged and the activation/deactivation of the logging process depends on the inclusion/exclusion of the aspect on an application.

Aspects are created through AOP instances of the class *advices*[2]. The *advices* are implemented into MiddLog through *interceptors*, per application type (eg. Web service, EJB, etc.), which contain the logging code, that can be orthogonally applied to the application and a specification that identifies in which joinpoints the aspects are applied. The joinpoints are defined through a configuration file managed by the integration layer, as presented in section 3.1.2.

Interceptor on the server side. Interception on the server side aims to monitor the applications (Web services, Servlets, etc.) that the developer deploys in the application server. The interceptor is implemented as a middleware component and it is "plugged" in the architecture of the application server, acting as one more service in the runtime environment. In other words, it extends the application server container with functions for capturing information about running applications. The interceptor for Web services builds on two major mechanisms: SOAP message handler for XML-based Remote Procedure Calls and XML Messaging for XML-based documents [14].

A SOAP message handler is a component that can be associated with an entire Web service or with a particular Web service interface during deployment. A handler intercepts both request and response SOAP messages of Web services. It receives the request message before invoking the service implementation as well as it processes the response message before it is returned to the client. During the request, a handler verifies which *joinpoints* must be treated and applied to the service.

XML Messaging [3,14] provides a mechanism that allows the transfer of complete business-level documents between two separate Web services on an asynchronous way. This mechanism is implemented as a component that consumes SOAP messages sent by a client application. This component intercepts the SOAP message in both the request and response of the Web services. It is deployed and connected to a service provider, previously installed on an application server. This provider receives the SOAP messages request and redirects it to the Web services. Thus, the interceptor assigned to the provider intercepts the request and verifies which *joinpoint* should be treated and applied to the service.

Interception delay and Joinpoint verification. Although MiddLog uses a queue to dispatch collected data to the Processing layer, it should not insert delays in the component execution on the application server during the interception process.

The solution for this problem is to adopt asynchronous communication in the process of capturing and sending the data collected by the interceptor. The capture process is accomplished through an internal queue in the interceptor, which is controlled by a *thread*. For example, when a SOAP message is intercepted, data are extracted and formatted in this context, according to the adopted data model. The formatted data are added to the interceptor internal queue, releasing the client component to continue the normal flow of processing. Whenever the thread is executed, a copy of this queue is ready for processing so that the queue becomes empty again and can receive new messages. Simultaneously, the thread removes each message of this copy for *joinponts* verification and sends these messages to the MiddLog queue.

Interceptors on the client side. Client side interceptors aim to monitor applications running on client stations. Their goal is to help the application developer to perform his/her application monitoring, even if the application is not running on an application server. The big hindrance in client side environments is their execution context. Differently from application server execution environments, which offer resources for interception as part of their own architecture, on the client side the application is directly executed by the operational system (for applications written for example in C/C++) or by a virtual machine (for languages such as Java - JVM- and .net-CLR).

In this context, the adoption of AOP technique is again an important element in the proposed framework. Relevant works [17] have been conducted in this area, like *AspectJ, AspectC#, JBossAOP Framework, AspectWerkz* and others, which facilitate building interceptions to be applied in client applications. In these environments, in opposition to the server side environments, the client application goes through a pre-compilation process where its binary code (*byte-codes*) is manipulated to be linked to the aspects, according to the aspect definitions included by the developer in the describer file.

public interface Interceptor	```<?xml version="1.0" encoding="UTF-8"?>```

public interface Interceptor
{
    public String getName();
    public Object invoke(Invocation invocation)
    throws Throwable;
}
	```<?xml version="1.0" encoding="UTF-8"?>```
	```<aop>```
	    ```<bind pointcut="all(test)">```
	        ```<interceptor```
	```factory="middlog.interceptor.TraceInterceptor"/>```
	    ```</bind>```
	```</aop>```

Fig. 3. Interface and description file for an interceptor on JBossAOP

The client side aspect offered by MiddLog (Fig. 3) is implemented by an interceptor based on JBossAOP Framework [5]. The choice of this framework was motivated by some of its capacities, namely: it supports middleware services of JBoss application server; it allows definition of interception points by description files; it allows *advices* to be implemented as interceptors; its implementation is independent of the application server.

In the same way as in interception on the server side, the act of sending the data package is done through the remote invocation of a component service *APIMessage,* belonging to the *Integration layer.* The use of the component *APIMessage,* brings, among other benefits, its usage by an interceptor created by an application developer and the message sent to MiddLog queue through a local or remote invocation, providing extensibility to the framework.

Interception delay and joinpoint verification. Different from interceptors on the server side, in the client side implementation there is no need to include the necessary program for joinpoints verification of where the aspect (interceptor) will act. As seen before, the verification is performed during the application compilation. This approach brings advantages and disadvantages to the process. The advantage is the gain in the interceptor performance, because it already knows where to act without wasting time in joinpoints verification. The disadvantage is that whenever the developer wishes to include a new point of interception he must include it into a descriptor file and recompile his application.

3.3 Message Processing Layer

The Message Processing Layer, represented in Fig. 2, is responsible for receiving and handling all messages sent by interceptors, before storing them in log files. This layer is composed of two main services: Message queue and Logging framework.

Message queue. MiddLog message queue supports data capturing and sending through the Interception layer in an asynchronous way. This queue is created in the message provider of the application server and it is used by an interceptor component or directly by an application, through the APIMessage component, so that they can send data collected from the application to the log file.

The message processing of this queue is executed through a message-driven component, *MDmiddlog,* which is associated with the queue created in the application server. *MDmiddlog* component is responsible for receiving each message from the queue, verifying the type of the received message, as well as extracting from the message the application identification (ID) and the information to be sent to the log framework. The ID is used to associate an application with an instance of the log framework and also with the component *appender,* which is responsible for processing log outputs.

Logging framework. In the MiddLog architecture a low level framework is used to implement the logging mechanism. This framework is responsible for managing the receiving, from MDmiddlog component, of information related to the monitored application and the sending of such information to a previously configured device. From several logging frameworks available [6,7,16], Log4J [7] was chosen to be used in Middlog due to its flexibility, portability and popularity in the software development community.

3.4 Data Model

MiddLog architecture includes an extensible data model that seeks as a main goal to standardize the content and exposure of collected data from the application. The main advantages and benefits of the model are described below.

Extensibility. The extensibility of the data model is strong contribution of the proposal. By using Object-Oriented Programming, new types can be created from a base type or subtypes assuring the flexibility and re-utilization of the model without affecting the developed components and application.

The base type of the proposed model is the *logType*. This abstract type provides the minimum information for log generation and a mandatory method called *getXML,* that are used in subtype creation. The abstract method *getXML* is used so that the *interceptor* developers can format their outputs into log file (Fig. 4).

```
public abstract class logType implements java.io.Serializable {
... public abstract String getXML();
}
public class Component extends logType implements java.io.Serializable { ...
    public String getXML(){
        String strXML = "";   strXML += "<xslog:component idApp='"+getidApp()+"'";
        strXML += " description='"+getDescription()+"'"; ... ; strXML += "/>"; return strXML;
    }...
```

Fig. 4. Fragment of the data model implemented for a Java class

Information standardizing and exposure. MiddLog implements an XML-based [19] description language, named XSLog, to represent, validate and expose the proposed data model (Fig. 5). XSLog language extends the basic types offered by XML, providing a well-organized set of types and structures which can be used in the creation of log files.

```
<?xml version=" ... >
 <xs:element name="logEntry" type="xslog:logType" abstract="true"/>
 <xs:element name="log">
  <xs:complexType> <xs:sequence>
    <xs:element ref="xslog:logEntry" maxOccurs="unbounded"/>   </xs:sequence>
 </xs:complexType> </xs:element>
 <xs:element name="component" type="xslog:componentType"substitutionGroup="xslog:logEntry"/>
   <xs:complexType name="logType">
      <xs:attribute name="idApp" type="xs:string" use="required"/>  ...
   </xs:complexType>
   <xs:complexType name="componentType">
     <xs:complexContent>
      <xs:extension base="xslog:logType">
            <xs:attribute name="objeto" type="xs:string" use="required"/> ...
     </xs:complexType>. . .
```

Fig. 5. Fragment of XSLOG schema

4 Usage Scenario

This section presents an experiment that shows the logging process operation and the main features of MiddLog framework.

We have used a simple application that receives the name of a person and shows the word *"hello"* and the person's name on the user's screen. This application was developed using distributed components. The application has two parts: one component on server side implemented through a Web service [14,18] and a client application that uses this service.

```
public interface HelloWorld extends Remote {
    public String getHelloWorld(String name) throws RemoteException;}
    public class HelloWorld_Impl implements HelloWorld, ServiceLifecycle {
        public String getHelloWorld(String name) throws RemoteException { return "Hello " + name; }
...}
```

Fig. 6. Part of the HelloWorld Web service code

HelloWorld (Fig. 6) represents a business class that exposes its services to client applications. The offered service is: *getHelloWorld (*String name*)*, which returns the message "hello<name_of_person>" to client applications.

```
public class Client {  ....
    public static void main(String[] args) {
    try {    ServiceFactory factory = ServiceFactory.newInstance();
             Service service = factory.createService(new QName(qnameService));
             ....
             call.setOperationName(new QName(endpoint, "getHelloWorld"));
             call.addParameter("String_1", QNAME_TYPE_STRING, ParameterMode.IN);
             String[] params = { "Marcelo!" }; String result = (String)call.invoke(params);
             System.out.println(result);
    } catch (Exception ex) { ex.printStackTrace(); }    }  }
```

Fig. 7. Client application that invoke the Web service through RPC

| `<?xml version="1.0" encoding="UTF-8"?>`
`<configuration . . . >`
`    <application name="HelloWorld">`
`        <class name="*">`
`            <method name="*"/>`
`        </class>`
`    </application>`
`</configuration>` | `<xslog:component idApp='HelloWorld' description=' URI:`
`http://popshopdes:8080/simple-ws4ee/exactpath/jse'`
`Owner="        object='HelloWorld'       idObject='7298031'`
`interface="                        methodEvent='getHelloWorld'`
`argsmethod='(String_1=Marcelo) Return=(Hello Marcelo!) '`
`dateEvent='03/10/2005'        startTimeEvent='08:59:39,31'`
`endTimeEvent='08:59:39,125'/>`
`. . .` |

Fig. 8. *JoinPoint* configuration file and output generated in log

The client application is composed of a class, named *Client* (Fig. 7), whose main goal is to invoke Web services on the application server. It is important to note that there is no code to generate log information neither in the Web service code (Fig. 6) nor in the client application code (Fig. 7). To generate application log through MiddLog, the application must be registered in the *joinpoint* list so that MiddLog starts the process of monitoring and generating the log file (Fig. 8). However, MiddLog must be installed as a service in an application server. First, MiddLog is deployed in the server; secondly, a message queue is created in the message provider of the server; and finally, each interceptor component is associated with a specific *container* in the application server.

The main goal of this experiment is to show that MiddLog *logging* process can be easily used in applications running on application servers so that the developer does not need to modify his/her application source code and regenerate its byte-code. Furthermore, this experiment tried to evaluate the MiddLog impact on the execution of the client application in the server. This was accomplished by collecting time information before and after activating the *logging* process on the application. The hardware and software environment used for the experiment was: (i) Pentium 4 1Ghz with 256MB of RAM and HD 80GB; (ii) SO Windows2000- SP4; (iii) JBOSS 4.01 application server; and (iv) Jakarta Log4J 1.2.8. Table 1 presents the result of the experiment. It can be noted that there was no significant performance degradation in the application execution with the utilization of the MiddLog log service.

Table 1. The time evaluation of MiddLog (after 15 service calls)

Application	MiddLog monitoring	Start time	End time	Elapsed time
Web service	No	08:30,04,125	08:31:02,062	00:00:57,9
Web service	Yes	08:59:39,31	09:00:39,125	00:00:59,8

5 Conclusion

Current logging frameworks allow developers to include logging facilities in their applications without worrying about developing complex codes for log files management. However, the developer is still in charge of choosing monitoring points on his/her application and of including API calls in the code to send collected data to the log file.

MiddLog is a framework that extends the existing log frameworks with new functionalities, providing a complete and flexible set of logging mechanisms to the developer. MiddLog leverages the log management task to the level of a middleware service. MiddLog service layers are built through a component-based approach, thus facilitating its deployment and execution in application servers and exposing its services as Web services. The use of AOP techniques allows the implementation of component interceptors, which perform the application monitoring and the dynamic verification of *joinpoints* by using a declarative language. The performed experiments indicate that this combination allows the developer to include/exclude monitoring points in an application at any moment, without restarting the application server or the MiddLog framework, and also without significantly compromising the execution time of the application.

It is important to point out that, due to the Integration layer exposition through a Web service, client applications developed using any technology will be able to explore the framework features by using common Internet protocols. Furthermore, the MiddLog architectural approach provides easy integration to any other application server.

References

1. Cruz, S. M. S., Campos, L. M., Campos, M. L. M., Pires, P. F., A Data Mart Approach for Monitoring Web Services Usage and Evaluating Quality of Services. . In proceedings of XVIII Simpósio Brasileiro de Bancos de Dados, SBBD, pp 267-280, 2003.
2. Gregor Kiczales, *et.al.* Aspect-Oriented Programming. In proceedings of ECOOP, Finland. Springer-Verlarg LNCS 1241. June 1997.
3. Hangin' with the JAX Pack, Part 2: JAXM. Publish on ONJava.com at: http://www.onjava.com/pub/a/onjava/2001/11/28/jaxpack2.html. Last access: June/2004.
4. Irani, R. Web Services Intermediaries – Adding value to Web Services. Available at: http://www.webservicesarchitec.com/content/articles/irani07print.asp.   Last   access: July/2003.
5. JBoss Aspect Oriented Programming. Available at: http://www.jboss.org/products/aop. Last access: November/2004.
6. JLog: A Java Logging Framework. Available at: http://www.adtmag.com/java/ articleold.asp?id=966&mon=8&yr=2000. Last access: July/2003.
7. Log4j Project – Available at: http://logging.apache.org/log4j/docs/index.html. Last access: May/2003.
8. Lowy J. Contexts in .NET: Decouple Components by Injecting Custom Services into Your Object's Interception Chain. Published in MSDN Magazine, March 2003.
9. Microsoft Distributed Transaction Coordinator. Available at: http://msdn.microsoft.com /library/default.asp?url=/library/en-us/mts/mtxpg03_27xu.asp. Last access: March/2005.
10. Object Managment Group – CORBA. Available at: http://www.omg.org. Last access: May/2003.
11. Ramnivas Laddad, Simplify your logging with AspectJ. Available at: http://www.developer.com/java/other/article.php/10936_3109831_4. Last access: July/ 2004.
12. S. Yajnik, D. Liang, J. C. Shih, C.-Y. Wang, and Y. M. Wang, DCOM and CORBA Side by Side, Step by Step, and Layer by Layer. Available at: http://www.research. microsoft.com/ ~ymwang/papers/html/dcomncorba/s.html. Last access: April/2003.
13. Shukla D., Fell S. and Sells C. AOP - Aspect-Oriented Programming Enables Better Code Encapsulation and Reuse. Publish at MSDN Magazine, March 2002.
14. Sun MicroSystem, Java 2 Platform, Enterprise Edition (J2EE). Available at: http://java. sun.com/j2ee/1.4/docs/index.html. Last access: June/2004.
15. Sun MicroSystem, Java Transaction Service (JTS). Available at: http://java.sun.com/ products/jts/. Last access: March/2005.
16. Sun Microsystems Inc, JSDK Logging. Available at: http://java.sun.com/_j2se/1.4/docs/ guide/util/logging/index.html. Last access: July/2003.
17. Tools for practitioners, Aspect-oriented software development. Available at: http://www.aosd.net/technology/practitioners.php. Last access: December /2004.
18. Word Wide Web Consortium (W3C) - Web Services Activity: http://www.w3.org/2002/ ws/. Last access: October/2004.
19. World Wide Web Consortium (W3C) – XML. Available at: http://www.w3.org/TR/2004/ REC-xml-20040204/. Last access: October/2004.

Specification of Access Control and Certification Policies for Semantic Web Services

Sudhir Agarwal[1] and Barbara Sprick[2]

[1] Institute of Applied Informatics and Formal Description Methods (AIFB),
University of Karlsruhe (TH), Germany
agarwal@aifb.uni-karlsruhe.de
[2] Department of Computer Science and Automation,
Indian Institute of Science, Bangalore, India
sprick@csa.iisc.ernet.in

Abstract. Web service providers specify access control policies to restrict access to their Web services. It turned out, that since the Web is an open, distributed and dynamic environment, in which a central controlling instance cannot be assumed, capability based access control is most suitable for this purpose. However, since practically every participant can certify capabilities defined in his/her own terminology, determining the semantics of certified capabilities and the trustworthiness of certification authorities are two major challenges in such a setting. In this paper, we show, (1) how certification authorities and their certification policies can be modeled semantically (2) how Web service providers can specify and check the consistency of their access control policies and (3) how end users can check automatically, whether they have access to a Web service.

1 Introduction

Semantic Web services promise dynamic business that can be offered and carried out in the Web. In such an open environment, access control plays an important role. Roughly, access control means that the users must fulfill certain conditions in order to gain access to certain functionality. Access control is not only important from the security point of view, but also from a legal point of view. In some cases, even if a Web service provider does not wish to restrict access to his Web service, he may be forced by law to do so. In our previous works [1,2], we have identified that capability based access control is much more suitable for Semantic Web services than identity based access control methods. In such systems, users prove their legitimacy for access by showing an appropriate set of credentials stating their capabilities. A Web service provider can verify, whether the shown set of proven credentials satisfy all the required constraints. In case, it does not, a Web service provider will not allow the user to access his Web service. However, there are still several open issues that need to be resolved in capability based access control in open environments. We identify three major roles a participant can play in such a setting, namely *user*, *web service provider* and *certification authority*.

K. Bauknecht et al. (Eds.): EC-Web 2005, LNCS 3590, pp. 348–357, 2005.

Users. Users want to access Web services. In case of restricted access they must prove their eligibility, e.g. by showing appropriate certificates (in a capability based setting). In some cases a user wishes to automatically infer whether he/she can fulfil the conditions imposed by the access control policy of a Web service. In another scenario, a user may compose some Web services that may belong to different administrative domains. He then wishes to know the access control requirements of the composed system. To support such use cases, the access control policies as well as the credentials have to be specified formally.

Web Service Providers. Web service providers want to restrict access to their services to only eligible users. For this, they specify and enforce access control policies. If these are specified in terms of capabilities that need to be proven by certificates, then the following questions need to be addressed:

- What is the meaning of the terminology used by CAs in their certificates?
- What is the certification policy of the CA that has issued the certificate?
- Which credentials of which certification authorities shall be trusted? On what grounds are the CAs authorized to certify the respective property?
- Are the credentials still valid or have they been revoked?
- Considering the certification policies of the CAs, is the specified ACP consistent with certain conditions and laws?
- Is the ACP satisfiable? That is, is it possible for any user at all to fulfill all the conditions and thus gain access to the Web service?

Certification Authorities. certify users certain properties by issuing certificates. Each certification authority defines its own terminology that it uses in its certificates, for example, the names of certifiable properties and the relation between certifiable properties.

Currently, certification authorities specify their certification policies explicitly in documents that are readable only for humans (see e.g. [3] for an extensive list of certification authorities). These documents are meant to be read by the service providers before they define the access control policies for their Web services. In this paper we show how certification authorities can specify their certification policies in a machine readable form and how they can publish the policy as well as their certification context, e.g. which properties have been certified to them. This approach has several advantages: When specifying their access control policies, Web service providers can use these certification policies to automatically check, whether the specified ACP fulfills certain (legal as well as self imposed) requirements. When verifying the access eligibility of a particular user on the grounds of a presented set of credentials, the Web service provider can make use of the published certification context to check the validity of the presented credential chains. Though revocation of certificates has been addressed in several papers, it is still a controversial issue (e.g. in the context of delegation) and important real life applications such as *tls* or *ssl* simply ignore the possibility of revocation. Our approach can support the CAs in the implementation and enforcement of revocation of certificates.

We begin with a description of an example scenario that serves as a running example throughout the paper in section 2. In section 3, we introduce a simple and novel approach, how a certification authority can specify explicitly and with machine understandable semantics which terminology it uses in the certificates that it issues and which relationships exist among the certified properties. In section 4, we show how Web service providers can specify the access control policies of their Web services based on their knowledge about certification authorities. We conclude in section 7 after discussing some related work in section 6.

2   Scenario

We now describe an example scenario that will be used throughout the paper as a running example. We consider the following organizational entities: (1) Outdoor Shop (*OutShop*), (2) Wildlife foundation (*WLF*), (3) Forest Department (*FD*), (4) Local Trekking Club (*LTC*).

The Outdoor Shop *OutShop* acts as Web service that maintains a list of approved trekking guides. To register as a guide, a user must be above 25 years old, have good trekking experience as well as knowledge in first aid. *OutShop* trusts the Wildlife foundation *WLF* and the Forest Department *FD* as well as their delegates to certify guidance experience.

The Wildlife Foundation *WLF* issues certificates about guidance experience *app_guide*. In its certification policy it does not relate this properties to any other properties. Furthermore, it allows the local Trekking Club *LTC* to act on its behalf and issue guidance experience certificates.

The Forest Department *FD*, too, issues certificates about guidance experience. However, it issues such certificates only to people who are above 25 years old and have knowledge in first aid (certified e.g. by the Red Cross). This restriction is specified in *FD*'s certification policy.

3   Specification of Certification Policies

In the Web practically every participant can act as *Certification Authority* (CA) autonomously and independent of other CAs. It is therefore unrealistic to assume that there is a global vocabulary of properties that every CA uses (in our example scenario for instance, the meaning of app_guide certified by the Forest Department is different from the meaning of app_guide certified by the Wildlife Foundation). Further, there may exist logical relationships among certification authorities (e.g. delegation) and among the properties they certify (e.g. inclusion/exclusion of other properties). For example the certification of the property app_guide is delegated from *WLF* to the local trekking club *LTC*, and the certification of app_guide by the Forest Department implies, that the grantee is above 25 years old and is experienced in first aid.

A signed set of properties that a certification authority certifies together with their relationships and dependencies with other properties (possibly certified by other CAs) is called a *certification policy* of the certification authority. A CA can specify its certification policy and propagandize its trustworthiness in the semantic Web with machine understandable semantics. To do so, the CA specifies

- its certification context in terms of certified properties. This ground can help a Web service provider to decide about the trustworthiness of the certification authority.
- the terminology it uses in the certificates that it issues. These certificates are referenced by a Web service provider in the specification of an access control policy.
- relationships among the properties, that it certifies and any axioms about them.

A certification authority is associated with a set of properties that it possesses and a set of properties that it certifies. In our example, the certification authority LTC possesses the property that it is delegated to certifiy property *app_guide* to users. This property is certified by the *WLF*. In order to talk about such properties and certification authorities more formally, we model concepts `Property` $\sqsubseteq \top$ and `CA` $\sqsubseteq \top \sqcap \exists$`possesses.Property` $\sqcap \exists$`certifies.Property`.

Delegation. Logical relationships between various CAs and the properties they certify can be specified through axioms, in particular class hierarchies over relevant instances of `Property`. Note, that the concrete properties used in an axiom by a certification authority C do not necessarily need to be the properties that are certified by C. Subclass relationship between two classes of different certification authorities can be used for specifying delegation structures. Consider for example, certification authorities C_1 and C_2 that certify properties P_1 and P_2, respectively. By defining the axiom $P_1 \sqsubseteq P_2$, the certification authority C_2 states, that anyone possessing the property P_1 also possesses the property P_2. In other words, the certification authority C_2 delegates the certification of the property P_2 to the certification authority C_1.

Enforcement. We propose to use two kinds of certificates for the enforcement of certification policies, namely *delegation certificates* and *property certificates*. Delegation certificates are meant for realizing the delegation. A delegation certificate is issued by a certification authority to another certification authority to allow the latter to issue certificates (delegation or property) about a property that is defined by the former. This certificate will be signed by the issuer and contain the public key of the recipient. A property certificate is a certificate that is issued by a certification authority to an agent certifying that this agent has a certain property. A property certificate is signed by the certification authority and contains the public key of the recipient.

3.1   Certification Policy - Example

Recalling our running example, we consider the certification authorities, namely the WLF, FD, LTC, GOV and $REDCROSS$ that we model as instances of the concept `CA` as `CA(WLF)`, `CA(LTC)`, `CA(FD)`, `CA(GOV)`, `CA(REDCROSS)`.

WLF defines and certifies the property "appguide" to approved guides, which can be modeled with the following axioms.

$$\text{Property(WLF.org;\#appguide)}$$
$$\text{certifies(WLF,WLF.org;\#appguide)}$$

Further, WLF defines

$$\texttt{LTC.org;\#appguide} \sqsubseteq \texttt{WLF.org;\#appguide} \qquad (1)$$

to specify the delegation structure which mean that the guides approved by LTC are also approved guides from the point of view of WLF. By specifying such an axiom, WLF delegates the certification of the property "WLF.org;#appguide" to LTC.

LTC and FD also issues certificates to approved guides. Government GOV certifies the property state.gov;#above25 to people who are above 25 years of age. Similarly, $REDCROSS$ issues certifies the property RedCross.org; #firstaid to persons who have experience in first aid.

$$\text{certifies}(\text{LTC}, \text{LTC.org};\#\text{appguide})$$
$$\text{Property}(\text{FD.org};\#\text{appguide})$$
$$\text{certifies}(\text{FD}, \text{FD.org};\#\text{appguide})$$
$$\text{certifies}(\text{GOV}, \text{state.gov};\#\text{above25})$$
$$\text{certifies}(\text{REDCROSS}, \text{RedCross.org};\#\text{firstaid})$$

Though on first sight the properties WLF.org;#appguide and FD.org; #appguidefd seem to be equivalent because of their names, they are quite different in their certification policies: The Forest Department certifies this propety only to guides who are at least 25 years old and who are knowledgable in first aid, certified by the government. This restriction can be expressed in the certification policy by stating the following axiom:

$$\texttt{FD.org;\#appguide} \sqsubseteq \texttt{state.gov;\#above25} \sqcap \texttt{RedCross.org;\#firstaid} \quad (2)$$

Note the difference between the two axioms (1) and (2): While in axiom (1) the conclusion of the axiom lies in the namespace of specifying CA, it is the assumption of axiom (2). In this sense, axiom (1) has more the character of a definition (of delegation) and may substitute a delegation credential. Axiom (2) is more a promise or an actual certification policy which says, that the CA FD "promises" to check the age and the knowledge about first aid before certifying a user that he is an approved guide. In case there is no axiom in the government's namespace delegating the certification of the property *age above 25* and in the namespace of the Red Cross delegating the certification of the property knowledgeable in First Aid, a potential Web service provider now has to decide whether to trust this policy or not.

4   Specification of Access Control Policies

We now turn our attention to Web service providers and consider the problem how they can restrict access to their services. In a capability based setting, access is granted or denied on the basis of certified properties. For a correct specification of the access control policy, a Web service provider faces the following two problems: (1) he must understand the meaning of credentials and certified properties and (2) he must trust the issuers of credentials. A Web service provider can understand the meaning of the credentials issued by a certification authority from the description of the properties that the certification authority certifies. On the basis of the description of the properties that a certification authority possesses, a Web service provider can build his trust in the certification authority.

We now show how a Web service provider can make use of certification policies as introduced in section 3 while (1) *specifying* the access control policy for his service and (2) *verifying* the eligibility for access of a particular user.

Specifying Access Control Policies. An *access control policy* for a Web service w is a set of *authorization terms* (p, w, f). Each authorization term has the intuitive meaning that a user being able to prove property p is granted access to functionality f of Web service w. The tuple $\langle w, f \rangle$ is called an *interface*, the set of all interfaces is denoted by I. We define the *expansion* $exp(p, w, f)$ of an authorization term to be the set $\{(s, w, f)|$ subject s can prove to have property $p\}$ and the expansion $exp(\Pi)$ of a policy Π to be the union of the expansions of elements of Π. An authorization term can be defined with DL axioms as follows:

```
AuthorizationTerm ⊑ ⊤ ⊓ ∃subject.ca-Property ⊓
                    ∃object.WebService ⊓
                    ∃authorization.WebServiceFunctionality
```

An approach for specifying and automatically composing access control policies using a policy algebra [4,5] has been proposed in [1,2]. The algebra allows to specify and compute access control policies of composite Web services from those of its component Web services.

Verifying Eligibility of a User. When a user requests access by showing his set of certificates the Web service provider must be able to verify the user's eligibility in order to decide whether to grant or to deny access to the user. To verify the eligibility of a user, he checks for each access requirement, whether the shown set of credentials (plus possibly published certification policies and delegation credentials published by relevant CAs) contain a valid certificate chain from some trusted CA to the required property. However, in this process, the service provider also needs to consider the possible revocation of one or more certificates shown by the user. This could either be a certificate directly issued to the user or a certificate in the certificate chain issued to one of the involved CAs. If the CAs publish their certification policies including the delegation credentials issued to them in machine readable form on the web, it might still be possible to automatically find a valid chain that proves the users' eligibility, e.g. via newly stated relationships or other published delegation certificates.

4.1 Access Control Policy - Example

Let us now consider our running example again to illustrate how a Web service provider can specify an access control policy using the knowledge he gains from the certification policies of the certification authorities.

The outdoor shop *OutShop* offers a registration service for approved trekking guides. For the registration they have the following access condition: Each trekking guide must be approved by either the Forest department *FD* or by the wildlife foundation *WLF*, must at least 25 years old and must be knowledgeable in first aid. This leads to the following access control policy:

$$ACP(P) := \{(WLF, \texttt{OS.edu}, \textit{trecking guide}), (FD, \texttt{OS.edu}, \textit{trecking guide})\}$$

where WLF and FS are defined as follows:

$$WLF \equiv \texttt{WLF.org;\#appguide} \sqcap \texttt{state.gov;\#above25} \sqcap \texttt{RedCross.org;\#firstaid}$$
$$FD \equiv \texttt{FD.org;\#appguide} \sqcap \texttt{state.gov;\#above25} \sqcap \texttt{RedCross.org;\#firstaid}$$

From the certification policy, the Web service provider can infer that whoever has the property `FD.org;#appguide` also has the properties `state.gov;#above25` and `RedCross.org;#firstaid`. At the time of specification of the policy, it allows him to relax the policy and thus reduce the number of certificates, a potential user has to present:

$$ACP(P) := \{(WLF, \texttt{OS.edu}, \textit{trecking guide}), (FD, \texttt{OS.edu}, \textit{trecking guide})\}$$

with FS being defined as

$$FD' \equiv \texttt{FD.org;\#appguide.}$$

At the time of verification it allows the Web service provider to verify, that a user, who has presented "only" a valid chain for `FD.org;#appguide` is still eligible for the registration.

5 Users

We now turn our attention to the third logical role, namely *users*. Users are mainly interested in accessing Web services. In case of secure semantic Web services, which is our main concern in this paper, any Web service discovery component must consider the user's certificates as well as the access control policies of Web services. Syntactical certificates description schemas, such as X509, KeyNote or SPKI/SDSI certificates make it difficult for a client side discovery component to perform matching based on functional as well as security aspects, because such a discovery component can not know the meaning of the certificates that the user has and hence can not know which properties has been certified to the user.

In our setting, an end user possesses a set of certificates meta-data about each certificate. The meta-data contains information about the properties that a certificate actually certifies and hence describes the semantics of the certificate. Note, that in many cases, a certificate certifies more than one property. The end users (1) have their goals in mind and want to discover and compose Web services, (2) want to access Web services that offer required functionality, (3) have certain properties certified to them and can use the certificates to prove their eligibility if access to a Web service is restricted.

5.1   Example

Consider an end user, who is an experienced wildlife and trekking guide and holds a certificate certifying him the property LTC.org;#appguide. The user wishes to register himself as an approved trekking guide in the Outdoor Shop *OutShop*.

In our example, the set of Web service descriptions that our end user obtains from an appropriate discovery component will contain the description of the Web service *OutShop*, since the matching software can infer from the certification policy of the wildlife foundation WLF that LTC.org;#appguide is subset of WLF.org;#appguide and hence a user possessing the propertyLTC.org;#appguideltc has access to the Web service *OutShop*

Now, our end user wants to register as a approved trekking guide. He finds out, that this functionality is accessible only for approved guides from the forest department FD and from the Wildlife foundation WLF, that are above 25 years old and are knowledgeable in first aid. By looking at the certification policies of WLF and FD he finds out automatically, that WLF has delegated the certification of property *app_guide* to the local trekking club TLC, which means, that it will be enough to hold the certificate LTC.org;#appguide rather then the certificate WLF.org;#appguide.

6   Related Work

In the area of service oriented computing there are already several approaches for declaratively modeling the user's objectives; mainly in terms of policies. On the one hand, there are XML-based approaches, like WS-Security, XACML, EPAL, etc. These approaches allow to model constraints about domain-specific attributes of a service. XACML has been approved by OASIS and that promises to standardize policy management and access decisions. However, XACML focusses more on technical issues and addresses how the access control can be enforced. EPAL and XACML specifications greatly overlap and do very similar things in slightly different ways. As a consequence, the user has to learn the different approaches and work with different policy tools. Furthermore, it is not possible to specify a policy that combines privacy and communication security concerns such as: send sensitive content over secured lines only. WS-Policy introduces a logic framework that allows domain-specific policy assertions to be plugged in. Nevertheless, the supported assertions are very simplistic in nature and still require the respective native policy interpreters. The major disadvantage of XML is that the semantics is contained implicity in the expressions. Meaning arises only from the shared understanding derived from human consensus. This leads to extra manual work for software engineers and could easily result in fragmentation.

Security-related ontologies to markup DAML-S [6] elements such as input and output parameters with respect to their security characteristics, such as encryption and digital signatures have been developed in [7,8]. [9] gives an short introduction to Rei, case studies, use cases and open issues. However, the mechanism described in the paper requires clients to send their privacy policies and permissions to a Web service provider, which is not always wishful. Nevertheless, the authors identify the enforcement problem as an open issue. [10] introduces an enforcement architecture based on a policy engine and the policy enforcement mechanism for pervasive environments. The policy engine reasons over policies described in Rei and uses Prolog for its reasoning engine. [11] discusses the policy language Rei in more detail. However, neither [10] nor [11] provide Rei's mapping to Prolog. So, it is not clear what the policy engine acutally does. Since Rei requires a special reasoner, it is not clear, what is the added value of Rei as compared to XML based approaches except that it is more expressive.

Our work is complementary to the existing approaches as it also addresses the need of machine understandable specification of certification policies that are specified by the certification authorities. It also presents how Web services providers can use such semantically-rich specifications for defining their access control policies. Consequently, our paper covers a broader spectrum and also shows the added value of specifications with formal semantics within the context of access control. We also address the issue of enforcement which can not be ignored while dealing with security related aspects. Finally, our approach is completely based on description logics which is the formalism behind the W3C standard OWL (Web Ontology Language). Consequently, we do not require the users and providers of semantic Web services to install a special reasoner.

7   Conclusion

In a capability based access control system a Web service provider specifies the access requirements for his service in terms of required properties. For gaining access, users have to prove that they satisfy these properties. To do so, they need to present certificate chains that prove a delegation chain from a trusted certification authority to the required property.

This approach faces several problems: revocation of certificates is still a controversial issue since the semantics is not fully clear in presence of delegation. The second problem is that one cannot always assume the existence of a "trusted" root CA, e.g. Verisign, as in principle everyone can act as CA. Potential CAs therefore publish their (signed) certification policies in order to establish trust in them. Thirdly, while composing Web services and access control policies automatically from those of its components, a Web service provider needs to check whether governmental- and self imposed laws are still met by those CAs trusted by the components. The Web service provider is then able to automatically check whether the trust structure of the component services is compatible with his trust structure. Our approach shows how certification policies can be specified in the semantic Web in a machine understandable way, which makes them suitable for automatic verification of the compatibility between access control policies and governmental or self imposed laws. Further, delegation structures of CAs can be made explicit in our approach, which allows CAs to handle revocation of (delegation) certificates in an online manner.

References

1. Agarwal, S., Sprick, B.: Access control for semantic web services. In: 1st International Conference on Web Services. (2004)
2. Agarwal, S., Sprick, B., Wortmann, S.: Credential based access control for semantic web services. In: AAAI Spring Symposium 2004 - Semantic Web Services. (2004)
3. Stefan Kelm, S.S.C.: The pki page – extensive list of certification authorities. http://www.pki-page.org/ (2004)
4. Biskup, J., Wortmann, S.: Towards a credential-based implementation of compound access control policies. Technical report, University of Dortmund (2003) http://ls6-www.cs.uni-dortmund.de/issi/publications.
5. Bonatti, P., de Capitani di Vimercati, S., Samarati, P.: An algebra for composing access control policies. ACM Transactions on Information and System Security (TISSEC) **5** (2002) 1–35
6. Ankolekar, A., Burstein, M.H., Hobbs, J.R., Lassila, O., Martin, D., McDermott, D.V., McIlraith, S.A., Narayanan, S., Paolucci, M., Payne, T.R., Sycara, K.: DAML-S: Web Service Description for the Semantic Web. In: ISWC2002: Ist International Semantic Web Conference, Sardinia, Italy. Lecture Notes in Computer Science, Springer (2002) 348–363
7. Denker, G., Kagal, L., Finin, T., Sycara, K., Paolucci, M.: Security for daml web services: Annotation and matchmaking. In: Second International Semantic Web Conference. Volume 2870 of Lecture Notes in Computer Science., Springer (2003)
8. Kagal, L., Paolucci, M., Srinivasan, N., Denker, G., Finin, T., and, K.S.: Authorization and privacy for semantic web services. In: Proc. of AAAI Spring Symposium on Semantic Web Services. (2004)
9. Kagal, L., Finin, T., Joshi, A.: Declarative Policies for Describing Web Service Capabilities and Constraints. In: W3C Workshop on Constraints and Capabilities for Web Services, Oracle Conference Center, Redwood Shores, CA, USA, W3C (2004)
10. Patwardhan, A., Korolev, V., Kagal, L., Joshi, A.: Enforcing Policies in Pervasive Environments. In: International Conference on Mobile and Ubiquitous Systems: Networking and Services, Cambridge, MA, IEEE (2004)
11. Kagal, L., Finin, T., Joshi, A.: A Policy Language for A Pervasive Computing Environment. In: IEEE 4th International Workshop on Policies for Distributed Systems and Networks. (2003)

Improving Reuse of Web Service Compositions

Carlos Granell[1], Michael Gould[1], Roy Grønmo[2], and David Skogan[2]

[1] Department of Information Systems (LSI),
Universitat Jaume I, E-12071 Castellón, Spain
{carlos.granell, gould}@uji.es
http://www.geoinfo.uji.es
[2] SINTEF Information and Communication Technology,
N-0314, Oslo, Norway
{roy.gronmo, david.skogan}@sintef.no
http://www.sintef.no

Abstract. We describe a methodology for assembling composite services based on three basic processes which are independent of the concrete implementation: Service Abstraction Process, Service Composition Process, and Translation Process. These processes share the concept of integrated component composed of two key aspects: a specific set of the Aalst's workflow patterns together with a component-style composition of complex services. We propose a novel approach that implements the steps of such methodology, providing an efficient manner for developing service compositions and enhancing the expressiveness of target composition languages like BPEL4WS. Here we focus on the description of the Service Abstraction Process, a critical step in order to enhance the service composition by facilitating the reuse of existing services.

1 Introduction

In the service oriented architecture field, several different approaches and platforms are being developed to address the common goal of web service composition [8]. Each provides unique perspectives to facilitate service integration, from static and dynamic approaches to manual or automated ones, and each approach defines its own manner for composing services, provides its specifications and languages, and introduces new specifications to the web service protocol stack[1]. In fact each of the possible service facets (addressing, discovery, context, etc.) normally carries a specification or even two or more potential specifications with no single consensus standard defined to date, leading to overlapping features [13]. This may lead to inter-compatibility issues among different approaches, complicating even further the service composition problem. In this work, rather than provide a new specification from the ground up, we prefer to build our approach, where possible, upon existing well-known web services specifications or *de facto* standards (like for example HTTP, WSDL, and BPEL).

Most similar approaches attempt to address service composition by composing *single* web services from scratch, ignoring reuse of existing compositions or parts of

---

[1] http://roadmap.cbdiforum.com/reports/protocols/

K. Bauknecht et al. (Eds.): EC-Web 2005, LNCS 3590, pp. 358–367, 2005.

compositions. In this sense, from a developer's perspective it is interesting to explore the reuse of existing services. It is expected that this higher level of service reusability will lead to more efficient, more structured composition process that will accelerate rapid application development.

In this paper we concentrate on how the service reuse can be exploited in the service composition process for developing more rapid and efficient web applications. First we describe a service composition methodology for developing applications composed of three steps, namely Service Abstraction Process (SAP), Service Composition Process (SCP), and Translation Process (TP). The SAP is charged with distinguishing abstract services from concrete services, ready for composition. The SCP provides the needed means for creating service composition reusing existing ones. At run-time, the TP translates the service composition description into a target composition language like BPEL4WS to be executed by a workflow engine. Secondly, we propose a service composition model using specific workflow patterns and a component-style composition of complex services. The set of workflow patterns is based on [1], adapted to the service composition context. The *integrated component* notion incorporates component aspects into web service concept. Integrated components together with workflow patterns become the fundamental blocks for application development by reusing and combining simpler components into more complex ones. In this paper we focus on the description of the SAP process within our model, the proposed workflow patterns set and its relationship to the integrated components.

The remainder of the paper is organized as follows. The proposed methodology is described in section 2. Section 3 presents the SAP process in detail, describes the integrated component concept, workflow patterns used, and how to design these integrated components on our model. Finally, section 4 concludes the paper.

2   A Service Composition Methodology

Our objective is to introduce a conceptual methodology supporting service reuse and composition. It consists of applying the following basic processes: the SAP for creating abstracts services or integrated components, the SCP for constructing complex applications (composite services) reusing abstract services, and the TP for converting complex services into a target composition language for deployment and invocation. The rest of this section describes each process presenting its purpose, the modules implicated, and their relationships.

2.1   Service Abstraction Process

The core of service-oriented architectures (SOA) is essentially collections of services (operations) described by an interface and provided to a user or client. Composing web services by means of *concrete* service interfaces leads to tightly-coupled compositions in which each service involved in the chain is tied to a web service instance. If current services are replaced by new or updated ones, changes in the underlying workflow may become necessary from, for example, slight modifications of bindings to wholesale redesign of part of the workflow description. Because of that, services

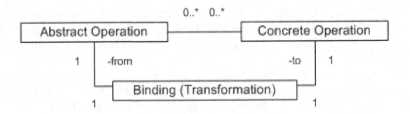

Fig. 1. Elements within the Service Abstraction Process

should be interpreted as abstract notions facilitating their independent composition. Figure 1 depicts a UML class diagram illustrating the elements and their relationships contained in the SAP.

The SAP is a process (abstraction process) which allows us to move service operations from terms of particular functions to shared and agreed domain concepts. In particular, ontologies and semantic properties are a basic ingredient in the abstraction process because these introduce meaning to services (for example semantic properties) and thus enable the reuse of these services and their independent composition. A minimum required attribute for describing the service functionality is its signature, composed of its operation name and its input and output parameters. The developer (or software module) should be able to represent different operation signatures as a (new or existing) single abstract signature, specified as the minimal signature required for a given functionality [6]. In this way, the resulting abstract operation associated with each domain forms the basis for the future composition process, which is carried out in terms of common abstract signatures instead of concrete signatures. From Figure 1, the SAP may be composed of the following modules:

–   *Abstraction module.* This module is charged with abstracting operations: to map operation and parameter names to comprehensible names defined by means of common vocabularies or taxonomies. The resulting abstract operation is made available in service registries. In fact, every abstract operation is actually a set of candidates operations with a given functionality, of which the execution results of just one will be considered at run-time by a workflow engine. We will ignore aspects concerned with the quality of service [7] although we realize all these properties – security, availability, efficiency, response time, etc. – play an important role for selecting the most appropriate operation for execution among the candidates.
–   *Binding module.* The abstraction process itself includes a gap between the abstract specification of an operation and how to access to an operation on a technical level. The binding description specifies how to map from abstract operations to concrete operations. The established bindings are meant for service invocation and should be kept separate from the description of the abstract and concrete operations, the three logical views of an operation - abstract, concrete and binding - remaining physically separate.

2.2 Service Composition Process

A composite service incorporates the business logic and functionality of several simpler services contained within [2]. The problem addressed is how to build and integrate such a composite service by reusing other simpler services.

A natural way of conceptualizing service composition is by means of composing single and composite services recursively [2, 8]. In this way, a composite service is defined as an aggregation of other single and composite services. The SCP suggests an extension of this idea by adding two new aspects. First, component technology [12] allows modular composition of software systems from reusable and independent code described by explicit interfaces. In essence, this approach is identical to others carried out within different contexts like for example component-based software development [11], in which the application logic is constructed by composing smaller software components. Therefore, the *composition process* constructs complex applications as integrated components by incrementally aggregating and reusing existing ones. Second, a specific set of workflow patterns defines the orchestration among the integrated components. This provides an added level of simplicity, independence, and reusability in the composition process.

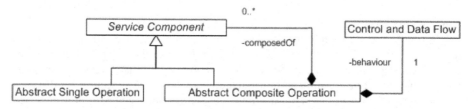

Fig. 2. Elements within the Service Composition Process

As depicted in Figure 2, the relationships among the tasks in a composition process starts from the level of abstraction defined by abstract single operations, which are previously created by the SAP. An abstract single operation is considered a basic element. An abstract composite operation is in turn an aggregation of other abstract (single or composite) operations, which are referred to as *service component*. The service component may comprise single or composite operations and specify the orchestration among the contained operations (service components), that is, the control and data flow description. The control flow establishes the partial order in which the service components should be invoked. The data flow captures the data dependences among such service components. Based on these relationships, the SCP may be composed of the following modules:

- *Composer module.* It handles the composition process by combining service components from single or composite ones. The resulting service component is also considered as an integrated component. Orchestration features among contained service components are also specified by this module. Therefore, the composition process consists of discovering existing abstract operations, designing the resulting composition, and registering it for future use.
- *Discovery module.* This module is concerned with selecting the required service components for composition.

2.3 Translation Process

Once a composition is created following the two processes mentioned, we use the TP to transform the composition into a target web service-oriented workflow language to permit users and external programs to execute it. The TP converts the integrated component(s) description to a workflow language (for example BPEL4WS) while also enhancing the expressiveness of these languages since the target process description is reached by following a component-style composition.

All these combined processes provide a methodological, an efficient way for developing applications by service composition and reuse. Users may create customized applications following the service composition methodology in three steps, using the underlying concept of integrated component with regard to its creation, composition, and translation: they first create abstract services as integrated components. Then, application development is performed by incrementally aggregating existing integrated components. Finally, these complex applications created are translated into executable descriptions for invocation.

3 Abstraction Process for Designing Integrated Components

Now that the service composition methodology has been introduced, we describe the abstraction process according to the SAP. The key elements are integrated components and workflows patterns. In section 3.1 we propose the integrated component concept for expressing services. Section 3.2 presents appropriate workflow patterns for selection of services within an integrated component. Finally, section 3.3 discuses the modeling of services based on such integrated components and workflow patterns.

3.1 The Role of Integrated Components

Expressing services as blocks of components is especially attractive within service composition contexts for different reasons. First, by definition, components are the sole ingredients of the composition process [12], which is a critical aspect to simplify the composition model as a useful and practical process. If we treat both single and composite services as components, recursive composition becomes an implicit and natural means for building complex services (compositions). Next, components must be units of replacement [12] avoiding external data dependencies. This means that a component is not dependent on the composition in which it is involved. It can be reused in others when the functionality that it exposes is required. Furthermore, it is clearly relevant for improving service reuse that components incorporate no implementation details, only metadata describing all service aspects involved in the composition process.

We adopt a component-based approach to model web services (earlier versions of this concept are found in [3, 4]). We define an *integrated component* as a service adopting the component technology's aspects explained above. It comprises either abstract single operations (SAP's outcome) or abstract composite operations (SCP's outcome). We consider either abstract (single or composite) operation is an integrated component. To accomplish that, all service aspects relevant for service composition need to be captured in abstract descriptions. From the set of layers for designing a service [10], we take into consideration the following service aspects for enabling integrated components: (i) *descriptive aspects* are metadata concerned with the context in which the service operation is performed; (ii) *functional aspects* detail the service capabilities in terms of operations, parameters, etc., that is, its functionality; (iii) *structural aspects* show how a service is internally structured as a combination of simpler services; (iv) finally, *binding aspects* establish relationships between abstract and concrete specifications required for service invocation.

An integrated component combines the component and services aspects into the single notion, maintaining the benefits of both, by two functional interfaces: public and private. The public interface expresses publicly the service's descriptive and functional aspects. The private interface represents an internal view of the integrated components encapsulating the structural features like control and data flow as well as the necessary transformations for binding.

3.2 Workflow Patterns

Workflow patterns also play a key role in our model because they describe the structural features of an integrated component. Firstly, this section selects a relevant set of workflow patterns for service composition. Then, it discusses which of those selected workflow pattern sets are applied in the abstraction process and their relationship with the integrated components.

The original 20 workflow patterns [1] provide a framework for comparing different workflow management systems according to their functionality (see Table 1). However, not all workflow patterns are relevant to the service composition context. Our choice is based on simplicity criterion where *sequence* (1), *parallel split* (2), *choice* (4, 6), and *replication* (9) constructs offer enough means to model complex patterns in any composition [9]. Counterpart patterns regarding synchronization (3, 5, 7, 8) are also significant in our model since the split and join combination aligns perfectly to the integrated components' hierarchical structure for building composition as stated in the previous subsection.

Table 1. Relevant and non-relevant workflow patterns (synomymous term in parenthesis)

No	Relevant Workflow Patterns	No	Non-Relevant Workflow Patterns
1	Sequence (*seq*)	10	Multi-merge
2	Parallel split (*and-split*)	11	Implicit Termination
3	Synchronization (*and-join*)	12-13	Patterns involving Multiples Instances (design time)
4	Exclusive choice (*xor-split*)	14-15	Patterns involving Multiples Instances (run time)
5	Simple merge (*xor-join*)	16	Deferred Choice
6	Multi-choice (*or-split*)	17	Interleaved Parallel Routing
7	Synchronizing merge (*or-join*)	18	Milestone
8	Discriminator (*disc-join*)	19	Cancel activity
9	Arbitrary circles (*loop*)	20	Cancel Case

The remainders of the workflow patterns (10-20) are not considered for service composition. Some irrelevant workflow patterns (10, 12, 13, 17) can be modeled with basic ones (Table 1, left column). For instance *multi-merge* (10) defines several parallel executions with a specific joining point can be represented by using *and-split* (2) and *and-join* (3) together. Others are not suitable for service composition as *deferred choice* pattern (16) since it assumes an external input in the workflow. As described in section 3.1, we prefer integrated components with lower levels of external data dependencies. The rest of workflow patterns (11, 14, 15, 18, 19, 20) have a great importance on the execution of the workflow, however they have no relevant meaning during the abstraction process described in this section.

Understanding how integrated components are related to workflow patterns is critically important since the composition process is generally considered to be the application of a composition operator [12]. In our model, workflow patterns play the role of *selection* operators in the SAP and of *composition* operators in the SCP. Here we focus on the selector role during the abstraction process.

Each and every resulting abstract operation, the abstraction process' outcome, is considered an integrated component. An integrated component comprises a set of candidate operations with similar functionality. An appropriate workflow pattern is needed to execute one operation from a potential operation set. The idea is to extend the functionality of the *alternative services* pattern proposed in [5]. Suppose that one service is selected for execution but that such a service becomes unavailable due to server or network troubles, failing the workflow execution. To prevent this, the alternative services pattern allows us to model alternative services in the workflow that perform the same task as the most appropriate service selected by quality, data or simply user preferences.

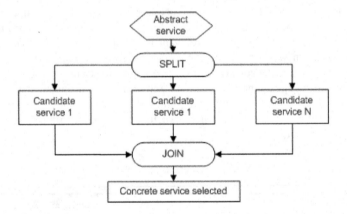

Fig. 3. Workflow pattern for service selection in the SAP

Figure 3 illustrates the service selection situation. Both the split and join conditions are needed for modeling the service selection into a target composition language. The split condition is concerned with the candidate operation set (inputs) whereas the join condition refers to the selected operation (output). From the relevant workflow patterns in Table 1, the inputs or-split and and-split are suitable whereas for the output we are interested in disc-join pattern because only one of them will be finally considered by the workflow engine. Therefore, the or-split with disc-join and and-split with disc-join pairs are appropriate in the abstraction process. The former is suitable when the user selection explicitly includes some conditions (for example, quality or pre-conditions) over the candidate operations taking them into account *a priori*. This selected set is modeled for execution [5] and only the first one to terminate successfully is considered and the others are ignored at run-time. We can say that two filters are applied: the first one concerned with criteria at design-time and the second one concerned with service availability at run-time. For the latter all candidate operations are considered for execution. In this case, only the service availability filter runs. Therefore, these selection workflow pattern pairs are reflected in the resulting workflow description to help assure that the composition is somewhat fault-tolerant due to multiple service availability.

3.3 Modelling Integrated Components

Building on the concept of integrated components in section 3.1 and the analysis of workflow patterns in section 3.2, here we detail the abstraction process for modelling integrated components.

The objective of this abstraction process is to build integrated components which will then be used for the composition process within the SCP. From the user perspective the public interface, the integrated component's functionality and descriptive aspects, is interesting and not how such a component is internally constructed. From the programmer or designer perspective, the private interface is also interesting because it shows how the component is internally structured. Therefore, modelling integrated components consists of specifying all service aspects stated earlier.

Figure 4 summarizes the major steps in the abstraction process in which a bottom-up design is necessary to reach the abstraction operation level of available concrete operations: (i) the definition of the required abstract operation in terms of is domain; (ii) the functionality associated with the abstract operation; (iii) the internal structure definition; (iv) the definition of the appropriate transformation between the abstract and concrete operations; and finally (v) the abstract operation registration. An integrated component is generated by steps (i) and (ii) which represent the public interface and by (iii) and (iv) which correspond to the private interface.

The first step (i) consists of finding an appropriate abstract operation that corresponds conceptually to a given concrete operation. At this moment two possibilities are possible: either an abstract operation already exists or does not. For the former, we specify the descriptive aspects of this new abstract operation which can be, for example, commerce classification, service category, or domain, such as are represented in an OWL-S service profile. For the latter, such a concrete operation is actually being assigned to an existing abstract operation then specifying the descriptive and functionality aspects are not necessary. Indeed, it is likely that several operations within a similar domain will belong to the same integrated component. For example, let us consider a couple of operations concerned with weather information (Get Wind and Get Weather Report), where the Get Wind operation returns only certain wind-related variables a complete weather report, including in addition to wind information, weather forecast features such as pressure, humidity, or temperature. In this case, the integrated component (Wind Info) should be formed by the minimal common information among them, hiding both operations under the same domain (the Wind concept). Similarly, in a complex operation like Get Weather Report, some parts of the same function may belong to several integrated

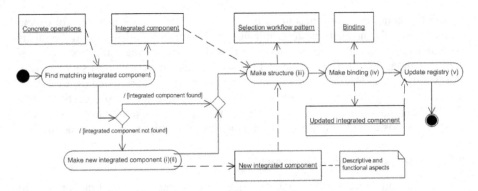

Fig. 4. UML activity diagram for the abstraction process in the SAP (numbers in parenthesis correspond to service aspects described in section 3.1)

components with different concepts (`Wind, Pressure, Humidity`, and `Temperature` concepts). Both service availability and reuse are improved by decomposing a given complex operation into its finer functionalities, leading to multiple logical views of the same operation. In step (ii), we specify the functionality aspects if necessary. In particular, service capabilities like inputs or outputs are described in terms of concepts in a certain domain. Both sorts of attributes form the public interface.

The next step (iii), structural aspects are introduced by specifying one of the selection workflow patterns described previously, ensuring that only one concrete service is successfully executed. For example, the invocation of `Wind Info` contains two concrete operations, `Get Weather Report` and `Get Wind`. One incoming operation must be completed before executing the following service in the chain. Both concrete operations are executed but only one is considered by the workflow engine. Suppose that an `and-split` with `disc-join` selection pattern is chosen and `Get Wind` would terminate before `Get Weather Report`. In this case the latter is ignored in the workflow execution. Binding aspects are specified in (iv) where the appropriate transformation between different levels of abstraction are described. In this case, the binding concept establishes relationships between the inputs and outputs concepts of the integrated component with the service description specification (typically WSDL). For example, it is necessary to declaratively specify a mapping from an integrated component (`Wind Info`) to its concrete operations (`Get Wind` and `Get Weather Report`) by specifying network protocol, message format and, optionally, more elaborated transformations such as filters or logical views. Structural and binding attributes form the private interface. Finally, step (v) consists simply of registering (updating) the abstract operation as an available integrated component for future reuse.

4 Conclusion and Future Work

In this paper we have presented a methodology for developing web applications using three basic processes for service composition, namely Service Abstraction Process,

Service Composition Process, and Translation Process. In order to better support service reuse, we introduced a model for service composition that implements such a methodology. We described the core elements in our model: workflow patterns and integrated components as building blocks for incrementally composing complex service compositions. Our ongoing work includes a toolset to support the integrated components definition and to explore service reuse during the composition process.

Acknowledgements

This work has been partially supported by the EU project IST-2001-37724, by the Spanish Ministry of Science and Technology project TIC-2003-09365-C02, and by Fundación Bancaixa-Castelló.

References

1. Aalst, W.M.P., Hofstede, A.H.M., Kiepuszewski, B., Barros, A.P.: Workflow Patterns. Distributed and Parallel Databases **14** (1), (2003) 5-51
2. Alonso, G. Casati, F., Harumi, K., Machiraju, V.: Web Services: Concepts, Architectures and Applications. Springer-Verlag, Berlin Heidelberg (2004)
3. Granell, C., Poveda, J., Gould, M.: Incremental Composition of Geographic Web Services: an Emergency Management Context. In: Proc. of the 7th AGILE Conference on Geographic Information Science, University of Crete Press, Crete, Greece, pages 343-348 (2004)
4. Granell, C., Ramos, J.F.: An Object-oriented Approach to GI Web Service Composition. In: Proc. of the First DEXA Workshop on GIM 2004, Zaragoza, Spain, pages 835-839 (2004)
5. Grønmo, R., Solheim, I.: Towards Modeling Web Service Composition in UML. In: Proc. of The 2nd Intl. Workshop on Web Services: Modeling, Architecture and Infrastructure (WSMAI), Porto, Portugal, pages 72-86 (2004)
6. Melloul, L., Fox, A.: Reusable Functional Composition Patterns for Web Services. In: Proc. of the IEEE ICWS 2004, San Diego, California (2004)
7. Menascé, D.A.: QoS Issues in Web Services. IEEE Internet Computing **6** (6), (2004) 72-75
8. Milanovic, N., Malek, M.; Current Solutions for Web Service Composition. IEEE Internet Computing **8** (6), (2004) 51-59
9. Milner, R.: Communicating and Mobile Systems: the Pi-Calculus. CUP (1999)
10. Sollazo, T. Handschuh, S., Staab, S., Frank, M.: Semantic Web Services Architecture – Evolving Web Service Standards towards the Semantic Web. In: Proc. of 15th International FLAIRS Conference. AAAI Press, pages 425-430 (2002)
11. Szyperski, C.: Component Software. Beyond Object-Oriented Programming. Addison-Wesley, New York (1998)
12. Szyperski, C.: Component Technology – What, Where, and How?. In: Proc. 25th International Conference on Software Engineering ICSE'03, pages 683-693 (2003)
13. Vinoski, S.: WS-Nonexistent Standards. IEEE Internet Computing **8** (6), (2004) 94-96.

Remote Data Access Scheme for Service Delivery and Invocation Based on SOAP Protocol

Byong-In Lim, Ho-Jin Shin, Seung-Hyun Lee and Dong-Ryeol Shin

School of Information and Communication Engineering,
Sungkyunkwan University
440-746, Suwon, Korea
+82-31-290-7125
{lbi77, hjshin, lshyun0, drshin}@ece.skku.ac.kr

Abstract. The Simple Object Access Protocol (SOAP) is a novel protocol which supports information exchange in a decentralized, distributed environment, which brings flexibility and extensibility to the communication and invocations among remote hosts. However, SOAP requires a high performance for collaboration such as service delivery and invocation. Furthermore, SOAP itself is not well suitable for mobile devices due to network bandwidth or resource-constraints problems. In this paper, we describe SOAP-based remote data access scheme which is comprised of XML and RPC technology. Especially, we focus on the scheme which is optimal over service discovery and invocation based on SOAP technology. Also, we apply the proposed scheme to LSD (Lightweight Service Discovery) which is a peer-to-peer, cache-based service discovery protocol for ad hoc environments.

1 Introduction

Modern technological changes have allowed the computing environment to become increasingly pervasive, ubiquitous [1], and mobile. Devices in this environment may constitute mobile ad hoc networks [2], in which devices are connected to each other through wireless connections. These devices are usually mobile, handheld or wearable. These aspects enhance information processing of large amount of data, and provide excellent mobile accessibility. However, heterogeneous network structures and the tremendous improvement of network resources create new challenges in supporting management and interoperability among these resources.

In this sense, efficient remote access to information has become a hot topic in ubiquitous environments. As a result, service discovery protocols are coming to play as an increasingly important role in ad hoc networks. Several service discovery protocols [3, 4, 5, 6] are proposed to facilitate dynamic cooperation among devices/services with minimal administration and human intervention. In order to be able to support the impromptu community, they should provide the means to announce its presence to the network, to discover services in the neighborhood, and to access services. While many of the architectures provide good foundations for

This work was supported by CUCN Grant, Korea.

K. Bauknecht et al. (Eds.): EC-Web 2005, LNCS 3590, pp. 368 – 378, 2005.

developing systems with distributed components in the networks, they do not adequately solve all the problems that may arise in dynamic domains such as ad hoc networks.

In this paper, we describe a remote service access scheme, for collaboration among heterogeneous devices in an ad hoc network, based on the SOAP [7] protocol. The SOAP-based system, enabling the system to become more flexible, providing extensible remote data access, can easily implement interoperability and XML based processes. In spite of this advantage, a trade-off in the computing environment is also emerging as a problem in SOAP based systems. For example, flexibility and extensibility is supported but high performance is required [8, 9] to operate XML encoding or decoding over a high load network. In LSD we occasionally use the SOAP protocol to abbreviate network traffic and to minimize XML operation. When LSD discovers a service, it exchanges the optimized packet with a minimum data size and invocation used to optimize SOAP messages. Thus a reduction in network traffic and an improvement of performance are to be expected.

The remainder of the paper is organized as follows. Section 2 describes the LSD architecture. Section 3 describes the service discovery procedure, including the discovery algorithm and cache management. Section 4 describes the service invocation scheme based on SOAP. Section 5 presents future work. Finally, this paper is concluded in Section 6.

2 LSD Overview

LSD can find services on remote hosts, uses Peer-to-Peer algorithms, supports the cache-based service discovery protocol for ad hoc environments, supports invocation, and serves as a ubiquitous media for information exchange.

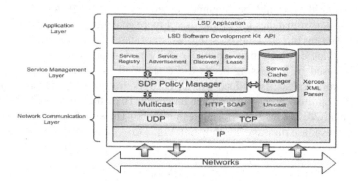

Fig. 1. LSD system architecture

Fig. 1 shows the LSD architecture and corresponding components in a single mobile device. The LSD consists of three layers: the application layer, the service management layer, and the network communication layer. The application layer provides the user with applications such as audio-video players and printing applications. The service management layer provides services associated with discovery. In the service management layer, we use a cache manager that registers information about services offered by peers in the network. The SDP Policy Manager in the layer is responsible for enforcing policies designed to control platform behavior. These policies are registered with the SDP Policy Manager, which is responsible for ensuring that all platform components are in compliance with the specified policies. The network communication layer is associated with network operations. We send advertise/request messages using UDP, and retrieve the data using the HTTP or SOAP based on TCP.

3 Service Discovery Procedure in LSD

3.1 Service Discovery Algorithm

To support service discovery and invocation in a decentralized, distributed environment, some procedures are required [10, 11, 12, 13, 14]. First of all, the service description must be able to describe the different aspects of heterogeneous services in a comprehensive and unambiguous manner, machine-interpretable in order to facilitate automation and human-readable to facilitate rapid user formulation. In LSD, service description is represented using XML. Secondly, the service advertisement process periodically provides service providers with advertising a registered service description in the cache, enabling network devices to provide services and to be aware of and use available services from other devices. After initial service description propagation, the service discovery process provides an important role for communication and invocations among remote hosts. When service consumers demand available services, they send a request message to neighboring devices via multicasting. Using this information, a device providing services must send reply messages via unicasting. When the service consumer has received several reply messages, a flexible and efficient matching algorithm would be required, based on their semantics, to maximize the number of positive matches giving the user a more eclectic choice of services for his or her needs. During the above processing, we must carefully consider limitations due to network topology, which may change rapidly and unpredictably. In particular, the packet size used in processing needs to be as small as possible so they can reduce overall network traffic. To reduce overall network traffic, LSD transmits the process message by optimizing a string packet based on TCP, then the receiver encodes the message in a XML DOM tree, storing it in a cache. The structure of the advertisement, request and response message are shown in Fig. 2 (a), (b) and (c), respectively.

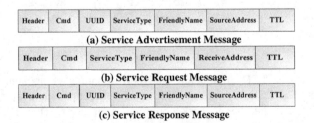

(a) Service Advertisement Message

(b) Service Request Message

(c) Service Response Message

Fig. 2. Message structure of LSD

In this paper, we assume that LSD devices, applications and resources within networks are all service based. A definition of the related factors shown in Fig. 2 is as follows.

Header : unique system message field for protecting message overflow coming from the same multicasting address from other systems
Cmd : form of message for deciding the received packet processing routine
UUID : provided service unique identifier
ServiceType : provided service in a matching module process
FriendlyName : flexible description of user friendly expressions.
SourceAddress : actual physical address of provided service
ReceiveAddress : address receiving reply regarding request message
TTL : increase service reliability through setting up lease time

LSD performs network service discovery through using message structure which is shown in Fig. 2. Fig. 3 shows the sequential process of the LSD discovery algorithm.

The definition of the terminology LC, DM, RDM and DML are in the order:

Local Cache (LC) stores the description of all services, which are provided by each device in the ad-hoc network.
The Delta Message (DM) includes information which does not exist in the advertisement received from the surrounding devices, but is contained in the service description in its own LC, alternatively, DM{S1, S3} = LC{S1, S2, S3} - advertisement{S2}.
Remote Delta Message (RDM) refers to DM messages received from surrounding devices.
Delta Message List (DML) is a temporary list of DMs, created or updated when advertisements are received from surrounding devices.

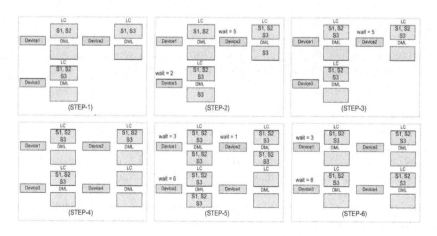

Fig. 3. LSD Discovery Algorithm

For ease of explanation for the LSD algorithm, the algorithmic procedure is reviewed step by step.

▶STEP 1

Suppose that an ad hoc network is made up of device 1, 2 and 3. Device 1 caches service information about S1, S2 and Device 2 about S1 and S3. Device 3 caches S1, S2 and S3.

▶STEP 2

Device 1 advertises (S1, S2) in its own LC. Device 2 and device 3 receive advertisement messages and then store the descriptions of the service which were advertised in their LCs. After that, they create DM (S3, S3) and await a random waiting time (5, 2).

▶STEP 3

The device 3 which was created with the least waiting time in Step 2 becomes activated first and it multicasts its delta message, S3. Device 1 stores the received service description in the LC: LC{S1, S2, S3} = LC{S1, S2} U RDM{S3}. Device 2 stores the received service description in the LC: LC{S1, S2, S3} = LC{S1, S2, S3} U RDM{S3}, and then deletes DM, S3, in its DML. The reason for deleting its DM here is to reduce the network load caused by redundant information transmission because the remote delta message that it received should also be received by other devices in the network. Thus, at this point, all devices reach the steady state, called 'state of convergence', and thus even though the device 2 is activated later at time 5, it does not operate any further because there is no more message to report to its DM.

▶STEP 4

All network devices are in the status of convergence, and device 4, which is now new, comes into the ad-hoc network. Device 4 advertises its dummy message.

▶STEP 5

Device 1, 2 and 3, which have all received advertisements, create DMs and await for a waiting time as they did in Step 2. The device 2 which was created with the least waiting time becomes activated first, and it multicasts its DM, which are S1, S2 and S3.

▶STEP 6

Device 1 and 3 which have received messages in Step 5 remove their DMs, which are now S1, S2 and S3. Device 4 stores the received description in its LC. As a result, all devices converge to the steady state, and thus device 1 and 3, even if activated, do not operate any more after checking that there is no more DMs that they have.

Figure 4 summarizes the LSD discovery algorithm of the sequential process exemplified in the Figure 3, in the pseudo-coded form. Define the related functions shown in Figure 4 as follows:

Delta[] : temporary storage space for created DM

wait(Randomtime(X)) : function used to generate random waiting time, in order to prevent a multicast storm

isEmptyDELTA() : function that determines if a service has been created in the DML

MakeDelta() : function that creates a new DM when an advertisement is received.

isEmptyDELTA() : function that determines if any DM has been created in the DML

EmptyDELTA() : routine that removes any DMs created in DML

LOCALCACHE <-- LOCALCACHE U {msg} : routine that adds the new service description to its LC when this is received

DELTA[] <-- DELTA[] - {msg} : routine that removes recently received data from the DML, which is waiting to be transmitted DM list

MINE.Description : refers to the service description which describes the device's own characteristics

```
DELTAMESSAGE     DELTA[cachesize]
receivemsg(msg)
{
    if( msg is advertisement message )
    {
        if( !isEmptyDELTA() )
        {
            LOCALCACHE <-- LOCALCACHE U {msg}
            DELTA[] <-- DELTA[] - {msg}
            return
        }
        LOCALCACHE <-- LOCALCACHE U {msg}
        DELTA[] <-- MakeDelta()
        wait( Randomtime(X) )
        if( isDeltaEmpty() )
            return
        else
        {
            Multicast( DELTA[] )
            EmptyDELTA()
        }
    }
    else if( msg is delta message )
    {
        LOCALCACHE <-- LOCALCACHE U {msg}
        DELTA[] <-- DELTA[] - {msg}
    }
    else if( msg is request message )
    {
        if( msg □ MINE.Description )
            Unicast( MINE. Description );
        else
            return;
    }
}
```

Fig. 4. A PseudoCode of Discovery Algorithm

As described above, all devices store information concerning all services available on the network, in their LC. As a result, the response time can be reduced and a more reliable service can be provided. When either a new advertisement or a DM is received , the device obtains the status of all devices stored in the LC with others information in the network, without sending or receiving any redundant data.

Therefore, removing the DM from its DML, improves overall efficiency, and is called to reach a convergence state.

3.2 Service Cache Manager in LSD

In a mobile ad hoc network, wireless nodes are mobile and do not use any preexisting fixed network infrastructure. Therefore, network topology may change rapidly and unpredictably. For this reason, we must consider the limitations of ad hoc network, such as high packet loss, intermittent connection, and frequent network topology changes. To overcome these limitations the LSD uses a local cache, managed internally in the LSD by service cache manager, for storing all available remote host service information. A service cache manager stores a local cache with service advertisement information from neighboring hosts. When LSD devices demand a service description from a neighboring host, the service cache manager searches the service in local caches at first. If information is found, requested service information is sent. In the event of an absence of information, users send a request message using multicasting. Therefore, the LSD can trim unnecessary service information request message, which is already stored in the local cache, to the extent of increased adaptation in dynamic ad hoc networks. However we must consider various problems such as cache accumulation, cache replacement and cache elimination, which may arise from a lack of cache space. When a LSD device joins an ad hoc network, firstly a decision is made regarding local cache size, taking into account the device storage capability. Then, the local cache is managed using a priority queue, considering usage of a service such as service advertisement messages and service request messages.

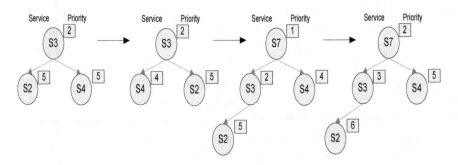

Fig. 5. A Sequential Process of the LSD caching operation

The priority queue is a First In First Out (FIFO) data structure, implemented using a heap data structure, and for efficient data management, allows data reordering. Fig. 5 shows the sequential process of the LSD caching operation. Suppose that a local cache in a mobile node is made up of S3, S2 and S4, their priorities are 2, 5 and 5 respectively. If the node receives an advertisement or request message regarding S4, its priority decreases 1, from an initial 4. Then, the node accomplishes tree-structure reordering. S7 is service information, running on the neighboring host. When the node receives information regarding S7, its priority is set at 1. Then, tree-structure reordering occurs. If an advertisement or request message regarding particular services has not been received for a long period of time, priorities are increased. In the case of a local cache queue overflow or priority of a particular service reaches a large value, service information is deleted in the order of local cache priority value. In the LSD, the priority levels of services is controlled by a cache manager and determined by the frequencies and service popularity in the network. Therefore, an increase in service hitting rate and service reliability for the service provider is expected by the preferential elimination of old or unused data.

4 SOAP Based Scheme for Flexible Service Invocation

In the above section, we have shown that the service discovery process enables LSD to detect other services in neighboring devices. After the service discovery process, service delivery and invocation processes facilitate service. Functions include transmitting commands from the user to the service provider and receiving results or invoking provided services. A flexible and extensible invocation mechanism is responsible for abstracting communication details from the user and executing a remote service in a dynamic scheme. In this subsection, we describe how to invoke the discovered service in the LSD. The LSD abbreviates network traffic and minimizes XML operation by exchanging the optimized packet with a minimum data size as shown in Fig. 2. As a result, the service information would be stored in a local cache.


```
<?xml version="1.0"?>
<ServiceCache>
  <ServiceAdv>
    <!-- Base information of printer device-->
    <ServiceID>UUID://54091b02-3763-46fc-a643-c0997397a21b</ServiceID>
    <ServiceType>printer</ServiceType>
    <FriendlyName>hp-printer</FriendlyName>
    <ServiceUrl>LSD://203.252.46.118:40001</ServiceUrl>
    <TTL>
      <StartTime>2004-10-15T10:50:40</StartTime>
      <EndTime>2004-10-16T10:50:30</EndTime>
    </TTL> </ServiceAdv> <ServiceAdv>
    <!-- Base information of audio device-->
    <ServiceID>UUID://87091b02-3763-46fc-a643-c0997397a21b</ServiceID>
    <ServiceType>audio</ServiceType>
    <FriendlyName>samsung-audio</FriendlyName>
    <ServiceUrl>http://203.252.46.236:40011</ServiceUrl>
    <TTL>
      <StartTime>2004-10-17T10:30:27</StartTime>
      <EndTime>2004-10-17T11:48:21</EndTime>
    </TTL>
  </ServiceAdv>
</ServiceCache>
```


(a) Service Description in Cache


```
<?xml version="1.0" encoding="UTF-8"?>
<lsdRoot xmlns="http://lsd.skku.ac.kr/LSD-Schema" xmlns:xsi="http://www.w3.org/2001/XMLSchema-instance"
xsi:schemaLocation="http://lsd.skku.ac.kr/LSD-Schema F:₩MyWorkspace₩LSD_ing₩LSD-schema₩LSD-new.xsd">
  <device>
    <generalInfo>
      <!-- device's property -->
      <deviceID>UUID://34b10c4c-65a1-417f-8af9-ce771e5fa3c3</deviceID>
      <location>urn:lsd.skku.ac.kr:device:something</location>
      <deviceType>printer</deviceType>
      <friendlyName>hp-printer</friendlyName>
      <manufacturer>hp</manufacturer>
      <model>
        <modelName>hp-s1024</modelName>
        <modelNumber>4526cfg</modelNumber>
      </model>
      <controlURL>http://nrlab.skku.ac.kr</controlURL>
      <TTL>
        <start>2004-10-15T10:50:40</start>
        <end>2006-10-16T10:50:30</end>
      </TTL>
    </generalInfo>
    <!-- available services and function -->
    <services>
      <serviceID>UUID://ed8a2c53-93c9-47dd-a483-7df819aa9607</serviceID>
      <serviceType>printing service</serviceType>
      <serviceDescription>set parameter for printing number</serviceDescription>
      <fuctionName>invokeprint</fuctionName>
      <parameterType>boolean</parameterType>
    </services>
  </device>
</lsdRoot>
```


(b) Service Description for LSD Service

Fig. 6. Service Description in LSD

Fig. 6-(a) shows the device information in the LSD local cache. If a service consumer wants to access and utilize the service, he or she activates a matching module using ServiceType and ServiceName in his or her device cache as shown in Fig. 6-(a). If the service consumer finds the adequate service, the service consumer requests service description, as shown in Fig. 6-(b), using ServiceURL in the cache using the HTTP. The description includes detailed service information, representing device and service characteristics. If no information is available locally, the consumer sends a Service Request Message as shown in Fig. 2-(b). Then, the service consumer acquires the location of the service description. Based on this information, the consumer requests service description. Then, the provider sends the service description as shown in Fig. 6-(b). In this Service Description, the upper side has information regarding the device's property, and the lower side has available services and function information for each device.

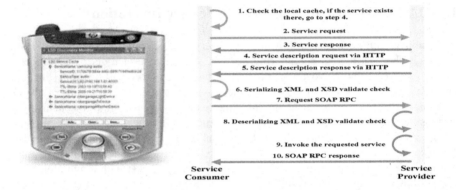

Fig. 7. A Sequence Diagram of remote data access scheme in LSD

Fig. 7 shows a remote data access scheme sequence diagram in the LSD. When using the remote service, the service consumer must know its functionality, parameter and characteristics. To resolve this problem, the transmitted description includes function name, parameter type and so on. From this information, he or she forms an XML document containing the URI of the service provider, the remote method name to execute and the parameters associated with that method. The XML document that is checked is based on XSD (XML Schema Definition) and is serialized into a SOAP message to be sent to the service provider using the HTTP. This XML document is the main interface used when executing the SOAP RPC invocation. The service provider is responsible for receiving and deserializing the XML document. When the service provider receives the SOAP RPC request message, the service provider invokes the function provided in the received request message, and then returns its results, the results are structured into a response XML document. The service consumer receives the SOAP RPC response message, containing the result of requested service invocation. In this scheme, the LSD can access remote services and supports flexibility and extensibility in communication and invocations among remote hosts, which is comprised of XML and RPC technology. The LSD system was implemented using Personal Java 1.2 and J2ME CLDC/MIDP. For this implementation, we used an IBM ThinkPad and WinCE based iPAQ's from Compaq. This architecture is only a preliminary version, and we are now in the process of completing implementation.

5 Future Work

In an environment with little route stability, such as an ad-hoc network, broadcast service discovery/advertisement is likely to be more effective, as shown in the LSD. Conversely, more stable networks, which can exploit the greater capability of their powerful nodes, may be able to take advantage of a structured P2P algorithm such as DHT. The agent platform also enhances the functionality of the service discovery mechanism. Based on this ideas [15], we combines these technologies in order to solve the open scalability, dynamicity and interoperability problems, susceptible in highly dynamic, heterogeneous environments, such as ubiquitous networks.

6 Conclusion

With the advancement of modern technology, and as increasingly large numbers of people start to use mobile devices, the ability to access remote information offered in a mobile ad hoc network is the major prerequisite for effective network usability. In this paper, we presented a novel scheme for service discovery and invocation in ad hoc environments, maximizing the effect of SOAP, and also discussed the advantages and disadvantages of using the SOAP. We are currently developing a more sophisticated LSD engine along with other associated mechanisms. Future work includes detailed simulations and performance evaluations for the developed systems.

References

1. M. Weiser "Some Computer Science Issues in Ubiquitous Computing. ACM, July. 1993
2. Jun-Zhao Sun., "Mobile Ad Hoc Networking: An Essential Technology for Pervasive Computing", MediaTeam, Machine Vision and Media Processing Unit, Infotech Oulu P.O.Box 4500, FIN-90014 University of Oulu, Finland
3. University Plug and Play Device Architecture Reference Specification. Microsoft Corporation.
4. Ken Arnold et al, The Jini Specification, V1.0 Addison-Wesley 1999. Latest version is 1.1 available from Sun.
5. Service Location Protocol Version 2, Internet Engineering Task Force, RFC 2608, June 1999.
6. Sumi Helal: Standards for service discovery and delivery, Pervasive Computing, IEEE, Volume: 1, Issue: 3, Pages:95 - 100 , July-Sept. 2002
7. M. Gudgin, M. Hadley, N. Mendelsohn, J.-J. Moreau, Canon, and H. F. Nielsen. Simple Object Access Protocol 1.1, June 2003. http://www.w3.org/TR/SOAP.
8. D. Davis and M. Parashar, "Latency Performance of SOAP Implementations", Proceedings of the 2nd IEEE/ACM International Symposium on Cluster Computing and the Grid, pages 407-412, 2002.
9. N. Abu-Ghazaleh, M. J. Lewis, and M. Govindaraju. Differential Serialization for Optimized SOAP Performance. To appear in the 13th IEEE International Symposium on High Performance Distributed Computing (HPDC-13), June 2004, Honolulu, Hawaii.

10. O. Ratsimor, D. Chakraborty, S. Tolia, D. Kushraj, A. Kunjithapatham, G. Gupta, A. Joshi, T. Finin, "Allia: Alliance-based Service Discovery for Ad-Hoc Environments," in ACM Mobile Commerce Workshop, 2002.
11. D. Chakraborty and A. Joshi, "GSD: A novel group-based service discovery protocol for MANETS," In IEEE Conference on Mobile and Wireless Communications Networks, Stockholm, Sweden, September 2002.
12. M. Nidd, "Service discovery in DEAPspace," IEEE Pers. Commun., vol.8, pp. 39–45, 2001.
13. C. Lee, A. Helal, N. Desai, V. Verma, B. Arslan, "Konark: A System and Protocols for Device Independent, Peer-to-Peer Discovery and Delivery of Mobile Services," IEEE System. Man. Cybernetic., vol. 33, no. 6, pp. 682-696, Nov. 2003
14. Rohan Sen, Radu Handorean, Gruia-Catalian Roman, and Christopher Gill, "Service Oriented Computing Imperatives in Ad Hoc Wireless Settings," Technical Report WU-CSE 2004-05, Washington University, Department of Computer Science, St. Louis, Missouri.
15. Kee-Hyun Choi, Ho-Jin Shin and Dong-Ryeol Shin, "D2HT: Directory Federation using DHT to Support Open Scalability in Ubiquitous Network", PWN 2005, March, 2005

Author Index

Lecture Notes in Computer Science

For information about Vols. 1–3531

please contact your bookseller or Springer

Vol. 3580: L. Caires, G.F. Italiano, L. Monteiro, C. Palamidessi, M. Yung (Eds.), Automata, Languages and Programming. XXV, 1477 pages. 2005.

Vol. 3579: D. Lowe, M. Gaedke (Eds.), Web Engineering. XXII, 633 pages. 2005.

Vol. 3578: M. Gallagher, J. Hogan, F. Maire (Eds.), Intelligent Data Engineering and Automated Learning - IDEAL 2005. XVI, 599 pages. 2005.

Vol. 3577: R. Falcone, S. Barber, J. Sabater-Mir, M.P. Singh (Eds.), Trusting Agents for Trusting Electronic Societies. VIII, 235 pages. 2005. (Subseries LNAI).

Vol. 3576: K. Etessami, S.K. Rajamani (Eds.), Computer Aided Verification. XV, 564 pages. 2005.

Vol. 3575: S. Wermter, G. Palm, M. Elshaw (Eds.), Biomimetic Neural Learning for Intelligent Robots. IX, 383 pages. 2005. (Subseries LNAI).

Vol. 3574: C. Boyd, J.M. González Nieto (Eds.), Information Security and Privacy. XIII, 586 pages. 2005.

Vol. 3573: S. Etalle (Ed.), Logic Based Program Synthesis and Transformation. VIII, 279 pages. 2005.

Vol. 3572: C. De Felice, A. Restivo (Eds.), Developments in Language Theory. XI, 409 pages. 2005.

Vol. 3571: L. Godo (Ed.), Symbolic and Quantitative Approaches to Reasoning with Uncertainty. XVI, 1028 pages. 2005. (Subseries LNAI).

Vol. 3570: A. S. Patrick, M. Yung (Eds.), Financial Cryptography and Data Security. XII, 376 pages. 2005.

Vol. 3569: F. Bacchus, T. Walsh (Eds.), Theory and Applications of Satisfiability Testing. XII, 492 pages. 2005.

Vol. 3568: W.-K. Leow, M.S. Lew, T.-S. Chua, W.-Y. Ma, L. Chaisorn, E.M. Bakker (Eds.), Image and Video Retrieval. XVII, 672 pages. 2005.

Vol. 3567: M. Jackson, D. Nelson, S. Stirk (Eds.), Database: Enterprise, Skills and Innovation. XII, 185 pages. 2005.

Vol. 3566: J.-P. Banâtre, P. Fradet, J.-L. Giavitto, O. Michel (Eds.), Unconventional Programming Paradigms. XI, 367 pages. 2005.

Vol. 3565: G.E. Christensen, M. Sonka (Eds.), Information Processing in Medical Imaging. XXI, 777 pages. 2005.

Vol. 3564: N. Eisinger, J. Małuszyński (Eds.), Reasoning Web. IX, 319 pages. 2005.

Vol. 3562: J. Mira, J.R. Álvarez (Eds.), Artificial Intelligence and Knowledge Engineering Applications: A Bioinspired Approach, Part II. XXIV, 636 pages. 2005.

Vol. 3561: J. Mira, J.R. Álvarez (Eds.), Mechanisms, Symbols, and Models Underlying Cognition, Part I. XXIV, 532 pages. 2005.

Vol. 3560: V.K. Prasanna, S. Iyengar, P.G. Spirakis, M. Welsh (Eds.), Distributed Computing in Sensor Systems. XV, 423 pages. 2005.

Vol. 3559: P. Auer, R. Meir (Eds.), Learning Theory. XI, 692 pages. 2005. (Subseries LNAI).

Vol. 3558: V. Torra, Y. Narukawa, S. Miyamoto (Eds.), Modeling Decisions for Artificial Intelligence. XII, 470 pages. 2005. (Subseries LNAI).

Vol. 3557: H. Gilbert, H. Handschuh (Eds.), Fast Software Encryption. XI, 443 pages. 2005.

Vol. 3556: H. Baumeister, M. Marchesi, M. Holcombe (Eds.), Extreme Programming and Agile Processes in Software Engineering. XIV, 332 pages. 2005.

Vol. 3555: T. Vardanega, A.J. Wellings (Eds.), Reliable Software Technology – Ada-Europe 2005. XV, 273 pages. 2005.

Vol. 3554: A. Dey, B. Kokinov, D. Leake, R. Turner (Eds.), Modeling and Using Context. XIV, 572 pages. 2005. (Subseries LNAI).

Vol. 3553: T.D. Hämäläinen, A.D. Pimentel, J. Takala, S. Vassiliadis (Eds.), Embedded Computer Systems: Architectures, Modeling, and Simulation. XV, 476 pages. 2005.

Vol. 3552: H. de Meer, N. Bhatti (Eds.), Quality of Service – IWQoS 2005. XVIII, 400 pages. 2005.

Vol. 3551: T. Härder, W. Lehner (Eds.), Data Management in a Connected World. XIX, 371 pages. 2005.

Vol. 3548: K. Julisch, C. Kruegel (Eds.), Intrusion and Malware Detection and Vulnerability Assessment. X, 241 pages. 2005.

Vol. 3547: F. Bomarius, S. Komi-Sirviö (Eds.), Product Focused Software Process Improvement. XIII, 588 pages. 2005.

Vol. 3546: T. Kanade, A. Jain, N.K. Ratha (Eds.), Audio- and Video-Based Biometric Person Authentication. XX, 1134 pages. 2005.

Vol. 3544: T. Higashino (Ed.), Principles of Distributed Systems. XII, 460 pages. 2005.

Vol. 3543: L. Kutvonen, N. Alonistioti (Eds.), Distributed Applications and Interoperable Systems. XI, 235 pages. 2005.

Vol. 3542: H.H. Hoos, D.G. Mitchell (Eds.), Theory and Applications of Satisfiability Testing. XIII, 393 pages. 2005.

Vol. 3541: N.C. Oza, R. Polikar, J. Kittler, F. Roli (Eds.), Multiple Classifier Systems. XII, 430 pages. 2005.

Vol. 3540: H. Kalviainen, J. Parkkinen, A. Kaarna (Eds.), Image Analysis. XXII, 1270 pages. 2005.

Vol. 3539: K. Morik, J.-F. Boulicaut, A. Siebes (Eds.), Local Pattern Detection. XI, 233 pages. 2005. (Subseries LNAI).

Vol. 3538: L. Ardissono, P. Brna, A. Mitrovic (Eds.), User Modeling 2005. XVI, 533 pages. 2005. (Subseries LNAI).

Vol. 3537: A. Apostolico, M. Crochemore, K. Park (Eds.), Combinatorial Pattern Matching. XI, 444 pages. 2005.

Vol. 3536: G. Ciardo, P. Darondeau (Eds.), Applications and Theory of Petri Nets 2005. XI, 470 pages. 2005.

Vol. 3535: M. Steffen, G. Zavattaro (Eds.), Formal Methods for Open Object-Based Distributed Systems. X, 323 pages. 2005.

Vol. 3534: S. Spaccapietra, E. Zimányi (Eds.), Journal on Data Semantics III. XI, 213 pages. 2005.

Vol. 3533: M. Ali, F. Esposito (Eds.), Innovations in Applied Artificial Intelligence. XX, 858 pages. 2005. (Subseries LNAI).

Vol. 3532: A. Gómez-Pérez, J. Euzenat (Eds.), The Semantic Web: Research and Applications. XV, 728 pages. 2005.